TWENTIETH-CENTURY RELIGIOUS THOUGHT

The Frontiers of Philosophy and Theology, 1900-1970

JOHN MACQUARRIE

SCM PRESS LTD

334 01702 5
First published 1963
by SCM Press Ltd
58 Bloomsbury Street, London WC1
Revised edition 1971
Fourth impression 1978

Printed in Great Britain by
Fletcher & Son Ltd, Norwich

TWENTIETH-CENTURY
RELIGIOUS THOUGHT

To
John Michael,
Catherine Elizabeth
and
Alan Denis

CONTENTS

Sociological Interpretations of Religion

XI Pragmatism and Allied Views

XII Philosophies of Personal Being

XIII The Religious Consciousness and Phenomenology

PREFACE

FOUR years ago some members of the editorial staff of Messrs Harper and Brothers suggested to me over lunch that I should write the story of religious thought in the present century, with special reference to the relations of philosophy and theology. At first I shied away from so wide and laborious an undertaking. But on reflection, it occurred to me that if I were to make the attempt—and surely someone ought to make it—then even if no one else were to profit from my book, I should at least educate myself a little better in writing it. When once I had begun, I found that in spite of the labours involved, the task was a fascinating one, and if some people get from the reading of this book even a fraction of the interest and pleasure that I have had from the writing of it, I shall be well satisfied.

In a book such as this, exposition is of primary importance. I have tried to be fair to everyone and to caricature no one. Obviously, however, no single person can have a detailed knowledge of every corner of so wide a field as the one surveyed here. While it has been my constant endeavour not to impute to anyone views for which I could not find—as it seemed to me—clear warrant in his own writings, I have no doubt been guilty of wrong emphases and plain misunderstandings. Yet these are risks that have to be taken if we think it worthwhile to break out sometimes from our narrow specialisms in order to see and evaluate these in the context of the whole picture.

It would be a dull book which merely recorded who said what, and so a large part of the text is taken up with analysis and criticism of the views expounded. Here I have felt no inhibitions whatever. But the criticism has been, in the main, kept separate from the exposition, and I hope that most of it is fair criticism and not just the expression of my own emotional reactions.

It is impossible to study what has actually been said about the problems of religion without at the same time studying the problems themselves. The ultimate purpose of a book of this kind must be to throw some light on the problems themselves. This does not mean that the reader will be conducted to any firm conclusions at the end. The purpose of the book will have been served if it kindles the reader's interest in the problems, and enables him to see what these are, and what roads towards their solution still appear to be open.

So far as I am aware, there is no other book which covers quite the same field as this one. There are, however, many books which overlap various parts of the field. I have profited from several of these, and I hope that full acknowledgement has been made, both in the text and in the bibliography.

Professor Daniel Day Williams, of Union Theological Seminary, New York, read the whole book in typescript, and suggested many improvements. Further valuable comments were received from Professor John McIntyre, of the University of Edinburgh, and Professor Ian T. Ramsey, of the University of Oxford. Mr. William Newton Todd gave assistance in reading the proofs. To all of them, I wish to express my warm thanks.

J. M.

University of Glasgow,
November, 1961

PREFACE TO THE NEW EDITION

A chapter has been added giving an account of developments in religious thought in the lively if confused decade, 1960–70. Some paragraphs in this chapter echo passages from a survey of recent theology which I wrote for *The Expository Times,* vol. lxxviii.

J.M.

University of Oxford,
January, 1971

I

INTRODUCTORY COMMENTS

1. Scope, Method and Purpose of the Inquiry

IT is neither desirable nor necessary to weary the reader with a long introductory discussion of the methods and principles which will be employed in this inquiry. If they are employed with any success, they will become plain enough in the pages that follow. Nevertheless, anyone who is rash enough to embark on so vast a theme as the one announced in the title of this book may be expected to say at the beginning what he intends to include in his survey, how he proposes to investigate his theme, and what purpose his investigation is supposed to serve.

We must first then delimit our territory, which we have described as 'religious thought'. The expression 'religious thought' is used here to include all serious reflection of a philosophical nature on the central themes of religion. It will include 'philosophy of religion', understood as that branch of philosophy which concerns itself with interpreting and evaluating religion, and also 'philosophical theology', understood as that branch of theology which concerns itself with elucidating and examining the philosophical implications of a religious faith. It will usually exclude those areas of philosophy which have no direct bearing on religion, and those dogmatic and ecclesiastical concerns of theology which lack any direct philosophical interest. It is obvious, however, that we must allow ourselves some freedom here, since a philosophical point of view which has nothing to say about religion may have important repercussions on religious thought, while a purely dogmatic theology which disclaims any connection with philosophy may nevertheless carry its own hidden philosophical implications.

Our subject-matter thus takes shape as a frontier—the boundary between philosophy and theology. We must explore what has been happening along this frontier in the present century, though in order to understand this we may have to make occasional trips into either the philosophical or the theological hinterland. A great many different kinds of activities go on along a frontier. There is peaceful trade and commerce.

Thus we shall find exchanges of ideas between philosophers and theologians. The philosopher may find the expression of a truth in a religious dogma or even in a myth, while the theologian may welcome the conceptual apparatus of a philosophy for the explication of religious faith. There may also be a certain amount of smuggling. A philosopher may set out on his philosophizing with theological motives which may be hidden even from himself and which destroy the freedom of his inquiry, while a theologian may be so intent on conforming his faith to a philosophy that he distorts this faith in the process. A frontier may also be the scene of violent warfare. We must take into account negative evaluations as well as positive ones, whether they are pronounced by the philosopher against the theologian, or by the theologian against the philosopher. Even when the frontier is very quiet, and philosophers seem completely indifferent to religion or theologians to philosophy, we must ask the reasons for this state of affairs, and what judgments are implied in it.

As well as being confined to religious thought in the sense which has just been explained, our subject will be limited in two other ways. As indicated in the title, we shall confine ourselves to the twentieth century. Since, however, it is impossible to draw a hard and fast line between one century and another, we must take notice of those thinkers who were still alive and active in the early years of our century, even if much of their work had already been done in the preceding one. We shall further confine ourselves to religious thought in Western culture. In doing this, we certainly do not intend any disrespect to other cultures. Indeed, men like S. Radhakrishnan of India and D. T. Suzuki of Japan—to mention only two whose works are well-known in the West—would take a high place among philosophers of religion in our time. But Western culture constitutes a certain unity, and to try to extend our survey beyond it— even if we were competent to do this—would land us in almost insuperable complications.

Having thus demarcated our territory, we must now turn to the question of the method by which we can best explore it. Here a number of problems arise—problems of selection, of exposition, of comparison, of criticism, of chronology. We must indicate very briefly how we intend to deal with each of these points.

The field which confronts us is a vast one, and our first problem must therefore be one of *selection*. From the host of philosophers and theologians who have written during the present century on topics which are relevant to our theme, which are we to choose for the purpose of exhibiting the trends of religious thought during the period? No two people would make the same choice, and obviously any selection must be influenced by subjective factors—not least among these factors being the limitations of the selector's own knowledge. Our aim will be to make the selection as catholic as possible, so that the less well-known points of view get a hearing alongside those which have attracted widespread attention. Only in this way can we hope to get a balanced and comprehensive picture which will show us the many colours in the spectrum of recent and contemporary religious thought.

When we come to *exposition*, the aim must be, above all, fairness. This however is by no means easy. It must always remain something of an impertinence to attempt to summarize in a few paragraphs complex ideas for the proper expression of which their authors required several volumes. We shall best be able to guard against doing injustice to writers by sticking as closely as we can to their own writings, employing their own terminology and citing where possible their *ipsissima verba*.

Selection and exposition are only the beginnings of our task, since it would be a dull book which merely recorded who said what. We must pass on to the *comparison* of the various thinkers, showing what they have in common and where they differ. In this way, we can bring them together into groups, each of which represents a more or less distinct type of thought. In some cases the group may be so definite as to constitute a clearly defined school; in other cases the group may be so loosely bound together that it is little more than a convenient device for the treatment of our theme. In any case, there is overlapping, so that we must proceed to the comparison of the groups themselves, and show how one type of thought flows into another.

The kind of *criticism* which we shall offer will not be made on the grounds of any preconceived idea of what a philosophy of religion ought to say. It will be confined to such questions as to whether a particular interpretation of religion makes sense, whether it is adequate to the phenomena with which it purports to deal, whether it ties in with what we know from other sources, how far it depends on uncriticized presuppositions, and so on. In saying this, we are simply announcing our intention of endeavouring to be as fair as possible. We are not claiming to pronounce with some kind of Olympian detachment, for such a claim would obviously be both presumptuous and absurd. No one can write on these matters except from a point of view, and the present writer will disclose his own point of view before we reach the end of the book. But he will try not to obtrude it upon the reader, so that each point of view can be considered on its own merits.

The question of *chronology* is one of the most difficult of all. Just as the various types of thought interpenetrate each other in their ideas and treatment, so they overlap in time. We cannot draw sharp lines, and say that after such and such a year certain types of thought were replaced by others. We propose, however, to distinguish three phases in the religious thought of our century. The first phase continues into the twentieth-century ideas which were already developed in the nineteenth. In the second phase, we find new movements which distinctly belong to the twentieth century but which, at least in their original forms, have already passed their zenith and have either declined or been transformed and differentiated into still newer movements. In the third phase we find those movements which hold the field at the present time. Continuity will be given to our story by transitional chapters which will convey us from one phase to the next.

Such are the methodological considerations which we shall endeavour to keep in view. As a consequence, our investigation will assume a form rather like that of Mussorgsky's well-known musical composition, *Pictures from an Exhibition*. In this composition, Mussorgsky takes us through a collection of pictures, describing each one and recording his impressions, while continuity is provided by a recurring 'promenade' theme as we are conducted through the galleries.

Finally, we may ask what is the purpose of such a survey as the one upon which we are about to embark. It may, of course, have its uses as a kind of guide-book or quick reference-book. Or again, in these days of excessive specialization, it may be said that it is useful to get a broad view of any subject, so that we can rid our minds of provincialisms. However, we should keep an even more important purpose in view. It is impossible to study the history of any problem without studying the problem itself. From the study of what men have actually said on the problems of religion, one may hope to arrive at a clearer understanding of these problems, and see which roads towards their solution are open and which are closed. But how far this more ambitious purpose will be realized can be judged only at the end of our investigation in the light of our conclusions—if indeed we are lucky enough to arrive at any.

But enough has been said for the present on these general considerations of the scope, method and purpose of our investigation. We must now turn to the subject-matter itself, and have a first look around.

2. A First Look Around

If anyone was reflecting about religion on the first day of the twentieth century, presumably his thoughts would not be very different from those which had been entertained in the later part of the nineteenth century. The first phase of our story, as already stated, is the continuation in the present century of ideas which had been already developed in the preceding one.

When we look back upon the views which were held at that time, they may well seem to us to be dated, or even to have come out of another world. Yet there was certainly no dreary uniformity about them. They displayed very considerable variety. Let us listen to what the English philosophical theologian, J. R. Illingworth, had to say about the diversity of thought in the early years of the century: 'A really complete survey of contemporary opinion would disclose in it variety rather than unity—a multitude of incoherent and often incompatible points of view, all of which may in a sense be called modern, but none of which can claim to be typically representative of the age, views which approximate and inter-lace and then diverge—currents and cross-currents and rapids and back-waters of thought.'[1]

Presumably we can date these views because, in spite of the variety of types of thought represented—idealism, spiritualism, naturalism, mater-ialism, and so on—there were certain characteristics which were common to most of the types of thought current in those days. These characteristics are apparent to us as we survey the scene from a distance, and perhaps they stand out all the more clearly because they would not readily commend themselves to much of our thinking to-day. Our way of looking at things has changed, so that when we pick up a book on our subject written around the beginning of the century, we get a certain impression of strangeness as we read. Whether the change is for the better or the worse, we cannot, of course, say. But we cannot fail to notice that there has been a fairly radical change, and our task will be to trace the various shifts and intermediate stages which lead from the points of view prevailing in Western religious thought at the beginning of the century to those which we know to-day.

Among the characteristics common to most types of thinking in the early years of the century, but by no means so readily acceptable to us, is optimism. It is, of course, only too easy to make superficial and trivial generalizations with so slippery a word as 'optimism'. It is surely true to say, however, that a certain buoyancy of spirit was evident in most schools of thought at the beginning of the century, and that this buoyancy has been more and more weighed down as the world has become increasingly disjointed and unstable. Whereas optimism mirrored the relatively secure and expanding civilization of earlier days, a sober caution reflects the

[1] *Divine Transcendence*, pp. 1–2.

anxieties of our own time. At the present day there will be no ready response to the optimism of idealists like Sir Henry Jones, who concluded his Gifford Lectures by assuring his audience of 'the friendliness and helpfulness of man's environment';[1] or like Josiah Royce, who asserted that 'the world, as a whole, is and must be absolutely good'.[2] Now that science has shown itself to be an ambiguous blessing even in the field of material well-being, we should hesitate to share the different kind of optimism expressed by Sir James G. Frazer, who thought it 'not too much to say that the hope of progress—moral and intellectual as well as material—in the future is bound up with the fortunes of science'.[3] Our contemporary theologians, perhaps because of some of the horrors which we have witnessed in the twentieth century, tend to dwell on the sinfulness of human nature, and few of them would subscribe to the optimistic view of man implied in Adolf von Harnack's exhortation that we should 'with a steady will affirm the forces and the standards which on the summits of our inner life shine out as our highest good'.[4] Of course, one could find pessimistic utterances as well, but in general, optimism prevailed. The isolated sentences which we have just quoted from writers of the period would need to be studied in their contexts to be properly understood—and we hope to do more justice to these writers in due course—but these sentences nevertheless point to a kind of optimism which was prevalent at the beginning of the century and has now largely disappeared.

This optimism was closely linked with another idea characteristic of the period—the idea of development or evolution. This idea might be given a more Hegelian or a more Darwinian flavour, but in one form or another it recurred in different types of thought. It is prominent in writers so divergent as Edward Caird and Ernst Haeckel. The idea of evolution is, of course, still one to which we ascribe a high value. But we have come to distinguish more critically between evolution as a scientific hypothesis which we accept in its own field, and evolution as a philosophical generalization, of which we may be doubtful. We may be especially doubtful of it, if it is inflated into the idea of a general and inevitable progress in which the later is the more advanced, and the more advanced is somehow the better and the truer.

In spite of these evolutionary ideas, the notion of 'substance' was still dominant in most of the thinking done at the beginning of the century. Substance might be spiritual or it might be material, there might be one substance or many substances, substance might even be conceived as

---

[1] *A Faith that Enquires*, p. 360.　　　[2] *The Religious Aspect of Philosophy*, p. 444.
[3] *The Golden Bough*, p. 712.　　　[4] *What is Christianity?*, p. 301.

active, but essentially 'substance' is a static idea, and has for its explanatory model, so to speak, solid enduring thinghood. Whether or not some notion of 'substance' may be indispensable is debatable; but there is no doubt that philosophical interest has nowadays shifted from substance to such dynamic concepts as events, processes, function, life and the like.

Philosophies in those days were also characterized by comprehensiveness. Their authors usually aimed at systematic treatment. According to Wilhelm Windelband, the term 'philosophy' in the usage current around the turn of the century meant 'the scientific treatment of the general questions relating to the universe and human life'.[1] The analytical philosopher of our own day who occupies himself with limited problems would shrink from such a definition of his subject. Because of its comprehensiveness, any philosophy at the beginning of the century usually devoted some attention to the problems of religion. Theologians on their side frequently sought confirmation of their beliefs in philosophy. Thus there tended to be a fairly close association between the two. Dean Inge went so far as to claim that 'the goal of philosophy is the same as the goal of religion—perfect knowledge of the Perfect'.[2] Even if recently we have seen philosophy and theology beginning to draw together again, for the most part in our time the two have gone their separate ways, and there has been nothing like the close relations which subsisted between them at the beginning of the century. We may notice also that a comprehensive systematic philosophy tends to assume a certain air of finality. Referring to the tasks of philosophy, Bernard Bosanquet remarked: 'I do not conceal my belief that in the main the work has been done.'[3] It is only fair to Bosanquet to add that before the end of his life he was facing up to the new tendencies which had meantime appeared. But for us who can look back over the last sixty years and see how idealism has faded away, how long-established traditions have broken down, and how new movements of thought have taken shape, everything seems transitory and in flux.

Such are some of the recurring characteristics which we find in the first phase of twentieth-century religious thought, and they catch our eye just because they are found much more rarely in the thinking of our own day. But, as we have already noted, this first phase—comprising those types of thought which, already full-blown in the nineteenth century, still had plenty of life in the opening years of the twentieth—displayed remarkable variety. How can we classify its different manifestations?

[1] *A History of Philosophy*, vol. I, p. 1.
[2] 'Philosophy and Religion', in *Contemporary British Philosophy*, Series 1, ed. J. H. Muirhead, p. 191.
[3] *The Principle of Individuality and Value*, Preface, p. 5.

The most obvious dividing line is between idealistic or spiritualistic types of thought on the one hand and naturalistic types on the other. But terms like 'idealism' and 'naturalism' are little more than convenient labels, the meanings of which vary in different contexts. The term 'idealism' in its wide sense can be applied to movements so diverse as the speculative idealism of the neo-Hegelians and the critical idealism of the neo-Kantians, two groups which were both in vigorous life at the turn of the century. Among the neo-Hegelians themselves, a division appeared between absolute idealists and personal idealists. And there was a considerable group of thinkers of spiritualistic or personalistic type whose relation to traditional forms of idealism was very loose. Thus we can disinguish five main types of religious thought in the first phase of our story.

If we arrange these types between the extremes of speculative idealism on the one hand and positivistic naturalism on the other, our survey of the first phase will cover the following topics: the neo-Hegelian movement in British and American philosophy, culminating in absolute idealism, together with the influence of this movement in theology (Chapter II); the personal idealism which arose within neo-Hegelianism by way of reaction against the tendency to submerge personality in the Absolute, again with its theological counterpart (Chapter III); a group of philosophies found in various countries and against various backgrounds, all of which philosophies may be broadly characterized as spiritualistic, theistic and personalistic (Chapter IV); neo-Kantian philosophy and the allied Ritschlian theology, found chiefly in Germany, and centring its interpretation of religion in the idea of value (Chapter V); naturalistic and positivistic interpretations of religion in terms of biology, anthropology and psychology (Chapter VI).

II

ABSOLUTE IDEALISM

3. IDEALISM IN THE ENGLISH-SPEAKING COUNTRIES

THE term 'idealism' is used to describe a variety of philosophies which all in one way or another regard physical objects as existing only in relation to an experiencing subject, so that reality is conceived in terms of mind or experience. In the type of idealism which we are about to consider, physical objects are referred to an all-embracing or absolute experience, in which our finite human minds are somehow included.

This type of idealism flourished in Germany in the early part of the nineteenth century, but long after it had passed its zenith in its native land, it underwent a remarkable revival in the English-speaking countries, where it had become the dominant type of philosophy by the beginning of the twentieth century. The new idealism, however, was not just the restatement of an older philosophy. It speedily acquired its own distinctive characteristics. In the words of a neutral commentator, Guido de Ruggiero, it is not 'a matter of a simple repetition of foreign ideas, but of an absolutely original movement which receives its initiative from Hegel but transforms his doctrine radically'.[1]

To begin with, German idealism began to infiltrate into the English-speaking world through the influence of poets and men of letters, of whom Coleridge and Carlyle in Britain, and Emerson in America, may be mentioned as outstanding examples. Only in the last third of the nineteenth century did idealism establish itself among English-speaking philosophers, as distinct from those who were primarily men of letters. Among the pioneers of the movement were J. H. Stirling and T. H. Green in Britain, and W. T. Harris in America. The whole German idealist movement, from Kant onwards, made its influence felt, and perhaps the diversities within the German movement, coming together, help to account for some of the distinctive characteristics of Anglo-American idealism. It would be true to say, however, that it was Hegel

[1] *Modern Philosophy*, p. 261.

who above all influenced the new movement, and however difficult and complex his system of philosophy may be, an attempt must be made here to summarize its most salient features.

Hegel's idealism maintained that reality is rational. The world is the manifestation of a spiritual principle. This does not mean that material things are illusory, but that they are correlative to a spirit which realizes itself in and through the processes of nature. In man, spirit attains self-consciousness. Hegel thus finds room in his system for the idea of development or evolution, but this is interpreted as a spiritual process in which the lower is explained in terms of the higher rather than the higher in terms of the lower. Hegel was not only an idealist but also a monist, that is to say, he held that reality is one. But this unity does not preclude difference. Rather, the development of the absolute spirit involves differentiation, but in such a way that the differences are held together in a more comprehensive unity. A favourite illustration used by Edward Caird to explain this principle of identity in difference is that of a society which, as its development proceeds, involves increasing division of labour; yet this division of labour heightens the unity of the society, increasing the mutual interdependence of its members. For Hegel, reality is so much a unity that no individual fact can be fully understood except in its relation to the whole. We must penetrate behind the representation of any particular to the universal concept or notion that it exhibits, and which has its place in the articulated system of reason. As development produces differentiation, the differences conflict, but in truth they are complementary, and are reconciled in a higher unity. This is the famous Hegelian dialectic, whereby the conflict of thesis and antithesis is resolved in a higher synthesis.

What these doctrines imply for the interpretation of religion will become clearer as we proceed. They formed the matrix of ideas from which Anglo-American idealism was built up. There can be no doubt that theological motives played a considerable part in the thinking of many of the early English and American idealists. They saw in idealism an alternative to the naturalism and agnosticism which seemed to be undermining religious faith, and regarded themselves as defenders of the faith. For this reason, their ideas were soon taken up by theologians. Hegelian influence is evident in the English theologians who contributed to the symposium *Lux Mundi* in 1889, and in contemporary American theologians such as Elisha Mulford. As time went on, however, the new idealism shook off its subservience to theology, and developed with that independence which is proper to philosophy. The ambiguous bearing of Hegelianism upon Christianity became increasingly apparent, and those theologians who had embraced idealism either resiled from it or were driven into increasingly unorthodox positions or looked for new formulations of idealism more in accord with traditional Christian teaching.

In the present chapter we shall consider first two British philosophers who taught a fairly unadulterated Hegelianism, though with their own distinctive emphases (Section 4). Next we shall look at the high-water mark of the British neo-Hegelian movement in the absolute idealism of Bradley and Bosanquet (Section 5). Then we must direct our attention across the Atlantic to the greatest of the American idealists, Josiah Royce (Section 6). Having surveyed the philosophers, we shall then examine some of the theological and religious writers of idealist tendency (Section 7). We shall conclude with a critical summary (Section 8).

4. British Neo-Hegelianism
E. Caird, H. Jones

One of the most influential and probably the most respected of British philosophers in the opening years of the twentieth century was Edward Caird[1] (1835–1908). Though he followed the ideas of Hegel pretty closely, he gave to his own version of idealism a definitely theistic character, and laid stress on the idea of development or evolution. The resulting philosophy of religion, if not exactly orthodox, is at least highly compatible with Christianity.

Caird begins from the belief that 'the world is a rational or intelligible system'.[2] Everything from the physical processes of nature to the highest spiritual activities of man is in principle capable of rational explanation. The mode of explanation, however, must be adequate to what is explained. We cannot explain the higher in terms of the lower, and in a world which has brought forth the spiritual life of man the ultimate principle of explanation must be spiritual. This unifying with the God of religion. Reason and religion come to the same goal, so that religion needs neither a special revelation nor a mystical intuition. 'Every rational being as such is a religious being.'[3] Religion is thus a conscious relation to God, and God in turn is the absolute spiritual principle which manifests itself both in nature and in man, and is the unity underlying all differences.

In working out this view of religion, Caird makes use of two ideas. The first is that of *the unity of man*, which depends on his self-consciousness

[1] Professor at Glasgow, 1866–93; Master of Balliol College, Oxford, 1893–1907.
[2] *The Evolution of Religion*, vol. I, p. 4.   [3] *Op. cit.*, vol. I, p. 68.

and his sharing in a common rationality. Since man is one, his religion is one, and the data for an understanding of it must be drawn from the whole field of its varied manifestations, from primitive as well as from advanced religion, from non-Christian as well as from Christian. The second idea is that of *development or evolution*. This is conceived as a process of differentiation and integration, one in which 'difference continually increases, not at the expense of unity, but in such a way that the unity also is deepened'.[1] Thus the diverse manifestations of religion must be understood in the light of the unitary process of development. In this process, what is lower is to be understood in terms of what is higher. If it is objected that the definition of religion as 'a conscious relation to God' is inapplicable to primitive religion, it must be replied that primitive religion contains the germ of higher religion. The knowledge of God is at once the presupposition and the end of our thinking, and in the development of religion it is brought more and more clearly to consciousness.

There are three elements in consciousness. Man can look outwards upon the not-self, the *object*; he can look inwards upon himself, the *subject*; he can look upwards to the unity which embraces the cleavage of subject and object and is presupposed in the difference between them, the absolute principle of unity or *God*. While these three elements are always present in consciousness, one or other of them may be dominant at any particular stage of man's development. Thus we find three stages in the development of religion. In *objective* religion, illustrated in the religion of Greece, God is represented primarily in objective terms. He is conceived as immanent in the natural world, and this type of religion moves through polytheism to pantheism, when everything finite is submerged in the whole. By way of reaction, *subjective* religion, typified in the religion of Israel, turns to the inner life of man and finds God more clearly manifested in the moral consciousness than in nature. Such religion culminates in monotheism, in which God is conceived as transcendent and external to the world. The opposition between subjective and objective religion is overcome in *universal* religion, of which Christianity is the type. This religion unites the immanence of pantheism with the transcendence of monotheism, and establishes the kinship of man's inner life with nature by referring them both to a wider unity. Yet this all-embracing unity is not one in which differences disappear, and the finite spirit of man is assured of immortality on the basis of its participation in the absolute spirit.

While we said that Caird's philosophy of religion is compatible with Christianity, it is clear that for him Christianity is esteemed only as the

[1] *Op. cit.*, vol. I, pp. 175.

manifestation of universal religion. This is the permanent element in Christianity which he sought to disentangle from whatever is transitory and particular. Again, we said that Caird gives a theistic interpretation to Hegelianism, but although this was certainly his intention, it is not clear that he escapes pantheism. His stress is on immanence rather than transcendence. He rules out miracles and divine interventions, or rather he would say that all is miracle, since everything manifests God. Thus the incarnation of God in Christ is not a unique or discontinuous event. Christ is to be revered not so much for himself as for the idea which he represents—the idea of a divine humanity, of the union of God and man and the incarnation of the divine in all human life. 'The general idea needs, so to speak, to be embodied or incarnated, "to be made flesh and to dwell among men" in all the fulness of realization in a finite individuality, before it can be known and appreciated in its universal meaning.' Then, however, we may proceed 'to detach the idea from accidents of time and place and circumstances, and present it as a general principle'.[1] Though this account of religion may nowadays seem speculative and intellectualist, the comprehensiveness of his thought and the nobility of this mind make Caird one of the great British religious thinkers of recent times.

Caird's relatively pure Hegelianism continued for another generation to have adherents, but none of its later exponents presented it with the lucid persuasiveness of Caird himself. We may glance briefly at one of his disciples, Henry Jones[2] (1852–1922). For Jones, idealism has itself become a religion, a 'practical creed' which he preached with enthusiasm as the way forward for the modern world.[3] In their deepest significance, the dogmas of Christianity agree with idealism. Thus, as in Caird, the dogma of the incarnation is held to signify the immanence of God in all men.[4] Such dogmas are to be regarded not as authoritative revelations but as the embodiment of hypotheses which find their rational confirmation in philosophy.

Jones restates the typical Hegelian teachings. 'Let man seek God by the way of pure reason, and he will find him.'[5] Rational inquiry will show beyond the differences of the world the underlying spiritual unity which

---

[1] *Op. cit.*, vol. II, p. 221.

[2] After holding academic posts at Bangor and St Andrews, he succeeded Caird as Professor at Glasgow, 1894–1922.

[3] See his lectures, *Idealism as a Practical Creed*.

[4] There is a well-known story of Jones relating to the days when, as a young man, he used to preach in Welsh chapels. It was explained to him that he had not been invited back to one of these chapels because he was said to deny the divinity of Christ. He replied: 'I deny the divinity of Christ! I do not deny the divinity of any man.' See Sir H. J. W. Hetherington, *The Life and Letters of Sir Henry Jones*, p. 43.

[5] *A Faith That Enquires*, p. vii.

is immanent both in nature and in man, and which assures man of the friendliness and co-operation of this world. Special emphasis is laid on the moral life. This is no vain striving after an unrealizable ideal, but 'a process that always attains'.[1] In the pursuit of the good, man realizes himself. No one does a morally good action without the gain of becoming a better person. Evil, on the other hand, is self-defeating. Thus our world favours the moral life, which is fulfilled in religion as the doing of the divine will.

God is identified with the Absolute of philosophy, and the stress is upon his immanence. There are no providential interventions. God is the world-process, yet as self-conscious and personal he is said also to transcend the universe. His is no static perfection, for in a changeless world the pursuit of the good would be unreal. However difficult the conception may be, we are to think of God as the perfect in process, as a dynamic progress from perfection to perfection, as the never-resting realization of ideals of goodness.

It is interesting to notice how Jones has to defend the traditional Hegelianism which he had inherited from Caird against the new developments which were taking place in British idealism. On the one hand, he opposes those who so stressed the finitude of man that there is nothing left for him but absorption into the Absolute. Jones denies that the contrast between finite and infinite is an ultimate one. As with other contrasts, its terms can be reconciled in a higher unity. Man has in his spiritual life something of the infinite, while the Absolute must cherish and maintain rather than extinguish the elements which have a place in it. The relation of the Absolute to the individual human being is better understood in terms of love than of absorption, and this love assures us of immortality. On the other hand, Jones equally opposes those idealists who tried to preserve individual personality by dissolving the universe into a republic of spirits. Jones adheres strictly to monism. God is immanent in the human spirit, he is the source of man's bent towards goodness, and our common life in God enhances rather than destroys individual personality. Perhaps the optimism of idealist philosophy reached its peak in the teaching of Jones.

5. BRITISH ABSOLUTISM AND SUPRARATIONALISM
F. H. Bradley, B. Bosanquet, C. A. Campbell

The expression 'absolute idealism' was defined at the beginning of this chapter in a wide sense which includes all those forms of idealism which

---

[1] *Op. cit.*, p. 152.

conceive the world as dependent on or correlative to an all-embracing or absolute experience. In this sense, Jones could call his doctrines 'absolute idealism'.[1] The expression, however, is also used in a narrower sense for the particular kind of idealism found in Bradley and Bosanquet, and which, to avoid confusion, may be called 'absolutism'. This absolutism may therefore be regarded as a species of absolute idealism, alongside and distinct from the neo-Hegelianism of Caird and Jones. The name 'absolutism' draws attention to the teaching that complete reality belongs only to the Absolute, while everything short of the Absolute is reduced to the status of appearance. There is the further point, however, that the Absolute is now claimed to be beyond rational description, and this doctrine of suprarationalism, as we shall see, has continued to be taught long after many other elements in the philosophies of Bradley and Bosanquet have been discarded.

The leading spirit in this new development was Francis Herbert Bradley[2] (1846-1924), undoubtedly the most brilliant of the neo-idealists and probably the greatest British philosopher of any school in recent times. Bradley proposes to embark on a metaphysical inquiry, by which he understands 'an attempt to know reality as against mere appearance'.[3] We are impelled to such an inquiry both by the need of our own nature to go beyond the region of ordinary facts to a more comprehensive view, and by the need to guard ourselves against uncritical acceptance of false or inadequate views of the world. 'Our orthodox theology on the one side and our commonplace materialism on the other side vanish like ghosts before the daylight of free sceptical inquiry.'[4] The aim of metaphysics is to satisfy the intellect. The intellect is satisfied only by that which is one and free from contradiction; this is *reality*. The intellect is not satisfied by that which is fragmentary and infected with contradiction; this is *appearance*.

The sceptical part of Bradley's argument consists of a hunt for contradictions in our thinking about the world. As soon as we pass beyond the level of immediate experience to discursive thinking, we are involved in relations. But the notion of 'relation' proves, on examination, to be unintelligible and one that lands us in insoluble contradictions. 'A relational way of thought must give appearance and not truth.'[5] Once this point is reached, there is no turning back. The various areas of our thinking are explored, found to be riddled with contradiction, and handed over one by one to the realm of appearance—space and time, motion

[1] *Idealism as a Practical Creed*, p. 12.
[2] Fellow of Merton College, Oxford 1870–1924.
[3] *Appearance and Reality*, p. 1.   [4] *Op. cit.*, p. 4.   [5] *Op. cit.*, p. 28.

and change, selfhood and personality, are alike shot through with incon-
sistencies. The moral life too has its contradictions, which it seeks to overcome by passing into religion. But even God and religion fall short of
reality, for religion implies a relation between God and man, so that man
stands over against God and God is therefore less than the Absolute.
Yet religion also demands that God should be all in all, and if God were
to pass into the Absolute, he would cease to be the God of religion, and
religion would disappear. Thus God too is an appearance, an aspect of
the Absolute.

If so much is appearance, what then is reality? Only the Absolute has
reality in the full sense. Can we, however, know anything about it? We
can have some positive knowledge of the Absolute, because we have a
positive criterion for reality—freedom from contradiction. Thus we can
say that the Absolute is *one*, for a plurality of reals would lead to contradiction. The differences of the universe must belong within one
integral harmonious system. Further, the Absolute is *experience*. Bradley
holds to the idealist thesis that to be real is to fall within experience. The
absolute experience, however, must be different from our finite experience.
It must be one experience in which all contradictions are resolved in a
harmonious whole. We are said to get a clue to the nature of this experience from that unbroken wholeness of immediate feeling which lies below
the level of relational thinking. 'From such an experience of unity below
relations we can rise to the idea of a superior unity above them.'[1] It is
also asserted that the Absolute is *spiritual*. It is not, however, personal.
We have already seen that the notion of personality belongs to appearance, as a bundle of discrepancies. More than that, since a person exists
in virtue of his relations to what is outside of himself, personality must be
finite, and Bradley holds that infinite personality is a meaningless idea.
Yet it would be a grave mistake to think that the denial of personality to
the Absolute means that it is below the level of personality. Rather, it is
suprapersonal.

What now becomes of the realm of appearance, to which so much was
consigned? Appearances are not illusions. The Absolute needs its appearances and would be nothing without them. Even the meanest of them has
its place in reality. Nothing is lost, for all is reconstituted in the absolute
experience. This, however, involves a transformation which we can only
dimly understand. Since what we value most still falls short of reality,
even the good must be transformed into something higher in the Absolute,
and we cannot properly speak of the Absolute as good. At the other end
of the scale, evil also is taken up in the Absolute and transmuted so that

[1] *Op. cit.*, p. 462.

it contributes to the richness and perfection of the whole. Of special interest is the question of the destiny of the finite self. A self, as we have seen, is not independently real. It has an adjectival status within the all-comprehending whole. It too is taken up in the Absolute, but must be so transmuted that anything like personal immortality is improbable. Thus all appearances find their fulfilment in the perfection of the Absolute—a static perfection which admits neither progress nor regress. The Absolute contains many histories, but has no history of its own.

The rigour of Bradley's metaphysic is somewhat mitigated by his doctrine of degrees of truth and reality. All appearances are not on the same level. Some stand nearer to reality than others, and require a less drastic transformation in the Absolute. The test is that of comprehensiveness and coherence. Thus good has more reality than evil, and it is more true to call the Absolute good than evil. In general, what is higher for us is higher also for the Absolute. Thus Bradley can allow that 'there is nothing more real than what comes in religion' and that 'the man who demands a reality more solid than that of the religious consciousness seeks he does not know what'.[1] As a practical affair, religion does not provide ultimate truth, and theologians should not pretend that it does. For instance, a personal God is not the ultimate truth of the universe. Metaphysics does deal with ultimate truth, and in this respect stands higher than religion. But since we are not merely theoretical beings, religion stands higher than philosophy in so far as religion attempts to express the complete reality of goodness through every aspect of our beings. For Bradley himself, metaphysics has something of the character of a religion. He says that for some people it is a way of satisfying the mystical side of our nature and of experiencing the Deity, but he disclaims that this way is superior to others, or that it could be for any but a very few.

In one of his essays, Bradley remarks: 'There is, I should say, a need, and there is even a certain demand, for a new religion.'[2] Philosophy cannot supply this, but Bradley visualizes the possibility of a religion not itself founded on metaphysics but with a creed which metaphysics could justify; and this might come about by 'modification' of the religion which we already have. This suggests that Bradley's metaphysic would be compatible with a drastically transformed and idealized version of Christianity. Nevertheless, one must say that with his powerful and original contribution to philosophy, the earlier alliance between neo-idealism and theology ended.

Almost inseparable from the name of Bradley is that of Bernard

[1] *Op. cit.*, p. 398. [2] *Essays on Truth and Reality*, p. 446.

Bosanquet[1] (1848–1923). Though he perhaps fell short of Bradley in ability, he surpassed him in the breadth of his interests. Whereas Bradley in the main confined himself to the central philosophical disciplines of logic, metaphysics and ethics, Bosanquet wrote not only on these but also on such themes as art, religion and the state. He was, in addition, much taken up with social work. Philosophy, he believed, needs both the best of logic and the best of life.

Bosanquet's central doctrines are very close to Bradley's, but he introduces a somewhat different terminology and draws out the wider implications of absolutism. In particular, he makes extensive use of two terms, neither of which was specially prominent in Bradley—'individuality' and 'value'. We usually think of an individual as that which is distinct, separate, particular, and especially we use the term for a single self or person as a supposedly independent unit. This, however, is far from Bosanquet's usage. He thinks that we are too prone to take a negative criterion for individuality—to call something 'individual' just because it is not something else. We need a positive criterion, and this criterion is ability to stand by itself, freedom from contradiction, or, in a word, self-completeness. When we recognize this, we see that individuality does not belong to that which is separate or fragmentary, such as an isolated self, but only to a system or a 'world'. We get a clue to the nature of individuality from, say, a picture in which the artist has combined separate elements into a harmonious whole; or from the state which, on the Hegelian view, is more truly an individual than any one of its citizens. A work of art or a state, however, is still a finite individual, not wholly self-complete. We are driven on towards the doctrine of absolutism. 'In the ultimate sense, there can only be one individual, the Absolute.'[2] Individuality is also the criterion of value. We ascribe value to whatever gives us satisfaction, but this does not mean that values are merely subjective, in the sense that we cannot argue about them. Enduring satisfaction is found only in what is self-consistent, so that in the last resort value, like individuality, belongs in the full sense only to the Absolute.

In finite existence therefore we have only degrees of individuality and value, but these point us to their completion in the Absolute. In its quest for full individuality and satisfying value, the finite self (the so-called 'individual' in the ordinary sense of the term) must go outside of its separate selfhood and identify itself with the whole of which it is a member.

---

[1] Professor at St Andrews, 1903–8; he devoted most of his life to writing and philanthropic work.

[2] *The Principle of Individuality and Value*, p. 68.

'The greatest men leave little more than a name, because their work has blended with cosmic forces from which it cannot be separated for estimation.'[1] Jesus and Socrates are cited as examples—we know little of their 'persons' apart from their 'worlds' and the 'movements' which they initiated.

Three stages are distinguished in the pilgrimage of finite selves towards their destiny. The first is *the moulding of souls*. The world is a 'vale of soul-making', in Keats' expression. The universe is such that it brings forth finite spiritual beings who are moulded by nature and who at the same time mould both themselves and their environment and aspire to pass beyond a merely natural existence. The second stage consists in *the hazards and hardships* of finite selfhood. Here Bosanquet's view may be contrasted with that of Jones. Whereas Jones, with a somewhat facile optimism, viewed morality as 'a process that always attains' and man as 'realizing himself' in the pursuit of the good, Bosanquet draws attention to the failures and contradictions involved in the strivings of the finite self for an infinite satisfaction. Such a self 'is always a fragmentary being, inspired by an infinite whole which he is for ever striving to express in terms of his limited range of externality. In this he can never succeed.'[2] The way to the third stage, *stability and security*, can lie only through self-transcendence. In the religious consciousness, man recognizes himself for the dependent being that he is. He must give up every vestige of independence. Self-transcendence means the surrender of his separate finite selfhood in his membership of the Absolute, the true individual and the ultimate value. Thus the destiny of the finite self is neither destruction nor immortality, but rather transmutation in the Absolute. Nor is this something that is merely future. The perfection of the Absolute is timeless. Transmutation of the finite self, like 'eternal life' in the Fourth Gospel, can be here and now. The evanescence of the limits of personality and absorption in a deeper experience belong to everyday life. It is in this way, according to Bosanquet, that human destiny gets fulfilled.

The Bradleian tradition has been continued, though with many far-reaching modifications, in the philosophy of Charles Arthur Campbell[3] (1897–   ). In his early book, *Scepticism and Construction*, Campbell takes as his starting-point Bradley's sceptical doctrine that the Absolute is beyond relations and so beyond rational knowledge. It is, in Campbell's terminology, 'suprarational', and 'must remain opaque to the categories of the intellect'.[4] Moreover, while Bradley based his argument on an examination

---

[1] *The Value and Destiny of the Individual*, p. 264.
[2] *Op. cit.*, p. 304.
[3] Professor at Bangor, Wales, 1932–8; Glasgow, 1938–61. [4] *Op. cit.*, p. 3.

of the nature and demands of knowledge, Campbell claims that when
we turn to different forms of experience, we get striking corroboration
of the essential result of the epistemological argument. He examines
not only cognitive experience, but also the experiences of self-activity,
morality and religion, and finds that in each case the very nature of the
experience compels us to affirmations which imply the conviction that
reality is beyond knowledge.

Are we then reduced to an utter metaphysical scepticism? Bradley
mitigated his scepticism by his doctrine of degrees of truth, but Campbell
rejects this. He puts in its place a doctrine which distinguishes 'noumenal'
and 'phenomenal' truth. Noumenal truth, which would give absolute
intellectual satisfaction, is utterly precluded from our finite minds, and
with it, knowledge of ultimate reality. Phenomenal truth gives satisfaction
in so far as that is attainable by finite minds, and philosophy can even
discover final phenomenal truths. There is an affinity between noumenal
and phenomenal truth since both are related to the intellect's quest for
satisfaction. Phenomenal truth is not to be despised just because noumenal
truth is unattainable, and indeed phenomenal truth provides the only
possibility for constructive philosophy.

The detailed application of these ideas to the problem of religion is
carried out by Campbell in his Gifford Lectures. The religious relation has
two terms, the soul and God, and Campbell begins by asking whether
the self can be regarded as a soul in any sense that would be religiously
satisfying. An examination of the experiences of the self leads him to
conclude that it is a relatively abiding, active, spiritual entity, as against
the view that it is a mere concatenation of experiences. We may notice
that here also Campbell parts company from Bradley who assigned to the
self a merely adjectival status.

From selfhood the argument goes on to Godhood. Rational theism is
found to be internally inconsistent, so we are driven to consider the
question of suprarational theism. Campbell introduces this with a discussion of Otto's doctrine of the 'numinous'[1] as an overplus of meaning
which transcends our rational concepts. This means that our language
about God is not literally applicable, but is symbolic of a reality which is in
itself unknown. But if our talk of God is not to be utterly empty, we would
need to suppose that there is some affinity between our symbols and what
they symbolize.

Here we come back to the philosophical argument for a suprarational
Absolute. And now a striking parallel emerges between the symbols of
religion and the phenomenal truths of philosophy. For both religion and

[1] See below, p. 214.

philosophy, 'the ultimate reality transcends all possible conception. But for neither does this entail sheer, blank ignorance of its nature. For the religious consciousness, there is an affinity between its object and certain rational qualities, which justifies the symbolic representation of its object. For the intellectual consciousness, there is an affinity between that perfect unity in difference which must characterize reality, and the most comprehensive and coherent unities actually attainable under the conditions of finite experience.'[1] Campbell argues further that the symbolical knowledge of God of which he speaks is no more agnostic, it would seem, than the knowledge permitted by scholastic philosophy's doctrine of analogy.

The conclusion of his argument leads us therefore to a Being who is infinite and eternal, the sole ultimate reality, the creator of the finite temporal world, and the source of the moral law; such a Being utterly transcends all human power of conception, but may be legitimately symbolized as a Spirit of the highest goodness, wisdom and power.

6. AMERICAN ABSOLUTE IDEALISM

J. Royce

In America absolute idealism developed on independent and original lines, and found an exponent of the first rank in Josiah Royce[2] (1855–1916). In an early work, while acknowledging his 'great debt' to Hegel, he added that 'it is a mistake to neglect the other idealists just for the sake of glorifying him'.[3] In his later writings he moved further away from Hegelianism, and Gabriel Marcel has gone so far as to claim that in Royce's thought we see a transition from Absolute idealism towards existentialism. This is an exaggeration, and it is better to regard Royce as an idealist who worked out the teachings of the school in a very original way.

Royce was interested all his life in the problem of religion. It was however his custom not to express an opinion until he had reached a clear understanding of the issue involved. As he says himself, 'A philosophical student waits for light, and does not teach a doctrine until he finds light about that doctrine.'[4] Consequently his view of religion took shape gradually over the years as he advanced from one group of problems to another, and we can best expound it in three stages.

The foundation was laid in an early work in which Royce tells us that the religious problems first drove him to philosophy, and declares that

---

[1] *On Selfhood and Godhood*, p. 403.   [2] Professor at Harvard, 1882–1916.
[3] *The Religious Aspect of Philosophy*, p. xiv.   [4] *The World and the Individual*, vol. II, p. xiv.

these problems 'deserve our best efforts and our utmost loyalty'.[1] The central problem is stated in the following terms: 'Is there then, anywhere in the universe, any real thing of infinite worth?'[2] When we examine the answers which have been traditionally given to this question, it might seem that we cannot avoid falling into complete scepticism, for on all sides we find conflict, doubt and error. But now Royce makes the daring and original move which, as he believes, brings the solution of the problem. The very fact that there can be error implies that there must be absolute truth. Error is commonly taken to be the failure of my thought to agree with its intended object. Since, however, I cannot step outside of my thinking to compare my thought with the reality which I intend to think about, the recognition that I can be in error implies that there is a higher thought which includes both my thought and its intended object. The assumption on which all rational thinking proceeds—that objective truth and error are possible—implies the Absolute, the all-embracing thought which includes my thought and all thoughts and objects as subordinate parts or elements. 'All reality must be present to the unity of the Infinite Thought.'[3] Thus, among other things, a perfect knowledge of good and evil belongs to the Absolute, so we may conclude that 'the world, as a whole, is and must be absolutely good, since the infinite thought must know what is desirable, and knowing it must have present in itself the true objects of desire'.[4] The existence of evil is no evidence against this, for just as error implies absolute truth, so evil implies absolute goodness, and is overcome in the Absolute. Having established the Absolute as the foundation of religion, Royce was content to leave aside for the time being such questions as that of the destiny of finite selves. 'Whatever happens to our poor selves, we know that the Whole is perfect. And this knowledge gives us peace.'[5]

Fifteen years later this problem of 'our poor selves' and their relation to the Absolute was attacked by Royce in his Gifford Lectures. The Absolute is now conceived in terms of will rather than of thought. Ideas are said to be volitional as well as cognitive entities—they embody purposes (their 'internal' meaning) as well as standing for facts (their 'external' meaning). Internal meanings seek external realization, while external meanings demand to be appropriated as the satisfaction of internal meanings. Only in God or the Absolute are all ideas completely fulfilled; and since Royce defines 'individuality' in terms of purpose or will,[6] this means that for him, as for Bosanquet, the Absolute is the only perfect individual,

[1] *The Religious Aspect of Philosophy*, p. ix.   [2] *Op. cit.*, p. 8.
[3] *Op. cit.*, p. 433.   [4] *Op. cit.*, p. 444.
[5] *Op. cit.*, p. 478.   [6] *The World and the Individual*, vol. I, pp. 335–9.

'the Individual of Individuals'. Finite selves aspire to individuality, but they never approach it so long as they remain isolated. They progress towards it as their purposes become wider and more inclusive, and as they realize their unity with other selves, with nature, and with God. But Royce differs sharply from Bosanquet's view that the finite self is an appearance which must be transmuted in the Absolute. Royce's Absolute is rather an absolute self which is constituted by the infinity of finite selves in which the Absolute represents itself. It is 'not a barren Absolute which devours individuals, but a whole that is just to the finite aspect of every flying moment, and of every transient or permanent form of finite selfhood —a whole that is an individual system of ethically free individuals who are nevertheless one in God'.[1] Thus every finite individual has his unique place in the Absolute.

This social conception of the Absolute leads to Royce's final view of religion, which found mature expression a dozen years later in his exposition of Christianity as a religion of loyalty. He defined 'loyalty' as 'the willing and thoroughgoing devotion of a self to a cause, when the cause is something which unites many selves in one, and which is therefore the interest of a community'.[2] What chiefly impressed Royce in the New Testament was not the person of Jesus but the Pauline churches, for whom Christ was the symbol for the Spirit uniting their members. The cause to which these communities were devoted was not sectarian or partisan, but had in view a world-wide community of the faithful, and so engaged a genuine loyalty. The ultimate principle is loyalty to loyalty, which means rising above selfish and limited interests to the service of the whole community of mankind. Royce supports these views by bringing forward a complex philosophical theory of interpretation. He holds that interpretation is as fundamental to cognition as are perception and conception, but interpretation is peculiar in that it is a relation which always involves three terms—what is interpreted, the interpreter, and the one to whom the interpretation is given. Thus interpretation brings us into a community of interpretation. The world itself is constituted by an endless series of interpretations. 'Every act of interpretation aims to introduce unity into life, by mediating between mutually contrasting or estranged ideas, minds, and purposes.'[3] Now, the charity or love taught by St Paul is not only an emotion but an interpretation, leading towards the realization of the ideal community. The doctrine of an unending movement towards the ideal community is not meant to be an abandonment of the Absolute. The community after which we aspire is the expression

---

[1] *Op. cit.*, vol. I, p. 42.   [2] *The Problem of Christianity*, vol. I, p. 68.
[3] *Op. cit.*, vol. II, p. 286.

of the divine on earth, and though still invisible, is perfectly real.

It is not easy to see how all the elements in Royce's thinking about religion hang together. If he had been able to reflect for another decade or so, would he have presented us with a more systematic statement? Or is it more likely that he would have disturbed us by some fresh departure? Perhaps just this is creative philosophizing.

7. ABSOLUTE IDEALISM IN THEOLOGICAL AND RELIGIOUS WRITERS
J. R. Illingworth, R. J. Campbell, R. W. Trine

When we turn from the philosophers of Anglo-American absolute idealism to the theologians and religious writers who were influenced by the movement, we experience something of an anticlimax, for among them we do not find any thinkers comparable in stature to Bradley and Royce, or to the great German Hegelian theologians of an earlier time. Nevertheless, as we have already noted, the new idealism had soon made its influence felt in theology. This influence expressed itself chiefly in an emphasis on the doctrine of divine immanence. We shall look briefly at three writers who, around the turn of the century, exhibit in varying degrees the influence of absolute idealism.

With John Richardson Illingworth[1] (1848–1915), one of the most competent English philosophical theologians of his day, the influence was a moderate one, so that his theology remains substantially orthodox. Beginning from the common distinction between body and soul, or matter and spirit, Illingworth points out that however different these two may be, we always know them in combination.[2] Matter is always correlative to a knowing mind, while spirit, as we know it, is always embodied. But though the two are always conjoined, a certain primacy belongs to spirit which uses matter for its purposes.

Illingworth next draws attention to our awareness of an indwelling Spirit in the material world of nature—an awareness which belongs to the religious consciousness and which is claimed to be a fundamental fact of human experience. He illustrates this awareness by a chain of quotations drawn from both the Christian and non-Christian religions. In this he makes clear his adherence to the idealist doctrine of the unity of man, and of man's religion. Elsewhere he states plainly that in the non-Christian religions no one 'can fail to recognize the ring of true religion', and he compares the Christian revelation to a superstructure based on natural

---

[1] Rector of Longworth, near Oxford, 1883–1915.   [2] *Divine Immanence*, pp. 2ff.

religion and dependent upon it.[1] If we now ask how the universal Spirit is related to matter, we are told first that they constitute a unity in which spirit has the primacy. The best clue to the relation of the divine Spirit to the material order is found in what we know of ourselves, 'the starting-point of all our knowledge'. We transcend matter, and are to some extent its masters; but we are also immanent in matter—essentially immanent in our bodies and secondarily immanent in the environment which we mould to our purposes. Similarly the divine Spirit transcends the material order and yet indwells it. To the question whether God indwells it as his body or his work, 'it is obvious that no answer can be more than conjectural or hypothetical'.[2] The Christian revelation, however, points to an answer. God is completely immanent in Christ, as we are in our bodies, and he is secondarily immanent in his whole creation, as we are in our works—except that whereas we can be only impersonally present in our works, God really does animate the universe. Furthermore, God is also immanent in man, who is regarded as a part of nature.

Illingworth has no objection to calling this God 'suprapersonal', provided we include in this term 'the essential attributes of personality'.[3] Sometimes, however, he prefers to speak of human personality as imperfect, a replica in the finite of the divine archetypal personality;[4] and sees in the triune constitution of the human personality as thought, desire, and will, a reflection of the divine Trinity.

Though obviously willing to go pretty far with absolute idealism, Illingworth always regarded Christianity as a historical revelation, and laboured hard to maintain the uniqueness of the incarnation in Christ and even the belief in miracles. Towards the end of his life he thought it necessary to correct the immanentist trend of his theology by stressing the divine transcendence and developing a doctrine of ecclesiastical authority.[5] Such a theme takes us outside of philosophical theology, and here we must bid farewell to this able and learned theologian.

Less erudite than Illingworth but also less inhibited by the claims of orthodoxy was Reginald John Campbell[6] (1867–1956). He became famous as a preacher in one of London's leading nonconformist chapels, and in his sermons worked out the so-called 'New Theology' which was the subject of much controversy in the first decade of the century. A major ingredient in this theology was absolute idealism.

[1] *Personality Human and Divine*, pp. 161–2. [2] *Divine Immanence*, p. 72.
[3] *Op. cit.*, p. 158. [4] *Personality Human and Divine*, p. 216.
[5] In his book, *Divine Transcendence*.
[6] Minister of the City Temple, London, 1903–15; returned to the Church of England (in which he had been confirmed), 1916; after holding various offices, became Canon of Chichester, 1930–46.

Campbell is almost echoing Bradley[1] when he says that the danger to religion and to mankind 'arises from practical materialism on the one hand and an antiquated dogmatic theology on the other'.[2] There is a certain bitterness in Campbell's frequent attacks on the traditional theology. He thinks that its chief defect is its conception of a God who is separate from the world, and that its statements, if taken at all literally, amount to a *reductio ad absurdum*. Thus he ironically writes: 'This God is greatly bothered and thwarted by what men have been doing throughout the few millennia of human existence. He takes the whole thing very seriously, and thinks about little else than getting wayward humanity into line again. To this end he has adopted various expedients, the chief of which was the sending of his only-begotten Son to suffer and die in order that he might be free to forgive the trouble we had caused him.'[3] Campbell writes much more in the same strain.

Campbell's own starting-point is the immanence of God in the universe and in mankind. God is the all, the infinite Spirit present in every atom of the universe, the unity in all multiplicity. There is no sharp distinction between divinity and humanity. The spirit of man is a manifestation of the one divine Spirit, and Campbell speculates whether the subconscious reach of the mind may not be the factor which unites men with each other and all mankind with God. In the light of these ideas—for which, like other idealists, he disliked the term 'pantheism'—he restated the underlying meaning of the traditional Christian doctrines. The fall does not signify a fall of man, who is rising all the time, but the fall of the infinite into the finite, the process by which the divine life realizes itself in limited existences. This process involves sin and suffering, but these are means to a great end. The consubstantiality of Christ with the Father does not mean that Christ was a uniquely constituted being. Jesus is indeed historically unique. He is the standard of human excellence, and brought to light the unity of God and man. But there is no gulf between him and the rest of mankind. Christhood is a potentiality for all men, since all are of the substance of God and all human history is divine incarnation. The atonement is not the once-for-all satisfaction of an outraged God. Jesus' self-sacrificing love shows us the way to realize our unity with God, and is an atonement only when the sacrifice is repeated on the altar of the disciple's heart. The kingdom of God must be conceived in terms of immanence as belonging to his present world, and Campbell embraced socialism as the means to its realization.

Campbell's arguments are often superficial and rhetorical, but he was honestly striving to make Christianity intelligible to modern minds, and

[1] See above, p. 29.   [2] *The New Theology*, p. 2.   [3] *Op. cit.*, pp. 18–19.

many people were undoubtedly helped by his teaching. Yet he resiled from his views, and eventually became a cathedral dignitary.

America had its idealist theologians as well as England, but for an illustration of the influence of absolute idealism on American religious thought, we propose to go outside of Christian theology to a representative of the heterodox movement known as 'New Thought'. This had many sources, and was not specifically Christian but sought to express the truth in all religions. It sometimes ran into extravagances, but deserves to be judged by its best representatives. In any case, our survey must take note of some writers of a more popular sort, to show how philosophical and theological ideas have broken out of narrow professional circles to make their influence felt on large numbers of ordinary people.

The representative whom we have chosen is Ralph Waldo Trine[1] (1866-   ). He enjoyed the respect of William James, while James Leuba wrote of him as 'one of the ablest and sanest writers of "New Thought" '.[2] He was deeply influenced by Emerson, who, as we have noted, was one of the pioneers of idealist teaching in America. Trine himself may be regarded as a mystic rather than a philosopher, for he tells us that though reason is not to be neglected, the highest wisdom comes from interior illumination. He sets forth a view of the world which is in its essence a popular version of absolute idealism, combined with elements from Christianity, the Asian religions, and the current psychology.

'The great central fact of the universe', he writes, 'is that Spirit of infinite life and power that is behind all, that animates all, that manifests itself in and through all; this Spirit is what I call "God".'[3] Nothing is outside of God. The material universe represents God's thought, while men themselves are partakers of the divine life. Men do not differ from God in essence or quality, but in degree. They are individualized spirits, while God is the infinite Spirit which includes them.

The essential message of Christianity is the same as that of the other great religions, so that one should be able to worship equally well in a Catholic cathedral, a Jewish synagogue, or a Buddhist temple. This universal message of religion is the summons to come into conscious realization of our unity with the infinite Spirit. To come into such conscious realization is to be changed from a mere man into a God-man. Recognition of our own divinity makes available the dynamic of religion and gives mastery over life. Since God is literally among us, salvation works itself out in this world, and is said to include not just peace of mind

---

[1] Author of a series of books on religion and the conduct of life.
[2] *A Psychological Study of Religion*, p. 300.
[3] *In Tune with the Infinite*, pp. 11–12.

but physical health as well. Trine's own remarkable longevity would seem to be a tribute to the practical efficacy of his teaching.

The obvious weakness of a doctrine such as Trine's is that since it lacks a critically examined intellectual basis, it may easily slip into sentimentalism and groundless optimism. Trine himself is saved from the worst extravagances by a certain vigour and commonsense in his thought. That his teaching obviously met a need of the day is attested by the fact that the book from which we have quoted (and which is still in print) sold over a million copies and was translated into a score of languages. The astonishing popularity of Trine's uncritical optimism may lead us to suspect that the optimism of the idealists in general was as much a reflection of the optimistic spirit of their times as the rationally founded conclusion which they suppose it to be.

8. SUMMARY AND CRITICISM OF ABSOLUTE IDEALISM

The leading characteristics of the absolute idealist interpretation of religion may be summarized as follows. It was *metaphysical*. The essence of religion is found in a world-view, according to which everything is referred to the absolute spirit as the sole ultimate reality. Reality might be conceived as rational (Caird, Jones) or as supra-rational (Bradley, Bosanquet, C. A. Campbell) or as combining thought and will (Royce); reason might be supplemented by revelation (Illingworth), joined with cosmic emotion (R. J. Campbell) or subordinated to mystical illumination (Trine); but religion is basically conceived in an intellectualist way, as founded on a metaphysical belief about the universe. It was *monistic*. Reality is one, and all dualisms and pluralisms are resolved in the comprehensive unity. The dualism between God and the world is overcome by a doctrine of divine immanence, often amounting to pantheism. The plurality of finite individual selves is usually overcome by regarding them as manifestations, adjectives, fragments or what you will of the one Spirit which indwells them all. There is consequently a tendency to depreciate the philosophical status of personality, which is imperfect in the finite form in which we know it, and may therefore be predicated only metaphorically of God.[1] Since monism rules out any 'beyond' or crude supernaturalism, there is a tendency to conceive the practical benefits of religion

[1] This last point is often misunderstood. To say that God is not personal does not mean that he is subpersonal—on the contrary, the writers who talk in this way insist that he is suprapersonal. If we are going to permit ourselves to indulge in such speculations at all, this is surely a plausible contention. Even so orthodox a theologian as Illingworth was prepared to accept it. (See above, p. 39.)

in this-worldly terms, as moral, social and even physical well-being. But perhaps the most important religious consequence of monism is the removal of a hard and fast barrier between the divine and the human— God and man are essentially one. The type of view which we are considering is also characterized by its concern for the *universal*. Anything which is particular is of interest only in so far as it illuminates a 'world' in which it finds a place. The religious consequence here is a tendency to depreciate history—for instance, belief in a particular incarnation is of interest not as the assertion of a once-for-all happening but as a parable of the timeless truth of the union of God and man. Finally, we note the characteristic of *optimism*. Evil is taken up and resolved in the perfection of the whole. The problem of evil is a difficult one for any philosophy of religion, but it was specially difficult for the absolute idealists who had to maintain both that the whole is perfect and that the moral life is important. Their attempted solutions took such various forms as the idea of progress from perfection to perfection in the Absolute (Jones) or that evil is an appearance (Bradley) or that it is the necessary accompaniment of the 'fall' of the infinite into limited existences and is outweighed by the good to which this process leads (R. J. Campbell).

No one would wish to deny the impressiveness of the absolute idealist interpretation of religion.[1] Yet perhaps its very comprehensiveness has proved to be its undoing. In taking reality as a whole, absolute idealism invites us to take its own system of thought as a whole also. Thus if we find a few cracks or weaknesses in its closely knit structure, we are tempted to abandon the whole thing.

This is indeed what has happened. Rival philosophies have drawn attention to weaknesses in absolute idealism, and the whole movement has faded away. Of these rivals, personal idealism began as a reaction within the idealist camp itself. It contended that idealism, as a philosophy of spirit, should take as its norm not the speculative notion of an absolute spirit but the idea of personality, the only form of spiritual life of which we have direct experience, and it drew attention to the difficulty of understanding how a person can be included in God. Outside of idealism altogether, pragmatism directed its attack against the intellectualist bias of absolute idealism. We are more than contemplative beings, our life is acting and willing, and perhaps these should guide our understanding rather than pure thought. Already in the voluntaristic colouring of Royce's version of idealism we see a concession to the pragmatists.

---

[1] Least of all the present writer who acknowledges that if he has any interest in or understanding for the problems of philosophy and religion, he got it from thinkers of this school.

The new realism was another enemy. Not only did it challenge the whole idealist thesis, but by demanding an analytical rather than a synthesizing approach to philosophy, it drew attention to the woolliness of some of the sweeping assertions made about the Absolute. Outside of philosophy, the trend of events and the coming of the First World War made any optimistic philosophy less easy to accept. Thus absolute idealism has gradually declined.

The tradition has still indeed its representatives. As late as 1957, my own teacher, C. A. Campbell, who resolutely refuses to conform to the current enthusiasm for empiricism and analysis, was defending some of Bradley's central doctrines, though making it quite clear that he certainly would not wish to defend all the doctrines of the absolute idealists or 'the imprecise and rhetorical language'[1] in which they were often expressed. Campbell's suprarationalism, however, while it stands in the idealist tradition, departs so radically from the older varieties that it has ceased to be 'idealism' in the strict sense, and obviously escapes some of the strictures passed above on absolute idealism. The breach begins with Bradley himself, for in demonstrating the failure of thought to grasp reality, he had departed from the basic idealist tenet that the real and the rational are the same.

But Bradley's remaining admirers are few. More often than not, he is perfunctorily dismissed or left on the shelf. Idealist theologians are likewise in eclipse, and the doctrine of divine immanence has been replaced by a stress on transcendence. Of course, it is a question whether, if the Western world should come through its present turmoils—political, social, and intellectual—to a settled and stable period once more, something like absolute idealism may not reappear. For the present, however, it is out of favour, and is not even seriously discussed, much less defended. A prediction made about it by George Santayana away back in 1911 has been fulfilled: 'Nothing will have been disproved, but everything will have been abandoned.'[2]

---

[1] *On Selfhood and Godhood*, p. 39.　　　　[2] *Winds of Doctrine*, p. 211.

III

PERSONAL IDEALISM

9. THE STATUS OF PERSONS

PERSONAL idealism arose as a reaction against absolute idealism, but as a reaction which was still within the Anglo-American idealist movement and which, in many instances, still largely looked to Hegel for its inspiration. Both forms of idealism conceived reality as spiritual. Absolute idealism laid the stress upon the one all-embracing Spirit, the Absolute, in which finite spirits or persons were supposed to be somehow included; and thus there was often a tendency to deny full reality to persons and to think of the Absolute as suprapersonal. On the other hand, personal idealism takes its clue to the nature of spirit from the spiritual life of persons—which is, after all, the form of the spiritual life most readily accessible to us; and it tends to think of God or the supreme Spirit as personal also. Thus we find something like a Hegelian dialectic working itself out in neo-Hegelianism itself. The stress shifts from the one Spirit to the many spirits. There is a movement from monism in the direction of pluralism. Where God or a supreme Person is recognized, reality may still be conceived as one, and we do not have an extreme form of pluralism. But in all the personal idealists, there is a movement away from what they regarded as the too thoroughgoing monism of the absolute idealists.

The motives behind personal idealism were, however, not purely philosophical. Theological motives undoubtedly played a part with some of the writers whom we shall consider. We have noted already how some of the pioneers of neo-Hegelianism were attracted to idealism because they supposed it to be an ally of religion against naturalism and agnosticism. In Bradley and Bosanquet, idealism had taken a turn which estranged it from theology. In Illingworth, though he went pretty far with the absolute idealists, we already see an attempted defence of personality in the interests of religion. Now the stress on personality comes to the fore. This is the category which is to cement the alliance between idealism and Christianity. Yet once again we find philosophy asserting its independence, and personal idealism in its most brilliantly original formulation—

the atheistic idealism of McTaggart—carries us even further from Christian orthodoxy than absolute idealism had done.

Another motive in personal idealism, especially among its American exponents, was the democratic interest. It was felt by some that an absolutist metaphysic is inappropriate in a free society. Democracy rests upon a belief in the worth of the individual person, and the interest of some philosophers was to find a metaphysical basis for the democratic way of life.

It is likely that some non-philosophical motives are present, either consciously or unconsciously, in every philosophy. Provided that they are kept within check, they need not distort the philosophy to the point where it loses all interest and value. Whatever the motives which may have been at work, we find some very acute thinkers among the personal idealists.

In our survey of the movement, we shall look first at some philosophers who retained a monistic basis and whose position is a mediating one (Section 10). Next we shall turn to more extreme and avowedly pluralistic theories (Section 11). The impact of personal idealism on the thought of some prominent theologians will then be considered (Section 12). The chapter will end with a summary and critique of the movement (Section 13).

10. MODERATE PERSONAL IDEALISM
A. S. Pringle-Pattison, W. E. Hocking

The teaching of the Scottish philosopher Andrew Seth Pringle-Pattison[1] (1856–1931) provides a good introduction to personal idealism. Beginning as a Hegelian, he soon came to criticize some of the Hegelian doctrines,[2] and as a consequence divided the British idealists into the two camps of absolute idealism and personal idealism. His criticism was that the cold logic of the Hegelian system failed to do justice to the reality of persons, each one of which is unique and qualitatively distinct. In particular, he attacked the idea that personal selves can somehow be included in an absolute Self. 'The radical error both of Hegelianism and of the allied English doctrine I take to be the identification of the human and divine self-consciousness, or, to put it more broadly, the unification of consciousness in a single Self.'[3] Pringle-Pattison holds that each self is perfectly *impervious*—and 'impervious in a fashion of which the impenetrability of matter is a faint analogue'. Thus personality is characterized by autonomy

---

[1] Professor successively at Cardiff, 1887–91; St Andrews, 1891–1919; Edinburgh, 1919–31. He was known as Andrew Seth until 1898 when he took his additional surname.

[2] In his early work, *Hegelianism and Personality*.   *Op. cit.*, p. 215.

and exclusiveness. 'I have a centre of my own—a will of my own—which no one shares with me or can share, a centre which I maintain even in my dealings with God himself.'[1] It is maintained that personality in God on the one hand and the dignity and immortality of finite personality on the other are both postulated by the religious consciousness, and that both had been denied or seriously compromised in absolute idealism.

In later life Pringle-Pattison worked out his own metaphysical system[2] which, in the typically Hegelian manner, attempts to exhibit reality as a rational whole. His metaphysic conserves the two cardinal tenets of his early writing—the personality of God and the indestructible worth of human personality; but we find that he avoids the sheer pluralism to which his doctrine of exclusive selves seemed to point.

Nature, man and God form an organic whole so that any one of these three, taken in isolation, is an abstraction. Thus nature is not to be properly understood in isolation from man, who has arisen out of it. We cannot be content to think of a purely mechanical nature as something that is complete in itself. Man is a child of nature, not an excrescence on the surface of the universe, and his spiritual life cannot be regarded as alien to nature. 'The characteristics of the ethical life must be taken, therefore, as contributing to determine the nature of the system in which we live.'[3] The spiritual personalities which nature brings forth and towards which it tends are free, autonomous and immortal. Yet these finite subjects, in turn, are not to be taken in isolation from God and 'have no independent subsistence outside of the universal Life which mediates itself to them in a world of objects'.[4] Philosophy cannot rest in any explanation which stops short of God.

In his turn, however, God 'becomes an abstraction if separated from the universe of his manifestation'.[5] We are not to think of God as a pre-existent Deity who called the world into being by an arbitrary act of will. The world is God's eternal manifestation rather than a creation which he could do without. Just as human personalities need God, so God needs them. Such finite personalities are not mere adjectives of the Absolute, nor can we think of them as created in the way that things are produced. They are members or incarnations of the Absolute. Yet Pringle-Pattison stops short of the idea that finite selves are coeternal with God. To say that personality is immortal and has no end does not mean that it has no beginning—'it is emphatically something that must be won before there can be any question of its conservation'.[6] Thus he turns aside before the

---

[1] *Op. cit.*, p. 217.   [2] See *The Idea of God* and *The Idea of Immortality*.
[3] *The Idea of God*, p. 156.   [4] *Op. cit.*, p. 314.
[5] *Ibid.*   [6] *The Idea of Immortality*, p. 196.

more radical consequences of personal idealism, and there is some justice
in Rudolf Metz's criticism that 'Pringle-Pattison's position is a half-way
one',[1] lacking the consistency of either rigid monism or thoroughgoing
pluralism.

A similar avoidance of extremes is found in the American philosopher,
William Ernest Hocking[2] (1873–1964). On the question of monism and
pluralism, for instance, he tells us that 'the monism of the world is such
only as to give meaning to its pluralism; our belonging to God such only as
gives us greater hold upon ourselves'.[3] His philosophy has an eclectic
character, as he seeks to do justice to opposing points of view and to
modify idealism in the light of rival theories. Yet he holds that idealism is
not so much a type of philosophy as the essence of all philosophy. For he
believes that every philosophy must assume that the universe has a meaning which is already there for us to discover, and because it possesses
meaning, reality must have a mental or spiritual character.

This spiritual character is discovered to be that of a Self. And if we ask
whether selfhood may not be the manifestation of something higher, we
are told: 'No. For there is nothing higher than selfhood and nothing
more profound.'[4] Rejecting the notion of a finite God, Hocking maintains
that God cannot be less than the Absolute. In the idea of God, the Absolute
'is raised to the level of personality and moral quality'.[5] Personality is
deep and wide enough to include such impersonal aspects as we may find
in reality, and it is explicitly denied that there can be anything above or
beyond personality. Finite persons may be said to be in God, as dependent
on him and created by him. They are also said to be imperfect images of
the whole cosmos. Nature is the bridge by which selves communicate with
each other. The scientific understanding of nature as a self-contained
entity is an abstraction which must be supplemented by the mystics'
experience of nature as the communication to us of the divine Mind.
Nature is a function of mind, and through it God communicates with us,
and makes possible our social communication with each other. Nature is
thus necessary to selfhood, both in God and man, though we may also
think of it as created.

This idealist world-view provides the philosophical foundation for a
natural religion. Man's pursuit of values and his spiritual aspirations do
not have their setting in an alien world. Along with the demand for right
living goes the sense of certain attainment, which flows from faith in God.
Religion is described as 'anticipated attainment'; or, more fully, as 'the

---

[1] *A Hundred Years of British Philosophy*, p. 389.   [2] Professor at Harvard, 1914–43.
[3] *The Meaning of God in Human Experience*, p. 181.   [4] *Types of Philosophy*, p. 441.
[5] *The Meaning of God in Human Experience*, p. 207.

present attainment in a single experience of those objects which in the course of nature are reached only at the end of infinite progression'.[1] Religion begins as an emotional response, but it is driven to seek an intellectual foundation in a world-view such as that which idealist philosophy provides. 'Mighty religion and mighty strokes of speculation have always gone together.'[2]

Hocking, however, criticizes those idealist philosophers who offer to us an abstract 'religion in general', lacking the concreteness of the actual religions practised by man. There can be only one true religion, yet such a religion is powerless if it lacks the concreteness of the positive religions known in personal and social experience. These considerations sent Hocking in quest of a world faith which would be at once universal and concrete. The way to such a world faith, he tells us, cannot lie through the radical displacement of other religions by one particular religion, or through any superficial syncretism. The way must be through reconception, a process of mutual learning among the world's religions. Such reconception will conserve what is best in each tradition. The unique contribution of Christianity is its declaration 'that history is in fact *personalized* in its invisible structure, in such wise that each life may achieve dignity and power'.[3]

Hocking's constant endeavour to find a middle way may leave us the impression that, like Pringle-Pattison, he has brought us to a half-way house. But in any case, there is no doubting his genuine insight into the concrete realities of religion.

11. PLURALISTIC PERSONAL IDEALISM
G. H. Howison, J. M. E. McTaggart

A much more radical variety of personal idealism was expounded by the American philosopher, George Holmes Howison[4] (1834–1916). In early life he was associated with W. T. Harris and other pioneers of American neo-Hegelianism, but he became the opponent of monism and worked out his own highly original and strongly personal type of idealism. In a criticism of Royce, Howison argued that absolute idealism, by including finite selves in the Absolute, denied personality in the genuine sense both to man and to God, and thus struck at the very foundations of the Western democratic way of life and of the Christian religion which inspires it.

---

[1] *Op. cit.*, pp. 31, 51. [2] *Op. cit.*, p. 59.
[3] *Living Religions and a World Faith*, p. 268.
[4] After various appointments, he became professor in the University of California in 1884.

Western civilization is founded on personal responsibility, while Christianity teaches a moral relation between God and man, as real and distinct persons. Absolute idealism is a reversion to oriental pantheism—a type of belief whose 'monotonous theme was the ineffable greatness of the supreme Being and the utter littleness of man' so that its tradition 'lay like a pall upon the human spirit'.[1] In protest against a monism which, as he believed, obliterated the distinctness of moral persons, Howison expounded his own pluralistic metaphysic, and seems to have been the first philosopher to employ the description 'personal idealism' for the type of theory which he embraced.

The outlines of Howison's positive teaching are straightforward enough. He declares his adherence to idealism, which he defines as 'that explanation of the world which maintains that the only thing absolutely real is mind, and that all material and all temporal existences take their being from mind, from consciousness that thinks and experiences'.[2] There is not, however, one all-inclusive Mind or Absolute, but a plurality of minds. A mind is a free and self-active unit, an independent centre of origination, which begets space and time and the material world, and which recognizes other minds. Such a centre of mind is a person, and since the essential characteristic of these centres is that they are free and self-active sources, we cannot think of them as having been produced or created. They have no origin—they just *are*. Thus there is an eternal plurality of indestructible persons. 'Not even divine agency can give rise to another self-active intelligence by any productive act.'[3]

God is therefore not the creator of spirits, but is to be understood as the central member of the circle of minds, *primus inter pares* in the society of coeternal persons. He governs not by power and authority, but by light and reason, in virtue of his worth as the fulfilled type of every mind.[4] Howison puts the same point in another way by saying that God's causation is not efficient but final—he does not offend against personality by compelling men, but attracts them by love and reason. The central meaning of Christianity is said to lie in the faith that God and man are reciprocally and equally real, not identical; and consequently this religion is to be interpreted as one of aspiration rather than of submission—each

[1] See the symposium by Royce, Howison and others, entitled *The Conception of God*, p. 60.

[2] *Loc. cit.*, p. 53.

[3] *The Limits of Evolution*, p. 289.

[4] On this 'democratic' conception of God, see John Passmore, *A Hundred Years of Philosophy*, p. 74, n. 1, where one of Howison's disciples is quoted as saying that 'there is no place in a democratic society for such radical class distinction as that between a supreme Being favored with eternal and absolute perfection and the mass of beings doomed to the lower ways of imperfect struggle'.

person is drawn towards God as the realized ideal of his own personal being.

The picture of reality which emerges from Howison's pluralistic idealism is therefore that of a republic of free and eternal spirits—a restatement of the classic idea of the City of God. The plurality of persons is harmonized in the republic not by simultaneity or contiguity—for time and space are begotten by minds—but by a common rationality. Persons are held in union by logical and moral bonds, and the centre of reference is provided by God. One can hardly refrain from questioning, however, whether God is at all necessary to Howison's metaphysic. We have been brought at least well on the way to a type of personal idealism which could dispense altogether with the idea of God.

Such an atheistic type of personal idealism we do in fact meet in the British metaphysician, John McTaggart Ellis McTaggart[1] (1866–1925). Though very strongly influenced by Hegel, he gave to idealism an atheistic and pluralistic turn, and constructed a metaphysic so original that it may be doubted whether anyone apart from McTaggart himself has ever held it. Yet the sheer originality of his thought and the systematic formulation which he gave to it entitle him to a place among the top thinkers of Anglo-American idealism. Furthermore, we should notice that although McTaggart's atheism is anti-Christian, it need not therefore be anti-religious. He himself defines religion as 'an emotion resting on a conviction of a harmony between ourselves and the universe at large'.[2] If religion is thus defined, then the dogma which asserts the existence of a personal God is not essential to religion. McTaggart's system is in fact an illustration of religious atheism. Some dogmas, however, would be essential to religion, since otherwise we could scarcely have the conviction of being in harmony with the universe. A 'dogma' is taken to mean 'any proposition which has a metaphysical significance' and 'metaphysics' signifies 'the systematic study of the ultimate nature of reality'.[3]

In his critique of religious dogmas, McTaggart considered the ideas of God, freedom and immortality. Beginning with the immortality of the self—which was indeed the chief preoccupation of his whole philosophy—he declared his conviction that there are arguments strong enough to justify such a belief.[4] At this stage of his philosophizing, however, he did not advance such arguments, but contented himself with rebutting the common arguments against immortality and with clarifying what is involved in the belief in the immortality of the self. It is argued in detail that the self is not merely an activity of its body; and even if the body

[1] Fellow of Trinity College, Cambridge, 1891–1925.
[2] *Some Dogmas of Religion*, p. 3.   [3] *Op. cit.*, p. 1.   *Op. cit.*, p. 77.

were regarded as a necessary accompaniment of the self (a view which cannot be conclusively established), it might be the case that on the destruction of one body, the self passes to another body; furthermore, we cannot argue from the transitoriness of material things to the transitoriness of the self which is quite differently constituted. The allusion in these arguments to the possibility that the self may pass from one body to another is developed in McTaggart's further exposition of the idea of immortality. The common idea of immortality in the Western world is that our present life will be succeeded by an unending life after death. McTaggart, however, holds that any arguments which support immortality are as likely to support a belief in pre-existence as in a future life. Thus if man is immortal, it is probable that his present life lies between a life that has been and a life that is to come. There is no reason for confining ourselves to the thought of three lives. It is more probable that there is a plurality of lives, and that each man's existence before and after his present life would be divided into many lives, each bounded by birth and death. Death brings forgetfulness, but this does not break the continuity of a self. The continuity is not that of consciousness, but of a substance and its attributes. What is gained in one life—for instance, love—may be preserved and strengthened in a further life, though there is no memory of the former one. It is claimed that there is an attraction in this doctrine of a plurality of lives, for we can hope to make good the deficiencies and failures of any particular life in the succession of lives which will lie ahead.

After discussing the idea of freedom and criticizing indeterminism, McTaggart passes on to the idea of God. If by 'God' we mean—as Western thinkers usually mean—a being who is personal, supreme and good, then we have two cases to consider. The first case is that in which 'supreme' means 'omnipotent'. 'An omnipotent person', says McTaggart, 'is one who can do anything',[1] and we are to understand this statement in an utterly literal fashion. If there is an omnipotent will, it must completely determine everything, and its possessor should even be able, if he wished, to alter the laws of thought or the multiplication tables. McTaggart dwells on the difficulties of conceiving such omnipotence, and argues that omnipotence is incompatible with personality (which requires something existing outside of its own will), and irreconcilable with goodness (in view of the evil in the world). If the idea of an omnipotent God breaks down, there remains the second case, where 'supreme' means 'most powerful', but not 'omnipotent'. There may be something attractive in the idea of a finite God striving after the good, and we could believe such a God to be personal, good, and even supreme in the sense of having

[1] *Op. cit.*, p. 202.

more power than any other being. But such a God could not ensure the triumph of goodness, and there is in any case no evidence for his existence. Thus belief in God is rejected. But this belief is by no means necessary to support a belief in immortality or the conviction that the universe is spiritual and harmonious. 'If all reality is a harmonious system of selves, it is perhaps itself sufficiently godlike to dispense with a God.'[1]

The results of this critique of religion are mainly negative. If religion is to be rehabilitated, this can be done, McTaggart thinks, only on the basis of a complete system of metaphysics which would show that the universe is good on the whole and the kind of universe with which we can stand in harmonious relations. Such a complete metaphysic he proceeded to construct. He begins with a rigorous *a priori* deduction of the characteristics which must belong to whatever exists, and then applies the results to our experience.

McTaggart endeavours to show that time and matter are unreal, and that the only existence are the spiritual substances which we call 'persons' or 'selves'. In time these selves pass though innumerable lives, but since time is unreal we must view the ultimate reality *sub specie aeternitatis* as an eternal system of selves united in the harmony of a love 'so direct, so intimate, and so powerful that even the deepest mystical rapture gives us but the slightest foretaste of its perfection'.[2] The stress is on a pluralism of spiritual substances, but we may also think of one substance, the Absolute. This, however, is not an all-inclusive Self, since no self can include another self, nor is it in any sense God; it is simply the system. The explanatory model is that of a college, whose members have more reality than the college itself. This metaphysic of McTaggart, though atheistic, remains almost passionately religious. It might be compatible with some oriental religions, but it marks the furthest remove of Anglo-American idealism from Christian theology.

12. PERSONAL IDEALISM IN THEOLOGY
H. Rashdall, C. C. J. Webb

Personal idealism in its more moderate formulations had naturally a strong appeal for theologians. Among those who were influenced by it, we may notice Hastings Rashdall[3] (1858–1924), an exceptionally able theologian who wrote with distinction on a wide range of subjects. Having embraced the idealist philosophy, Rashdall became in 1902 a contributor

---

[1] *Op. cit.*, p. 250.   [2] *The Nature of Existence*, vol. II, p. 479.
[3] Tutor at Oxford, 1888–1917; Dean of Carlisle, 1917–1924.

to the symposium *Personal Idealism*.[1] This was a kind of manifesto issued
by the personalist wing of the British idealist movement and directed
against both naturalism and absolutism, which—in the words of the editor
—'are the adversaries against whom the personal idealist has to strive'.
The views put forward by Rashdall at that time are essentially the same
as those which he developed in more detail in his later writings.[2]

Rashdall suggests certain criteria for personality. By a 'person' we mean
a consciousness which thinks as well as feels; which has a certain permanence or unity; which distinguishes itself both from the objects of
experience and from other persons; and which is a source of action. If we
accept these criteria, then it would seem that we cannot deny some kind
of rudimentary personality to animals. Even if we were to add the criterion
of morality, it would be hard to say exactly where morality begins. Thus
Rashdall thinks that there are degrees of personality. Even personality
at the human level does not fully satisfy the criteria—for instance, unity
would seem to depend on memory, and this is never complete in any
human person. If there is any being who fully satisfies the criteria of
personality, it can only be God.

The existence of God is established on Berkleian lines. The world is
mind-dependent, but it is obviously not dependent on your mind or
mine. We must therefore assume a divine Mind which creates both the
world and our human minds. The usual objections to ascribing personality
to a divine creative Mind fail when it is recognized that God is personal
in the highest degree—free from the deficiencies which always belong to
personality at the human level, yet not on that account anything other
than personal.

God, however, is not the Absolute. We have seen that it is a mark of a
person to distinguish himself from other persons, so that one person can
never be included in another. Thus created persons are not included in
God but stand outside of him. Both God and the souls are included in the
Absolute, which cannot therefore be itself a Person but is rather a society
of persons. God is less than the Absolute, and Rashdall frankly accepts the
doctrine of a limited God—though a God who is limited only by his own
creation. Such a doctrine eases the problem of evil, but it raises the
question whether such a God can ever overcome evil. Rashdall's reply is
that although not omnipotent, God is the strongest power in the universe,
and since he is a rational and moral Person, we can have grounds for
optimism. Yet Rashdall also acknowledges that there is 'a real warfare

[1] Edited by Henry Sturt.

[2] Rashdall's contribution to the symposium was entitled 'Personality, Human and
Divine'. His views are restated in more detail in *The Theory of Good and Evil* and *Philosophy
and Religion*.

with a real evil', that 'the victory cannot be won without our help', and that 'we are called upon to be literally fellow-workers with God'.[1]

These philosophical ideas are clearly seen in Rashdall's treatment of theological themes. He believed in a continuous divine revelation given in personal, that is to say, moral and rational terms. The culmination of this process of revelation is the life and self-sacrificing death of Jesus Christ, but 'all human love, all human self-sacrifice is in its way and degree a revelation of God'.[2] Rashdall repudiated as irrational, immoral and subpersonal those traditional views of the death of Christ which saw in it an expiation or satisfaction or anything of the sort. He held that Christ's life and death must be understood together as saving men by moral influence. Salvation is simply the attainment of spiritual life, and it begins now as men follow the ideal exhibited in Christ; but if this ideal is indeed the revelation of God's own loving nature, we must suppose that the spiritual life which men begin to attain on earth is continued and perfected beyond death. In Rashdall the 'liberal' theology inspired by neo-idealism reaches perhaps its finest expression.

Differing considerably from Rashdall, yet equally concerned with the idea of personality, was another eminent theologian of the Church of England, Clement Charles Julian Webb[3] (1865–1954). He tried to steer a middle way between the absolute and personal idealists, but the importance which he assigned to the idea of personality places him closer to the second of these two groups. His basic convictions are rather similar to those of Hocking. A God who is worthy of the name cannot be finite, but must be the Absolute. Yet the God who is known in religious experience—and especially Christian experience—is personal. Thus Webb chooses a more difficult route than Rashdall, and sets out to show that God is both personal and identical with the all-inclusive Absolute. He says: 'About the problems involved in the questions: "Is God the Absolute? Is the Absolute God?" my thoughts continually revolve.'[4]

Webb acknowledges that divine personality cannot be precisely the same as human personality. We would, however, be justified in speaking of a personal God if it might be supposed that 'we could stand in personal relations with him'.[5] But if God is the Absolute, how can we have personal relations with the Absolute? We are included in the Absolute, and it is not easy to see how a personal relation is possible between two entities one of which is included in the other. Webb's reply is that we must

[1] *Philosophy and Religion*, p. 86.
[2] *The Idea of Atonement in Christian Theology*, p. 449.
[3] Tutor, 1899–1920, then professor, 1920–1930 at Oxford.
[4] *Contemporary British Philosophy*, Second Series, p. 349.   [5] *God and Personality*, p. 73

distinguish between the relation of man to man in social experience and the much more complex relation of man to God in religious experience. Both are personal relations, but the first is one of mutual exclusion, while the second is one of mutual inclusion. In religion God dwells in us and we dwell in God, yet in such a way that we preserve our distinctness and a genuine personal relation is possible.

Such a personal relation would be impossible if God were merely immanent or merely transcendent. In the first case, finite spirits would be emanations of God, identical with him and lacking the distinctness required for reciprocal personal communion; in the second case, they would be mere products so distant from God that personal relations would again be ruled out. God must be both transcendent and immanent if personal relations with him are to be possible. Webb finds a clue to these complex structures in the thought that there are personal relationships within the Godhead itself—a thought which finds expression in the religious idea of a Mediator. The Mediator is integral to the Godhead, yet distinct from the Father. The Mediator is also said to be the archetype of finite spirits which, in union with him, have a personal relation to the Father. This personal relation, which is neither a proud claim to identity with God nor a mere abject servility before him, is the sole ground on which we can entertain a belief in immortality. Thus Webb sought to reconcile the ideas of personality, God and the Absolute. But perhaps he was attempting an impossible task.

13. SUMMARY AND CRITICISM OF PERSONAL IDEALISM

In common with the absolute idealists, the personal idealists had in the main a speculative and metaphysical approach to the problems of religion. Both groups tried to account for religion in terms of an all-embracing world-view, according to which the ultimate reality is mind. The personal idealists, however, tried in various ways to move away from the idea of a monolithic Absolute, and to find room in their world-view for the value and importance of personality.

No doubt the idea of personality is of high importance to religion, at least in the Western world. Yet it may be doubted whether the personal idealists made any major advance towards giving us a convincing account of religion. The most successful versions of personal idealism were the more extreme ones—those of Rashdall, Howison and McTaggart. But they save personality at the expense of diminishing God, or even causing him to disappear altogether. Less successful are the mediating views of

Pringle-Pattison, Hocking and Webb, who, so to speak, want to make the best of both worlds by combining monism and pluralism, and by clinging both to the Absolute and to personality. In fairness, it must be said that any mediating view is more difficult to formulate consistently than an extreme view, just because the mediating view will notice factors which the extreme position has ignored or underestimated. Yet the mediating positions which we are discussing at the moment seem to break down at one particular point. They cannot give a clear answer to the question: 'How can one person be included in another person?'

The strength of personal idealism lies in its stress upon personality as the highest kind of being known in our experience, and in its protest against the tendency of some absolute idealists to depreciate personality. On the other hand, the weakness of personal idealism seems to be its assumption that because personality is the highest kind of being known to us, it must therefore also be the highest in the universe. It is, however, possible or even probable that God transcends personality by, let us say, as much as man transcends mere animality. This would be especially probable if God is identified with the Absolute.

Our study of the theories surveyed in this chapter may raise in our minds a more serious question. Did the idealist attempt to grasp reality as a rational whole—an attempt common to the absolutist and personalist wings alike—have any hope of success? Are the solutions really convincing? It surely must give us pause when we reflect that Howison, the American democrat, awards to the universe a constitution not unlike that of the United States while McTaggart, the Cambridge lecturer, has the vision of reality as the ideal college. These views may avoid the woolliness which characterized absolute idealism, but they reflect too clearly the environments whence they are sprung. We may even be reminded of Xenophanes' taunt that if horses could reflect on the semblance of the gods, they would portray them as horses. The ambitious speculations of the idealists inevitably provoked a reaction, and in the next chapter we shall consider some views in which we can hear at least certain murmurings against what was regarded as an excessive rationalism and intellectualism.

IV

PHILOSOPHIES OF SPIRIT

14. REALITY AS SPIRITUAL

HERE we are using the expression 'philosophies of spirit'[1] in a very wide sense to designate a number of loosely associated views which, like idealism, regard spirit as the ultimate reality, but which stand apart from the main idealist tradition. It is indeed difficult to draw hard and fast lines, and in particular some forms of personal idealism tend to shade off into our so-called 'philosophies of spirit'. Both are inclined to interpret reality in theistic, personal and ethical terms. But the philosophers of spirit cull their ideas from a much wider area of the history of philosophy than the idealist tradition, understood in the narrower sense, and in principle some distinctions can be made.

Several of the philosophies of spirit trace their lineage not through Hegel but through such thinkers as Lotze and Leibniz. Both of these philosophers recognized a kind of hierarchy of spiritual beings. At the apex of the hierarchy stands God; at a lower level are finite selves, each one of which is a microcosm or a kind of mirror of the universe; below the level of human selves and extending right down through nature are lower grades of spiritual being. Leibniz supposed that there is a continuous line of active substances, which he called 'monads', stretching from God at the top down to the lowest monad, which is next to nothing. Such a notion is obviously different from the common idealist position. As Lotze put it, if one recognizes that reality is spiritual, then one must either adopt the idealist view that the world of things is a phenomenon dependent on mind, or else one must hold that things commonly regarded as

---

[1] Some of these philosophies were formerly—and sometimes still are—designated by the term 'spiritualism', but the popular usage of this word has nowadays so much overshadowed its quite distinct philosophical usage that it has become misleading to employ it as a philosophical term. 'Ethical theism' would be a correct description of the philosophies discussed in this chapter, but this description is so broad that it would cover, for instance, many forms of idealism as well. 'Personalism' would have been a useful description for most of the views presented here, but it is customary to use this word specifically for the views of the American school founded by B. P. Bowne. (See below, p. 65.)

inanimate have actually in varying degrees a spiritual life of their own. Lotze himself accepted the second of these alternatives—the doctrine usually called 'panpsychism'. There were other notable nineteenth-century advocates of this doctrine, such as Fechner. But though most of the thinkers to be considered in this chapter owe something to Lotze, only a few of them explicitly accept his panpsychism.

A further difference from idealism is seen in the stress which the philosophies of life lay upon activity as the distinguishing mark of spirit. These philosophies often complain that idealism is too intellectualist and rationalist in its approach. Idealism tends to understand spirit as the thinking *subject*, and over against this we find the philosophies of spirit emphasizing the idea of spirit as the *agent* or source of action—though obviously some idealists had stressed this aspect too. The philosophies of spirit set alongside thought the whole range of the spiritual life in its moral, religious and aesthetic activities.

Unlike most of the idealists, some of the thinkers whom we are going to consider were keen students of the natural sciences, and their philosophies have a strongly empirical flavour. Instead of laying down the characteristics of the real *a priori*—as, for instance, that it must be rational—they construct their philosophies in the light of what they learn from our experience of the world. They are even prepared to find room in their world-views for contingent alogical elements if these are demanded by experience. They reject a merely mechanical interpretation of nature, and think that for an adequate interpretation of the results of science we must call to our aid the concept of purpose. The fact that nature demands a teleological interpretation is evidence of its basically spiritual constitution.

Not all of the characteristics mentioned—such as panpsychism, activism, an interest in natural science—will be found in each of the philosophies of spirit to be discussed, for these philosophies form a very heterogeneous group, drawn from various backgrounds and having only certain basic similarities in common. We shall therefore group them somewhat arbitrarily. First, we shall consider some continental philosophies of spirit, with examples from Germany, Italy and France (Section 15); then we shall turn to their counterparts in the English-speaking countries, where what we call 'philosophies of spirit' are closely akin to the forms of personal idealism considered in the preceding chapter (Section 16); a group of philosophers who set out from moral experience and take as their specific concern the ethical approach to theism will next engage our attention (Section 17); philosophical theology will be represented by a British theologian whose approach has much in common with the philosophies of spirit (Section 18); and we shall end with an evaluation (Section 19).

15. CONTINENTAL PHILOSOPHIES OF SPIRIT
R. Eucken, B. Varisco, E. Boutroux

Rudolf Christoph Eucken[1] (1846–1926) is the best-known German representative of a spiritual type of philosophy in the early part of the present century. He enjoyed an extraordinary vogue even beyond his own country. He was a Nobel prizewinner for literature, and most of his works have been translated into English. Eucken's position in Germany re-sembled in some ways that of Sir Henry Jones in Britain—that is to say, he was not a particularly original or systematic thinker, but regarded his philosophy as a practical creed, and gained his reputation by the enthusiasm with which he proclaimed his views as a message for the times. For this reason, Eucken is often considered to have been more a preacher or prophet than a philosopher.

Of the characteristics of philosophies of spirit mentioned above, the one which is most clearly exemplified in Eucken is activism. Rejecting intellectualism and a speculative approach to the problems of philosophy, Eucken holds that truth must satisfy the requirements of the whole of life. This approach he calls the 'noological' method. The speculative method deals 'with shadows of the living content and concreteness of reality. On the contrary, the noological method understands the par-ticular out of an encompassing and basal whole of life.'[2]

The creed which Eucken develops on the basis of this method is straightforward enough. On the one hand, man may lead a *natural* existence, that is to say, an existence in which he is preoccupied with the satisfaction of biological needs and with material and economic values, and in which he is related only externally with other men. Such an existence is at bottom meaningless and empty, yet Eucken believed that it is the kind of existence towards which modern civilization is tending. He speaks of the 'impersonal' character of modern civilization which makes men its instruments and 'ties them ever more securely to the visible world'.[3] On the other hand, human existence acquires significance in so far as it becomes a *spiritual* existence. In such an existence, man relates himself to and co-operates with the universal Spirit. The life of spirit is essentially deed, action and struggle, so that the spirituality of man is not

---

[1] Professor at Basel, 1871–74; at Jena, 1874–1920.
[2] *The Truth of Religion*, p. 180.   [3] *Op. cit.*, p. 46.

so much an eternal truth about man as something which man must continually gain and develop.

The function of religion is not to be just one activity among others but to pervade all activity by holding up to us the whole spiritual life as over against the immediate natural environment. Religion conduces to our entering into the spiritual life, and in religious experience the universal Spirit is known as a personal God, and there is intercourse with him 'as between an I and a Thou'.[1] Like the idealists, Eucken speaks of an absolute religion, which is related to the historical religions as truth is to its appearances. He finds in Christianity the highest manifestation of absolute religion and an unassailable nucleus of truth, but believes that Christianity must be purged of many of its transient and accidental features.

A philosophy of spirit of the Leibnizian type is well illustrated in the writings of the Italian thinker, Bernardino Varisco[2] (1850–1933), whose major works are available in English. Originally a teacher of scientific subjects, Varisco turned to philosophy in an attempt to reconcile the scientific and religious views of the world. He begins from the multiplicity of subjects, each of which has its own particular view of the world. A subject is 'principally a centre of conscious activity'.[3] A person is a highly developed rational subject, though what is clearly and presently conscious in such a subject is said to be surrounded by a much vaster sphere of subconsciousness. Below the level of persons are the sentient subjects of animals. 'Everything leads us to believe' that at a lower level still there is an infinite number of embryonic subjects and that 'what we call inert matter might be reduced to an aggregate of such subjects'.[4] These subjects, of course, are very primitive, and they are probably more like our unconsciousness than our consciousness.

Variations are continually taking place in the subjects, and these variations are of two kinds. Some arise from the spontaneous activity of the subjects themselves. This spontaneity is not restricted to developed subjects, and it implies an *alogical* factor in the world. Other variations arise from the mutual interference of the subjects. They interact in regular ways so that there is an ordered universe and the multiplicity of subjects constitutes a unity. This implies a *logical* factor.

To account for the unity, Varisco introduces the idea of 'being'. It is said that being unifies the particular subjects because, in the first place, it is the concept which, explicitly or implicitly, is common to every thinking subject; and in the second place, it is the character common to every

[1] *Op. cit.*, p. 430. [2] Professor at Rome, 1905–25.
[3] *The Great Problems*, p. 96. [4] *Op. cit.*, p. 216.

object which determines thought. It is argued that being is the universal subject which thinks itself in the particular subjects and the world, and becomes determinate in them.

Is this somewhat nebulous universal Subject to be identified with the God of religion? Or is it just a purely immanent ground which would be nothing apart from its particular determinations? Varisco was an honest thinker, and although he himself accepted the traditional concept of God, he acknowledged frankly that on the basis of the argument summarized above 'the existence of a personal God appears to us an unjustified hypothesis'.[1] He believed that the evidence of purpose in the world and the apparently providential conservation of value point to a theistic conclusion, but more would be needed to justify this conclusion on rational grounds. In his later writings, Varisco argued that the universal Subject is indeed a personal God, but a God who limits himself in power and prescience so that men are free to co-operate with him in the work of creation. This philosophy, he believed, vindicates the fundamental positions of religion, and especially of the Christian religion.

In France a distinctive tradition of spiritual philosophy had maintained itself throughout the nineteenth century in the face of naturalism and positivism, and the chief representative of this tradition in the opening years of the present century was Emile Boutroux[2] (1845–1922). He too was a figure of international repute and was Gifford Lecturer at Glasgow in 1903, though unfortunately his lectures were never published. Boutroux well illustrates the type of philosophy of spirit which is preoccupied with the relations of religion to the natural sciences. He tries to meet the sciences on their own ground, and to show that the understanding of the world which they offer needs to be completed by a spiritual interpretation of nature.

Purpose and freedom, essential to the life of spirit, seemed to be excluded on the nineteenth-century scientific view of the world as a web of phemomena rigidly determined by necessary laws. Boutroux proceeds to a critical examination of the methods of science to find out whether the deterministic scheme of laws under which science represents nature is an exhaustive account, or whether there is not in the reality of nature something more, which is irreducible to the scientific transcript, and which he calls 'a certain degree of contingency'.[3] He finds that there is indeed such a contingent element. Science selects such data as conduce to the establishment of general laws, and always leaves something out. As we pass from physics to biology and from biology to the study of human activities, the

---

[1] *Op. cit.*, p. 270.   [2] Professor at the Sorbonne from 1888.
[3] *On the Contingency of the Laws of Nature*, p. 4.

element of irreducible contingency keeps on increasing. There is genuine novelty at each new level, and this cannot be described in terms of the lower level. Boutroux was as well aware as anyone of the danger of trying to set up religion in the gaps in scientific knowledge. He maintains, however, that the element of irreducible contingency which appears as a limit to science is not a mere negative finding, but a positive one. It directs us to seek the creative principle in nature.

In order to do this, we must take into account what science leaves out. 'Science consists in substituting for things symbols which express a certain aspect of them.'[1] Because of its abstract intellectuality, the scientific understanding must be distinguished from human reason in the wider sense—the reason which takes account of the wholeness of things in their quality, value and significance for life. This wider use of reason opens the way to a spiritual interpretation of the world, and makes possible the religious attitude alongside the scientific attitude.

In religion, man rises to the creative principle of life. Both belief and practice are involved in religion—belief in God as the ideal Being, and the practice of love as the expression of communion with God. Thus understood, religion is entirely conformable to reason in that wider sense in which reason is distinguished from a bare scientific understanding. Reason in this wider sense sees in nature more than a mere mechanism and, by analogy with life, is able to form the conception of 'a Being who is one and multiple—not like a material whole but like the continuous and moving infinity of a mind, of a person'.[2] Although there may often be tensions between the scientific attitude and the religious attitude, both are sanctioned by reason, both are creative activities of spirit, and both are needed for the fullest development of human life.

16. ANGLO-AMERICAN PHILOSOPHIES OF SPIRIT
J. Ward, B. P. Bowne, E. S. Brightman

Those American and British philosophies which we may designate as 'philosophies of spirit' were naturally influenced by the idealism which, as we have seen, flourished in the English-speaking countries. In particular, we shall find that the idea of personality plays a large part in the views which we are about to consider, and that these views have a close kinship with personal idealism. Nevertheless, because of the stress which they lay on activity and the experience of life, it seems better to include them among the philosophies of spirit.

[1] *Science and Religion in Contemporary Philosophy*, p. 361. [2] *Op. cit.*, pp. 393–4.

In England, we find the spiritual type of philosophy ably represented by James Ward[1] (1843–1925), a disciple of Lotze. In addition to being a philosopher, Ward was a noted psychologist, and was well versed in the biological sciences. He had the very rare distinction of being appointed Gifford Lecturer on two separate occasions, and was regarded in his day as one of the most acute critics of naturalism and one of the most powerful defenders of theism. In his philosophy, he draws upon his knowledge of psychology and biology to construct a world-view in which the ultimate reality is active spirit.

Among the various strands that go to make up Ward's thought, we find reiterated all the major themes which we have met in the continental philosophers of spirit already considered. He claims that experience as a whole, rather than theoretical thinking, is the best guide for philosophy; he points to the abstract character of the natural sciences; and he asserts that nature, when it is taken concretely, demands a spiritual interpretation. Ward's reflections on psychology had led him to emphasize the essentially practical and purposeful character of experience, in which conation is more fundamental than cognition. The theoretical subject is a bare abstraction from the organic unity of experience. Of experience itself, he says: 'In a word, it is life—life as it is for the living individual.'[2] This emphasis on concrete experience underlies Ward's criticism of the mechanistic naturalism which flourished in the nineteenth century—one of the most searching criticisms that it received at the hands of any philosopher. Ward finds naturalism wanting because it concerns itself with a partial aspect of the concrete reality known in experience, and sets up this aspect as if it were the whole reality. Its error is said to be that of 'ascribing objective existence to abstractions'.[3] We must return from the network of necessary relations into which science has resolved the world, to the fullness and variety of that concrete reality from which science itself sets out before its abstractive procedure comes into play.

The concreteness which is lacking in the natural sciences Ward finds in history. We may note that Ward's appeal to history shows how his thought links up with that of such German philosophers as Windelband and Dilthey. Although it 'affords little foothold for positive and exact science', he claims that 'the historical is what we *understand* best and what concerns us most'.[4] What history discloses is not a dead mechanical world, but a spiritual world of conative subjects striving for ends and realizing values.

---

[1] Fellow of Trinity College, Cambridge, from 1875, and professor at Cambridge from 1897.

[2] *Naturalism and Agnosticism*, vol. II, p. 111.

[3] *Op. cit.*, vol. II, p. 66.   *Op. cit.*, vol. II, p. 280.

Since this realm of ends and values cannot be included in nature as abstractly interpreted by the sciences, we must rather ask whether nature cannot be assimilated to the realm of ends, and given a spiritual, more concrete interpretation. This is in fact what Ward proceeds to do. 'There is nothing in nature that is incompatible with a spiritualistic interpretation.'[1] Science discovers no clear-cut lower limits to consciousness and life, and there is a presumption that nature is continuous and shows no sudden leaps. Hence if we interpret from above downwards, we meet no impassable barrier to a spiritual interpretation. We are led to a doctrine of panpsychism. Nature is teleological throughout. Even supposedly inanimate things have some sort of rudimentary spiritual life, and the realm of the historical extends below man throughout nature. It is claimed that 'nature thus resolves into a plurality of conative individuals'.[2]

We cannot, however, rest content with a pluralism. The unity and order of the world point to a doctrine of theism. God is at once the source of the spiritual world and the end towards which it moves. God is personal, and both transcendent and immanent. In creating free conative subjects, he has imposed a certain limitation on himself, but this is not to be regarded as a diminution of God, for the more freedom he has given to his creatures, the greater must he be. God's purpose is love, and evil will be overcome. But love cannot be ready-made; it arises freely, and men work together with God for the realization of his purpose. These teachings of Ward afford us one of the clearest and most comprehensive statements of the fundamental themes of the philosophies of spirit.

Another disciple of Lotze was the American philosopher, Borden Parker Bowne[3] (1847–1910). He came to formulate a type of philosophy which he called 'personalism'. This still has many adherents in the United States, where it constitutes a distinct school of thought. But it should be noted that Bowne was not the first to use the term 'personalism', and that the word is often employed in a wider sense for any type of philosophy which upholds the value of personality.

Following Lotze, Bowne thinks of the real as that which can act or be acted upon. 'Things are distinguished from non-existence by this power of action and mutual determination.'[4] Now what entities can satisfy this criterion of reality? According to Bowne, only personal selves, which are at once abiding and changing, afford an adequate conception of the real. Personal life is the active ground of the world, and the key to the problems of philosophy is found in personality.

Reality, it is argued, consists of a system of persons related through

[1] *The Realm of Ends*, p. 20.   [2] *Op. cit.*, p. 21.
[3] Professor at Boston, 1876–1910.   [4] *Metaphysics*, p. 40.

God as the supreme Person. The existence of God as the supreme Person is established in various ways. One line of argument is in effect a restatement of the classic cosmological proof of the divine existence. It is argued that for everything that exists, there must be a sufficient cause; thus the existence of persons is to be attributed to a cause which cannot itself be less than personal, that is to say, to a supreme creative Person. Another line of argument begins from the categories which we employ in understanding the world. These categories are taken from our experience as persons. Causal efficiency, for instance, is known from our own active self-experience. Persons initiate change and act upon things. We cannot find efficient causation either in lifeless atoms or in impersonal laws, for it is bound up with the purpose and intelligence of personality. Those categories which we draw from self-experience apply to the world because the world proceeds from a source which has kinship with ourselves—that is to say, it is dependent on the causal activity of the divine Person. The other categories like substance, unity in multiplicity, and so on, are likewise said to be bound up with personal experience.

God is conceived as active and creative. 'Our God is not an absentee apart from the world in self-enjoyment, but he is present in the world, in life, in conscience and history, carrying on a great moral campaign for the conquest and training of the human will, and its establishment in righteousness'; God is also said to be 'the great and everlasting Worker'.[1] The material world, as we have seen, is dependent on the divine causal activity, and it serves as a training ground for persons. Thus nature is properly understood only in relation to persons, and, like Ward, Bowne carried on a vigorous polemic against naturalistic philosophies, especially the views of Herbert Spencer. Finite persons themselves, though creatures of God, are said to preserve a 'mutual otherness and relative independence'.[2] Religion is primarily concerned with the pursuit of righteousness, and though religious belief is supported by philosophy, the certainty of faith is attained not through speculation but through trust and obedience.

Bowne's philosophy thus turns out to be a fairly orthodox version of theism. It is clear, however, that he was a thoroughly honest thinker, and did not shrink from examining in the light of experience the philosophical implications of theistic belief. Himself a Methodist, he is credited with having exercised a liberalizing influence on American Protestant theologians, and with having stimulated their interest in the philosophical problems of religion.

Among Bowne's successors in the American personalist school may be

[1] *The Essence of Religion*, pp. 7, 254.   [2] *Personalism*, p. 277.

mentioned Edgar Sheffield Brightman[1] (1884–1953). He tells us that he began from a position substantially the same as Bowne's, and one of his arguments for theism is essentially like one we have already met in Bowne —namely, that the fact of personality can be adequately accounted for only on the supposition that there is a cosmic creative Person.[2] Brightman's general line of argument for theism is of a kind with which we have become familiar in this chapter—an appeal to experience as a whole, where fact is not disjoined from value, and where moral and religious experience is taken into account as well as natural science.

It is however his frank examination of experience that leads Brightman to modify the traditional theistic doctrine in one important respect. God is creative, supreme and personal, but he is also, according to Brightman, limited or finite. Four kinds of evidence are adduced to show that God is limited. Firstly, there is evolution, with its waste as well as its progress. It suggests 'a power that is achieving its ends in the face of what seems to be opposition'.[3] Moreover, since Brightman, like Bowne, has no use for an absentee God, he believes that a God who is really involved in cosmic evolution must be one 'into whose very being time enters'.[4] Such a God is not one of finished perfection. Secondly, there is the evidence of personality itself. A free personality is impossible without a definite structure, or nature, which is given. If God is a person, this must be true of him also. We do not suppose, for instance, that God could make a round square. His own rational nature sets limits to his will. More generally, as Brightman sees it, there are passive as well as active elements in the divine nature. Thirdly, it is maintained that all existence exhibits conflict and duality, and we must suppose that even the divine existence includes struggle and victory over opposition. Fourthly, Brightman claims support from religious experience itself. This points to a God whose nature includes suffering, and redemption by a cross.

Such, Brightman thinks, is the kind of God required by the facts of experience. God is not limited by anything external to himself, but by the 'given' in his own nature. This looks like the traditional theological doctrine of the 'aseity' of God—the doctrine that God cannot act against his own nature; he cannot, for instance, make a round square, because his nature is rational. But Brightman's 'given' seems to go well beyond what theologians have included under 'aseity'. And although we are told that God increasingly masters the given in himself, we can hardly refrain from asking: 'Who or what gives the given? Is there some more ultimate power behind Brightman's God, like the fates behind the Greek gods?'

---

[1] Professor at Boston from 1919.
[2] *The Problem of God*, p. 157.
[3] *Op. cit.*, p. 126.
[4] *Op. cit.*, p. 129.

Brightman raises difficult questions, but he makes a very honest contribution to the problems of theism.

17. THE ETHICAL APPROACH TO THEISM
W. R. Sorley, A. E. Taylor, W. G. de Burgh

In the philosophers considered in this chapter, we have noted the repeated demand that our interpretation of the world must be based not on the abstract schema presented by the natural sciences, but on the whole range of experience, including morality, religion, and whatever else may be reckoned under what we commonly call 'spiritual' experience. We must now consider some philosophers who made it their specific concern to explore the avenues which lead from moral experience towards a theistic interpretation of reality.

A good starting-point is provided by the ideas of William Ritchie Sorley[1] (1855–1935). Again we meet the influence of Lotze, and also that of the Baden school of neo-Kantianism.[2] These influences make Sorley's thought more akin to the philosophies of spirit considered in this chapter than to the idealist philosophies discussed earlier, though of course it is also close to some of them.

Sorley proposes to reverse the method of philosophical inquiry that was current in his day; that is to say, instead of first seeking a metaphysical interpretation of reality and then drawing the ethical consequences of the view reached, he intends 'to inquire into the bearing of ethical ideas upon the view of reality as a whole'.[3] He quotes in support of this procedure a sentence of Lotze: 'The true beginning of metaphysics lies in ethics.' Thus Sorley's point of departure is moral experience.

Such experience introduces us to the idea of 'value', and, like Ward, Sorley notes that value is taken into account in the historical sciences but is left out in the natural sciences. The obvious difference between the historical sciences and the natural sciences is that the former direct attention to unique individual cases, whereas the latter generalize and seek universal causes. Individuality, although in its completeness it may be said to belong only to reality as a whole, is much more clearly exhibited in persons than in things. Persons are, indeed, the bearers of value. Goodness, for instance, may be said to belong *instrumentally* to things, but *intrinsically* it belongs only to persons. It is argued that any complete view of reality must find room for the values which the historical sciences discover in individual persons, as well as for the causal connections which the

---

[1] Professor at Cardiff, 1888–94; Aberdeen, 1894–1900; Cambridge, 1900–33.
[2] See below, p. 77.   [3] *Moral Values and the Idea of God*, p. 1.

generalizing sciences discover both in persons and things. Persons are as much a part of reality as things are, and it is claimed that our experience of moral values is no less objective than our knowledge of natural facts.

Thus the problem becomes one of bringing together in a single view of reality the order of values and the order of causes. A naturalistic philosophy which has no place for values cannot offer a solution, while the various idealist and spiritualist philosophies offer a whole range of solutions, from a pluralism of spiritual substances or monads to a monism of an all-inclusive spiritual substance. The best solution to satisfy all the facts of experience is, according to Sorley, a theism which avoids the extremes of pluralism and monism. We need the idea of a personal God who is both the creator of the existent world and the source and bearer of value. Sorley frankly recognizes the difficulties of this solution, especially the difficulty occasioned by the presence of evil in the world. This difficulty he attempts to meet like Rashdall, by supposing that God is limited by his own creation. But whatever the difficulties, Sorley denies that we can be content with any philosophy which cannot find room for value as well as fact, or which leaves them disjoined. 'If we are unable to reach a view of reality *as a whole*, then we have attained no philosophy.'[1]

We pass to Alfred Edward Taylor[2] (1869–1945), perhaps best-known as an authority on Plato. His early *Elements of Metaphysics* expounds an idealism strongly influenced by Bradley, but in his much later work, *The Faith of a Moralist*, with which we shall be concerned here, Taylor like the other thinkers discussed in the present chapter has broken away from a close association with orthodox idealism, and we meet in him such diverse influences as Plato, St Thomas Aquinas and Bergson.

Taylor's intention is to show that moral experience points for its completion beyond itself to religion. He prefaces his argument with a thesis now familiar to us in this chapter—that in the concretely experienced world, facts and values are never separated. This point is essential to the subsequent argument, for if ethics had to do with values that are divorced from facts, no possible inference could be made from ethics to the nature of reality.

The argument proper begins by asking about the nature of the good at which the moral life aims. Is it a temporal good or an eternal good? Even to be aware of the temporal nature of our life on earth is to have begun to transcend the form of temporality. The moral ideal cannot be satisfied by temporal goods, for these are defective in that they can be attained only successively and never all simultaneously. Thus the moral life points us to an eternal good. The next question is whether man of himself can attain

---

[1] *Op. cit.*, p. 500.   [2] Professor at St Andrews, 1908–24; Edinburgh, 1924–45.

to an eternal good. Taylor, who perhaps took more seriously than some other philosophers of his generation the gravity of sin and guilt, answers the question in the negative. But it does not follow that the moral life is doomed to frustration, for he now introduces what he calls 'the initiative of the eternal'[1]—that is to say, the divine grace which reaches out to man and enables his moral attainment. The moral life thus finds fulfilment in the life of religion. A further consequence to be drawn is the immortality of the individual, who is destined for an eternal good.

Thus if we take the moral life seriously, we find that it implies a natural theology of God, grace and immortality. But the question is now raised whether such a minimal theology does not, like morality, point beyond itself for completion. Do not its bare bones, so to speak, need to be covered with the flesh and blood of an actual historical religion? Like Ward and Sorley, Taylor is impressed with the concreteness of history, and maintains that, in spite of the metaphysician's addiction for the abstract and universal, it is reasonable to look for the completion of natural theology in a positive historical revelation.

The last of our trio of ethical theists is William George de Burgh[2] (1866–1943). His book, *From Morality to Religion*, was written after those of Sorley and Taylor, and de Burgh acknowledges his indebtedness to these two thinkers. But his own contribution to the problems of the ethical approach to theism is perhaps the most original of the three.

Religion implies personal communion with God, whereas morality is possible apart from belief in an other-worldly order. Morality, de Burgh thinks, is essentially a practical affair, while in religion action is subordinate to the vision of God and has as its specific motive the love of God. Like Taylor, de Burgh believes that an examination of morality shows the need for its completion in religion. He maintains that morality exhibits certain antinomies which cannot be resolved on the level of morality itself. One such antinomy is the dualism of ethical principles. 'Human actions are open to two different types of valuation, according as their motive is the sense of duty or the desire of good.'[3] That is to say, a man may act morally by fulfilling an obligation, such as paying a debt; but he may also seek the realization of some object which he considers good, though he has no obligation to seek it. De Burgh does not think that any ethical theory can resolve this antinomy by subsuming either type of conduct under the other. Another antinomy is of a more practical sort. This is the well-known fact that everyone falls short in the moral life. 'For all our striving, we remain to the end unprofitable servants.'[4] We neither perfectly fulfil the

[1] *Op. cit.*, vol. I, pp. 211ff.   [2] Professor at Reading, 1907–34.
[3] *Op. cit.*, p. 37.   [4] *Op. cit.*, p. 67.

moral law—the classic statement is by St Paul—nor do we consistently and successfully realize the good.

These antinomies, de Burgh argues, can be resolved only on the level of religion. The two types of ethical principle converge upon the idea of God. The type of action that is motivated by desire for the good—action *sub ratione boni*—tends of itself to pass into religion, as we move from the pursuit of finite goods to the vision of an infinite and eternal good. Here the argument is reminiscent of Taylor. Now the appeal of the good is to man's rational nature, but human nature is also sensuous, and pursuit of the good is wayward. So we have the second path, that of duty, which leads upwards from the immediate duties of my station to the thought of duty universal as God's will for man. Only beyond time and place do the two paths come together in the service that is perfect freedom, the religious synthesis of duty, goodness and God.

On the practical side, moral failure and impotence prepare the way for religion. The antinomy of a striving which, on the human level, is doomed to frustration, is resolved by the supervention of the divine grace which perfects nature. De Burgh expounds St Thomas Aquinas' doctrine of the *virtus infusa* which springs from the love of God—a love in which God himself is on both sides of the relation. It is maintained that such *virtus infusa* does not violate but rather fulfils the moral life. So again we are invited to the conclusion that morality leads to theistic religion.

How much weight can we attach to these ethical arguments for theism? We should note that those who advance them, while certainly attaching high importance to them, recognize the limitation which must belong to an argument from one sector of experience. Sorley and de Burgh both say that the argument for theism is cumulative, and that the ethical approach needs to be supplemented by other approaches. Taylor, as we have seen, suggests that the natural theology derived from ethics gets filled out by revelation. On the other hand, some moral philosophers take quite a different view of the relation of ethics to theism.[1] But it must be acknowledged that the three philosophers considered here, whether taken singly or together, present an impressive case for completing morality in theistic religion.

18. ETHICAL THEISM AND THEOLOGY
F. R. Tennant

To the theologically-minded philosophers whom we have considered in the preceding sections of this chapter, we may add a philosophically-minded theologian who had much in common with them—Frederick

[1] See, for instance, W. G. Maclagan, *The Theological Frontier of Ethics.*

Robert Tennant[1] (1866–1957). He was a pupil of Ward, for whose psychological work in particular he had a sincere and even exaggerated respect; and, like Ward, he was well acquainted with the biological sciences. Tennant believed it to be the duty of the theologian to get to know the findings of psychology and the natural sciences, to study the methods and limitations of science, and to acquaint himself with epistemological and metaphysical theories. This may sound like an impossible demand, but it sprang from Tennant's conviction—surely a defensible one—that the intellectual status of theology must be tested by seeing how it stands up in the light of these various fields of study. Faithful to his principles, Tennant wrote a vast work on the philosophical presuppositions of Christian theology, and attempted to show their reasonableness.

The basic presupposition of Christian theology is taken to be ethical theism. This involves three factors which are distinct and yet which are not comprehensible apart from each other—God, the soul, and the world. 'God, man, and the world constitute a chord, and none of its three notes has the ring of truth without the accompaniment of the other two.'[2] Tennant endeavours to establish this position by a strictly empirical method. There is no special religious faculty to provide a short-cut. We have to go to the facts of experience, and draw from them whatever conclusions they render probable.

God comes first in the order of being, but he is last in the order of knowing. Experience begins with the self and the world, and the knowledge of these two advances *pari passu*. It is argued that the self implies a soul, which is substantial, enduring and active. The world, in turn, cannot be exhaustively described in mechanistic terms, but invites teleological interpretation. The appeal is to a 'wider teleology', which differs from such pre-evolutionary teleologies as Paley's in citing not isolated instances of adaptation but whole areas of experience which seem to give evidence of purpose. The cumulative argument passes in review the intelligibility of the world to human reason, the suitability of the environment to life and moral development, the aesthetic value of nature, and finally the interrelated organic structure of the whole. The total picture is said to point to an intelligent and purposeful Creator. Tennant goes on to clinch the argument by taking man and the world together in a synoptic view. Man is continuous with nature, but he is also personal and moral, and his moral life is to be taken into account in any estimate of the world that has brought forth man. Thus the moral argument becomes the coping-stone of the cumulative teleological argument, and we are led to belief in a personal moral God as the ground of the world, to an ethical theism 'which

---

[1] Lecturer at Cambridge, 1907–31.   [2] *Philosophical Theology*, vol. II, p. 259.

takes the realization of personality and of moral values to be the *raison d'être* of the world'.[1] This conclusion cannot, indeed, be logically demonstrated, but it is said to have that reasonable probability which is as much as we can expect in such matters.

While ethical theism is thus established as the philosophical presupposition of Christian theology, it is also used by Tennant for the criticism and reconstruction of Christian doctrine itself. He believes that much that has passed for theology offends against ethical theism. He criticizes notions of election and predestination as belittling personality in man, and as destructive of a personal ethical relation between man and God. Unethical too is the traditional doctrine of the divine immutability, for it takes as its model inert matter, not active spirit; God is immutable only in the constancy of his moral purpose. Likewise Tennant rejects the traditional doctrine of original sin, on the ground that sin must be ethically conceived as 'moral imperfection for which an agent is, in God's sight, accountable'.[2] Thus his ethical theism not only defends but at the same time criticizes Christian theology.

19. ASSESSMENT OF PHILOSOPHIES OF SPIRIT

The philosophies which we have considered in this chapter undoubtedly provide a congenial background for a religious attitude to life, and in particular for an ethical version of Christianity. The fact that some of these philosophies may have been expressly constructed in order to provide just such a background need not prevent us from trying to assess them fairly.

They have undoubtedly a number of merits. Avoiding *a priori* speculations on the nature of reality and appeals to intuition or special faculties, they set out from the firm ground of common experience, and most of them try to do justice to the results of the empirical sciences. Avoiding vicious abstraction, they take experience in the concrete, point to the limits of scientific method, and claim a place for history and the human studies alongside the natural sciences. Avoiding an excessive intellectualism, they make room for the fact that man is not just a cognitive subject but a being who is active, evaluating, and engaged in the realization of ends.

Yet these philosophies themselves tend to speculate beyond the limits of experience. To take one example—and admittedly he is one of the most intellectualist of the thinkers we have considered here—Bowne, in spite of the undoubtedly activist strand in his philosophy, looked like a rationalist in the eyes of William James, himself a thoroughgoing empiricist.

[1] *Op. cit.*, vol. II, p. 258.   [2] *The Concept of Sin*, p. 245.

James writes: 'See how the ancient spirit of Methodism evaporates under those wonderfully able rationalistic booklets of a philosopher like Professor Bowne.'[1] Though some of the philosophers we have been discussing complained about abstract intellectualism, they did not altogether extricate themselves from it.

The doctrine of panpsychism, which we met in Varisco and Ward, is an obvious example of a speculative idea. It can indeed, as we have seen, be supported by plausible arguments, and we shall meet it again in other contexts.[2] But even allowing for the force of the argument about the abstract character of natural science, it is rather surprising to find panpsychism reappearing in modern guise after science has stripped nature of animistic interpretation. Of course, the modern versions of the doctrine are much more sophisticated than Thales' reputed teaching that 'everything is full of gods'. Again, it may surprise us to find among some of the thinkers whom we have been considering the reappearance of the teleological and cosmological arguments for the existence of God. Such arguments seem to take us back to the kind of natural theology which prevailed before Kant. It may, of course, be possible to restate these arguments cogently, and many attempts to do so have been made. There is no universal agreement about them. For instance, de Burgh criticizes Tennant for making too much of the teleological argument, and too little of the cosmological.[3] But both Tennant and de Burgh would agree that the arguments for theism are cumulative and establish no more than a degree of probability.

In any case, we must agree with Clement Webb that 'it would be extremely unjust to look upon these writers'—he has in mind Ward and Tennant, but his remarks would apply to others in this chapter—'as merely reproducing an obsolete and pre-Kantian manner of philosophizing'.[4] We may indeed equally well think of them as pointing forward to such developments as philosophies of value and culture, pragmatism, neovitalism, and even existentialism. What we have called the 'philosophies of spirit' are themselves unsatisfactory because they are too speculative to have the force of philosophies of action, and not sufficiently intellectualist to be able to claim for their speculations the strictness which belonged to idealist metaphysics. We have now to turn to a line of thought which makes a more definite break with metaphysical speculation, and which, following out ideas of which we have already come across echoes in Sorley, tries to justify religion in terms of moral value.

---

[1] *The Varieties of Religious Experience*, p. 492, n. 2. [2] See below, pp. 258–77.
[3] *From Morality to Religion*, p. 153.
[4] *Religious Thought in England from 1850*, p. 161.

V

THE IDEA OF VALUE IN PHILOSOPHY
AND THEOLOGY

20. NEO-KANTIANISM AND RITSCHLIANISM

IT was mentioned above that the Hegelian type of idealism established itself in the English-speaking countries only after it had declined in Germany itself.[1] In the latter country, speculative idealism had fallen into disfavour, and in the last thirty or forty years of the nineteenth century there was a revival of the critical idealism of Kant. Closely allied to this neo-Kantian philosophy was the Ritschlian school of theology. Both centred their interpretation of religion in the idea of value, and especially moral value.

Kant, as everyone knows, showed in his *Critique of Pure Reason* that human understanding is limited to the phenomena of sensory experience. When we try to go beyond these and ask questions about transcendent objects—God, freedom, immortality—we land ourselves in contradictions. The ultimate reality is unknowable, and rational metaphysics is impossible. These negative conclusions are, however, mitigated in his *Critique of Practical Reason*. As Kant himself put it, he removes knowledge in order to make room for faith. The ideas of God, freedom and immortality which cannot be established by the theoretical reason, find their justification in the practical reason or conscience which directs the moral life. As moral agents, we act as if these ideas were true, though we are impotent to establish them on purely rational grounds.

The neo-Kantians did not, of course, simply reiterate the teachings of Kant. They drew their initial inspiration from Kant but developed their own distinctive philosophy, just as the neo-Hegelians did. Into this developed philosophy other influences entered, notably that of Lotze who was much preoccupied with the idea of value. Lotze held that our ultimate convictions are of three kinds. We may be convinced of logical necessities, of facts of experience, or of determinations of value. These convictions are all independent of each other. As well as basing his philosophy of religion

[1] See p. 24.

on the spiritualistic metaphysic mentioned in the last chapter,[1] Lotze argued that religion is not primarily an intellectual matter but involves judgments of value which are irreducible to judgments of fact or necessity, and are therefore not to be tested by purely theoretical canons. He believed further that in God there is a synthesis of necessity, fact and value.

When we turn to the theological side, we find that Ritschl owed much both to Kant and to Lotze. Ritschl had begun as a Hegelian, but he came to reject metaphysics as a distorting influence for religion and theology. The traditional formulations of ecclesiastical dogma he likewise rejected, as an illegitimate mixture of metaphysics and religion. Religious assertions are not to be taken as disinterested statements of fact, but as value-judgments. Thus, for instance, the assertion of Christ's divinity is not to be understood as a metaphysical statement about Christ's nature (as in the traditional formulae of the Church) but as the judgment that for the believing community Christ has the value of God. Ritschl did not indeed deny what may be called a 'supernatural' element in religion, but there is a definite positivist tendency in his thought. He says: 'I, too, recognize mysteries in the religious life, but when anything is and remains a mystery, I say nothing about it.'[2] The theology which he developed is therefore dominated by ethical rather than metaphysical categories. The religious estimate of the historical Christ as God perfectly revealed arises from the ethical estimate of Christ's moral perfection; while the aim of the Christian religion is the realization of the kingdom of God, which is both the highest religious good and the moral ideal for men.

The various disjunctions which we have met in Kant, Lotze and Ritschl —between knowledge and faith, fact and value, the theoretical and the practical—reappear in the thinkers whom we are about to consider. By their stress upon the practical, these thinkers link up with the activist tendencies of the philosophies of spirit on the one hand, while their aversion to metaphysics relates them on the other hand to the positivists who will be considered in the next chapter. We shall find here also pointers to various pragmatist, historical and sociological interpretations of religion, to be considered later.

By the beginning of the present century, both neo-Kantian philosophy and Ritschlian theology were just about the peak of their development, so that already a wide range of divergent tendencies had made itself apparent. Among the philosophers, some stressed the positive side (the assertion of values) while others stressed the negative side (the denial of metaphysical knowledge). Among the theologians, some were driven by

[1] See above, pp. 58–9.
[2] *Justification and Reconciliation*, p. 607, n. 1.

the repudiation of metaphysics to fall back on the importance of revelation, while others preferred an undogmatic ethical version of Christianity. In the survey which follows, we shall look first at some representative neo-Kantian philosophers (Section 21), then at some of the more important Ritschlian theologians in Germany (Section 22) and America (Section 23), and thereafter proceed to an estimate (Section 24).

21. SOME NEO-KANTIAN PHILOSOPHERS
W. Windelband, H. Cohen, H. Vaihinger, H. Höffding

The beginnings of German neo-Kantianism are dated by Windelband around 1865—just about the time when neo-Hegelianism was making its appearance in British philosophy. Windelband remarks: 'The philosophical revival of Kantianism presents a great variety of views, in which we find repeated all shades of the opposing interpretations which Kant's theory met at its first appearance.'[1] There was indeed a bewildering variety of thinkers who seem to have had little in common beyond the fact that they all appealed to Kant as the great philosopher of modern culture, and that each one claimed to be expounding the really important truths in Kant's philosophy. While some of these thinkers—like those who belonged to the schools of Marburg and Baden—were relatively orthodox in their Kantianism, others interpreted the master in ways which led towards empiricism, positivism and even pragmatism. In the present context, we must be content to select a few philosophers whose views attracted international attention and who had something important to say on our own particular theme, the interpretation of religion.

Perhaps the most distinguished of the neo-Kantians, and certainly the one who is best-known beyond the confines of Germany itself, is the philosopher whom we have just quoted, Wilhelm Windelband[2] (1848–1915). He was the chief representative of the Baden school which found the main problems of philosophy in axiology, or the science of values. A pupil of Lotze, Windelband is famous as a historian of philosophy. He regarded the history of philosophy as itself a philosophical discipline, and saw in neo-Kantianism a movement to reconcile the implications of nineteenth-century natural science with 'the demands of the heart'. This movement had resulted in the emergence of the problem of value as the central problem of philosophy. It is worth quoting a few sentences

[1] *A History of Philosophy*, vol. II, p. 642.
[2] Professor successively at Zürich, 1876–77; Freiburg, 1877–82; Strasbourg, 1882–1903; Heidelberg, 1903–15.

from the concluding pages of his monumental survey of philosophical thought: 'Philosophy can live only as the science of values which are universally valid. It has neither the craving to know over again from its standpoint what the special sciences have already known from theirs, nor the desire to compile and patch together generalizations from the results of the separate disciplines. Philosophy has its own field and its own problem in those values of universal validity which are the organizing principle for all the functions of culture and civilization and for all the particular values of life. But it will describe and explain these values only that it may give an account of their validity; it treats them not as facts but as *norms*.'[1]

Such Windelband took to be the philosophical task of his time, and he himself approaches it from the intimate connection between the theoretical and the practical interests in man—a connection which he finds most clearly expressed in Kant among modern philosophers. All our knowing is bound up with willing, and so with those values which characterize the ends towards which the will is directed and in which it finds satisfaction. 'The general lines of the solution of problems and the answers to questions are for the most part determined by ideas of value.'[2] Windelband illustrates this by analysing the judgment, in which, he says, all our knowledge is found. 'To judge means not merely to connect ideas with each other, but to affirm this connection as valid and true; or in negative judgments, to reject it as false.'[3] Truth is not, as the untrained mind supposes, the correspondence of ideas with facts. This criterion would in any case be inapplicable to many kinds of judgment. Truth is itself a value, the satisfaction of the demands of a subject. While there are no values apart from evaluating subjects, this does not mean that values are merely subjective. A value consists of a relation between a subject and an object to which the subject directs itself, and it is obvious that such a value as truth must claim universal or intersubjective validity. Hence Windelband holds that there must be a 'logical consciousness in general' whose demands are satisfied by truth. The logical demand involves a necessity which is satisfied by truth, but this logical necessity is not like the necessity of a law of nature; it is not the necessity of what must be, but of what ought to be.

Windelband goes on to discuss these views in relation to the various sciences, and in the course of the discussion he makes a distinction which explains the importance which, as we have seen, he attaches to history. It is a distinction which we have already met in Ward and which we shall meet again in Dilthey and the philososphers of history—the distinction

---

[1] *A History of Philosophy*, vol. II, p. 680.
[2] *An Introduction to Philosophy*, p. 29. [3] *Op. cit.*, p. 170.

between the natural sciences which look for general laws, and the historical sciences which study individuals in so far as these individuals manifest some cultural values.

Alongside truth or logical value, Windelband sets ethical and aesthetic values, and it is argued in a similar fashion that these values also possess the characteristic of universality. Although we find that ethical and aesthetic judgments vary from individual to individual and from race to race, we speak nevertheless of higher or lower standards of morality or taste in different people, races or periods, and this implies that we try to set up some final standard of evaluation. But where can we find the standard of absolute values? To get away from the relativities of individuals and races, 'it seems necessary to pass beyond the historical manifestations of the entire human mind to some *normative* consciousness, for which these values are values'.[1] Just as we had to posit a 'logical consciousness in general' to account for the universal validity of truth, so it is now suggested that we must posit a normative consciousness as the foundation of universally valid ethical and aesthetic values. We are told, however, that this notion of a sovereign order of absolute values, transcending the human order, is a postulate and not something metaphysically known.

This talk of a transcendent realm of values introduces the theme of religion. The threefold scheme of logic, ethics and aesthetics, as well as repeating the pattern of Kant's philosophy, also corresponds to the threefold division of mental activities into knowing, willing and feeling, so that the list of universal values is complete. Religion is not a fourth realm of value, nor is the holy a distinct value to be set alongside the true, the good and the beautiful. Religion is rather concerned with the quest for a final synthesis, and identifies the normative consciousness postulated by the various realms of value with God or the holy, conceived as a transcendent reality in which all values are realized and what ought to be coincides with what is. This demand of religious faith is, however, not metaphysically demonstrable, and indeed it presents baffling problems. If God is the single principle of all things, why are facts and values rent asunder in the world? Again, if all values were realized, everything would be motionless in a state of eternal completion and valuation would cease, for the will needs the duality of fact and value as the condition of its activity. The problem of religion is the final problem to which we are conducted by the problem of values, but this final problem is insoluble. 'It is the sacred mystery, marking the limits of our nature and our knowledge.'[2]

The Marburg school of neo-Kantianism may be illustrated with

[1] *Op. cit.*, pp. 215–16.   [2] *Op. cit.*, p. 358.

reference to the thought of Hermann Cohen[1] (1842–1918). His interest in religion, especially in Judaism, makes him particularly relevant to our survey. Indeed, in the first two decades of the present century, Cohen came to be esteemed as a kind of modern Jewish prophet or sage, as Buber came to be at a later time; and Cohen's influence, like Buber's, extended far beyond the Jewish community.

Cohen's neo-Kantianism is of the most thoroughgoing rationalistic variety. Reality is identified with the object of rational thought. Thus when he comes to religion, Cohen endeavours to purge it of all irrational and mythological elements, and finds its justification solely in so far as it gives expression to the values of a rational ethic.

His general philosophy, like Windelband's, falls into three parts, in accordance with the Kantian scheme. The first part is a logic, dominated by mathematical conceptions, and it is chiefly for this part of his work that Cohen has been esteemed among professional philosophers. The second part is an ethic, in which he develops a form of socialism—not, indeed, the materialistic socialism of Marx, but a socialism which is guided by Kant's principle that persons are to be treated as ends, never as means, and which has as its ideal the unity of all mankind. The third part is an aesthetic, in which Cohen tries to work out a science of pure feeling.

This threefold scheme, like Windelband's, is exhaustive, so we must now ask where religion comes in, if anywhere. Cohen thinks that the Kantian ethic is the philosophical formulation of the ethical monotheism which finds expression in the Hebrew scriptures. The justification for religion is its ethical content, and Cohen virtually absorbs religion into ethics. God himself is simply an idea, immanent in reason. He is the centre of all ideas, the idea of truth. 'The concept of God and his existence mean only that it is not an illusion to believe in the unity of mankind.'[2] To ascribe to God life or personality is to slip back from rational philosophy into myth and anthropomorphism.

The strictly rational and ethical conception of religion which Cohen delineates is seen by him as the philosophical essence of the teaching of the Hebrew prophets and their successors, when this teaching is emptied of the last remnants of mythology; and his rationalistic interpretation of Judaism may be compared with that of another great Jew of modern times —Einstein.[3]

A more radical and much more activist form of neo-Kantianism is found in the works of Hans Vaihinger[4] (1852–1933). He is often counted among the pragmatists, but such a classification is not strictly accurate.

---

[1] Professor at Marburg, 1876–1912.　　[2] *Ethik*, p. 55.
[3] See below, p. 245.　　[4] Professor at Halle from 1884.

As Vaihinger himself points out, there is a fundamental difference between the principle of pragmatism that an idea which is found useful in practice is therefore proved to be true in theory, and the principle of his own fictionalism that an idea recognized to be theoretically untrue may nevertheless have practical value. His views represent an extreme development of neo-Kantianism. He professes to trace them back to some fundamental ideas which he learned from Kant—the impossibility of metaphysics, the supremacy of practical reason, the function of metaphysical ideas as regulative principles—and he regarded himself as bringing to light the essential teaching of Kant.

Vaihinger calls his doctrine 'positivist idealism', by which expression he indicates his view that thought is limited to the sphere of sense-experience. He also calls his doctrine the 'philosophy of "as if" ', by which he means that when thought oversteps its limits—as it may do—and forms ideas which cannot be other than false, we may sometimes accept these ideas *as if* they were true, because we find that they have a practical value. Such ideas Vaihinger calls 'fictions'. They are to be distinguished from hypotheses, which have some relation to facts, whereas fictions have no such relation and are unverifiable. They do not represent anything in the world, but they may nevertheless be useful. Here we must note that Vaihinger insists that theoretical interests are subordinate to practical interests. This is his interpretation of Kant's teaching on the practical reason, reinforced by Schopenhauer's teaching on the primacy of the will. Thought is purposeful. Ideas, judgments, the whole apparatus of thought, are simply means in the service of the will to live. Thought may indeed become an end in itself, and may set itself impossible theoretical problems, but when it does so, it runs into the false and contradictory ideas called 'fictions'. We should not expect our ideas to give us 'a portrayal of reality —this would be an utterly impossible task—but rather to provide us with an instrument for finding our way about more easily in the world'.[1] A fiction may be helpful in this respect, and if so, it has value for us in spite of its theoretical falsity. Its value is utility for life—not just life in a crudely biological sense, but richer and fuller life. And here we may notice a pessimistic strain in Vaihinger. He says: 'The real tragedy of life is that the most valuable ideas are, from the point of view of reality, worthless.'[2]

Vaihinger proceeds to show that fictions enter into most areas of our thinking. There are many of them in mathematics—such as the square root of minus one—and they may prove very useful. Other fictions are traced in physics, economics, jurisprudence, philosophy, and many other

[1] *The Philosophy of 'As If'*, p. 15.   [2] *Op. cit.*, p. 44.

branches of study—ideas which are all in one way or another contradictory or erroneous, but which nevertheless have the value of utility in some particular field. In the case of some of these ideas, their fictitious character is clearly understood by those who make use of them. In other cases, the fiction is mistaken for a hypothesis or is even converted into a dogma.

Vaihinger consigns to the realm of fictions the basic religious ideas— God, the soul, and so on. It is, however, claimed to be an advantage to recognize the fictitious character of these ideas, for then one will no longer be distressed about trying to make sense of them or to free them from contradictions, as would be necessary if they were hypotheses capable of verification. The value of fictions is not affected by their theoretical falsity. Vaihinger suggests that the Church might have saved itself a lot of trouble and time spent in trying to elucidate such ideas as the relationship of Christ to the Father if the fictitious character of these ideas had been recognized. We may ask whether these religious ideas would not lose their value for life if once we had decided to regard them as fictions. Vaihinger does not seem to think so. Religion is not a theoretical belief that the kingdom of God is coming, but a practical belief in the kingdom, that is to say, acting *as if* by our action the kingdom could be brought into being. The 'dignity and sublimity' of the religion of 'as if' is said to lie precisely in the fact 'that a good man does good although theoretically he does not believe in a moral world-order; he acts *as if* he did believe in it. This religion of "as if" is built up on a positivistic and at the same time pessimistic basis.'[1]

Still another expression of the neo-critical philosophy is found in the Danish thinker, Harald Höffding[2] (1843–1931). Like Windelband, he makes much of the idea of value, while, like Vaihinger, he leans far in the direction of positivism. Höffding is of special interest for our study because of the attention which he devoted to the problem of religion. He bases his treatment of this theme on the distinction between *explanation* and *evaluation*, and he tells us that for this distinction we are indebted to the philosophy of Kant.

Religion has its theoretical motives, and in an age of faith it satisfies man's quest for knowledge as well as his other spiritual needs. It offers an explanation both of particular events and of the world as a whole by referring everything to a single principle—God. Then alongside religion there arises science which offers a different kind of explanation. Particular events are explained in terms of other events within the same causal order, while no explanation at all is offered for the world as a whole. Gradually the scientific way of understanding particular events displaces

[1] *Op. cit.*, p. 326.   [2] Professor at Copenhagen, 1883–1915.

the religious way. There might still be the possibility that the two ways of explanation could be reconciled, the scientific explanation being appropriate to the parts and the religious explanation to the whole. Indeed, the fact that scientific explanation seems to presuppose a principle of unity in things might suggest that it points in the direction of a religious explanation. But this is not the case. Scientific explanation never attains finality, and its principle of unity remains an ideal. Religion steps in with its own principle of unity, but this is not the unity of phenomena as presupposed by science, but a God who stands over against the world. So far is this religious idea from being a final explanation that it rather raises new problems. Thus religion cannot be justified as explaining anything.

If religious ideas cannot be accepted as explanation, can they be justified in another way? Here we must turn from explanation to evaluation, and ask whether the religious ideas may not express something in the spiritual life other than understanding. In fact, Höffding thinks that the intellectual element has a very subordinate place in religion, and that what is important in the conception of God is that it gathers up the highest known values. He defines a value as 'the property possessed by a thing either of conferring immediate satisfaction or serving as a means to procuring it'.[1] He declares that 'the conservation of value is the characteristic axiom of religion', and the principle of the conservation of value is identified with God.[2] Conservation of value is analogous to conservation of energy in the physical world, and means that no value perishes out of the world. This is, of course, not demonstrable, but is rather a postulate.

The highest values are ethical values, and religion is based upon ethics, although many people think that the contrary is the case. The major development in the history of religion, according to Höffding, was not the transititon from polytheism to monotheism, but the transition from natural to ethical religion. The discovery and production of value belongs to ethics, and religion is concerned only with conservation. All the dogmas and myths of religion are symbols of the principle of conservation. Values change in the course of evolution, but in the higher religions ethical values are paramount. Thus the function of religion seems to be that of encouraging the moral life. 'Faith in the conservation of value will inspire us with courage not to give up things too easily for lost, but to continue our search for value, for hidden sources, until we discover how even the least maintains its place in the garland of life.'[3]

[1] *The Philosophy of Religion*, p. 12.
[2] *Op. cit.*, pp. 10, 384.
[3] *Op. cit.*, p. 344.

22. SOME RITSCHLIAN THEOLOGIANS
W. Herrmann, T. Haering, J. Kaftan, A. Harnack

A consideration of Ritschlian theology in the early years of our century may begin from the writings of Wilhelm Herrmann[1] (1846–1922). He well illustrates the distinctive characteristics which Ritschlianism shared with neo-Kantianism in the interpretation of religion—the repudiation of metaphysics and the practical emphasis on moral values—and furthermore he occupies a fairly central position in the Ritschlian school, so that by comparison with him we can see how the other representatives of the school group themselves in two opposing wings—a more conservative wing (Haering and Kaftan), and a more radical wing (Harnack).

According to Herrmann, metaphysics can never succeed in solving the problems which it sets itself, nor can it attain to objective truth, as the sciences can. Herrmann thinks that behind metaphysics there is a practical motive, the desire of man to find his orientation in the world. This desire is satisfied not by metaphysics but by religion. Unfortunately, religion and metaphysics have been confused in the past. The confusion may be seen in traditional ecclesiastical dogmas, which were a mixture of metaphysics and religion—for instance, theologians have taken an idea of God derived from Greek speculation and have superimposed it on the Christian idea of God. Such dogmas must be abandoned, but the possibility is not ruled out of a different approach in which 'Christian doctrine is only to be understood as the expression of new personal life'.[2]

This new approach is based not on metaphysical speculation but on faith, understood as an experience in which God reveals himself to man and a communion between them is established. Herrmann does not deny that there is some revelation of God in the general religious experience of mankind, even the most primitive, but he finds the revelation above all in the historical Jesus. The revelation lies in the 'inner life' or spiritual consciousness of Jesus, and not in such biographical details about him as his virgin birth, his miracles or his resurrection. These details are of secondary importance. It is the 'inner life' of Jesus, as preserved in the New Testament, that lays hold on us as it did on the first disciples, or, as Herrmann puts it, makes an 'impression' on us. The impression is such that we are brought into communion with God and constrained to acknowledge that Christ is God. If we ask about the exact nature of this impression, we get no clear answer, for Herrmann says that 'the inner life

---

[1] Professor at Marburg from 1879.
[2] *Systematic Theology*, p. 64.

of religion is a secret in the soul'.[1] It is claimed, however, that we have two objective grounds for the faith built upon this impression. The first is 'the historical fact of the person of Christ'.[2] We arrive at God not through any doubtful speculation but through Christ as a historical fact within the range of human experience. This fact is, Herrmann believes, sufficiently attested in the New Testament, at least as far as the all-important 'inner life' of Jesus is concerned; and further, this 'inner life' has an enduring character, so that we experience its power today as the first disciples did. The second objective ground is that 'we hear within ourselves the demand of the moral law'.[3] If we are going to live as specifically human beings, we must accept the objective validity of this law. Our inner moral convictions are realized in Christ, and he is also the founder of the kingdom of God, understood as the universal moral community which claims our consciences. These ethical valuations are expressed in the confession of Christ as God.

Thus the reality of God which metaphysics fails to establish is assured on the ground of the communion which we have with him in Christ. This communion is not mystical, if by 'mysticism' is understood an exclusively 'inner' experience of the individual, for the communion is centred in the historical Jesus, in whom we are said to get a positive view of God. Our idea of God should be derived only from this positive view. 'We do not merely come through Christ to God. It is truer to say that we find in God himself nothing but Christ.'[4] Other Christian doctrines, such as that of the person of Christ, must likewise be purged of alien metaphysics and interpreted as implications of the central fact of the believer's communion with God in Christ.

The exploration of these 'implications' of faith was fully carried out by Theodor Haering[5] (1848–1928), and the result was a massive and fairly conservative dogmatic system. Herrmann, like Ritschl himself, had spoken with reserve of the more speculative Christian doctrines. He regarded them as subordinate to the practical interest, and stated that any Christian dogmatics based on the Ritschlian approach would be shorter than the old dogmatic systems. This somewhat ambiguous attitude to doctrine had led to misunderstanding, and it was supposed in some quarters that Ritschlian theology, by subordinating questions of fact to judgments of value, was headed in the direction of a purely immanentist ethical and undogmatic view of religion, such as some of the neo-Kantian philosophers

[1] *The Communion of the Christian with God*, p. 19.

[2] *Op. cit.*, p. 102.   [3] *Op. cit.*, p. 103.   [4] *Op. cit.*, p. 32.

[5] Professor successively at Zürich (1886–1928); Göttingen, 1889–95; Tübingen from 1895.

taught. Such was not the intention of either Ritschl or Herrmann, and the misunderstanding is explicitly countered in conservative Ritschlians like Haering.

Haering finds a twofold foundation for religious faith. 'On the one hand, there is the satisfaction of our highest needs; on the other hand, there is the self-manifestation of God.'[1] This statement implies that both value and reality are involved. 'In Jesus, God shows himself to us as the reality of greatest value.'[2] We begin from a value-judgment of the moral consciousness, but corresponding to it is not just a subjective ideal but a reality, 'a power which transcends our consciousness and is independent of it'.[3] There is revelation of reality, an actual approach of God in the real world, though we recognize this approach for what it is only because it corresponds to our highest valuation.

Haering rebukes those Ritschlians who hesitated to explore the reality revealed to faith, and who ignored important traditional doctrines. The reality, however, must be understood from the point of view of its religious significance, and as an implication of the revelation, and Haering is cautious and moderate in his appraisals. Nevertheless, he goes through the whole gamut of dogma, from creation to angels and eschatology. Whether so much can be acknowledged as an implication of the revelation or whether a metaphysic is regaining admission by the back-door is a matter for discussion. But it certainly seems to be the case that Haering has moved from that 'positive view' of God of which Herrmann spoke, and has gone far towards reinstating the more speculative doctrines of traditional Christianity, such as angelology.

Yet, like the other Ritschlians, Haering has a strong ethical interest, and gives an important place to the idea of the kingdom of God. Doctrine and ethics form a single whole. 'Doctrine shows us how the kingdom of God becomes to us an assured personal possession as God's *gift* by faith in Christ; ethics how this faith is our incentive and motive-power to co-operation in the *task* of realizing the kingdom of God.'[4] Haering was a pioneer in the detailed application of Christian ethical principles to the moral and social questions of his day.

Also to be reckoned as belonging to the conservative wing of the Ritschlian school is Julius Wilhelm Martin Kaftan[5] (1848–1926), though in some respects he stands rather apart from the mainstream of Ritschlian thinking. Thus Kaftan gives an important place to mysticism, which had been suspect in the eyes of both Ritschl and Herrmann. Again, Kaftan

---

[1] *The Christian Faith*, p. 228.   [2] *Op. cit.*, p. 229.   [3] *Op. cit.*, p. 26.
[4] *The Ethics of the Christian Life*, p. 4.
[5] Professor at Basel, 1881–83; Berlin from 1883.

insists explicitly on the supramundane character of the kingdom of God, while still retaining for it an ethical foundation. He was an admirer of Kant, whom he regarded as the philosopher of Protestantism, and he sets out from the common neo-Kantian and Ritschlian starting-point of value-judgments, but his results stand at the furthest remove from that *merely* ethical, immanentist view of religion which was characteristic of many of the neo-Kantian philosophers.

Quite in the neo-Kantian and Ritschlian manner, Kaftan rejects speculative metaphysics, upholds the primacy of the practical reason, and maintains that 'in religion it is not theory that is the essential matter, but feeling and will'.[1] We cannot properly speak of the truth of a feeling or of a moral injunction, but we can speak of the truth of religion, for Kaftan holds that faith carries with it its own knowledge, the knowledge of God. This is not indeed an objective knowledge of God as he is in himself, such as speculation seeks to provide, but it is a genuine theoretical knowledge of God as he has revealed himself to us. Although religion is primarily a practical matter and begins from value-judgments, the knowledge which belongs to faith does not, according to Kaftan, consist in value-judgments but in theoretical judgments based upon value-judgments.

Thus, although Kaftan rejects the old dogmas which mingled speculative and religious thinking, he believes that the Church cannot do without dogma, and he visualizes a new kind of dogma which will be both theoretical and yet based on the practical experience of the apprehension of God's revelation in faith. Kaftan illustrates the difference between the two types of dogma by contrasting the interpretation of the Christian revelation in terms of the speculative idea of the Logos—an interpretation which 'unconditionally yields first place to knowledge'— with its interpretation in terms of the idea of the kingdom of God— an interpretation which gives first place to 'the moral righteousness which has to be realized in the world'.[2] The system of dogma is to be constructed by developing the central insight of faith into its finest details, and the reasonableness of this knowledge is held to be based on the correspondence of the Christian idea of the kingdom of God to the practical reason's ideal of a chief good, and on the fact of the historical revelation of the kingdom of God in Jesus Christ.

Kaftan himself interprets the kingdom of God as not merely an ethical ideal to be realized *within the world*, but as a transcendent reality *above the world*. Hence just as essential to the Christian religion as its moral endeavour is its mystical side which turns away from the world and is the

[1] *The Truth of the Christian Religion*, vol. I, p. 8.
[2] *Op. cit.*, vol. I, p. 93.

life of the soul hidden with Christ in God, a blessedness which lifts the believer above the world.

In contrast with the more or less conservative versions of Ritschlianism just considered, we find that the practical emphasis common to all the Ritschlian theologians is given a more radical turn by Adolf Harnack (1850–1931),[1] who stresses the ethical side of Christianity, reduces doctrine to a bare minimum, and has come to be regarded as the typical exponent of liberal Protestantism. One of the most erudite theologians of modern times, Harnack had a meticulous knowledge of early Christian history and literature. His brilliant gifts of exposition are attested by the enthusiastic reception given to his famous lectures on Christianity, delivered at Berlin in the winter of 1899–1900, and then published and republished many times in the following years.

Religion, according to Harnack, is a practical affair, and is concerned with the power to live a blessed and holy life. In Christianity, this power is traced back to the historical revelation of God in Jesus Christ. Although religion is practical, it involves some beliefs about God and the world, and it seeks to make these beliefs explicit.

The tendency to formulate religious beliefs led in Christianity to the rise of dogmas—propositions which were supposed to express the content of the Christian religion, and acknowledgement of which was required from members of the Church as the condition of their participation in the blessedness offered by their religion.

The rise of dogma, however, is regarded by Harnack as a perversion of the true nature of Christianity. The wells of true religion have become ₊hoked with theological and metaphysical garbage, and the history of the Church's thinking has in the main been the story of the obscuration and deterioration of Christian truth, rather than of its development and unfolding. The perversion seems to have begun in apostolic times when the early preachers, instead of repeating the preaching of Jesus concerning the kingdom of God and instead of reporting the historical events of his life, began to preach about the significance of his person and introduced such ideas as pre-existence. The process is accentuated with the spread of Christianity into the Hellenistic world, and its absorption of Greek ideas such as that of the Logos. The dogmas of the early Church are regarded as the work of the Greek spirit on the soil of the Gospel, 'the formulation of Christian faith as Greek culture understood it and justified it to itself'.[2]

In his monumental history, Harnack traces the development and

---

[1] Professor successively at Leipzig, 1876–79; Giessen, 1879–86; Marburg, 1886–88; Berlin from 1888.

[2] *History of Dogma* vol. I, p. 11.

variations of dogma on through the story of the Catholic Church. At the Reformation, Luther made some attempt to return to primitive Christianity and to emancipate religion from dogma, but this was only a beginning, and the attitude of Protestantism to dogma has remained ambiguous. Thus the rise and development of dogma have been, in Harnack's view, a smothering and obscuration of the essence of Christianity. Yet, in spite of all, the essence still survives as a kind of kernel in the husk.

This essence alone can satisfy modern men who are merely baffled by the unintelligibility and the incredibility of ecclesiastical dogmas. In his quest for the essence, Harnack tries to penetrate back through the theological accretions of the centuries to the concrete Jesus of history and his Gospel. Harnack believed that we can still get from the New Testament a sufficiently plain account of Christ's teaching and of his life as issuing in the service of his vocation. The teaching of Jesus is the original Gospel, and its elements are simple enough—the fatherhood of God, the infinite worth of the human soul, the ethical ideal of the kingdom of God. The essence of Christianity is therefore the ethic of Jesus in its theistic setting. 'How great a departure from what he thought and enjoined is involved in putting a christological creed in the forefront of the Gospel!'[1]

The Gospel as Jesus proclaimed it, we are told, has to do with the Father, not the Son. Harnack seems to think of Jesus as the religious genius of the human race who enjoyed a unique filial relation to God. His teaching and his life fulfil the highest aspirations of our moral consciousness, and so we are convinced of the truth of his message. Speculation on the ultimate problems gives us today as uncertain an answer as it did two thousand years ago. 'But if with a steady will we affirm the forces and the standards which on the summits of our inner life shine out as our highest good; if we are earnest and courageous enough to accept them as the great reality and direct our lives by them; and if then we look at the course of mankind's history and follow its upward development, we shall become certain of God, of the God whom Jesus Christ called his Father, and who is also our Father.'[2]

23. RITSCHLIANISM IN THE UNITED STATES
H. C. King

Like neo-Kantian philosophy, Ritschlian theology was primarily a German movement, but both movements had, of course, an influence in the English-speaking countries. On the British side of the Atlantic, the

[1] *What is Christianity?*, p. 147.   [2] *Op. cit.*, p. 301.

philosophy of W. R. Sorley, considered in the preceding chapter,[1] has obviously much in common with neo-Kantianism; while among theologians, the interest in Ritschlianism is attested by the publication of such notable studies as A. E. Garvie's *The Ritschlian Theology* and J. K. Mozley's *Ritschlianism*, and is also evident in John Baillie's early work, *The Interpretation of Religion*. But although there was this interest in Ritschlianism, the movement won few outright adherents in Britain. The case was rather different in the United States, where perhaps Ritschlianism had an appeal for the practical temper of the American people. We have to remember too that the idea of the kingdom of God, so central in Ritschlian thinking, had also for long occupied an important place in American Christianity, as is shown by H. R. Niebuhr in his book, *The Kingdom of God in America*. In any case, the Ritschlian theology met with a sympathetic response from several notable American theologians.

One of these was Henry Churchill King[2] (1858–1934). During a sojourn in Germany, he had become keenly interested both in the philosophy of Lotze and the theology of Ritschl. When we compare King with Bowne, that other American follower of Lotze, we find that both make much of the idea of personality. However, King's ways of speaking about 'reverence for personality' and 'the primacy of the personal' make it clear that for him personality is not so much regarded as the key to metaphysical problems, as it was with Bowne, but is chiefly considered as the source and principle of value. King claims that 'love for Christ as a person has, as a matter of fact, proved the mightiest of historical motives to noble living'.[3] This practical emphasis is evident in his theology, where, expressing dissatisfaction with traditional formulations, he contrasts the personal and ethical understanding of Christian doctrine with the metaphysical understanding, to the detriment of the latter.

As an illustration of this, we may notice what he has to say on the doctrine of the person of Christ. King states that Christ was at one with the Father in a moral and spiritual sense, that is to say, Christ was absolutely unique in his perfect response to the will of God. It may also be said that Christ is at one with God in a metaphysical sense, that is to say, he is of the same essence as God 'when essence is interpreted teleologically'. King goes on: 'The newer and the older, the personal and the metaphysical forms of statement would thus fall together. But there can be no doubt that the personal and practical form of the confession of Christ's divinity is, for the vast majority of men, much the more sure and rational test.'[4]

---

[1] See above, p. 68.

[2] Professor from 1891 at Oberlin College, Ohio, and President of the College, 1902–27.

[3] *The Ethics of Jesus*, p. 19.   [4] *Reconstruction in Theology*, p. 248.

The same kind of approach holds for other doctrines. Even such un-promising material as eschatology is given an ethical interpretation, on the ground that it implicitly emphasizes the worth of men. King's whole approach stresses the practical and active character of religion, and leads to a liberalizing of traditional doctrines. Thus although he uses the notion of personality in a rather different way from Bowne, he arrives at much the same results.

The practical bearing of Christian doctrine extends to the social order, and the prominence which the Ritschlian theologians gave to the idea of the kingdom of God reappears in King's interest in the relation of theology to the social consciousness. Thus King's thought merges into the American 'Social Gospel', a movement in which, as we shall see later,[1] Ritschlian ideas played an important part.

24. Critical Remarks on Neo-Kantianism and Ritschlianism

The views which we have considered in this chapter have the great merit of bringing into the forefront the ethical character of religion, and presumably there is no advanced religion worthy of the name which does not exert moral power in its devotees. It may even be the case, as both neo-Kantian philosophers and Ritschlian theologians suggest, that religion is primarily a practical affair, and that religious beliefs arise out of religious practice. On the face of it, this seems more plausible than the supposition that religion is primarily a world-view from which a way of life is then deduced.

But if, as Windelband has stated, one of the motives of neo-Kantianism was to reconcile the scientific understanding of the world with the demands of the heart, it is not at all clear that this end has been achieved. Rather, we seem to be left with two worlds on our hands—a real world of facts and a somewhat ghostly world of values—and the connection between them remains obscure. Here we may contrast with the neo-Kantians those British philosophers considered in the preceding chapter who strongly insisted that fact and value must not be separated. Among the others, Windelband comes to a halt before the impenetrable mystery of the duality of fact and value. Höffding is agonistic about the ultimate reality but exhorts us to realize values in the faith that they will not perish. Vaihinger is frankly pessimistic, and tells us that what is of most value to us is of no account in reality. Cohen, and other members of the

[1] See below, p. 163.

Marburg school, such as Natorp, lead us towards an immanentist view of religion, in which it is virtually identified with ethics. It is a religion without God, or at least, without a God who is more than an idea, a *focus imaginarius* of values. But even if it is conceded that religion is primarily a practical affair, it is surely no longer religion when it has been so utterly divested of its transcendent beliefs. The name may have been saved, but hardly the reality which most people have in mind when they think of religion.

Is the case any different with the Ritschlian theologians? They too reject the possibility of a metaphysical knowledge, but they believe in the reality of God and of a transcendent order, and they claim a knowledge of this transcendent order—a fairly detailed knowledge in the case of Haering and Kaftan, a more guarded knowledge in the case of Herrmann, and little more than a few general convictions in the case of Harnack. This knowledge of the transcendent, inaccessible by way of metaphysics, is claimed on the basis of revelation. It is surely, however, a desperate expedient when theology denies that there can be any knowledge of God apart from a special revelation. The Scottish theologian, W. P. Paterson, had the Ritschlian theologians in mind when he wrote: 'It is not natural, and it may even be thought a psychological anomaly that the same mind should be able to oscillate between the doubts of the sceptical philosopher and the childlike trustfulness of the humble believer. To say that in the strength of my Christian faith I believe that there is a God, almighty, all-wise and all-good, the Creator and the Governor of the world, and to go on to declare that nothing of these truths can be collected from an examination of the arrangements of the universe, the constitution of man, and the course of history, seems to be to pay to God the poor compliment of likening him to one of his earthly children who should be told that he had a lofty genius which unfortunately his writings did not reveal, or a noble character which was belied by all the details of his conduct.'[1] This curious mixture of scepticism and romanticism is, of course, not peculiar to the Ritschlian theologians but is found in some of the neo-Kantian philosophers as well—Natorp, for instance, combined a rationalistic approach to philosophy with a devout belief in the spiritual supremacy of the German people, and busied himself during World War I in writing books on the civilizing mission of Germany to mankind.

Guido de Ruggiero, after characterizing the Ritschlian conception of God as 'the exaltation of an arbitrary and isolated fact in the life of humanity', remarks that 'the God of Harnack, like the God of Ritschl, cannot be worshipped, loved or feared, but only criticized as a logical

---

[1] *The Nature of Religion*, pp. 6–7.

error'.[1] This may seem a harsh verdict, but if we reflect upon it we are bound to admit that there is good reason for it. While we may agree with Höffding about the importance of ethical religion, and while we have already applauded the stress laid by both neo-Kantians and Ritschlians on the ethical side of religion, we must beware of the danger of making our conception of God *exclusively* ethical, or he then becomes an abstraction. A God who can be exhaustively characterized in moral terms is a humanized God, lacking those elements of mystery and majesty for which the deeper aspirations of worship seek. The character of Deity which is variously designated as the 'numinous' (Otto) or the 'suprapersonal' (the idealists) or the 'wholly other' (Barth) is not indeed explicitly denied by the Ritschlians, but it is excluded from consideration. It may be an exaggeration to say that the Ritschlian God cannot be worshipped, but it is true to say that this conception of God is too thin to answer to the deepest needs of the religious consciousness. Obviously this line of criticism would apply more forcibly to Herrmann and Harnack than it would to Haering and Kaftan.

But leaving aside the question of how far the Ritschlian God can be worshipped, we have to face the question whether, as de Ruggiero alleges, his conception of God is a logical error. Can philosophical scepticism be combined with faith in a real God in the way which the Ritschlians desiderated? Can one pass from judgments of value to the assertion of a transcendent reality as easily as they supposed? Or is it not rather the case that the logical conclusion of Ritschlianism is to be found in the 'as if' of Vaihinger?

Of course, the Ritschlians point to the Jesus of history as the positive revelation of God and as the realization within history of the ideals of the practical reason. This positive revelation is supposed to provide the bridge which leads from value to reality, and firmly unites the two. Through the fog of metaphysical and theological speculation about Christ's person, the Ritschlians believed it possible to discern the actual historical Jesus as a positive fact. But now to the criticisms of the philosophers, we have to add the strictures of New Testament scholars who have attacked this side of the Ritschlian teaching. It is now claimed that even St Mark's Gospel presents a theologically coloured picture of Jesus, and that we cannot get behind it. Harnack has been compared to a child peeling an onion in the hope of getting to the core. What has he left when he has finished?

The detailed criticism of the Ritschlian picture of the historical Jesus has taken various forms in different biblical scholars. Alfred Loisy[2]

---

[1] *Modern Philosophy*, p. 93.   [2] See below, p. 182.

demands to know why the essence of Christianity should be sought only in its beginning and not in the fullness and totality of its life. Albert Schweitzer[1] and others have brought the New Testament picture, which the Ritschlians tended to consider in isolation, into the setting of contemporary religious movements, and have argued that the kingdom of God, so far from being the ideal of practical reason to be realized by moral endeavour, meant for Jesus an eschatological event, conceived in terms of Jewish apocalyptic and to be realized by a catastrophic intervention in history.

Some of the criticisms of the idea of a 'Jesus of history' have no doubt been exaggerated in the course of the violent theological swing away from Ritschlianism. But even when we allow for some overstatement, we see that the pictures of the historical Jesus which we find in writers like Herrmann and Harnack are not nearly so positive and objective as their authors supposed them to be. They are at least in part the projection of the moral ideals of these theologians themselves upon the figure of Jesus. In short, these pictures are idealized constructions, and have perhaps as little claim to be positively factual as has the metaphysical description of Christ in the Chalcedonian formula, which the Ritschlians so much disliked. But if this is so, the Ritschlians are left with no avenue of escape from the circle of their subjectivity, and are driven towards the same immanentist view of religion that we met in the neo-Kantian philosophers. The bizarre mixture of scepticism and faith from which the Ritschlians set out proves in the end—as we might have expected—to be an unstable foundation for religion.

The tendency which we have observed in the writers considered in this chapter has been to stress the practical and subjective factors in religion, and to minimize or to take away altogether any knowledge of reality which religion might claim. This tendency is carried a stage further in the various forms of positivism and naturalism to which we shall now turn.

[1] See below, p. 145.

VI

POSITIVISM AND NATURALISM

25. The Claims of Natural Science

THE astonishing advance of the natural sciences might well claim to be regarded as the most notable feature of the nineteenth century, and this advance has continued without interruption in our own century. As a consequence of the success of science, the claim was bound to be made that the natural sciences should have a greater part, or even a definitive part, in shaping our philosophical ideas. The champions of such claims were able to point to the relatively secure and unanimous findings of the sciences as compared with the uncertain and conflicting speculations of metaphysicians and theologians. The claim was made both in respect of the empirical methods of science, which, it was supposed, might be extended to fields formerly regarded as lying beyond the scope of science; and in respect of particular scientific hypotheses, such as that of evolution, which might be capable of application outside of the special sciences in which their usefulness had been demonstrated.

There are several types of philosophy which claim to base themselves upon the natural sciences, and although these types tend to shade off into one another, they are at least in principle distinguishable.

'Positivism'—which we have already met among the neo-Kantians—at once restricts and extends the claim on behalf of the sciences. It restricts this claim by denying that the sciences give us any knowledge of ultimate reality. They provide knowledge only of the connection and order of phenomena. It extends the claim of the sciences by denying that there is any knowledge outside of them. In particular, there is a condemnation of metaphysics in any form. We are to renounce the attempt to know reality, and content ourselves with the only kind of knowledge possible for us—the knowledge of phenomena which is provided by the sciences. The name of 'positivism' is especially associated with the French philosopher, Comte. This thinker distinguished three stages in human thinking—first, the theological stage, at which events are referred to divine agency; next, the metaphysical stage, at which events are referred to speculative causes;

and finally, the positive stage, which does not take us outside of observable and measurable phenomena, and which is the highest development of human intellect.

'Naturalism' is itself a metaphysic—it is the identification of reality with nature. Since the various aspects of nature are studied in the special sciences, the function of philosophy would seem to be the co-ordination of the findings of the sciences. Thus one of the greatest naturalistic philosophers of the nineteenth century, Spencer, tells us that 'science is partially unified knowledge; philosophy is completely unified knowledge', or 'knowledge of the highest generality'.[1] The term 'nature', however, is such a vague one that naturalism can take many different forms. If nature is supposed to be, in the last analysis, composed of material atoms in motion, then naturalism becomes 'materialism'. There were some thorough-going materialists in the nineteenth century, such as Buechner, the author of the famous book, *Force and Matter*. Normally, however, naturalism does not assume a purely materialistic form, and indeed none of the thinkers to be considered in this chapter were materialists in the strict sense. It may, for instance, be supposed that energy is the ultimate stuff of nature, and that energy may manifest itself as mind or matter. Or it may be that the ultimate source of nature is left undefined, as was the case in Spencer's 'agnosticism'—a view which merges into positivism. On the other hand, some naturalists find room for spirit in nature, but they would accept the common naturalistic thesis that there is nothing beyond nature, so that spirit is to be regarded as belonging to the data of nature, with nothing 'supernatural' about it.

It may be asked how this last position differs from that of idealists like Edward Caird, who, it will be remembered,[2] laid stress on the immanence of spirit and rejected talk of the 'supernatural'. The difference is that for Caird the evolutionary process is one in which the lower must be understood in terms of the higher, so that it is a process which is to be understood throughout as the manifestation of spirit. The naturalist, on the other hand, seeks to explicate what is higher in the evolutionary process in terms of what is lower; spirit is regarded as a product of nature, rather than nature as a manifestation of spirit.

Positivism and naturalism do not exclude some account of religion, or even some appreciation of religion. Comte, as is well-known, crowned his positivist system with a form of religion in which humanity takes the place of God as the object of worship. The naturalist, while he could not admit a transcendent God outside of nature, might nevertheless think of nature

[1] *First Principles*, pp. 132, 134.
[2] See above, p. 26.

itself as deiform. Spencer sought to reconcile science and religion by assigning to religion the realm of the unknowable.

Whatever the solution proposed, however, religion is treated as a natural phenomenon. Now it is obvious that religion is at least in part a natural phenomenon, and that in so far as this is the case, religion may be studied as a natural phenomenon. In fact, just about the turn of the century, recently developed branches of study were carrying out a scientific investigation into the phenomena of religion, and their findings added strength to the naturalistic case. In 1896 the University of Oxford founded a chair of anthropology, thereby recognizing the coming of age of a science which had already carried out wide-ranging investigations into the cultures of primitive peoples and, among other things, into the genesis of religious ideas. Meantime, the science of archaeology was tracing the history of religion back into remote times. Another group of investigators, chiefly in America, began to study the psychology of religion and were able to show the natural factors which enter into the formation of religious attitudes. Thus it began to seem possible to give a naturalistic account of religion in terms of biological, social and psychological factors without any appeal to God or revelation or any 'supernatural' factor at all.

In surveying positivist and naturalist views current at the beginning of the century, we shall begin with examples of scientific positivism (Section 26) followed by an example of a naturalistic metaphysic (Section 27). Then we shall consider the influence upon the interpretation of religion first of anthropology (Section 28), then of psychology (Section 29). We shall end with a critical review (Section 30).

26. SCIENTIFIC POSITIVISM
E. Mach, K. Pearson

Ernst Mach[1] (1838–1916), a scientist turned philosopher, may be regarded as one of the pioneers of modern scientific positivism. On his view, the units of experience are sensations—colours, sounds, pressures and so on. Our understanding is confined to the realm of sense-experience, and so we see that Mach's starting-point is close to the neo-Kantian positivism which we have already encountered. What we call 'bodies' and what we call 'minds' are in each case simply relatively stable complexes of sensations. A 'person' is said to be 'merely an indifferent symbolical thread' on which are strung 'the real pearls of life'—namely, the

---

[1] Professor at Graz, 1864–7; Prague, 1867–95; Vienna, 1895–1901.

everchanging contents of consciousness.[1] Thus there is at bottom no difference between the physical and the psychical, for both are constituted by sensations.

Science has been developed for practical purposes. By means of its concepts and hypotheses, we are enabled to predict and to cope with experience. Science does not explain *why* anything happens—such explanation was the mistaken endeavour of metaphysics, which tried to go behind sensations to 'things in themselves', whether bodies or minds. Science describes only *how* events happen, that is to say, it describes the regular connections between sensations.

Mach tried to purge the language of science from any terms which might be suspected of having a metaphysical or animistic flavour. He says, for instance: 'I hope the science of the future will discard the idea of cause and effect, as being formally obscure; and in my feeling that these ideas contain a strong tincture of fetishism, I am certainly not alone. The more proper course is to regard the abstract determinative elements of a fact as interdependent in a purely logical way, as the mathematician does.'[2] Similarly, the idea of force in nature suggests a comparison with our experience of willing; but Mach thinks it would be more proper to reverse the procedure, and describe the will itself by comparison with the acceleration of masses. We may contrast these views with those of such personalists as Bowne.[3]

Science, as we have seen, has a practical motive. On the basis of past experience, its laws restrict the possibilities which we may expect in future experience. It aims at economy, that is to say, at bringing wide areas of experience under as few concepts and hypotheses as possible, and as it succeeds in its task, we can better adapt ourselves to the environment and manage our experience. Thus science becomes 'the natural foe of the wonderful. The sources of the marvellous are unveiled, and surprise gives way to calm interpretation.'[4] The question of 'why' is solved by ceasing to ask this question and by confining ourselves to the facts of phenomenal experience. If we ask whether we can rest content with this 'phenomenalism', as Mach's view is sometimes called, he replies: 'The endeavour to confine oneself to *facts* is often censured as an exaggerated fear of metaphysical spooks. But I would observe that, judged by the mischief which they have wrought, the metaphysical are, of all spooks, the least fabulous.'[5]

Similar views were taught in England by Karl Pearson[6] (1857–1936),

[1] *Popular Scientific Lectures*, pp. 234–5.
[2] *Op. cit.*, p. 253.   [3] See above, p. 66.   [4] *Op. cit.*, p. 224.
[5] *Op. cit.*, p. 222.   [6] Professor at London, 1879–1933.

and from his writings we get a clearer understanding of the bearing of phenomenalism on the questions of religion and theology. Most of Mach's leading ideas are repeated—science is a practical affair, an instrument in the struggle for existence; bodies and minds are simply complexes of sensations; scientific language is to be purged of such metaphysical notions as 'causality', 'force', 'matter' and the like; science does not explain why, it merely describes how. So far this is merely a clearing up of science, and even a limitation to its possible claims.

On the other hand, Pearson goes beyond Mach in his aggressive insistence on the omnicompetence of science. Though scientific knowledge is not 'ultimate', it is the only kind of knowledge accessible to us and nothing lies beyond its scope. 'The whole range of phenomena, mental as well as physical—the entire universe—is its field. The scientific method is the sole gateway to the whole region of knowledge.'[1] Pearson disliked the term 'positivism', because it seems to suggest that there is a limit to what science may discover. Just as in the past science has opened up fields that have outrun all expectations, so in the future it may take us beyond anything of which we may dream at present.

The claim which Pearson makes, it should be noted, is twofold. There is the affirmation of the right of science to investigate all fields of knowledge, as against the attempts of theologians and metaphysicians to restrict science to those areas which they consider appropriate to the exercise of the scientific method. There is also the denial that there can be any knowledge outside of science, which means that theology and metaphysics have no contribution to make.

Such fields as religion and ethics must therefore be wrested by the scientist from the theologian and the philosopher, and investigated in a rational way. Religion is defined as 'the relation of the finite to the infinite'. For conventional religion, which fills up our ignorance of this relation with a myth, there must be substituted a scientific religion. 'The pursuit of knowledge is the true worship of man—the union between finite and infinite, the highest pleasure of which the human mind is capable.'[2] Ethics must be liberated from dependence on the sanctions and taboos of traditional religion, and put on a scientific basis as the rational pursuit of the welfare of human society. As Rudolf Metz has put it, 'Pearson's laudation of the scientific spirit is carried to the point of apotheosis.'[3]

[1] *The Grammar of Science*, p. 24.
[2] *The Ethic of Freethought*, p. 23.
[3] *A Hundred Years of British Philosophy*, p. 116.

27. EVOLUTIONARY NATURALISM
E. Haeckel

While the views which we have just considered make large claims for science, they condemn metaphysics and insist that science does not provide ultimate explanations. In striking contrast is the naturalistic metaphysic of Ernst Haeckel[1] (1834–1919)—'a rounded philosophical system', as he called it, in which he boldly expresses his conviction that the discoveries of nineteenth-century science bring the solution of the enigmas which have perplexed mankind through the centuries. Like Mach and Pearson, Haeckel was a scientist turned philosopher. His best-known book, *The Riddle of the Universe*, published just at the turn of the century, seemed to catch the popular imagination as an expression of the scientific outlook of the time, and—like the very different book of R. W. Trine mentioned in an earlier chapter[2]—had in the succeeding years an astonishing sale of hundreds of thousands of copies in all the leading countries of the world.

The outlines of Haeckel's philosophy are simple enough. Reality is identified with nature or the universe, which is conceived as infinite in both space and time. This universe is determined throughout by 'the great eternal iron laws'. Of these laws, two are fundamental. One is the law of substance, which affirms the constancy of matter and force in the universe. The other is the law of evolution, which affirms that all phenomena, including life and consciousness, are stages in the evolution of the one substance of the universe. While evolution goes on in some parts of the universe, devolution and disintegration are taking place in other parts, so that the overall picture is presumably much the same at any given time.

Haeckel calls his system 'monism', in opposition to all dualisms which would differentiate God and nature, soul and body, or spirit and matter. In his view, there is a single substance which manifests itself both as matter and energy or body and spirit. Every material atom has a rudimentary soul which is far below the level of consciousness. In the course of evolution, the rudimentary psychical character of substance gradually advances to consciousness, which is therefore a purely natural phenomenon. Monism implies that there is no matter without spirit or energy, and no spirit without matter. Haeckel rejects materialism equally with spiritualism, but since for him 'spirit' means much the same as 'energy', his monism is closer to materialism than it is to the panpsychism which

---

[1] Professor at Jena from 1864.
[2] See above, p. 42.

we met in Varisco and Ward[1] and to which Haeckel's view has an apparent resemblance.

This monism, said to be founded on the demonstrable results of science, solves the riddles of existence. In particular, it gives negative answers to the traditional problems of God, freedom and immortality. These three ideas are all based on a mistaken dualism. There can be no God apart from the universe. An invisible God who thinks, speaks and acts, would be, in Haeckel's famous phrase, a 'gaseous vertebrate'[2]—an impossible conception. A monistic and deterministic cosmos has likewise no room for the immortality of the soul or the freedom of the will.

Haeckel, however, proposes to compensate us for the loss of these beliefs with a new religion of monism. This is to be a pantheism in which God is identified with nature. It turns out to be a religion of science, accompanied by a scientific ethic, rather as we found in Pearson though differing in details. The first international monistic congress did in fact meet in 1912. But this first congress was also the last. The faithful assemble themselves no longer—if indeed any faithful remain.

28. ANTHROPOLOGY AND RELIGION
E. B. Tylor, J. G. Frazer, S. Reinach

The naturalistic interpretation of religion gained support from the developing science of anthropology which made possible the comparative study of human institutions and in particular showed the link between some of the beliefs and practices of advanced societies with those of primitive groups. If, for instance, modern religious beliefs can be shown to be descended naturally from primitive superstitions, it would no longer seem necessary to postulate any special supernatural 'revelation'; indeed, it might seem as if such beliefs had been discredited. Here, however, we must guard against any facile conclusions which would involve us in a genetic fallacy, and we remember that thinkers like Edward Caird fully accepted the evidence of anthropology on the evolution of religion without coming to naturalistic conclusions.[3]

Although most of his work had already been done in the nineteenth century, we may begin with the ideas of Edward Burnett Tylor[4] (1832–1917), who at the beginning of the present century had recently become Oxford's first professor of anthropology. Paul Radin credits Tylor

---

[1] See above, pp. 61, 65.   [2] *The Riddle of the Universe*, pp. 10, 235.
[3] See above, pp. 26ff.
[4] Reader, 1884–96, then professor, 1896–1909, at Oxford.

with having 'created the new science practically from its foundations'.[1]

Tylor makes two initial assumptions. One is that human culture—including knowledge, art, religion, custom and the like—has its laws which may be scientifically studied; in culture as in nature, we find 'the uniform action of uniform causes'.[2] The other assumption is that the various grades of culture found in the human race can be exhibited as stages in a process of development or evolution. Tylor draws attention to the phenomenon of 'survival'. An idea or a custom, once it has got established, tends to persist, and it may continue on into later stages of culture where it has become meaningless.

Tylor's principal contribution was his famous theory of 'animism'—the belief in spiritual beings. Confronted with such phenomena as death, sleep, dreams and so on, primitive man accounted for them in terms of a spirit separable from the body. From this he went on to believe in other spirits throughout all nature, some of these spirits having the rank of powerful deities. Since such spirits were supposed to control events and to affect human lives, it was natural that men should reverence them and seek to propitiate them. Thus we have the beginnings of religion, with the belief in spiritual beings as its minimal condition.

The higher religions—and our modern philosophies as well—have, in Tylor's view, developed out of the matrix of primitive animism. The superiority of the higher religions lies in their moral ideas, which are almost entirely lacking in primitive religion. These moral ideas have turned out to be the abiding fruit of animism. But alongside them, even in the higher religions, there are survivals that have outlived their usefulness, so that these religions stand in need of reformation. Indeed, Tylor says that 'the science of culture is essentially a reformer's science'.[3] He urges the theologian to consider along with the anthropologist each item of worship and belief. To which of the three following categories does it belong? 'Is it a product of the earlier theology, yet sound enough to retain a rightful place in the later? Is it derived from a cruder original, yet so modified as to become a proper representative of more advanced views? Is it a survival from a lower stage of thought, imposing on the credit of the higher by virtue not of inherent truth but of ancestral belief?'[4] Surely this is a modest enough claim that Tylor makes for the anthropologist.

Another British anthropologist with a special interest in religion was James George Frazer[5] (1854–1941). His best-known work, *The Golden*

---

[1] In his introduction to the 1958 edition of *Primitive Culture*.
[2] *Primitive Culture*, p. 1   [3] *Op. cit.*, vol. II, p. 539.
[4] *Op. cit.*, vol. II, p. 538.   [5] Professor at Liverpool, 1907–22.

Bough, written over a period of twenty-five years, was only a part of his vast output. It is nowadays perhaps chiefly prized as a mine of information about the myths and folklore of peoples all over the world, and the interrelations among them; and it is esteemed also for the writer's great literary skill. It was however intended to present a definite thesis on the way by which man has progressed from savagery to civilization, and to indicate the place of religion in this progression.

This thesis is to the effect that we can distinguish three stages in the mental development of mankind—magic, religion and science.[1] Of course, Frazer did not mean that each of these three follow one another in a clear-cut succession. A lower stage may persist alongside a higher stage, or there may be a lapse from a higher stage back to a lower stage. But on the whole, the movement is from magic through religion to science.

At the magical level, man depends on his own strength to overcome the difficulties that beset him and to gain his ends. He believes in a certain order of nature which he can learn to manipulate for his purposes by occult means. Experience teaches him that he is mistaken, and the keener minds now turn to religion. This is distinguished from magic by the fact that in religion man no longer relies on himself but seeks the aid of invisible beings who, he believes, possess that power to control natural events which magic failed to gain. Religion is defined as 'a propitiation or conciliation of powers superior to man which are believed to direct and control the course of nature and of human life',[2] and, like Tylor, Frazer thought that religion had probably originated in beliefs concerning the spirits of the dead. The religious attitude supposes that there is some elasticity or even caprice in the course of nature, but again experience teaches man his mistake. The 'rigid uniformity' of nature is discovered, and 'religion, regarded as an explanation of nature, is displaced by science'.[3] In science, man reverts to the self-reliance which characterized magic, but he now applies the rational methods of exact observation in place of the vain imaginings which belonged to the primitive stages of his development. Frazer speculates that in course of time yet another way of looking at the phenomena may come to supplant science, but so far, after groping in the dark for ages, man has found his first real clue in science, and Frazer expresses the belief that man's future progress, moral as well as material, is bound up with the fortunes of science.

The French scholar, Salomon Reinach[4] (1858–1932), was both an

---

[1] These three stages may be compared with the three which Auguste Comte suggested —see above, pp. 95–6.

[2] *The Golden Bough,* p. 50.   [3] *Op. cit.,* p. 712.

[4] In charge of national museums from 1886, after archaeological work in Greece.

archaeologist and an anthropologist, and his researches in these subjects were largely devoted to the investigation of religion. He believed that the time was ripe for a science of religion. In religion, as everywhere else, secular reason must exercise its right to investigate, and Reinach's aim was to consider religion 'as a natural phenomenon, and nothing more'.[1]

Religion is defined as 'a sum of scruples which impede the free exercise of our faculties'—a definition which, we are told, 'eliminates from the fundamental concept of religion God, spiritual beings, the infinite, in a word, all we are accustomed to consider the true objects of religious sentiment'.[2] These scruples have arisen from the irrational taboos of primitive societies, where they were associated with an animistic view of the world. The higher religions, including Christianity, have a natural origin in these primitive ideas, and not in any alleged revelation. Through the ages, a process of selection has gone on. Those scruples which have proved useful have persisted, and have tended to be transformed into rational rules of conduct; while those which have shown no such usefulness have sunk into the background. Thus human progress has taken place through the gradual secularizing of elements which were originally all enveloped in the sphere of animistic beliefs. This process has taken place not only in the transformation of taboos into moral rules but also in the development of science out of magic. Religion was the very life of nascent societies, and out of it has come our civilizations, though only through a process which has more and more limited religion and secularized the areas which once belonged to it.

Reinach visualizes further progress as lying in the direction of education and the extension of the rational outlook. But he concedes an indefinite future to religion, for the tasks of science will never be finished. Though he regards Christianity as a purely human institution and spends much time in criticizing the superstitions, follies and fanaticisms which have entered into its history, he regards it as the greatest of the religions. It is said 'to suit the temper of progressive and laborious nations, to teach the world the only moral lessons accessible to everyone, and to cleanse and soften the animal instincts of the human race'.[3] The time may be ripe for a science of religion, but apparently it is not yet ripe for the supersession of religion, for Reinach believes that the beneficent influence of Christianity is a thing not only of the past but of the future.

[1] *Orpheus*, Preface, p. vii.   [2] *Op. cit.*, p. 3.
[3] *A Short History of Christianity*, Preface, p. 5.

29. PSYCHOLOGY AND RELIGION
J. H. Leuba, S. Freud, C. G. Jung

The naturalistic interpretation of religion received a further stimulus from the development of the psychology of religion. The methods of psychology afforded the means for a scientific investigation of religious experience in terms of the factors immanent in such experience itself. The earlier investigators concentrated on particular aspects of religious experience, such as conversion, and employed such methods as the questionnaire and the comparative study of the journals and auto-biographies of religiously minded persons. Later, the newer techniques of psychoanalysis were applied. It became evident that much or even all of religion can be described in terms of the purely natural needs and yearnings of the human soul and the attempt to satisfy them. It would still be a question, of course, whether this positive account of religion would be the whole truth of the matter.

From the pioneers in this field of study, we select as an example James Henry Leuba[1] (1867–1946). His writings did not indeed achieve the same fame as *The Varieties of Religious Experience* of William James, but they are more strictly psychological, and it is Leuba who better represents the naturalistic point of view. Consideration of James will be deferred until we turn to pragmatism.

Leuba's thesis is summed up in this sentence: 'The reason for the existence of religion is not the objective truth of its conceptions, but its biological value.'[2] Let us consider, for instance, the belief in a personal God. Leuba notes that at an earlier time theologians had put forward metaphysical arguments for the existence of such a God, such as the argument from design. The advance of the physical sciences has destroyed the force of such arguments. Now theologians have shifted their ground—Leuba is thinking especially of the Ritschlians—and, rejecting metaphysics, appeal to inner experience. But in this case they have to contend with psychology, which carries the scientific method into the inmost experiences of the soul. So far are these inner experiences from establishing the existence of a personal God that they rather show how belief in such a God has arisen from the gratification it provides for affective and moral needs. 'It is precisely because no other form of available belief satisfies

---

[1] Born in Switzerland, he completed his education in the United States, and became professor in Bryn Mawr College.

[2] *A Psychological Study of Religion*, p. 53.

so easily and so completely certain urgent needs of the human heart that the idea of God the Father remains among us.'[1]

Leuba paid special attention to mystical experience, often supposed to be the citadel of religious experience and to provide those who practise it with an immediate and indubitable experience of God. In his detailed examination of mystical experience, Leuba seeks to account for it in psychological and physiological terms, as by assigning it to the sublimation of the sexual passion in the ascetic life, by comparing it with the states of consciousness induced by certain drugs, by showing its affinity with such pathological conditions as hysteria and epilepsy, and in other ways. He concludes that 'for the psychologist who remains within the province of science, religious mysticism is a revelation not of God but of man'.[2] None of its phenomena, whether voices or visions, illumination or sense of communion, can seriously demand that we look to some transcendent cause.

What is true of mysticism holds of religion in general—it is brought, so Leuba claims, wholly within the domain of the natural. One can therefore no longer assent with intellectual honesty to such a religion as Christianity with its transcendent beliefs. Yet man is so constituted that his religious needs are real and demand satisfaction. This must come about in a natural religion which takes account of scientific knowledge. Leuba recommends as a 'religion of the future' a blending of Comte's religion of humanity with Bergson's philosophy of creative evolution: 'Humanity idealized and conceived as a manifestation of creative energy possesses surpassing qualifications for a source of religious inspiration.'[3]

In the words of his biographer, Sigmund Freud[4] (1856–1939) 'went through his life from beginning to end as a natural atheist'.[5] This is worth remembering in assessing Freud's view of religion. He had dismissed religion as an illusion before he began his great researches into the human mind. His results were used to confirm a view which he already held and were not, as is sometimes supposed, the starting-point from which he reached his view of religion. Indeed, however revolutionary his discoveries in psychology may have been, Freud's understanding of religion remained essentially that of the deterministic naturalism of the nineteenth century.

Freud's name is inseparably connected with the discovery of the

---

[1] *Op. cit.*, pp. 265–6.   [2] *The Psychology of Religious Mysticism*, p. 318.

[3] *A Psychological Study of Religion*, p. 335.

[4] Practised psychiatry in Vienna most of his life, until forced to flee to England at the time of the Nazi annexation of Austria.

[5] Ernest Jones, *Sigmund Freud*, vol. III, p. 376.

unconscious mind. Strictly speaking, this was not a discovery, since the unconscious had often been hinted at before, or even used as a philosophical concept, as by Eduard von Hartmann. But just as Darwin transformed the idea of evolution from a philosophical speculation into a scientific hypothesis, so Freud opened up the unconscious and made it accessible to scientific investigation. Many of his major discoveries had been made before 1900, but in the exposition which follows we shall employ some of the terminology which he adopted only at a later stage of his thinking.

Freud divides the mind into three provinces. The vastest of these is the *id*—the unconscious region in which the basic instincts[1] of our nature jostle together with no sense of order or value. The *ego* is the much narrower region of consciousness. It maintains contact with the external world and aims at self-preservation, selecting some of the *id's* demands for satisfaction and rejecting others, according to circumstances. The third factor, the *superego*, which is the deposit of the parental influences of childhood, exercises a further control by banning those activities which are socially undesirable.

Knowledge of the unconscious is obtained through the analysis of its disguised manifestations in dreams, and through the various techniques of psychoanalysis. The unconscious contains not only the primal instincts or drives of human nature, but also *repressed experiences*—that is to say, experiences which were once present to consciousness but which, because of their unpleasant nature, have been pushed back into the unconscious— forgotten, as we say. However, these repressions still live on in the unconscious, and they may manifest themselves in strange ways. These manifestations of the repressed material are *neuroses*, and we shall see that Freud's conviction is that religion is to be understood on the model of such a neurosis.

To understand this, we must first turn to Freud's theory that before the emergence of adult sexuality there is a first sexual efflorescence in early childhood. The boy's first sexual feelings are directed towards the mother, and these feelings are accompanied by jealousy towards the father. Yet his feelings for the father are ambivalent, and may pass over into admiration. He wants to be like the father and to take his place. This is the Oedipus complex, called after the Greek tragic hero who murdered his father and married his mother.

[1] On the question of instincts (*Triebe*), Freud stated his latest position thus: 'After long doubts and vacillations we have decided to assume the existence of only two basic instincts: *Eros* (the love-instinct) and *Thanatos* (the destructive instinct). The aim of the first is to establish ever greater unities—in short, to bind together; the aim of the second, on the contrary, is to undo connections and so to destroy things.' See *An Outline of Psychoanalysis*, pp. 5–6.

In his book, *Totem and Taboo*, Freud applies these ideas to the origin of religion. In primitive times, he supposes, human beings lived in small groups, each under the domination of a father who possessed all the females. The sons were driven out or killed as they excited the father's jealousy. But they banded themselves together, slew the father, and partook of his flesh so as to share in his power. The sons would quarrel among themselves for the father's place, but experience of the futility of such struggles led to a new social organization and to the first taboos, forbidding incest. Meantime the memory of the father who had been both feared and admired was preserved in a strange way. Periodically a strong animal, suggestive of the father, was slain and eaten by the group. Here we have the origin of the totem.

These ideas, Freud believed, can be traced in the various religious mythologies, though myths, like dreams, disguise the underlying content. In one of his latest books, *Moses and Monotheism*, he tried to trace the same pattern in biblical religion. Moses, he supposed, first taught the Hebrews monotheism, which he had learned from the heretical Aton cult in Egypt. Following the speculations of some Old Testament scholars, Freud further supposed that Moses had been murdered by the Hebrews during their desert wanderings. Memory of the crime was repressed, and monotheism was given up. But after an interval, the repressed material returned as a kind of national neurosis, with the teaching of the Hebrew prophets, and the re-establishment, as Freud supposed, of the monotheism first taught by Moses. The murdered father of the people had triumphed in the long run. The story is pursued into Christianity. In the mind of St Paul, the death of Jesus stirred the latent sense of guilt, and this death was conceived as the atonement made by the Son for the ancient crime against the Father.

Thus the idea of God turns out to be at bottom a magnified version of the image of the human father. The transformation of the father into God takes place both in the history of the race, in the manner summarized above, and in the history of individuals who, in adult life, project upon the world the infantile memory of the father, and raise this image to the rank of a Father God. The father who gave them life, protected them, and demanded their obedience, becomes the God who is similarly creator, preserver, and lawgiver. As Freud himself acknowledged, this theory is more easily applicable to some forms of religion than to others. The main point that he wishes to make, however, is that a religious belief is determined by the psychological history of the person who holds it, and that such a belief is essentially infantile and neurotic. It is a projection of the nursery upon the world, and is thus a flight from reality. For Freud, as we have already noted, the real world is the rigidly determined atheistic cosmos of nineteenth-century naturalism. No Father God reigns over it, but—as he expresses it—'dark, unfeeling and unloving powers determine human destiny'.[1]

Next to Freud, the best-known among the psychoanalysts is Carl Gustav Jung[2] (1875–1961). Around 1912, he broke away from the Freudian circle, developed his thought along independent lines, and even gave up the term 'psychoanalysis' in preference for 'analytical psychology'. Nowhere is the difference between Freud and Jung more clear-cut than in their respective attitudes to religion. The difference at this point is twofold. In the first place, Jung does not share Freud's dogmatic atheism. 'It was', he says, 'a great mistake on Freud's part to turn his back on philosophy', for this has resulted in Freud's accepting 'a view of the world that is uncriticized or even unconscious'.[3] Jung's own view appears to be a Kantian agnosticism which leaves the ultimate nature of reality an open question. He is however quite clear that what we call 'spirit', though we do not know what this is 'in itself', cannot be derived from instincts or explained in terms of anything other than itself. In the second place, whereas Freud thought of religion as essentially neurotic, a failure on the part of the religious person to resolve his problems, Jung says that he attributes a positive value to all religions. His attitude is made clear in the following statement: 'Among all my patients in the second half of life—that is to say, over thirty-five—there has not been one whose problem in the last resort was not that of finding a religious outlook on life. It is safe to say that every one of them fell ill because he had lost that which the living religions of every age have given to their followers, and none of them has been really healed who did not regain his religious outlook.'[4] For Freud, religion is pathological, but for Jung, it is or ought to be health-giving.

It should at once be noted, of course, that Jung's view of religion, equally with Freud's, is a naturalistic one—at least, in one sense of the

---

[1] *New Introductory Lectures on Psychoanalysis*, p. 214. The words quoted here presumably do no more than assert the common thesis of nineteenth-century naturalism that the universe is indifferent to human aspirations and hopes; but Freud has chosen language which might suggest to the careless reader some sinister and even demonic power in the world. In this connection, we may notice that some logical analysts criticize psychoanalysis for the imprecision of its language and for drawing much of its terminology from mythology and metaphysics. This is said to obscure its genuine empirical content, and its relation to other scientific researches. See, for instance, A. J. Ayer, *Language, Truth and Logic*, p. 152. On the other hand, it could be argued that the subject-matter of psychoanalysis demands some such special kind of language.

[2] Psychiatrist in Zürich.

[3] *Modern Man in Search of a Soul*, p. 135.

[4] *Op. cit.*, p. 264.

word 'naturalistic'. Jung does not subscribe to a naturalism of the re-
ductionist type, and, as we have already seen, he explicitly denies that
spirit, whatever it may be, can be explained in terms of anything other
than itself. But on the other hand, he also repudiates any alliance of his
views with a theistic metaphysic. In accordance with his Kantian rejection
of metaphysics, Jung thinks that the problem of God's existence as a
superempirical reality is unanswerable, and it is certainly not one for
psychology. God can be *known* as a psychological reality, but the *belief*
that he has some other or 'higher' reality cannot be established. It is
probably in the light of this remark that we should interpret a statement
of Jung in a television interview a few months before his death; asked if
he believed in God, he replied that he did not *believe*, he *knew*. Jung's
appreciation of religion is based upon the consideration of it as a natural
factor in the life of the psyche. The 'truths' of religion are not objective
metaphysical truths, but truths of life.

What leads Jung to place a positive valuation upon religion? Like
Freud, Jung thinks of the conscious part of the mind as a relatively
narrow area which, on the one side, looks out on the external world, and
on the other side is backed by the vast region of the unconscious. Psychical
energy, or the *libido*, is given a wider interpretation by Jung than by
Freud—it includes not only sexuality but the entire will to live. There
are various polarities or oppositions in life, and different types tend
towards one or the other pole. There is the polarity of extraversion—
concern with the external world—and introversion—preoccupation with
one's own inner life; or again, the polarity of thought and feeling. Transcending all these is the polarity of conscious and unconscious. What one
fails to be in conscious life is potentially there in the unconscious. The goal
of life is individuation, the realization of one's own complete and unique
selfhood, and this is to be accomplished by bringing forth the latent
potentialities of the unconscious.

This unconscious, according to Jung, has various strata. The topmost
layer is the *personal unconscious*, formed in our individual lives. Below this
is the deeper region of the *collective unconscious*, the deposit of the collective
experience of the race, inherited by each individual. Jung was led to
believe in this collective unconscious because of the similarities which he
found between the imaginings of his patients and the symbols of ancient
myths. Within the collective unconscious he finds *archetypes* or primordial
images, the deposits of ages of experience. Myth is the language of these
archetypes, which express the truths of life. Their function is to predispose
us to meet the situations of life. Thus in men, where the consciousness is
male, the feminine element of the psyche forms an unconscious archetype

which prepares for the experience of women and affords the capacity for loving relationships. Among these primordial images Jung finds the archetype, God. Thus religion, so far from being an aberration, is an archetypal predisposition in man, and we can now understand why Jung thinks that religion must have its place in the well-rounded personality. God is within us as a psychological reality, the denial of which distorts our life.

What kind of religion does Jung recommend to us? We have seen that it is a natural religion. The transcendent objects of traditional religion are psychic contents which have been projected into metaphysical space. Christianity has lagged behind the mental development of mankind, and no longer meets men with understanding. Yet Jung thinks 'that we might still make use in some way of its form of thought, and especially of its great wisdom of life'[1] and that there are many people whose natural home is still within the Church. This residual value which Jung allows to Christianity has, of course, nothing to do with its professed revelation of God and the supersensible, but consists in whatever efficacy it still possesses as a therapy for the soul. Increasingly, as Jung sees it, men will turn from collective dogmatic forms of religion to private religions, in which each individual works out independently his own solution of the religious problem.

30. Criticism of Naturalistic Interpretations of Religion

At first glance, it might seem as if the positivists and naturalists whom we have considered in this chapter have a strong case in their interpretation of religion. The strength of their case rests on the claim that it is based on verifiable facts brought to light by scientific investigation. Yet when we examine this claim, we find that it is an extremely shaky one, and so the whole naturalistic case becomes equally shaky. One of the points which Pearson makes is that the scientific approach leads to unanimous findings, whereas theologians and philosophers are notorious for their disagreements. We have not, however, found unanimity among the thinkers whom we have considered. Are we, for instance, to follow Mach or Haeckel? Is Freud right, or Jung? The truth is that the facts must be interpreted, and that the thinkers whom we have considered— all of them were scientists of one kind or another by training—have, in so far as they move from the findings of their particular sciences into the sphere of philosophical interpretation, introduced presuppositions,

[1] *Psychology of the Unconscious*, p. 45.

speculations and even prejudices which need to be brought into the open and examined.

This remark does not apply with equal force to all of the thinkers under review. Some are commendably cautious in what they say. Tylor makes moderate claims for anthropology, Jung does not pronounce on the ultimate questions, Mach was interested in scientific method and explicitly says that science must not turn into a 'church', as he expressed it. But others are much less cautious. Science does turn into a 'church' with Pearson and Haeckel. There is more than a touch of fanaticism—Pearson prefers to call it 'enthusiasm'—both in their polemics against Christianity and in their apotheosis of science. To us who look back over sixty years of troubled world-history, however, there is also something pathetic in the faith of some of these men in scientific enlightenment, and their expectation that with the increasing diffusion of such enlightenment, the twentieth century would be an era of unprecedented contentment. Haeckel even believed that before long the monists would begin to take over the churches, as the Protestants had done at the Reformation, and that their wholesome teachings would transform the world. Sir James G. Frazer, though he also placed his trust in science, was more cautious, and events have justified his caution. Science has turned out to have potentials for evil as well as good, and education alone has not proved to be the answer to moral problems.

The major criticism of naturalism, however, is that it involves us in a gigantic one-sided abstraction. It takes a segment of experience—the segment which is amenable to measurement and quantitative analysis—and represents it as the entire reality. There are of course varieties of naturalism, as we noted, and the charge of one-sidedness is more applicable to the cruder mechanistic varieties than it would be to the naturalism of Jung, for instance, who finds room for spirit in nature, and might escape the charge of abstraction. On the other hand, a positivist like Pearson would not escape the charge, for when he says that there is no way of knowing anything apart from the scientific way, he is not confining himself to the scientific point of view and has in fact, in Bradley's phrase, become a 'brother metaphysician'. The abstraction and one-sidedness of naturalism was adequately exposed by such critics as Boutroux and Ward.[1] Here it may be added that the same kind of abstraction is to be seen in what the naturalists have to say in criticizing traditional religion. Just as they isolate the cognitive aspect of our experience of the world, so they concentrate on the element of belief in religion. They seem to think of religious beliefs as offering an explanation of the world, perhaps a rival

[1] See above, pp. 62, 64.

explanation to the explanations of science, whereas these beliefs can be understood only in the setting of the whole religious life, which involves conative and affective elements as well. Haeckel's amusing picture of God as the 'gaseous vertebrate' illustrates more than anything his own misunderstanding of the idea of God. On the other hand, the more naïve conceptions of theologians and the more childish beliefs of religious people offer sitting targets to the naturalists. Nevertheless, we must conclude that the abstract schema presented by the naturalists as the whole reality ignores some facts and exaggerates others, so giving a distorted picture.

When we turn to the special question of the light thrown by anthropology on the nature of religion, it should perhaps first be said that nowadays no sensible person would doubt that the higher religions of today are the lineal descendants of primitive faiths, and still retain many features which have come down, perhaps in disguised form, from savage times. The great American archaeologist, J. H. Breasted, concluded his study of the development of ancient Egyptian religion by comparing the processes of religious evolution to the slow geological processes in the earth's crust. And he remarks: 'Religion is still in the making, the processes which brought forth inherited religion have never ceased, they will continue as long as the great and complex fabric of man's life endures.'[1] Anthropology and archaeology, then, teach us that present-day religions have arisen from humble origins, and that the process of transformation and development may be expected to continue in the future. The facts are not in doubt. But how do we interpret them?

The first point on which we must be clear is that the origin of any particular belief or practice does not determine the question of its validity in its present form. After all, any human activity goes back to humble beginnings—presumably to animal beginnings in the last resort. We do not think any the worse of astronomy because it has grown out of astrology. But this point is not always remembered in the case of religion. Reinach delights to show the connection of Christian institutions with primitive superstitions, and gives the impression that he thinks he is thereby discrediting them. We must, however, judge things by what they are today, not by what they have grown out of. This is clearly recognized by Tylor, who sees that something derived from a cruder original may have acquired quite a new status and meaning.

Does not the picture of gradual evolution presented by anthropology strike at the theological idea of revelation? It does indeed strike at the idea of any one exclusive revelation, and if there are Christians who think that their own religion possesses the exclusive truth about God, they must

[1] *Development of Religion and Thought in Ancient Egypt*, p. 370.

find anthropology a very disquieting subject. But there is no reason why Christians should think in this way, and many reasons why they should not. For Christians who think of the revelation given in their own religion as continuous with a general revelation of God to mankind, there is nothing at all disturbing in the facts brought to light by anthropology. The point at issue with the naturalist is really whether in the process of development we are to understand the higher in terms of the lower, or the lower in the light of the higher—whether belief in God is merely the survival of primitive superstition, or whether these primitive beliefs are to be understood as the first glimmerings of an idea which has increased in depth and luminosity. This is a question which anthropology itself is quite incompetent to settle. But we may say that it would seem rather odd if someone told us that an acorn gives us a far better idea of an oak-tree than the grown tree itself.

Similar remarks apply to the psychology of religion. It is a most valuable study, but it does not and indeed cannot be determinative for the validity of religion. Just as religious beliefs have had their history in the race, so they have their history in the individual. No doubt we tend to believe what we want to believe. Yet the psychological criticism of belief can be carried only so far, or it ends up in a scepticism which engulfs the psychologist himself, and makes rational argument impossible. When the history of a belief has been demonstrated, we still have to ask the question of its truth or falsity.

Freud in particular seems to think that by tracing the history of the idea of God in the projecting of the father image, he discredits belief in God. As already noted, his theory is not applicable to religion in general, but only to those religions which recognize some kind of 'Father God'. More than that, the application of his ideas to Judaism and Christianity is by way of an almost baseless speculation about the history of Moses. Yet even if these points were accepted, what emerges? Simply that men think of God in terms of the human father—a point which theologians have discussed for centuries under the problem of analogical language. The question as to whether this analogue stands for any reality, or, if it does so, worthily represents it, is one on which psychoanalysis sheds no light whatever. Leuba also gives the impression that he thinks that religious beliefs can be discredited on the grounds of their psychological history. But when the British psychologist, R. H. Thouless, charged him with this fallacy,[1] Leuba replied that his intention had been misunderstood. Jung is of course quite clear that the objective validity of religious beliefs is not a question for psychology.

[1] *An Introduction to the Psychology of Religion*, p. 261.

While the foregoing remarks on naturalism have been of a critical nature, we must not be blind to the merits of this approach, and certainly we should not wish to defend any crass 'supernaturalism'. The naturalistic attitude has delivered mankind from many follies and superstitions—if it had never been taken up, we might still think that the gods are angry when it thunders or that we should try exorcism when the baby falls ill. What is being criticized is the attempt to extend a crudely naturalistic view to all reality and to subsume the higher under the lower. Jung's type of naturalism avoids this, and we shall find that the new naturalisms which appear later in the twentieth century avoid the grosser errors of the old. Again, the valuable insights of anthropology which places each particular religion within the general course of religious development, and of psychology which relates religion to the other activities of the psyche, are taken up in the philosophies of history and culture to which we shall shortly turn. But meanwhile, we have completed what we somewhat arbitrarily designated the 'first phase' of twentieth-century religious thought, and the time has come to pause and take a preliminary look at the way which lies ahead.

VII

SOME COMMENTS BY THE WAY

31. FROM THE FIRST TO THE SECOND PHASE

W E have now completed our survey of the first phase of twentieth-century religious thought. This first phase, it will be remembered, was said to consist of those philosophical and theological interpretations of religion which had already been worked out in the nineteenth century and which have continued to make their influence felt in the present century. Perhaps the first impression which we get from passing in review the various schools and individuals is that of a *plenum* of opinion, one view shading almost imperceptibly into the next so that we seem to have an almost unbroken continuity stretching from the high metaphysical speculations of the absolute idealists to the various forms of positivism, naturalism and agnosticism with which we ended. This impression of continuity could have been heightened by the inclusion of more names and of still finer gradations and transitions of thought, but it has not seemed proper to mention names without giving at least a brief exposition of what these names stand for, and a sufficient number has been mentioned to give a fair representative impression of the views that were held, and to indicate the broad sweep of these views. It might seem that only a bold man would pick and choose among them. We have certainly found confirmation of the remark made by a thinker of those days and quoted above[1] that 'a survey of contemporary opinion would disclose in it a multitude of incoherent and often incompatible points of view which approximate and interlace and then diverge'.

Yet we have also found confirmation of those common features which, it was suggested,[2] were to be found in most of the points of view current in the early part of the century. Generally speaking, we have found optimism, whether it rested on the perfection of the Absolute and the kinship of the world with the human spirit, or on the confidence inspired by the power of science and the belief in the perfectibility of mankind through scientific enlightenment. Generally speaking too the philosophies

[1] See above, p. 19.   [2] See above, pp. 19–21.

of those days had a certain comprehensiveness—they aimed at 'the treatment of the general questions relating to the universe and human life',[1] and almost as a matter of course gave some account of the religious problem. Many philosophers, as we have seen, thought of themselves as defenders of religion. Even the naturalists, while rejecting Christianity, usually put in its place some 'natural' religion of their own—a fact not without significance, since it at least recognizes a religious disposition in man and makes some provision for it. On the other hand, the theologians were ready to listen to the philosophers—some of them indeed merely echoed the philosophy of the day. Even the Ritschlians, though they rejected metaphysics, had a respect for philosophers like Kant and Lotze, and though they relied on revelation, they acknowledged the practical reason and did not fly openly in the face of logic and common-sense.

The weakening or even the disappearance of the features mentioned marks the second phase of religious thought in our century. It is impossible to say just when this second phase begins—it grows up alongside and within the first phase, and its roots go back also to the previous century. No doubt the outbreak of the First World War was a major factor in bringing about a shift in Western thinking, but it accelerated rather than initiated the change. Looking back on his student days in the Oxford of 1912, Leonard Hodgson indicates that idealism was already on the way out: 'A fading Hegelianism was characteristic of the world of philosophy as I knew it in 1912 . . . we were coming to the end of a period in which that system had been on trial.'[2] Back in this same pre-war period, George Santayana not only predicted the end of idealism[3] but asserted something more serious—that the whole civilization of Christendom had entered a critical phase, and was on the way to being replaced by a new kind of civilization. 'Our whole life and mind is saturated with the slow upward filtration of a new spirit—that of an emancipated, atheistic, international democracy.'[4] The threat to established ways and confident systems had, of course, been heard uttered by a few isolated voices back in the nineteenth century. Nietzsche spoke of a transvaluation of values, Burckhardt predicted the crisis of the West, and another voice, forgotten in 1900 but soon to be heard again, was that of Kierkegaard.

Twenty years after Santayana wrote the words quoted above, the First World War had come and gone, and the changed intellectual climate had by now become much more apparent. Here is how E. S. Brightman saw it: 'Theistic belief may be represented by a declining curve which seems rapidly to be approaching a zero value. The contrast between pre-war and

---

[1] See above, p. 21.
[2] *For Faith and Freedom*, vol. I, p. 39.
[3] See above, p. 44.
[4] *Winds of Doctrine*, p. 1.

post-war philosophy is a startling commentary on this curve. Before the (First) World War, the chief philosophers in the English-speaking world were such men as Ward, Rashdall, Bosanquet, Bradley, Royce, Bowne and James, the great majority of whom were theists. If we name the chief philosophers of the English-speaking world today, we think of Russell, Santayana, Broad, Dewey, Perry, Hocking and Whitehead, only one or two of whom could possibly be regarded as theists, and most of whom are open opponents of theism.'[1] But Brightman immediately goes on to point out that the old-fashioned naturalisms, inclining as they did towards a mechanistic and materialistic view of the world, had also gone out of favour. The new conceptions of science had meant a rethinking of what nature is. So he writes: 'Traditional theism has been treated very roughly; but it has not been subjected to any worse treatment than has naturalism.'[2] The new naturalisms of Bergson, Alexander, Whitehead and others turned out to be very different from the older varieties.

Just as the stable and secure background of the nineteenth century was disrupted by the violent upheavals of the twentieth, so the forms of thought which had grown out of that background were questioned and were dismissed by many as inadequate. In the flux of new currents of thought, the old dividing lines—such as that between idealistic and naturalistic theories, which we made the basis for the classification of schools belonging to the first phase[3]—become blurred and indistinct, as new problems arise and new formulations are looked for. Men in the twentieth century have the experience of themselves as pilgrims and strangers on the earth in a way which they did not have among the solid systems and landmarks of the last century. We must now try to set down some of the more obvious characteristics of this second phase of our story.

32. SOME CHARACTERISTICS OF THE SECOND PHASE

In the second phase of twentieth-century religious thought, as has been already indicated,[4] we find a number of movements which belong distinctively to our own century and yet have already either passed their full flowering or been transformed into still newer movements. In saying that these movements belong distinctively to our own century, it is not meant that they suddenly appeared after 1900. Most of them have roots in the nineteenth century, but—unlike the movements of the first phase which were already full-blown before 1900—these movements of the second

---

[1] *The Problem of God*, p. 29. [2] *Op. cit.*, p. 30.
[3] See above, p. 22. [4] See above, p. 18.

phase exerted their greatest influence after the turn of the century. Again, in saying that they have passed their full flowering or been transformed, it is not meant that they have lost vitality, but simply that the original formulations have been superseded or are no longer widely current. But these movements have proved determinative for subsequent development. As a concrete example, there may be mentioned the new realism of Moore and Russell. This had its antecedents before 1900 in the thought of Brentano and Meinong. Yet it belongs distinctively to the twentieth century, as one of our most influential philosophical movements. The original formulation of the views of Moore and Russell, however, is no longer current and belongs to the history of philosophy. Yet the spirit of their movement continues to be influential as, for instance, in logical empiricism.

The movements which we are about to consider are therefore, for the most part, of a transitional nature. In them we see twentieth-century man attempting to re-orient his thought as he lives in the light of new circumstances and as he addresses himself to new problems. We shall reserve until the third phase the relatively stable currents which seem to have emerged out of the flux of the second phase.

The features which we notice as characterizing the second phase are very largely the opposites of those which we found in the first phase, and have arisen by way of reaction. Thus we shall find that optimism has given way, if not to downright pessimism, at least to a much more sober and realistic attitude. The world is no longer judged by ideals but by facts— and the facts have often been depressing enough in our century. We shall find this spirit in thinkers of the most diverse sorts—Spengler proclaiming the inevitable decline of our civilization, Inge deploring the direction in which our modern world is heading, Unamuno finding the essence of life in suffering, Russell counselling us to build on the basis of despair. Theologians tend to take a more pessimistic view of human nature, and stress man's finitude and sinfulness. Even the idea of God may be transformed in a less optimistic direction. We have already met with the notion of a finite God among some of the personal idealists, and this notion becomes commoner—God is a suffering God, or perhaps an evolving God —a young God, so to speak, who has not yet got round to running the world properly. This too reflects the movement of interest from substance to process.

Along with the withdrawal from optimism goes the limitation of philosophy. It renounces its more comprehensive aims, and in particular it renounces metaphysics. It may confine itself to some particular sector, as in philosophies of history and culture; or it may concern itself with its own method, as in phenomenology; or it may believe that its business is simply that of analysis and clarification. The movement is away from the comprehensive problems to problems of limited scope, from synthesis to analysis.

In some cases, the anti-metaphysical bias goes so far as to become anti-intellectualist—perhaps in reaction against the dominance of science. In vitalism and pragmatism, and in their most notable theological counterpart, Catholic modernism, theoretical questions are subordinated to practical considerations. The anti-intellectualist tendency comes out even more strongly in the revival of interest in Kierkegaard, and in the philosophies of personal being which are the precursors of contemporary existentialism. These have been particularly influential in theology.

Still another feature to be noted is the increasing divergence between philosophy and theology. Concerning themselves with limited problems, with analysis and questions of method, philosophers no longer feel themselves called upon to pronounce about God and religion. They may even studiously avoid such questions—though in such cases it may nonetheless be necessary for us to take note of what they say, because of its implications for the religious question. According to one's point of view, this secularization of philosophy may either be hailed as its final deliverance from the leading-strings of theology, or blamed as its failure to face up to the deepest problems of human life. On the other hand, theologians have equally tended to become introverted. They have been jealous to defend the autonomy of their subject, to steer away from philosophical interests, and to base their findings on revelation or faith or inner experience—as indeed the Ritschlians had to some extent tried to do.

The full effects of this divorce will be seen only when we come to the third phase—though here again it must be said that the phases overlap and merge into one another, and that no sharp dividing lines can be drawn. The third phase in particular will be found to consist in the main of a continuation and accentuation of some of the tendencies present in the second phase.

Within this second phase, the following themes will be discussed: philosophies of history and culture (Chapter VIII) and theological movements associated with them (Chapter IX); sociological interpretations of religion (Chapter X); vitalism, pragmatism and various types of theological modernism (Chapter XI); philosophies of personal being, and their influence in theology (Chapter XII); phenomenology, and allied approaches to religion (Chapter XIII); the new realism (Chapter XIV); and finally the problems of science and religion, as seen by some twentieth-century scientists and theologians (Chapter XV).

VIII

PHILOSOPHIES OF HISTORY
AND CULTURE

33. MAN AS THE THEME OF PHILOSOPHY

WE turn now to a group of philosophies which take as their theme man himself, as he is revealed in his history and in the cultures which he has developed. We have already met pointers to this approach, both in Windelband, for whom the problem of value was paramount and the history of philosophy was itself a way of philosophizing,[1] and in Ward, who stressed the concreteness of history as over against the abstractness of the natural sciences.[2] We find the philosophical interest in history and culture continuing to grow, and perhaps it reached its peak in the period after the First World War.

In the last chapter, it was said that, in general, philosophy no longer takes for its province the whole of existence, but restricts itself in various ways, one of which is to study a sector of reality, such as history or culture.[3] Yet perhaps most of the thinkers at whom we are about to look would not wish to think of their interest in history or culture as a restriction, because in one way or another they believed that these fields supply us with a clue to reality which we cannot find elsewhere. Even if they renounce the aim of constructing a metaphysical system, they believe that the study of man's historical and cultural achievements affords a deeper insight into reality than, let us say, the study of nature can give.

Thus history and culture get a certain privileged status in the scheme of things, and in particular the claims of the human sciences are set over against those of the natural sciences. One writer goes so far as to find the motivation of historical and cultural philosophy in the desire to escape from the dominance of the natural sciences in philosophy. Helmut Kuhn writes: 'At the turn from the nineteenth to the twentieth century, German philosophy sought to put a check on the hegemony of the natural sciences by working out a system of human sciences.'[4] It is held that man, in his

[1] See above, p. 77. [2] See above, p. 64. [3] See above, p. 119.
[4] 'Ernst Cassirer's Philosophy of Culture', in *The Philosophy of Ernst Cassirer*, p. 549.

history and culture, must be studied by different methods from those which are employed in the natural sciences. At the same time, we must notice that some of the philosophers of history come much nearer to a naturalistic view of their subject-matter than others.

Religion is studied by these philosophies within the context of its historical and cultural setting. The evidence of anthropology and psychology may be relevant here, but it does not lead to the same naturalistic results that we found in writers like Reinach and Leuba. For anthropology and psychology are held to be human, as distinct from purely natural, sciences. Religion itself is taken to be one of the manifestations of man's spiritual life, which is of a different order and differently accessible from the purely natural phenomena of the physical world.

Varying degrees of value are assigned to religion by the philosophers of history and culture. In the present chapter, we shall consider the question in a general way, reserving until the next chapter the specific problem of Christianity in relation to the philosophies of history and culture.

The remainder of the present chapter falls into four sections. First, we consider some German philosophers who took history or culture as their leading theme (Section 34). Next, we turn to Italy where, as in the English-speaking countries, there was a late revival of Hegelianism, but a Hegelianism in which the idea of history was paramount (Section 35). Then we look at some English-speaking philosophers whose views have affinities with both the German and Italian groups (Section 36). A summary of the main points which emerge will provide the transition to the consideration of the influence of these philosophies on the problems of Christian theology (Section 37).

34. Some German Philosophers of History and Culture
W. Dilthey, O. Spengler, E. Cassirer

Wilhelm Dilthey[1] (1833–1911) is probably the greatest of those philosophers who have specially concerned themselves with man as he is revealed in his history and culture. Many influences entered into his thought, but like most German thinkers of his time, he had a particular interest in Kant, and in 1902 was entrusted with editing the definitive edition of Kant's works. Dilthey's aim was to write a *Critique of Historical*

---

[1] Professor successively at Basel, 1866–68; Kiel, 1868–71; Breslau, 1871–82; Berlin, where he succeeded Lotze in 1882.

Reason, but the work which he accomplished was, for the most part, fragmentary and unsystematic.[1]

Basic to Dilthey's point of view is the distinction which he makes between the natural and the human sciences. In the natural sciences we are, so to speak, spectators who look on from the outside. We observe the phenomena and describe their regularities without entering into them or knowing them in their inner reality. In the human sciences, on the other hand, we know the subject-matter—man's experience itself—from the inside, for we all live through experience. Of course, human behaviour can be studied from the outside also, but in that case we miss what is distinctive in it. By living through it, we can grasp its reality in a way in which we could never grasp the reality of that which can be observed only from outside, such as a physical or chemical process in nature. A priority is therefore claimed for the human sciences. 'The human studies have an advantage over all knowledge of nature in that their object is not a pheno-menon given in sensation, a mere reflection in consciousness of something real, but immediate inner reality itself, and this moreover in the form of a connected system enjoyed from within.'[2]

Thus the advantage of the human studies lies in the peculiarity of their subject-matter and its unique accessibility to understanding—a term which Dilthey uses in a wide sense for an activity of the whole personality. These human studies must use methods appropriate to their subject-matter, and thus we find Dilthey criticizing the kind of psychology which is conducted like a natural science on the grounds that it can tell us nothing about the higher activities of the mind. He proposes a wider kind of psychology which will 'add to the study of the forms of mental life a description of the reality of its process and content'.[3]

Yet if the human sciences seem to have an advantage over the natural sciences in one respect, they seem to be at a disadvantage in another. Since they deal with that which is particular and individual, how are they to attain universality and objective validity for their findings? It is here that we are led to perceive the place of history at the centre of the human sciences. In spite of the differences among types and individuals, the human spirit has a common structure and expresses itself in 'objective mind'. By this is meant 'the manifold forms in which the common back-ground subsisting among various individuals has objectified itself in the sensible world'.[4] This objective mind embraces instruments, towns,

---

[1] A short selection from his writings is available in English translation in the volume, *Wilhelm Dilthey—An Introduction,* by H. A. Hodges. References for passages quoted below are to this volume.

[2] *Op. cit.,* p. 125.   [3] *Op. cit.,* p. 130.   [4] *Op. cit.,* p. 118.

language, law, literary documents, cultural systems—indeed, everything that we understand as belonging to civilization and culture. History utilizes these objective expressions of mind to enter again into the minds which produced them. The historian 're-lives' the experiences which belonged to others, and this involves understanding in the fullest sense. There would seem to be a two-way traffic. I can enter into the experiences of others only because I live through experience myself; yet in entering into their experiences, I may first become aware of latent potentialities in my own experience. I am said to discover the 'I' in the 'Thou', and so to become aware of my own individuality. History thus becomes a seeking for the soul, an exploration of the human spirit. Dilthey's view of history brings him to the problems of interpretation, and he revived the science of hermeneutics, neglected since Schleiermacher's time. The possibility of interpretation, according to Dilthey, rests on an affinity between interpreter and author, on their sharing of a common experience, and this factor which arises from life itself and cannot be tied down by rules is just as important as the detailed historical, philological and literary knowledge which is also required for interpretation. We may notice that these views have had a considerable influence with some later New Testament exegetes, such as Rudolf Bultmann.[1]

Religion appears in Dilthey's scheme as one of the manifestations of the human spirit, an element of culture which varies in importance in different epochs. It is associated with the metaphysical consciousness, the awareness of the enigma of life and the quest for a comprehensive solution. Religion offers such a solution in the idea of God, but we can have no valid knowledge of such a transcendent reality. History is to be understood in terms of itself and of the human purposes which it reveals—that is to say, neither naturalistically nor in terms of an all-embracing divine purpose.

What history does show us is the relativity of all metaphysical systems. Three typical world-views are to be found running through history, and we may think of them as expressing different attitudes to life. The *naturalistic* world-view, running through Democritus, Lucretius, Hobbes, and the materialists and positivists of modern times, makes reason supreme. The world-view of *objective idealism*, as found in Heraclitus, the Stoics, Spinoza, Goethe and Hegel, gives the primacy to feeling and conduces to a pantheistic understanding of the world. The *idealism of freedom* is the third type of world-view, and is found in Plato, Christianity and Kant. It puts the will in first place, exalts personality, and forms the idea of a personal God. These world-views colour the religion, art,

[1] See below, p. 362.

literature and every other cultural manifestation which arises where any one of them predominate. They cannot, however, be reconciled, nor does any one of them fully and exhaustively express the variety of the human spirit. In recognizing that they are relative, and that nowhere is there absolute truth or value, the philosopher of history recognizes the relativism of his own point of view. Thus we end in a thorough-going relativism. But according to Dilthey, 'the last word of the mind which has run through all the world-views is not the relativity of them all, but the sovereignty of the mind in face of each one of them, and at the same time the positive consciousness of the way in which, in the various attitudes of the mind, the one reality of the world exists for us.'[1]

The relativism and historicism which appear in Dilthey come out much more strongly in the work of Oswald Spengler[2] (1880–1936). In him we also meet the chilly wind of twentieth-century pessimism, as he predicts the fall of Western culture. It is interesting to note that his book, *The Decline of the West*, though published in 1918, had been drafted before 1914.

Spengler not only turns away from the idea of history as a steady progress, but even from the idea that there is a unitary process of history. He returns to a cyclical interpretation of history, which he sees as a number of separate histories, each running through a determinate course. The historical unit is the *culture*, each one of which is self-contained. A culture has a life-span of roughly one thousand years, and by a 'comparative morphology' of the great cultures of the world, Spengler seeks to show that each goes through similar stages, which may be likened to the seasons of the year, ending inevitably in winter and death. Death, however, does not mean disappearance. The culture may continue as a mere *civilization*, which preserves the outer framework but is without the creative spirit—as we see, for instance, in the 'unchanging East'. The sensation caused by Spengler's book was due to his assertion that our Western culture has now reached the end of its life-span.

At the root of each culture lies a world-conception which is peculiar to the culture in question. There is for each culture a basic symbol which provides an understanding of the world, and all the manifestations of the culture are determined by the working out of this symbol. Spengler's account of the matter is decidedly naturalistic in flavour. The Classical culture arose in the clear Mediterranean atmosphere where everything is sharply defined, so the world is conceived as a cosmos of solid bodies. Sculpture flourishes, the gods are conceived in physical form, political organization is based on small independent city-states, science develops

[1] *Op. cit.*, p. 156.
[2] He spent most of his life in private study, without holding an academic post.

an atomic theory of hard massy particles. Spengler traces also a Magian culture, originating with desert-dwellers who, living under the dome of the sky, conceived the world as a cavern. This culture embraces both Byzantine Christianity and Islam, and its basic symbol appears in the domes and cupolas of their places of worship. In the dim forest lands of the north, Western culture arises and from the beginning takes infinite space as its symbol. The symbol of infinity leads to world-exploration, Copernican astronomy, Western imperialism, and so on. The West took over Christianity but made a new religion of it, entirely distinct from Byzantine Christianity. The difference is plainly exhibited in the new Gothic architecture whose spires and pinnacles reach out into space.

This brief sketch of his ideas shows us that for Spengler, religion, like every other cultural manifestation, is relative to the culture to which it belongs, and meaningful only within that culture. This radical relativism is extended even to science and philosophy. 'Truths are truths', says Spengler, 'only in relation to a particular mankind. Thus, my own philosophy is able to express and reflect *only* the Western (as distinct from the Classical, the Indian or any other) soul, and that soul *only* in its present civilized phase by which its conception of the world, its practical range and its sphere of effect are specified.'[1]

Another German thinker who conceived the task of philosophy to be that of understanding man himself was Ernest Cassirer[2] (1874–1945), though his approach to the problem differs considerably from Dilthey's. Beginning in the Marburg school of neo-Kantianism, Cassirer came to build up a philosophy of culture.

His first interest was in the philosophy of physics, of which he had a very thorough understanding. Physical science, he believes, does not give us a picture of reality. Rather, it has developed an increasingly refined *symbolism* by means of which the human spirit brings order into the manifold of the given and constructs its world.

But once we recognize the symbolic character of physics, we must abandon the idea that physical science has a uniquely privileged position and is able to offer us access to reality. On the contrary, we see that the human spirit employs many kinds of symbols besides those of physical science, and some of these symbols have a logic or grammar of their own, quite different from the rational ordering of the symbols of physics. In its richness and variety, man's cultural life shows many forms which cannot adequately be included under reason. 'Hence, instead of defining man as

---

[1] *The Decline of the West*, vol. I, p. 46.

[2] Professor at Hamburg, 1919–32; he left Germany when Hitler came to power, and after teaching at Oxford and Goeteborg, was professor at Yale, 1941–5.

an *animal rationale*, we should define him as an *animal symbolicum*.'[1] Symbolism is the peculiar dimension in which the human spirit moves, and Cassirer sets out to explore the wealth of 'symbolic forms' revealed in human culture.

Alongside science, religion finds its place, together with language, myth, art and so on, as elements within a diversified cultural life. Each element has its own peculiar symbolic form, but all of them by their symbols bring order to what is given in experience and appropriate it to the spiritual life of man. These symbolic forms cannot be reduced to a simple unity. On the contrary, each one has its specific character and structure. There are tensions and frictions among them, yet they all have a functional unity in human culture, where they complete and complement one another. Culture demands diversification, but this does not mean discord. It is a co-existence of contraries, a harmony of oppositions. 'Human culture taken as a whole may be described as the process of man's progressive self-liberation. Language, art, religion, science are various phases in this process. In all of them, man discovers and proves a new power—the power to build up a world of his own, an ideal world.'[2] None of the symbolic forms presents a picture of reality, but each one is justified to the extent that it contributes to man's cultural life and to the world which his mind constructs.

35. ITALIAN HISTORICAL IDEALISM
B. Croce, G. Gentile

While German philosophy looked in the main to Kant, the influence of Hegel was exerting itself in other countries. We have already seen the importance of the neo-Hegelian movement in the English-speaking countries. Now we turn to the neo-Hegelian movement in Italy, but we find it to be of a very different character. The most typical expression of British and American neo-Hegelianism was that which found reality in an unchangeable Absolute, but Italian idealism found the reality of spirit rather in action and history.

Its principal representative was Benedetto Croce[3] (1866–1953). He had wide interests in art, literature and politics, and worked out a system of thought in which philosophy is, to all intents and purposes, identified with history.

---

[1] *An Essay on Man*, p. 26.   [2] *Op. cit.*, p. 228.

[3] His life was spent in literary work. He was Minister of Education, 1920–21, went into retirement under Mussolini's régime, and again became Minister of Education in 1945.

Croce's philosophy gives expression to the liberal and humanistic point of view to which he was so passionately attached. Like the German philosophies which we have just considered, Croce's philosophy turns out to have for its theme the spirit of man himself, and it aims at self-knowledge. The approach, however, is very different in the two cases. Whereas Dilthey, for instance, gives priority to the human sciences on the ground that they alone have a subject-matter which is directly accessible, Croce goes much further. For him, the criterion by which we determine the priority of the human spirit is at bottom a metaphysical one. Spirit is the only reality, and therefore there is nothing else to compete with it for priority. In particular, it is denied that there is a nature independent of spirit, and the natural sciences are given a rather humble place in Croce's scheme of things. But if naturalism fares badly at his hands, so does theism. Spirit is conceived as a purely immanent process. The idea of a transcendent Spirit, or God, is rejected as firmly as that of an independent nature. Nothing is real outside of the process of spirit, and we see its highest manifestations in the spiritual life of man. Thus, as has been said, we have once again a philosophy which has man for its theme.

The world, then, is the process of spirit, an eternal stream of events in which there is nothing fixed or permanent. Action, movement, development, creative becoming are the characteristics of this process And since this spiritual development is exhibited in the life of man, it follows that philosophy is identical with history. It is said to be the methodology of history. Its business is to give a general description of the movements and activities of spirit as these are displayed in the history of the human mind.

Croce's own philosophy of spirit falls into four divisions. These are determined by two basic distinctions which he makes. The first distinction is between the *theoretical* activities of spirit—those in which mind understands and appropriates things—and the *practical* activities of spirit—those in which the mind creates and changes things. The second distinction is between two ways of knowing—the *intuitive* way, which is sensuous and has the particular for its object; and the *logical* way, which is rational and has the universal for its object. When we combined these two distinctions, we get a fourfold scheme of spiritual activity, and a corresponding fourfold division of the philosophy of mind. *Aesthetic* activity is theoretical, and concerned with the particular; *logical* activity is likewise theoretical, but concerned with the universal. *Economic* activity is the practical activity which concerns itself with individual aims—and it may be noted incidentally that the natural sciences are treated under this heading; *moral* activity is also practical, but here the aim is the general good. To each kind of activity belongs its own value—these are respectively beauty, truth, utility and goodness. In Croce's view, this scheme is an exhaustive one for the philosophy of spirit.

Does religion have a place in Croce's scheme, and if so, what place? We find that if he shows little respect for the natural sciences, he shows even less for religion. Since the fourfold scheme is claimed to be exhaustive, religion cannot be regarded as a fifth activity of spirit. 'Religion', we are told, 'is nothing but knowledge.'[1] It is, however, an imperfect and inferior kind of knowledge. With the development of spirit, its content has been changed, bettered and refined, and this process will continue, but its form remains the same—an imperfect mythological form which is surpassed by the rational form of philosophical knowledge. 'Philosophy removes from religion all reason for existing, because it substitutes itself for religion. As the science of the spirit, it looks upon religion as a phenomenon, a transitory historical fact, a psychic condition that can be surpassed.'[2] These strictures apply not only to the traditional religions but also to the various substitute religions devised by the naturalists, which Croce dismisses as 'the superstitious worship so recklessly lavished on the natural sciences'.[3]

I. M. Bochenski remarks that 'among all contemporary idealists, Croce is perhaps the one who shows least sympathy for religion'.[4] Yet while he rejects religion as a way of knowing and considers it to have been superseded by philosophy, Croce must still reckon with religion as a fact of history, as a stage or moment in the development of spirit. When it is viewed in this way, he seems willing to assign some value to it—for instance, he finds in the Christian ethic most of the true morality of spirit.

As a fact of history, religion is inescapable. It forms the entire intellectual patrimony of primitive peoples, and an important part of ours. In one of his essays, Croce argues that we in the Western world cannot help calling ourselves Christians. 'The name merely registers a fact.'[5] This has nothing to do with membership of a church or assent to a creed— it is simply the recognition that Christian ideals and values belong to our heritage, and have played a decisive part in the development of the human spirit. Ancient ethics and religion were taken up and dissolved in the Christian idea of conscience and of the God in whom we live and move and have our being. Christianity may in its turn be transcended, but this belongs to the future. 'This we know, that in our times, our thought inevitably works on the lines laid down by Christianity.'[6]

Thus Croce expounds a form of idealism which is opposed both to a

---

[1] *Aesthetic*, p. 63.   [2] *Op. cit.*, p. 64.   [3] *Op. cit.*, p. 63.
[4] *Contemporary European Philosophy*, p. 79.   [5] *My Philosophy*, p. 37.
[6] *Op. cit.*, p. 46.

naturalistic and to a religious interpretation of the world. Religion as a way of knowing is displaced by philosophy, its transcendent beliefs are rejected, and it is regarded as a purely immanent feature of man's history and culture, a transient phase in the unfolding of the human spirit.

Just as in English idealism we usually talk of Bradley and Bosanquet, so in Italian idealism the name of Croce is usually coupled with that of Gentile, though Giovanni Gentile[1] (1875–1944) followed a very different line of development. Whereas Croce was the lifelong liberal, Gentile became closely identified with Mussolini's government, and eventually met a violent death at the hands of his political opponents.

In Gentile's philosophy, we again meet with an idealism which is both activist and immanentist. It is *activist* because he holds that reality is not what is thought but rather the pure act of thinking itself. It is *immanentist* because there is no reality which transcends or stands outside of the activity of thinking. This is a creative act, and whatever we may think of—nature or other minds, even God, infinity and eternity—belongs within the act of thinking itself.

Within the act of thinking, three moments are distinguishable—the subject, the object, and the synthesis between them. On the basis of this, Gentile erects a threefold scheme of spiritual activity, which may be contrasted with the fourfold one of Croce's philosophy. We may affirm the subject, and, according to Gentile, *art* is the form of spirit whose essence consists in a liberating subjectivity. Or we may affirm the object, in which case we have *religion*, described as 'the exaltation of the object'.[2] Gentile has in mind the mystical experience in which the mystic loses himself in the being of God. Both art and religion are one-sided. They need to be integrated—though this does not mean that they are lost—in the higher activity of philosophy, the synthesis of subject and object, the complete actuality of self-conscious spirit. Philosophy, however, is identified with its own *history*, the creative process in which spirit becomes conscious of itself.

Though basically similar to Croce's, Gentile's philosophy allows a more important place to religion, and Gentile himself insisted that his philosophy is a religious one. Although he subordinates religion to philosophy, he claims that only within the synthesis of philosophy can religion be justified and retain its place; and he maintains the essential agreement of his philosophy of immanence with Christianity's stress on the principle of

---

[1] After holding academic posts at Palermo, Pisa and Rome, he became Minister of Education, 1923–24, in Mussolini's government, and remained the chief intellectual exponent of Fascism.

[2] *The Theory of Mind as Pure Act*, p. 147.

spiritual inwardness. But orthodox Christianity would scarcely welcome an alliance with Gentile's philosophy of religion, for the God of this philosophy is conceived as nothing but the infinity of which, in the course of his historical development, man becomes aware as immanent in his own spirit.

36. ENGLISH-SPEAKING PHILOSOPHERS OF HISTORY AND CULTURE
R. G. Collingwood, A. J. Toynbee, W. M. Urban, C. Dawson

Robin George Collingwood[1] (1889–1943) is the most outstanding representative of historicism in British philosophy. He was a noted archaeologist and historian as well as being a philosopher—his work on Roman Britain is considered authoritative—and his philosophical reputation has grown since his death, though his thought has little in common with the current trends in British philosophy. He was keenly interested in Croce and the Italian idealists, some of whose works he translated, but in some respects he has affinities with German writers like Dilthey and Cassirer, so that in Collingwood we find, as it were, a confluence of the two different streams of thought which we have already considered, the German and Italian approaches to the philosophical problem of history.

In an early work, *Religion and Philosophy*, published in 1916, we find Collingwood already suggesting that the problems of the philosophy of religion are to be pursued in the history of religion. A few years later, in *Speculum Mentis*, 1924, we find him adumbrating a kind of philosophy of culture which suggests comparisons with the views being worked out at about the same time by Cassirer. Philosophy, Collingwood tells us, is to take for its task a critical review of the various forms of human experience —art, religion, science and so on. We cannot carve out a particular province of experience for each of these, for each claims the whole of experience for its province. But we cannot say either that any one of them offers a true picture to the exclusion of the others. They are like maps of the same territory, but each map is in a different projection; or they are like so many mirrors, each one of which reflects with varying degrees of distortion the spirit's knowledge of itself. No one of them can be absolutized—religion, for instance, becomes mistaken if it takes its symbols for reality.

In Collingwood's further thought, history emerges as the master-study

[1] Fellow of Pembroke College, Oxford, 1912–34; professor at Oxford, 1934–41.

which helps us to co-ordinate the various distorting mirrors, and indeed, as with Croce, philosophy is practically merged into history. All human thinking is historically conditioned. The answers which we find are in part determined by the questions which we ask, and these questions, as Collingwood rightly saw, always carry with them certain presuppositions. The presuppositions are of an ultimate nature, they cannot be called either true or false, they are simply given with the historical situation in which the question is asked, and they change from one situation to another. This holds good even for the natural sciences. 'Natural science as a form of thought exists and always has existed in a context of history', so that 'no one can answer the question what nature is unless he knows what history is.'[1]

Collingwood's views on history itself resemble those of Dilthey. History, as distinct from mere change, is the history of human affairs. As a human action, any historical event has two sides to it—its 'outside', as an event in the physical world, and its 'inside', as an event in the mind of the agent. The historian cannot be concerned with either of these to the exclusion of the other. But 'his main task is to think himself into the action, to discern the thought of its agent'.[2] The event is to be re-enacted in the mind of the historian. Thus, as with Dilthey and Croce, history is concerned with the exploration of the human spirit, or, more briefly, it is for self-knowledge. This is said to include 'knowing what it is to be a man, what it is to be the kind of man you are, and what it is to be the man *you* are and nobody else is'.[3]

Religion is recognized by Collingwood as an important function of the human spirit, and it too must be considered from the point of view of its history. Its ultimate presuppositions, such as its belief in God, are historically conditioned, and, like all our ultimate presuppositions, cannot be shown to be either true or false. This leads to a radical relativism, which would make it impossible to ask about the truth of the religious beliefs held by any particular time, since these beliefs simply reflect the historical or cultural climate of that particular time. Yet he also tells us that our attitude to our own ultimate presuppositions is to be one of 'unquestioning acceptance'. Hence his friend and literary executor, T. M. Knox, remarks that 'while his final historicism has affinities with Dilthey and Croce, his doctrine of absolute presuppositions, with its religious and theological background, has affinities with Kierkegaard and even Barth'.[4]

At first glance, Arnold Joseph Toynbee[5] (1889–   ) seems to offer us a

---

[1] *The Idea of Nature*, p. 177.   [2] *The Idea of History*, p. 213.
[3] *Op. cit.*, p. 10.   [4] In his editorial preface to *The Idea of History*, p. xvii.
[5] Professor at London, 1919–55.

view of history very like Spengler's. In Toynbee, we come again upon the view that there is no unitary history of mankind, but a series of histories each of which fulfils its course within a particular society. The historian's interest is particularly directed to those societies which have passed the primitive stage and become civilizations. In his monumental work, *A Study of History*, Toynbee recognizes twenty-six of these civilizations, most of which have already run their course and belong to the past. Like Spengler, Tonybee is interested in the comparative study of these civilizations.

Collingwood criticizes Toynbee on the ground that he takes a naturalistic view of history: 'he regards the life of a society as a natural and not a mental life, something at bottom merely biological and best understood on biological analogies; he regards history as a mere spectacle, not experiences into which he must enter and which he must make his own'.[1] No doubt these criticisms are true up to a point. Yet Toynbee's view of history is certainly less naturalistic than Spengler's.

In the first place, Toynbee does not seem to think of the life of a society as merely that of an organism which runs a predetermined course from birth to death in accordance with natural laws. He detects in the life of a society a more specifically human pattern—that of 'challenge and response', as he calls it. A society has to face the challenge of various crises in its life, and its further development depends on the kind of response which it makes. To this extent, it has some responsibility for its own destiny.

In the second place, Toynbee does not think of the various societies as completely isolated from one another. There may be relations of affiliation among some of them. In the course of his studies, Toynbee came to attach more and more importance to religion. It may be the case that religion can pass on from one civilization to another, and be strengthened in the process. Thus Christianity arose out of the decline of Hellenistic society, and it may survive the decay of Western civilization. On this view, religion would not be just an aspect of civilization, as in Spengler. On the contrary, it is suggested that while the movement of civilization is cyclical, the movement of religion may be continuous from one civilization to another.

While Toynbee has a special regard for Christianity, he recognizes that all the higher religions have the same essence. In any particular religion, this essence is entangled with non-essential historical accretions. The essence of the higher religions consists in their recognition of a spiritual Presence higher than man himself in the universe, and in the

[1] *The Idea of History*, p. 163.

renunciation of self-centredness. When this essential unity is discerned amid the historical diversities of the higher religions, then we understand that 'the missions of the higher religions are not competitive; they are complementary'.[1] Toynbee advocates a kind of peaceful co-existence among them. We in the Western world must learn something of the tolerance of the Eastern religions so that 'we can believe in our own religion without having to feel that it is the sole repository of truth'.[2]

The American philosopher, Wilbur Marshall Urban[3] (1873–   ) recognizes a kind of *philosophia perennis* with which our Western culture and civilization are inextricably bound up. Plato, Aristotle, Aquinas, Leibniz —these great thinkers and others like them have been the exponents of this classic philosophy. But why do we recognize such men as 'great thinkers'? Urban's answer would seem to be that these men have built up the moral and political values on which our Western civilization is based, and which are of supreme importance to ourselves. The nineteenth century made the mistake of thinking that it could discard the classic philosophy of the West and retain the traditional values. This is not so, for the result is either a naturalism which in fact denatures man as the bearer of values, or else, by way of reaction, an irrational authoritative theology which equally offends against the nature of man. Hence for Urban the maintenance of our civilization demands the revival and re-statement of its classic philosophy.

This classic philosophy was both rational and religious. Its rationalism, however, was not the kind of rationalism that we meet in our own time. This modern rationalism is of a shallow, impoverished sort. The deeper, genuine rationalism of the West takes account of value. It makes possible a rational theology which sees in God the ground of human values, so that the perennial philosophy is religious as well as rational.

The destructive criticism of rational theology in modern times seems to be successful only because so much of our philosophy divorces facts from values, and treats the classic arguments for God as if they dealt with bare matters of fact. This attitude involves, among other things, an inadequate understanding of the function of language. Urban's *Language and Reality*, which owes much to Cassirer, is a major study of language as a sign or symbol of reality. The symbolic forms of the languages of poetry, science and religion are examined, and it is argued that what makes the world intelligible as a whole is the metaphysical idiom of the perennial philosophy—that traditional philosophy of the West, at once rational and religious, which is not indeed changeless or final, but which has in it

---

[1] *An Historian's Approach to Religion*, p. 296.   [2] *Ibid.*
[3] Professor at Yale, 1931–41.

something timeless and abiding. Religious language involves us in a symbolism which cannot be understood by a detached observer but only by one who is prepared to enter into the dimension of values into which it takes us. Religious language arises out of myth, in which value and existence are inseparable, but religious language differs essentially from myth in transforming the mythical material into a conscious symbolism. When the symbolic character of religious language is thus understood, we need to take another look at the classic arguments for God, and we find that the primary argument is that which proceeds from man as the value-bearer to God as the ground of value.

Thus Urban's philosophy of religion moves round the correlated ideas of humanity and deity. Since our talk of God is in terms of human symbols and values, 'the historical and therefore relative character of all religion is implied in the nature of its language'.[1] On the other hand, since such language grasps something of the eternal ground of values, it has a dateless quality. There are timeless elements not only in the perennial philosophy but in every revelation of God that has been handed down—'those who have been uniquely near to God at any time are nearer to us than our contemporaries.'[2]

We end this section by mentioning another thinker whose main interest has been in the philosophy of culture, and especially in the relation of religion to culture—Christopher Dawson[3] (1889–   ). In opposition to all theories which regard religion as simply a by-product of cultural or social factors, Dawson asserts that religion is the key to a culture, and plays a major part in shaping it. 'Even a religion which is explicitly other-worldly and appears to deny all the values and standards of human society may, nevertheless, exert a dynamic influence on culture and provide the driving forces in movements of social change.'[4] A religious faith introduces man to a wider range of reality than any human ideology which confines its attention to the finite and temporal world, and it has a correspondingly deeper influence, even though this may work unconsciously.

Religion is profoundly influential in any culture. In the great cultures of Asia, religion established a sacred social order, which might endure unchanged for centuries. Western culture differs markedly from Asian cultures in its dynamic and expansive character. Here there is no immobilization or worship of changeless perfection, but a restless spirit of change. We cannot account for the distinctive Western achievement in terms of

---

[1] *Humanity and Deity*, p. 473.   [2] *Op. cit.*, p. 474.
[3] Writer and lecturer on the philosophy of religion.
[4] *Religion and the Rise of Western Culture*, p. 7.

secular factors such as aggressiveness and acquisitiveness, which have always operated in human history. Dawson takes us back to the formative period of Western culture in the Middle Ages, and seeks to show by detailed studies of the medieval world that the driving force in Western culture is the spirit of Catholic Christianity, a spirit that strives to incorporate itself in humanity, and to transform the world.

It is true of course that Western culture has become increasingly secularized. By the nineteenth century men had even come to believe in a theory of automatic progress. The events of the present century, however, have shown us that progress is by no means automatic, and that the structure of culture and civilization is a fragile one which can easily fall back into barbarism. These reflections direct us again to the spiritual roots of our culture. 'It would be a strange fatality if the great revolution by which Western man has subdued nature to his purposes should end in the loss of his own spiritual freedom, but this might well happen if an increasing technical control of the state over the life and thought of its members should coincide with a qualitative decline in the standards of our culture.'[1] Religion continues to have a vital function, both as a principle of continuity and as a creative source.

37. Summary of Historical and Cultural Interpretations of Religion

We may now sum up the main characteristics of the views of religion which have been considered in this chapter. These views, of course, vary widely among themselves, but perhaps three important features may be mentioned as common to most of them.

1. These interpretations are, on the whole, *immanentist*—that is to say, their account of religion is confined to its place in the historical and cultural life of man. This statement is more true of some than of others. —it applies most to Croce, who expressly denies that there is any transcendent Spirit, and least to Urban who favours a rational argument for theism. But in each case the main interest is centred in interpreting religion as a factor in human life, and the ultimate metaphysical question may, as with Dilthey, be left aside. The assessment of religion is rather in terms of its value in the history and expression of the human mind. Even if religion is ultimately of the nature of a relation between the human spirit and a transcendent Spirit, there is much to be said for approaching it from the human side which is most easily accessible to us, rather than in

[1] *Op. cit.*, pp. 6–7.

trying to interpret it in the light of some preconceived metaphysic, whether idealistic or naturalistic.

2. The distinctively *spiritual* character of human life is, in general, recognized. For this reason, the immanentism of the philosophies of hitory and culture turns out to be very different from that of naturalism. Both types of philosophy think of religion primarily as a human affair, both are interested in the question of its development, but whereas the naturalist considers religion to be of a piece with natural phenomena in general, the philosophers of history and culture distinguish the activities of the human mind from mere natural happenings. Here also there are differences of degree. For Croce and Gentile, only spirit is real; Dilthey is content to stress the difference between spiritual activity and natural happening; Spengler perhaps comes nearest to a naturalistic point of view, though he says that neither idealism nor materialism is satisfactory.

3. Perhaps the most striking feature of most of the philosophies considered is their *relativism*. Such relativism is an almost inevitable conclusion when one embarks—as do Spengler and Toynbee—on the comparative study of cultures, or when one surveys the variegated patterns of history. This relativism impinges on religion in two ways. It suggests the relativity of all religious knowledge, which is historically conditioned (Collingwood) or expresses itself in particular symbols of human origin (Cassirer and Urban). It suggests also relativity among the great religions themselves, all of which express in their particular idioms a common matrix of teaching. The first of these relativities may be hard to accept for all religions, which have a tendency to identify their symbols with reality; the second of these relativities may be particularly hard to accept for Judaism, Christianity and Islam which, unlike the Eastern religions, have tended to claim, each one for itself, an absolute or exclusive possession of the truth about God. Yet the case for relativism made out by the philosophers of history and culture is a strong one, and cannot be ignored by theologians or philosophers of religion.

The philosophies which have just been summarized have possibly passed their zenith, at least in the form in which they were originally formulated. Their most fruitful ideas on man and his history and culture have been taken up by thinkers of more recent schools, such as Jaspers, Heidegger and Bultmann, who are more properly classed with the existentialists.[1] The contribution of the philosophies of history and culture to the interpretation of religion has, however, been an important one—perhaps just because they have been willing to take man at his face value into the subject-matter of philosophy, and to look at him and his

[1] See below, pp. 353ff.

religion as we find them, as far as possible without the distorting medium of either an idealistic or a naturalistic metaphysic; and perhaps also because they look at religion in all its varied historical and cultural manifestations, without prematurely absolutizing any particular form of it. But we must now consider more particularly how the historical approach impinges on Christianity and its theology.

IX

CHRISTIANITY, HISTORY AND CULTURE

38. HISTORY AND THEOLOGY

W E have now to consider those movements in theology and the interpretation of Christianity which run parallel with the more general philosophies of history and culture considered in the preceding chapter. In some cases we can see a direct influence of the philosophy of history upon theology—for instance, Dilthey exerts such an influence on the theology of Troeltsch. In other cases, the theological interest in history or culture arises independently.

There were good reasons for the rise of such an interest. In the nine-teenth century, the sacred literature of the great religions of the East had become accessible, through the labours of such great scholars as Friedrich Max Müller. For the first time, a comprehensive comparative study of religion became possible, and Christianity could be seen not as an isolated fact but within the context of the much wider religious history of the human race. More especially, much information was obtained about late Jewish speculation, Gnosticism, the mystery religions, and other currents of thought contemporary with the rise of Christianity, so that it became possible to see the New Testament in the setting of the Hellenistic world, and to trace its affinities with other religious ideas of its own time.

In Germany there arose a well-defined school of theology—the *Religionsgeschichtliche Schule*, or 'history of religion school'—which was flourishing from before the turn of the century till around 1920 and which, as its name implies, came to the problems of theology from the side of history. The interest of this school in history was, however, quite different from that of Ritschlians like Herrmann and Harnack. Whereas the Ritschlians sought to isolate what they supposed to have been the original religion of Jesus and to remove from it extraneous influences, the history of religion school sought rather to understand Christianity in relation to other religious movements and within the history of religion as a whole. As we shall see, the history of religion school dealt a severe blow to that picture of the 'Jesus of history' to which the Ritschlians had attached such importance.

Apart from this well-defined German school, there were other independent theologians and interpreters of Christianity whose interest in the relation of Christianity to history and culture was so pronounced that we are justified in including the consideration of them in this chapter.

The chapter will embrace the following topics: the general historical interpretation of Christianity (Section 39); the specific question of Christian origins and the historical Jesus (Section 40); some independent views of Christianity showing a special interest in its relations to history and culture (Section 41); some concluding remarks on the importance of these views and their consequences (Section 42).

39. The Historical Interpretation of Christianity
O. Pfleiderer, E. Troeltsch

For an introduction to the historical approach to Christianity we may go to the writings of the German theologian and philosopher of religion, Otto Pfleiderer[1] (1839–1908). A severe critic of Herrmann and the Ritschlians, Pfleiderer advocated what he called the 'genetic-speculative' method. In this he proposed to combine the insights of history and philosophy in their application to religion, for he contended that those who were conversant with the facts of the history of religion were usually destitute of philosophical ideas, while on the other hand no philosophical approach to religion can succeed without taking history into account.

Pfleiderer's philosophy of religion has therefore two sides to it. On the one hand, it traces the historical development of the religious consciousness, and this development is conceived as a purely immanent and continuous process from the first glimmerings of primitive religion up to the religions of the present day. Anything in the way of special revelations or miracles breaking supernaturally into the process is ruled out. We are to view the development of the religious consciousness within 'such a connection of causes and effects as is analogous to our general experience of what happens among men and in men'.[2] On the other hand, Pfleiderer's philosophy of religion seeks to provide a philosophical justification for the contents of the religious consciousness, for instance, the belief in God. We may think of the process of religious development as the progressive and continuous revelation of God, who, like the process itself, is conceived

---

[1] Professor at Jena, 1870–5; Berlin, 1875–1908.
[2] *Philosophy and Development of Religion*, vol. II, pp. 1–2.

primarily in terms of immanence. Pfleiderer recoils from a frank pantheism, but there is certainly no supernaturalistic distinction of God from
the world. God is 'the all-embracing whole' who nevertheless 'distinguishes himself from everything finite'; 'he neither disappears in the world,
nor is he excluded from it'.[1] Personality can be ascribed to him only in a
metaphorical sense.

Christianity is to be understood within this general framework of ideas,
and we must abandon the traditional idea that it had its origin in some
special or unique supernatural happening. 'The appearing of a heavenly
being for an episodic stay upon our earth breaks the connection of events in
space and time upon which all our experience rests, and therefore it undoes
the conception of history from the bottom.'[2] Christianity can be understood only as a phase in the general development of religion—a phase in
which the tendencies already at work came to liberation. In the prophetic
personality of Jesus men found their own growing spirit. Moreover, the
Jesus of history for whom Harnack looked is quite inaccessible to us, for
our only records do not permit us to go behind the mythical and religious
ideas which speedily gathered around him.

The process of development still goes on. Unfortunately, the Protestant
churches took over the supernaturalism and the dogmatic apparatus of
medieval Christianity, but they also incorporated into themselves the
principle of criticism, and they must go on reforming themselves and
freeing themselves from ideas which belong to past stages of culture. So
far as they do this, 'it may be a difficult task to recast their faith in harmony
with the knowledge of our time, but it cannot be an insoluble one'.[3]

The classic statement of the application of historicism to Christianity
is found in Ernest Troeltsch[4] (1865–1923), who, as already noted, owed
much to Dilthey. He states plainly that 'the investigation and assessment
of Christianity is to find its place within the framework of religious and
cultural history'.[5] The study of history, however, as Troeltsch had
learned from Dilthey, is to be sharply distinguished from the study of
nature. Both studies are scientific in their nature, and both concern
themselves with elucidating causal connections in their subject-matter.
But Troeltsch claims that the kind of causality is very different in each
case. Natural causality is a matter of the transformation and conservation
of energy, a continual reshuffling of patterns. Historical causality, on the

---

[1] *The Philosophy of Religion on the Basis of its History*, vol. III, p. 290.

[2] *Philosophy and Development of Religion*, vol. II, pp. 3–4.

[3] *Op. cit.*, pp. 354-5.

[4] Professor successively at Bonn, 1892–94; Heidelberg, 1894–1914; Berlin, 1914–23.

[5] In his essay, 'Ueber historische und dogmatische Methode in der Theologie', reprinted in *Gesammelte Schriften*, Band II, pp. 729ff.

other hand, is mainly a matter of psychological motivation. It is not just quantitative but qualitative, and is said to produce novelty in a way which is not possible where mere transformations of energy are concerned. The investigation of natural causality leads to the formulation of general laws, but in historical causality our interest lies in the individual and concrete. Like Dilthey and Collingwood, and also like the later existentialists, Troeltsch thinks that we must enter by sympathetic understanding into the concrete happenings of history. We try to make such a happening 'as intelligible as if it were part of our own experience'.[1]

Troeltsch lays down certain principles which are to guide us in our approach to history. One is the principle of *criticism*. Every tradition and every generally received interpretation of history must be sifted by criticism, and this is a work which is never finished. Fresh facts may come to light, or more careful criticism may upset the results of earlier investigation. It follows that the findings of history are able to claim only probability. They are always open to correction and revision, and always fall short of certainty. As far as Christianity is concerned, this principle simply sums up the results of all the historical research upon the Bible that went on in the century before Troeltsch. The events recorded in the New Testament and on which Christianity is supposed to be founded cannot be taken for certain. Some may appear more probable, others less so, but in any case we must keep an open mind about them—who knows whether next year an Arab boy may find in a cave by the Dead Sea some musty scrolls which will shed an entirely new light on the matter?

A second principle is that of *analogy*. We must go on the assumption that the events of the past are analogous to the events which we ourselves experience in the present. A report of past events which are analogous to present events must be deemed to have more inherent probability than a report of events for which we can find no analogies in our own experience. We have, for instance, no experience of miracles or wonders such as we read about in the Bible. We must therefore assume that the reports of such happenings are highly improbable. This principle of analogy is by no means an arbitrary one. If we did not assume that past events were similar in their nature to events that happen now, or that people thought and acted then in ways similar to those in which we think and act ourselves, then there would be no possibility at all of learning from history or of getting any understanding of the past.

A third principle is that of *correlation*. Every historical event is correlated with others in the same series. There is an integral continuity in history,

[1] See his article 'Historiography' in Hastings' *Encyclopedia of Religion and Ethics*, vol. VI, pp. 716ff.

so that everything which happens has to be considered as immanent in the immensely complex causal nexus. Troeltsch can even say that 'the history of mankind merges in the purely evolutionary history of the earth's surface',[1] but this naturalistic utterance conflicts with his sharp distinction between natural and historical causality. The point of the principle of correlation is, however, that although there may be distinctive events, and even highly distinctive events, all events are of the same order, and all are explicable in terms of what is immanent in history itself. Thus there can be no divine irruptions or interventions in history. God may indeed be at work in the process, or revealing himself in it, but if so his activity is immanent and continuous. It is not the special or sporadic intervention of a transcendent deity. Again, since all events are of the same order, it cannot be claimed that any particular event is final, absolute, unique or anything of the sort. The implication of this for Christianity is relativism. Christianity belongs within the sphere of religious and human history as a whole, and no absolute claim can be made for it. The life and work of Jesus Christ himself may be a very distinctive event, but it cannot be absolute or final or of a different order from other historical events.

Thus when Troeltsch's principles are applied to it, Christianity emerges deprived of certainty in its historical basis, shorn of its supernatural element, and denied any final or absolute character. It is true that in a discussion of the absoluteness of Christianity, Troeltsch acknowledges it to be the climax and point of convergence of religious development so far. But in one of his latest writings, he makes it clear that its definitive character holds only within a particular historical culture. 'It is final and unconditional *for us*, because we have nothing else. But this does not preclude the possibility that other racial groups, living under entirely different cultural conditions, may experience their contact with the divine life in quite a different way.'[2] Thus Christianity is not absolute, but it is sufficient for us. It may even be said that when Christianity is cut down to its proper dimensions as a phenomenon of history, and is seen within the framework of man's spiritual development as a whole, its true greatness becomes apparent. For man's history is conceived by Troeltsch as taking place against the background of an immanentist theism. God is the universal consciousness, the reality in which all things exist, and the ground of values. In the history of religion, the idea of God gains increasing content, and the contribution of Christianity has been an outstanding one.

What is the relation of Christianity to the historical culture within

[1] *Ibid.*   [2] *Christian Thought: its History and Application*, p. 26.

which it is set? Troeltsch discusses this question in *The Social Teaching of the Christian Churches*. He notes that Christianity itself exhibits various social structures, notably the 'church-type', which is open towards secular culture, and the 'sect-type', which is closed against it. While maintaining that theology and dogma are conditioned by historical social forces, he denies the Marxist thesis that religion is a product of such forces. Religious ideas originate in the autonomous religious consciousness, and can powerfully influence society by providing social ideals and the energy to pursue them. This aspect of Troeltsch's thought links the historical interpretations of religion to the sociological interpretations which will be considered in the next chapter.

40. PROBLEMS ABOUT THE JESUS OF HISTORY
J. Weiss, A. Schweitzer, A. Drews

While Pfleiderer and Troeltsch were engaged in the tasks of exhibiting Christianity within the general framework of the history of religion, other writers were concerning themselves with the more limited problem of relating Jesus and the origins of Christianity with contemporary religious ideas of the ancient world. These researches tended to confirm Pfleiderer's contention that the actual Jesus of history whom Harnack had sought is inaccessible to us, and that even our earliest documents are thoroughly saturated in the mythical and religious ideas of their time, so that they are not so much records of Jesus as records of what the early Christian community thought about Jesus.

Johannes Weiss[1] (1863–1914) related the preaching of Jesus to Jewish eschatology. At that time, the Jews were immersed in apocalyptic ideas. They looked for a catastrophic end of the age and the inauguration of a supernatural kingdom. According to Weiss, it is in the light of these contemporary Jewish ideas that the mission and message of Jesus is to be understood. The kingdom of God which Jesus proclaimed was not, as the Ritschlians mistakenly supposed, an ethical ideal of love to God and men, but the strange supernatural realm of Jewish eschatology. Jesus did not establish the kingdom but only proclaimed its coming. The missionary journey of his disciples was not intended to extend the kingdom, but only to warn men of its nearness. Disappointed with the response, Jesus gives his life as a ransom to hasten the coming of the kingdom, in the expectation that he himself would shortly return to have dominion in it, with all

[1] Professor successively at Göttingen, 1890–95; Marburg, 1895–1908; Heidelberg, 1908–14.

the splendour which Jewish apocalyptic writers from Daniel onwards had attributed to the Son of Man.

This view of Weiss makes the figure of Jesus utterly remote from us, and the gospel becomes a curious relic from a bygone culture whose ways of thinking are entirely foreign to ours. Actually Weiss came to acknowledge that his presentation of the case for an eschatological interpretation had been an extreme one, and that there are also ethical teachings in the gospel which are of lasting value.

In still another way, however, Weiss helped to destroy the picture of the historical Jesus as cherished by the Ritschlians. He is generally regarded as the pioneer of form-criticism—the approach to the Gospels which seek to analyse and classify the literary forms of the various sayings and narratives of which the gospels are made up, and to show how these served the apologetic and devotional purposes of the early Christian community. Weiss writes: 'Every narrative that has been preserved, every saying that has survived, is evidence of some particular interest on the part of the primitive Church. To this extent the selection of what was handed down serves to characterize the interest of the group whose need it satisfied. In far greater measure must we learn to read the gospels not only for what they tell us about Jesus, but also for what we can learn from them about the life and faith of the earliest Christians.'[1] Thus our documents do not show us Jesus himself, but the image of Jesus as coloured by the ideas and interests of those who had come to believe in him.

The most famous expression of the eschatological interpretation of primitive Christianity came from Albert Schweitzer[2] (1875–1965). Better known to the world at large as a missionary and philanthropist, he is also a considerable religious thinker, and his views deserve a respectful hearing if for no other reason than that he has lived them out.

In a critical survey of attempts to write the life of Jesus, Schweitzer notes that such attempts were motivated by the aim of setting Jesus free from the shackles of ecclesiastical dogma—and it may be noted in passing that Schweitzer himself has little use for such dogma. But the mistake had been made of trying to modernize Jesus. The Ritschlians had represented Jesus as the teacher of a universal message which is immediately applicable to our own age, but they had done this only by reading back their own ideals into the figure of Jesus. We have to recognize that Jesus belonged to his own time, and he must be understood in relation to his time. When we do understand him in this way, we see that his teaching

---

[1] *Earliest Christianity*, vol. I, pp. 12–13.

[2] Lecturer at Strasburg (then in Germany) from 1902 until 1913, when he gave up his academic career to found his hospital at Lambarene.

and his very life were centred in the eschatological beliefs of his age, and in his mistaken conviction that the end of the world was imminent. The historical Jesus belongs to a world whose ideas were quite different from ours, and so he 'will be to our time a stranger and an enigma'.[1] Schweitzer likewise finds that the thought of St Paul is impregnated through and through with the eschatological outlook.

If Jesus and the earliest Christianity belong to an outmoded world of thought, we may then ask—as Schweitzer himself does—what they can possibly have to do with us. Perhaps, says Schweitzer, the ideal would have been that religious truth should be expressed in a form independent of any connection with any particular period, so that it could be taken over simply and easily by one generation after another. But this is not the case. 'We are obliged to admit the evident fact that religious truth varies from age to age.'[2] The solution which Schweitzer proposes is to find in the teaching of Jesus a certain 'spiritual force' which he calls the 'religion of love' and which can remain essentially the same in connection with varying world-views—whether these be the world-views of Jewish apocalyptic, of Hellenistic times, of the Middle Ages, or of the modern period. 'The essence of Christianity is world-affirmation which has gone through an experience of world-negation. In the eschatological world-view of world-negation, Jesus proclaims the ethic of active love.'[3]

What this statement means can perhaps best be seen by considering briefly how Schweitzer combines the essential core of Jesus' religion of love with his own world-view. Schweitzer is pessimistic about the modern world, and in particular he is out of sympathy with the positivistic temper of the times. He declares his faith in rational thinking, and accepts the duty of thinking out man's relation to the world. The philosophy at which he arrives centres in the notion of 'reverence for life'.

We see that the world does not consist of mere happening, but contains life as well. Man knows that everything has, like himself, a will-to-live— and presumably the word 'life' is used here for a kind of universal striving rather than in a strictly biological sense. Man has both a passive and an active relation to the world. He has a passive relation, in so far as he is subordinate to world happenings; he has an active relation, in so far as he can affect the life which comes within his reach. The passive relation leads through a negative stage—that of resignation. But such resignation confers inward freedom, and so leads on to the stage of affirmation, which expresses itself in the ethic of love. Thus the essential pattern of Jesus'

---

[1] *The Quest of the Historical Jesus*, p. 397.
[2] *My Life and Thought*, p. 67.
[3] *Op. cit.*, p. 70.

teaching is disengaged from its eschatological setting and restated in the context of modern ideas.

While Weiss and Schweitzer connected Christian origins with Jewish eschatology, other writers linked them with different religious movements of the Hellenistic world, such as Gnosticism and the mystery religions. The idea that the gospels tell us more about the beliefs of the first Christians than about Jesus himself was carried by some to the extent of denying that there ever was a Jesus, and of explaining Christianity as simply a development out of the mythical and religious images of the ancient world. Such theories had already been advanced in the nineteenth century, but they received a new stimulus at the beginning of the present century, perhaps because of the uncertainty which had been introduced into the whole subject of Christian origins.

Of these twentieth-century Christ-myth theories, the one which attracted most attention—though it was not perhaps the most cogent— was that of Arthur Drews[1] (1865–1935). It is significant that in his approach to the New Testament Drews quotes extensively from Weiss, and presses the latter's form-criticism into service of the view that the gospels tell us only about the beliefs of the early Christians. The gospels contain no history, but consist of fragments of dogmatic, apologetic and devotional material. 'The Christ-myth method', says Drews, 'sets out from the fact that the gospels, on the admission of the theologians themselves, are not history books, but books for edification.'[2] They tell us nothing about a historical Jesus, but only about the purely mythical figure of that name who was reverenced in the early Christian cult and whose provenance can be traced in the myths of the ancient world.

But for the mythological background of the gospels Drews turned not to Jewish eschatology but to the astralism or cult of the celestial bodies which, he maintained, had formed the age-old material of Semitic religion. The figures in the gospel narratives are simply the mythical symbols for those imaginary figures which man's fantasy had read in the constellations of the sky. With astonishing ingenuity, Drews makes his identifications. Jesus himself is the sun. He is identified with Joshua, the ancient hero of Israel who is reported in the Old Testament to have commanded the sun to stand still. 'Jesus' is, of course, the Greek form of the Hebrew name 'Joshua'. This Joshua, according to Drews, had been worshipped as a sun-god in esoteric Jewish sects, and now re-appears as Jesus in primitive Christianity. The twelve apostles are easily identified with the signs of the Zodiac, St John the Baptist is Aquarius, Salome is

[1] Teacher in the Technical High School at Karlsruhe from 1898.
[2] *Die Christusmythe*, vol. II, p. 225.

Andromeda, and so on. The gospels reflect the galaxy, or rather, the myths which men had projected upon the galaxy.

These theories of Drews may sound fantastic, and perhaps they are, but we can understand why his thought should move in this direction when we consider the underlying philosophy which gave it direction. Drews' philosophy was a monism in which the world is conceived as a single process with God entirely immanent within it. It may be significant that at least in its stress upon divine immanence, Drews' world-view has affinities with those of Pfleiderer and Troeltsch. For Drews, then, the life of the world is God's life, the history of humanity is divine history, the passion of humanity is the passion of God himself who in the religious consciousness of the individual suffers and dies in order to overcome. The Christian myth contains this idea of redemption through suffering, but the idea is obscured when it is attached uniquely to a particular historical person who lived at a particular time. Hence Drews thought that he was serving the cause of true religion in denying the historical Jesus and transforming him and his particular history into a mythical symbol for the universal history of the divine world-process.

41. SOME INDEPENDENT THINKERS ON THEOLOGY, HISTORY AND CULTURE
W. R. Inge, F. von Hügel, F. Heiler

The men to be considered in this section were thinkers of such originality and with such a wide range of interests that it is impossible to classify them with any precision. Yet since they were all interested in various ways in the relation of theology to the general problems of history and culture, it seems convenient to group them together at this point in our survey.

We include among them William Ralph Inge[1] (1860–1954), whose biting and pessimistic utterances about modern society caused him to be known as the 'gloomy dean'. Inge scouts the vaunted progress of a technological civilization. Not material progress but the abiding spiritual values of truth, beauty and goodness can provide a stable foundation for our society. These values, however, are grounded in a transcendent God, so that Inge pleads for a religious and even a mystical interpretation of life, having as its climax the soul's inward ascent to God.

The point of view which Inge advocates is far from being an irrationalism, or a flight from the demands of science. On the contrary, he strongly

---

[1] Professor at Cambridge, 1907–11; Dean of St Paul's Cathedral, London, 1911–34.

condemned the irrationalist tendencies of the twentieth century. Reason is important for Inge, but, like Urban, he thinks of reason in a wider sense than is customary in modern times. Modern rationalism has become one-sided, whereas a genuine rationalism has wider horizons and considers facts and values together. A genuinely rational philosophy leads us to the same destination as religion. Indeed, in Inge's view, there is in the last resort no essential difference between religion and philosophy. The mysticism of which he speaks is no emotional subjectivism, but a controlled activity of the whole personality in which reason has its place. It is, moreover, not an abnormality but a fundamental tendency of the human spirit. Mysticism is thus a kind of spiritual philosophy, while on its side philosophy, in its higher reaches, becomes a dedicated quest. Thus mysticism and philosophy converge. 'The goal of philosophy is the same as the goal of religion—perfect knowledge of the Perfect.'[1]

There is one particular chapter in the history of philosophy which, as it seemed to Inge, realizes the ideal of combining rational thinking with a religious or mystical apprehension of God. This is neo-Platonism, especially as it is found in the thought of Plotinus. According to Inge, Plotinus achieved the almost complete fusion of religion and philosophy. Inge's own attitude towards him is not only that of a student but also that of a disciple. 'I have,' he says, 'steeped myself in his writings, and I have tried not only to understand them, as one might try to understand any other intellectual system, but to take them as a guide to right living and right thinking. He must be studied as a spiritual director, a prophet and not only a thinker. We can only understand him by following him and making his experience our own.'[2]

Why should Inge, a high dignitary of the Christian Church, have spoke in such exalted, even religious terms of a pagan philosopher? The answer must be that for Inge Plotinus' thought is not just another fascinating philosophical system, but rather the classic expression of the truth after which philosophy and religion alike aspire—the truth of the reality of God and the spirit, and the way by which man may realize his oneness with God. Plotinus' thought becomes for Inge the historical manifestation of a perennial philosophy.

Plotinus, of course, stands at the end of seven centuries of Greek philosophizing, and gathers up into his system the fruits of that long period of intellectual activity. Historically his thought combined with nascent Christianity, and so passed into the fabric of Western civilization as an indispensable factor in it. Platonism, Christianity and Western

[1] *Contemporary British Philosophy*, Series I, p. 191.
[2] *The Philosophy of Plotinus*, vol. I, p. 7.

civilization are bound by such historical ties that they have become mutually interdependent. 'We cannot preserve Platonism without Christianity, or Christianity without Platonism, or civilization without both.'[1] Hence Inge sees in the philosophy of Plotinus a living system and not a dead one. When it is adapted to modern needs and blended with Christianity, it can provide a sound and rejuvenating philosophy for the Western world, delivering it from the twin errors of a shallow rationalism on the one hand and the various forms of irrationalism on the other.

Akin in some respects to Inge is Friedrich von Hügel[2] (1852–1925), an Austrian nobleman who became one of the leading Roman Catholic thinkers of his day. For a time he was closely associated with some of the Catholic Modernists[3] but he always remained essentially loyal to the Catholic faith. His wide acquaintance with the history of religion, however, gave him a remarkable tolerance. He insisted upon 'the ready recognition, by any one religion, of elements of worth variously present in the other religions, together with the careful avoidance of all attempts at forced conformity'.[4]

Baron von Hügel's analysis of Western civilization discloses three chief forces in it.[5] First, there is Hellenism, the thirst for richness and harmony; next there is Christianity, the revelation of personality and depth; then there is science, the apprehension of fact and law. All three of these elements are necessary to the fullness of human life, and although the baron's interest lies primarily in the Christian element, he freely acknowledges that it cannot do without the others. In particular, he advocated free scientific biblical criticism at a time when his own Church frowned on it.

Religion itself is the apprehension of the reality of God. If we ask how we learn about God, the answer is that he is given or revealed to us in experience, and it is clear that for the baron himself God is more real than anything else. His writing about God is indeed profoundly impressive— one understands that here religion is being described from the inside. God is an immensely rich and complex reality. Our apprehension of God always falls short of the reality, and although we must formulate doctrines about him, these can never exhaust his nature. There is mystery in God —for instance, the baron frankly admits that there is no completely satisfactory solution to the problem of sin and suffering, which are like

[1] *The Philosophy of Plotinus*, vol. II, p. 227.

[2] Born in Florence, where his father was Austrian ambassador, he came to England in 1867 and spent most of his life in that country.

[3] See below, p. 181.

[4] *Essays and Addresses on the Philosophy of Religion*, Series I, p. 66.

[5] *The Mystical Element of Religion*, vol. I, ch. 1.

dark spots in our image of God. But he is convinced that we do sufficiently apprehend God to know him as the eternally perfect reality, who is above space and time and all the imperfections of the world.

Like Inge, the baron attaches importance to the direct mystical apprehension of God, but, also like Inge, he insists on the divine transcendence. The kind of mysticism which leads to pantheism or a doctrine of pure immanence is a mistaken mysticism which has got out of touch with other elements in experience. Although God himself transcends space and time, the religion in which we apprehend him lies within the context of our life in the world. We must recognize that religion cannot become a purely spiritual activity in isolation from the other activities of mankind. 'There is no such thing for man as a complete escape from history and institutions.'[1]

Religion therefore manifests itself in historical forms—in institutions such as the Church, and in sensuous media such as rituals, sacraments and the like. In these the divine is incarnated, the transcendent reality becomes immanent in earthly forms. For the baron, the finest historical expression of the religious spirit is the institution of the Catholic Church with all the richness of its worship and symbolism, but he does not deny value to any way in which the genuine apprehension of God has historically manifested itself.

Mention may be made here also of the German thinker, Friedrich Heiler[2] (1892–). Beginning as a Roman Catholic, he became a Lutheran —not, indeed, for the sake of attaching himself to a particular denomination, but because he had become interested in the ecumenical movement in the Christian Church and believed that in the Lutheran communion he would have a better opportunity of serving the cause of Christian unity. More than that, he looks beyond the Christian Church to the spiritual bond which unites all men. This truly catholic attitude arises in turn from the historical approach to religion—an approach which reveals an underlying unity of spirit beneath all the manifold local and temporal variations in which this spirit has manifested itself.

Heiler's special contribution lies in his study of prayer. Wherever there is religion, there is prayer, and the religion of any group or of any individual may be assessed from the prayers in which it expresses itself. 'Prayer', says Heiler, 'is the central phenomenon of religion, the very hearthstone of all piety.'[3]

Heiler surveys the whole history of prayer, from its forms in primitive

[1] *Essays and Addresses*, Series I, p. 15.
[2] Professor at Marburg from 1922.
[3] *Prayer*, p. xiii.

religion to the forms in which it expresses itself in the advanced religions. Although there is such a bewildering variety of forms, there runs through them a common essence, which is, according to Heiler, 'the expression of a primitive impulsion to a higher, richer, intenser life'.[1] This is true whether the prayer is eudemonistic or ethical, whether it moves in a realm of material or spiritual values.

Heiler shows a preference for the personal, dramatic, petitionary type of prayer as over against the more reflective, contemplative type which is associated with certain philosophical and mystical attitudes. The more personal type of prayer may be, by contrast, more non-rational and unphilosophical, but it is, in Heiler's view, the genuine type of prayer. The presupposition of such prayer is threefold: that there is a personal God who may be addressed as 'thou'; that this God is present to him who prays; and that a real fellowship may be established with this God. The realizing of this fellowship is indeed the centre of prayer. 'The miracle of prayer', says Heiler, 'does not lie in the accomplishment of the prayer, in the influence of man on God, but in the mysterious contact which comes to pass between the finite and the infinite Spirit.'[2] This fellowship or communion of prayer, Heiler asserts, is not merely a psychological phenomenon but a transcendent, metaphysical reality, a direct and indubitable contact between man and God. Hence the history of prayer is not merely the story of man's quest for God, but evidence of God's presence with men.

42. REMARKS ON THE HISTORICAL AND CULTURAL APPROACHES TO RELIGION

The great merit of the historical and cultural approaches to Christian theology surveyed in this chapter is that they help to deliver us from parochialism. The Christian religion is seen in the context of the whole spiritual development of mankind. Of course, the idealists had done much the same, but whereas they had done it on the basis of a metaphysic, the writers considered here base their case on less speculative grounds, and appeal to the historical facts which are open to empirical investigation. Moreover, they approach these facts free from the prejudices which accompany the naturalistic interpretation of the evolution of religion. It is, however, unfortunate that in more recent writers, such as Barth and his followers, there has been a reaction against the broadening influences

---

[1] *Op. cit.*, p. 355.
[2] *Op. cit.*, p. 357.

of the historical approach to Christianity, and that the ideas of exclusiveness, uniqueness and the like have come back again.[1]

The immanentist approach of Pfleiderer and Troeltsch, with its criticism of the mythological ideas of special revelation and miraculous intervention in history, effectively destroys the illusion that Christianity is something out of the blue. This approach by no means impairs the value of Christianity, but rather renders it a great service. For if Christianity were something absolutely isolated, an arbitrary insertion in history, so to speak, it would be unintelligible. All religion may indeed be mysterious, but there is a difference between mystery and sheer unintelligibility. It is hard to see how anyone could ever have become a Christian at all unless Christianity is itself a part of the wider religious history of mankind—a history which is still going on.

Weiss, Schweitzer and Drews, in their diverse ways, present us with the problem which arises when it is recognized that primitive Christianity drew its concepts and imagery from the various religious, mythical and philosophical ideas current at the beginning of our era. It is true that Drews offers us a fantastic picture, dictated more by his philosophical presuppositions than by genuine historical research. It is true also—as Weiss at least admitted—that the extreme eschatological interpretation of the New Testament is an exaggerated one. Yet the general principle has been established that the earliest Christian teaching is saturated in ideas which are quite foreign to modern ways of thinking. So it might seem that if Pfleiderer and Troeltsch help to make Christianity intelligible, Weiss and Schweitzer make it unintelligible! Yet Schweitzer himself, by his philosophy of reverence for life, shows how the essential spiritual content of Christianity can be disengaged from a primitive world-view and combined with a modern one. All these writers raise the problem of what Bultmann has later taught us to call 'demythologizing'.

The last group of thinkers whom we considered—Inge, von Hügel, and Heiler—take us into the very heart of religion in their sympathetic exploration of the historical manifestations of mysticism, devotion and prayer. They write not as mere observers or historians but as participants in the great spiritual experiences which they describe. Clearly there is some danger in this. Heiler, the weakest of the three philosophically, seems to leave us, in spite of his wide historical knowledge and his psychological insight, with the very dubious assertion that the experience of prayer is of itself sufficient evidence for the existence of a personal God. Yet these writers have fulfilled Dilthey's demand that the historian must enter into his subject-matter, and one would listen more readily to

[1] For a discussion of this point, see below, p. 335.

what they say than to the amateurish descriptions of religion which emanate from those naturalists who have never themselves tuned in, so to speak, on the religious wavelength.

It is only a step from the historical and cultural approaches to religion to the sociological approach, and to this we now turn.

X

SOCIOLOGICAL INTERPRETATIONS OF RELIGION

43. RELIGION AND SOCIETY

ACCORDING to Troeltsch, sociology is the history of the present, and since Troeltsch himself was interested not only in the historical interpretation of religion but also, as we have already noted, in its social application, he may be regarded as a linking figure between the theories considered in the preceding chapter and those which we are now going to examine. Whereas history concerns itself with the description, classification and elucidation of particular series of events, sociology aims rather at establishing the general laws of man's social life. It pays attention to the structure and function of human society, to the conditions under which social changes occur, and to the interaction of the various social groupings which exert checks and pressures upon each other.

It is clear that religion must come within the purview of the sociologist, for although some forms of religion, such as the broodings of the lonely mystic, are solitary, most religions are social in their nature. The great historical religions have taken the form of religious communities or churches, and have been powerful social forces, whether for good or ill. In some societies, the religious community is virtually indistinguishable from the civil organization. In modern societies, the religious community or church is usually one association among others within the body of society as a whole. Sometimes it is more important, sometimes less so, but some account must be taken of the part which it plays in the life of the society.

While almost every theory of religion would pay some attention to its social role, what we have called the 'sociological' theories of religion make the social aspect central in their interpretation. Even when this is done, there is still a wide range of possibilities. In the extreme case, it may be held that religion is *nothing but* a social phenomenon, that the gods themselves have been invented for social ends, and that they owe their genesis to the needs of the community. This would be a kind of sociological positivism. Or again, one might be agnostic about the truth of religious beliefs, and yet hold that in fact religion is best studied as a factor in the social development of mankind. At the other extreme, one might be firmly convinced of the transcendent and revelatory character of religion, and yet believe that in practice religion consists in the application and pursuit of the social ideals which arise out of the revelation. We have already met a tendency in this direction among the Ritschlians, who found the core of the Christian revelation in the idea of the kingdom of God and who, in varying degrees, made the kingdom of God an ethical ideal for humanity.

We must therefore bring together in this chapter some very divergent points of view which nevertheless agree in assigning a paramount place to the social function of religion. The topics to be considered are: sociology and the origins of religion (Section 44); the sociological theories of Max Weber (Section 45); Marxist views of religion (Section 46); the American movement known as the 'Social Gospel' (Section 47); some critical remarks on the sociological theories in general (Section 48).

44. THE SOCIAL ORIGINS OF RELIGION
E. Durkheim

Anthropological theories about the origins of religion got a new and sociological slant from the work of the French investigator Emile Durkheim[1] (1858–1917). His views constitute not just an anthropological or sociological theory, but a complete philosophy, known as 'sociological positivism'. The idea of society stands at the centre of this philosophy, and supplies the key for the understanding of philosophical problems. Truth and falsehood are objective in so far as they express collective and not individual thought. Even the laws of logic reflect the needs of civilized society, as we can see from the absence of such laws in the mythological mentality of primitive peoples. Society itself is not just the sum of the individuals included in it, but a peculiar kind of entity which is the source of constraints governing the thought and behaviour of its members.

Durkheim devoted special attention to the subject of religion in his social philosophy. The character of primitive religion, he believed, is best seen not in animism but in totemism, which Durkheim supposed to be a more fundamental and primitive form of religion. Totemism is certainly a widespread phenomenon, found in such widely separated groups as the

---

[1] Lecturer, 1887–96, then professor, 1897–1906, at Bordeaux; professor at Paris, 1906–17.

ancient Semites, the North American tribes, and the Australian aborigines, of whom Durkheim made a special study.

The totem—usually a species of animal, sometimes a kind of plant, rarely an inanimate object—stands in a peculiar relationship to a particular social group, normally a tribe or clan. According to Durkheim, the totem is for this group the type of the sacred, and the basis for the distinction of sacred and profane, which he takes to be the essence of religion. Usually the totem may not be killed or eaten except on special ceremonial occasions which may be followed by a period of mourning. There may also be some kind of sacramental communion with the life-principle of the totem. In some way, the life of the totem represents the life of the society itself, whose members occasionally regard themselves as descended from the totem.

Taking totemism as the type of religion, Durkheim concludes that religion is to be understood as a social phenomenon. 'When it is understood that above the individual there is society, and that this is not a nominal being created by reason but a system of active forces, a new manner of explaining men becomes possible.'[1] Religion serves the needs of the society in which it is practised, and the object of its cult, concealed under the figures of its particular mythology, is the society itself.

Durkheim rightly points out that earlier theories of primitive religion suffered from the defect of a one-sided concentration upon religious *belief*, whereas his own theory regards religion primarily from the point of view of *action*. For this reason he can claim that there is something eternal in religion, for although particular beliefs become outworn, any society must from time to time reaffirm itself, and such reaffirmation is essentially religious. Indeed, religion and society are so closely interwoven that religion is regarded as the matrix out of which other human activities, including science, have grown. Religion is by no means discredited by science, but it must always be looking for more adequate symbols in order to express its realities. In modern times we have come to understand that the ideas of divinity and of society are at bottom the same. So far, no new religion of humanity has displaced the traditional religion, but this may happen in due course. 'There are no gospels which are immortal, but neither is there any reason for believing that humanity is incapable of inventing new ones.'[2]

[1] *Elementary Forms of the Religious Life*, p. 447.   [2] *Op. cit.*, p. 428.

45. RELIGION AND CAPITALISM
M. Weber

The sociology of religion was specially studied by the German scholar, Max Weber[1] (1864–1920), a friend of Troeltsch.

Weber's aim was to exhibit the correlation in any given society between religious beliefs and social institutions. He contended that religious beliefs are much more closely linked with social development than we commonly recognize, and he illustrated his thesis by making a detailed study of the relation between Protestantism—especially in its Calvinist form—and the capitalist society which has arisen in the Western world.

The capitalism of the West, with its vast industrial empires and its widespread commercial enterprises, is unique in the world. Its rise cannot therefore be attributed solely to the acquisitive instinct which is universal among mankind. Moreover, modern capitalism breaks with the earlier tradition of the West, and erects what were once considered vices into accepted and respectable practices. How then are we to account for its rise?

Weber begins from certain empirically ascertainable facts. He notes, for instance, that in a mixed country like Germany the leaders of industry are overwhelmingly Protestant, and that English, Dutch and American Puritans have been the leading spirits in commercial enterprise. These facts are explained with reference to the change of beliefs which came about at the Reformation. The other-worldly asceticism of the medieval Church, expressing itself in the monastic life, was replaced by a this-worldly asceticism which is essential to capitalism. The Calvinist believed in a doctrine of election, and he assured himself of his own election by a life of self-control. 'The end of this asceticism was to be able to lead an alert intelligent life.'[2] It was to be a life not of impulsive enjoyment but of rational discipline, yet, in contrast to the monastic ideal, it was to be a life of discipline in the midst of worldly activity. Hence the Calvinist had a duty to his money, and must labour for its increase. A man's worldly calling becomes an exercise in ascetic virtue in which he must by his care and conscientiousness prove his state of grace.

Of course, Calvin himself had no prevision of this development of his doctrine, and Weber explicitly disclaims any intention of pronouncing on the *religious* worth of the Reformation. Also he disclaims any intention of showing that Protestantism *alone* is the root of capitalism. Yet he certainly

[1] Professor at Freiburg, 1894–97; Heidelberg, 1897–1903; Munich, 1919–20.
[2] *The Protestant Ethic and the Spirit of Capitalism*, p. 119.

maintains that the connection between Protestantism and capitalism is far closer and more potent than had been suspected.

Weber's method is, of course, applicable beyond this particular case, and he himself did in fact apply it to other situations, for instance, to Confucianism in Chinese society. If his approach is a valid one, then the sociology of religion becomes an important matter. Our whole social structure may be profoundly, if covertly, influenced by religious ideas, and indeed religious beliefs and social institutions may be correlative expressions of a single underlying attitude of mind.

46. RELIGION AND COMMUNISM
A. Kalthoff, K. Kautsky, V. I. Lenin

Like Weber, the Marxists think of religion in close association with the economic structure of society, but in a very different way. For whereas Weber traces the influence of religious ideas upon the economic system, the Marxists regard religion as simply a by-product of economic conditions; and whereas Weber does not pronounce on the value of religious ideas as such, the orthodox Marxist is hostile to religion.

Albert Kalthoff[1] (1850–1906) was a Lutheran pastor in an industrial city where he came under the influence of Marxist ideas. He came to advocate a new kind of Christ-myth theory, and his rejection of the historical Jesus was made explicitly on sociological grounds. 'To anyone who has learned to think sociologically, and to take account of the transitions, transformations and involutions which attend the rise of new forms of society, the idea that a suddenly converted Paul could in the space of twenty years have saturated Asia Minor and the Balkan peninsula with Christian societies by preaching as the Christ a Jesus hitherto unknown in these districts is a prodigy, alongside which all the miracles of the Church must look like child's play.'[2]

Kalthoff was not, of course, the first to appreciate the difficulty of accounting for a widespread Christian society in terms of an obscure historical figure who had lived in Palestine only a short time previously. The novelty of his view is that he looks for the origins of Christianity not in the philosophies and mythologies current at that time, but in social movements capable of giving rise to the new Christian society. He shifts the birthplace of Christianity from Palestine to Rome. There, he tells us, revolutionary forces and communistic ideas were at work among the

---

[1] Pastor in Bremen, and later an adherent of Haeckel's monism.
[2] *Dies Enstehung des Christentums*, pp. 25-6.

slaves and the oppressed masses. There was an important Jewish element in the proletariat, and this Jewish element contributed not only communistic ideas but also the apocalyptic hope of a Messiah and a good time coming.

Out of this ferment of social movements with a religious colouring arose Christianity, and its organization was to some extent ready-made in the communistic groups among the masses. Christ himself was the ideal hero of the new society, the mythical personification of its aspirations. The stories of his death and resurrection depict the struggling community's own experiences of persecution and renewal, while the belief in his coming gave hope for the future.

While Kalthoff rejected both the orthodox and the liberal interpretations of Christianity, he speaks of a Christianity which is claimed to be greater than either of them—'the secularized Christianity of the future'.[1] The Christ of this secularized Christianity is also a Christ of the future. He is not the Christ of the past, the Christ of the scholars or the Christ of the theologians, but the people's Christ, the Christ of the ordinary man who strives and suffers, the Christ who embodies the simplest and most natural and therefore divinest aspirations of the masses of humanity.

A similar view of Christian origins was expressed by the German socialist leader, Karl Kautsky (1854–1938). Although a devout Marxist—he had been private secretary to Engels and was editor of the works of Marx—even he could not stomach the excesses of Bolshevism, and he quarrelled bitterly with Lenin. Kautsky stood for a democratic as against a dictatorial socialism, and for this reason Lenin says about him that 'Kautsky beat the world record in the liberal distortion of Marx.'[2] Indeed, from the orthodox Marxist point of view, it is said that 'every phrase Kautsky utters is a bottomless pit of apostasy'.[3]

Nevertheless, as far as his writings on Christianity are concerned, Kautsky might seem to the unprejudiced observer to have succeeded fairly well in applying Marxist principles to the interpretation of Christianity. His aim, as he tells us, is to contribute 'to an understanding of those phases of Christianity which appear most essential from the standpoint of the materialistic conception of history'.[4] This conception of history looks to economic conditions for the explanation of events, whereas the traditional conception of history is said to have looked for the causes of events in abstract ideas and ethical aspirations. Further, Kautsky claims

[1] *Op. cit.*, p. 153.

[2] 'The Proletarian Revolution and the Renegade Kautsky' in *Marx, Engels, Marxism*, p. 452.

[3] *Op. cit.*, p. 450.   [4] *Foundations of Christianity*, p. 8.

that since he himself has been actively engaged in the struggle of the proletariat against the privileged classes, he may be in a better position than the professional scholar to understand the beginnings of Christianity, which he regarded as essentially a social movement among the impoverished classes.

Kautsky's account of the origins of Christianity resembles Kalthoff's in its main outlines, and we need not linger over points of detail. Christianity was not the work of an individual, but had its genesis in proletarian social movements, and particularly in the fusion of communistic and messianic ideas. But Christianity as we know it today is the reverse of the original Christianity, and its successes have been due to the fact that the original Christianity became transformed into its opposite. 'In its victorious course, the proletarian, beneficial, communistic organization became transformed into the most tremendous instrument of domination and exploitation in the world.'[1]

Such transformations are the rule in the dialectical process of history. Like the crucified Messiah, Caesar and Napoleon had their origin in democratic victories, and all ended by enslaving their own supporters. In the dialectic of history, every new struggle is different from the preceding ones, and so Kautsky does not share Kalthoff's sympathy for a secularized Christianity. We have to recognize that Christianity is now an obstacle in the way of the proletariat, and present-day socialism, in its different situation, must use different methods and aim at different results.

Since neither Kalthoff nor Kautsky can be considered an orthodox Marxist, we must turn for the unadulterated communist teaching about religion to Vladimir Ilyich Lenin (1870–1924), because Lenin has become in the eyes of the faithful the authoritative interpreter of Marx, and the Marxist-Leninist line is now upheld with a rigidity comparable to that which attaches to the dogma of the Roman Catholic Church or to the fundamentalism of some Protestant sects.

In a brief statement of the essence of Marxism, Lenin names as its first principle *materialism*, which he describes as 'the only philosophy that is consistent, true to all the teachings of natural science and hostile to superstition, cant, and so forth'.[2] This basic materialism is combined with the Hegelian idea of the *dialectic*, whereby the clash of thesis and antithesis gives rise to a synthesis which in turn becomes the thesis of a new opposition. Thus matter is not static, but eternally developing. This materialist

[1] *Op. cit.*, p. 381.
[2] 'The Three Sources and Three Component Parts of Marxism' in *Marx, Engels, Marxism*, p. 78.

philosophy is extended from nature to human society so as to become a *historical materialism*. History is to be understood in terms of *economic forces*, and its core is the *class struggle*. Man's 'various views and doctrines—philosophical, religious, political and so forth—reflect the *economic system* of society'.[1]

The Marxist attitude to religion is already implied in this summary, and it is stated more explicitly by Lenin elsewhere.[2] In the first place, religion is false, for its beliefs contradict the materialism on which Marxism is founded—'a materialism which is absolutely atheistic and resolutely hostile to all religion'. In the second place, religion is explained as a social organ which defends the interest of the ruling class in the present state of society—'all modern religions are instruments of bourgeois reaction that serve to defend exploitation and to drug the working class'.

There can be no question of any renovation of religion, or the replacement of traditional religions by a new religion, nor is socialism itself a religion. On the other hand, the struggle against religion must not be allowed to obscure the more fundamental struggle against capitalism, and must be subordinate to it; for, as we have seen, religion itself is simply a by-product of the basic economic factors at work in society, and it cannot be eradicated until society itself is transformed. Education can help to weaken religion, but in the end the dialectic process is itself the best educator. When the classless society is attained, religion will disappear because the social and economic conditions which give rise to religion will have been eliminated.

47. THE SOCIAL GOSPEL IN AMERICA
W. Gladden, W. Rauschenbusch, S. Mathews

In the early part of the century the social application of Christianity became a primary concern with some American churchmen, and we find in that country a definite movement known as the 'Social Gospel'. H. Richard Niebuhr has pointed out[3] that the idea of the kingdom of God has always been central to American Christianity, but in modern times it has been identified with a kingdom on earth, a social order. No doubt many causes contributed towards this identification—the general tendency of our times to secularize ideas, the social problems which immigration had created in the United States, the nationalist sentiment of America as the

---

[1] *Loc. cit.*, p. 79.
[2] See, *e.g.*, 'The Attitude of the Workers' Party towards Religion', *op. cit.*, pp. 273ff.
[3] In his book, *The Kingdom of God in America*.

young and coming country, the influence of Ritschlian ideas,[1] and so on. The three representative theologians whom we shall briefly consider show us different phases of the Social Gospel.

Washington Gladden[2] (1836–1918) thinks in social categories but retains a strong evangelical faith. Thus, in an essay on atonement,[3] he stresses social redemption: 'As the sin that separates us from God weakens the social bond and gives us on earth the substance of hell, so the love that brings us back to God restores the social bond and gives us on earth the substance of heaven.' Yet he also insists that 'the method of reconciliation is revelation', that the death of Christ is a judgment on human sinfulness, and that it is the 'saving work' of God in Christ that will bring social transformation. Again, while the kingdom of God is conceived as an earthly society—'that kingdom that we find, here on the earth, steadily widening its borders and strengthening its dominion'—he insists that this kingdom 'can be traced as directly to Jesus Christ as the St Lawrence River can be traced to its source in the mighty inland sea'.[4] Rejection of an other-worldly interpretation of Christianity does not mean for Gladden any denial of its supernatural character.

The kingdom of God includes all society and is a wider conception than the Church, which is ancillary to it. Yet the Church has an important function to perform. 'The problem is to make all life religious; but in order that it may become so, associations are needed whose function it shall be to cultivate religious ideas and feelings.'[5] The function of the Church is to be the spearhead, as it were, of the kingdom of God in the Christianization of society. It performs this function partly in its own life by ensuring that rich and poor come together within its fellowship and learn to care for each other. Just as the early Church reconciled Jews and Gentiles, so, Gladden hopes, it can still reconcile the labouring and capitalist classes. But partly the Church performs its function by being turned outwards upon society at large—and Gladden gave a practical example of this by serving on the city council and advocating his reforming ideals.

How did he conceive a Christian society? On the one hand, he strongly opposed any alliance of the Church with the privileged classes, and with what he regarded as 'predatory' wealth. In 1905, when the Congregational Church was offered a large sum of money for its missionary work by an oil corporation, Gladden called it 'tainted money', and declared that

---

[1] See above, p. 91.   [2] Congregational pastor at Columbus, Ohio, 1882–1914.
[3] In the symposium *The Atonement in Modern Religious Thought*, pp. 225–37.
[4] See 'Where is the Kingdom of God?', in *Burning Questions*, pp. 243ff.
[5] *The Christian Pastor*, p. 42.

if the Church accepts such money, she ought to perish with it. It has to be recorded that in spite of his protests, the Church took the money! On the other hand, Gladden does not think of a Christian society as communistic or egalitarian. Christianity does not abolish the natural differences between men, or the inequality of conditions or possessions, but it does bring them into a harmonious and reconciled society in which each helps the other.

Walter Rauschenbusch[1] (1861–1918) commits himself to a more radical political attitude. He can even quote Kautsky with approval. Whereas Gladden thought of the Church as embracing and reconciling all classes of society, Rauschenbusch advocates an alliance between the Church and the working class. Ameliorative measures and piecemeal reforms cannot bridge the cleavage in modern society between labour and capital, and if we are in earnest about overcoming the evils of industrial society we cannot, he argues, stop short of socialism. A socialist solution, he declares, 'should be hailed with joy by every patriot and Christian'.[2]

The original and essential purpose of Christianity, Rauschenbusch believed, was to transform human society into the kingdom of God by regenerating and reconstituting human relations. For various reasons, this fundamental purpose has always been bypassed or thwarted. In earliest Christianity, the disciples looked for the immediate return of Christ and were indifferent to a transitory world. Under the Roman Empire, there was no opportunity for social propaganda. Later, other influences supervened to divert the Church from its social purpose—monastic otherworldliness on the one hand, dogmatic and ecclesiastical concerns on the other. The sociological interpretation of Christianity has had a long time to wait, but now, according to Rauschenbusch, with the passing of older concerns and the rise of the urgent problems of modern industrial society, the time has come for the Church to turn to the long neglected social problem and so to carry out what he calls 'the fundamental purpose of its existence'.

Rauschenbusch himself attempted to restate Christian theology in detail from his sociological point of view. As we might expect, such a theology 'must not only make room for the doctrine of the kingdom of God, but give it a central place and revise all other doctrines so that they will articulate organically with it'.[3] Rauschenbusch points out that theologians have usually made one doctrine or another central in their schemes—St Athanasius did so with the incarnation, Martin Luther with justification

---

[1] Professor at Rochester Theological Seminary, 1897–1918.
[2] *Christianity and the Social Crisis*, p. 408.
[3] *A Theology for the Social Gospel*, p. 131.

by faith, Jonathan Edwards with the sovereignty of God. To give this central position to the kingdom of God is, it is claimed, to return to Jesus' own way of looking at things. The doctrine of the kingdom just is the social gospel, though it has been neglected for centuries and subordinated to churchly concerns. Yet although Rauschenbusch gives a this-worldly turn to Christian theology, he still retains, like Gladden, an evangelical faith and insists on the supernatural character of the kingdom. 'The kingdom of God is divine in its origin, progress and consummation; it is miraculous all the way, and is the continuous revelation of the power, the righteousness and the love of God.'[1]

We find a different formulation of the Social Gospel teaching in the writings of Shailer Mathews[2] (1863–1941), a leading representative of the Chicago school of theology. The prophetic evangelical faith which Gladden and Rauschenbusch retained as the background to their social teaching is replaced by a sophisticated evolutionary theology; though we may notice that politically Mathews was less extreme than Rauschen-busch, and preferred an enlightened capitalism to socialism.

'By the kingdom of God', says Mathews, 'Jesus meant an ideal social order in which the relation of men to God is that of sons, and to each other that of brothers.'[3] The individual human being is incomplete in himself and demands social union. Such union is possible for men not only with each other but also with God, and in teaching the fatherhood of God, Jesus meant to indicate a kinship between God and man. This kinship makes possible the social or personal relation of man to God, and this relation, in turn, works a moral change in man, just as intercourse between two friends might do on the level of ordinary human social relations. The relation with the divine life becomes the basis for progress in human relations towards the social ideal of brotherhood. Jesus himself is the decisive expression and exemplification of these relations.

Mathews sees in all religion the same kind of pattern of social relation-ships that we have noted as characterizing the kingdom of God. Religion is social behaviour in which men seek to extend the kind of relations that they have with each other to forces in the cosmic environment, in the hope of gaining help from such forces. The idea of God arises in this behaviour, and is not therefore a metaphysical absolute but an idea which changes with social advance. 'The meaning of the word "God" is found in the history of its usage in religious behaviour.'[4] This does not mean that God is merely the name for human ideals. God is a cosmic reality, and, as we

---

[1] *Op. cit.*, p. 139.
[2] Professor at Colby University, Maine, 1887–94; Chicago, 1894–1933.
[3] *The Social Teaching of Jesus*, p. 54.   [4] *The Growth of the Idea of God*, p. 210.

have seen from Mathews' teaching on the kingdom of God, the right ordering of human society itself depends on its relation to the cosmic reality of God. On the other hand, we can talk about God only in terms drawn from human social experience, as when we call him 'King', 'Judge', 'Father' and the like.

The traditional theistic idea of God as sovereign with men as his subjects is no longer acceptable. Mathews thinks of God in immanent terms as the power in the universe which brings forth personality, and so as the personally responsive element in the environment with which we are organically related. We can have a personal and social relation with this God, but it is a relation of co-operation rather than of subjection. So the idea of God is made both contemporary and democratic, though it should be mentioned that Mathews did not think that one can find a democratic pattern for the interpretation of atonement.

Some of the more sophisticated items in Mathews' modernist outlook may seem to us at first sight far removed from Jesus' preaching of the kingdom of God, but Mathews would say that they express in contemporary terms the same essential truths. To have a proper 'personal adjustment' to 'those cosmic activities which we know as God', to be 'fellow-workers in the process', entails a proper adjustment to our fellow-men and forwards the realization of the ideal society. 'We must live in harmony with our neighbor as truly as with God.'[1]

48. CRITICAL REMARKS ON THE SOCIOLOGICAL INTERPRETATIONS OF RELIGION

It is evident from the theories which we have just examined that religion is always deeply intertwined with numerous social factors, and that no account of religion which omitted the sociological aspect could be complete. Yet apart from this rather obvious truth, we get no clear guidance, for there are too many serious conflicts among the views we have considered. In particular, we have not been given any single convincing answer to the question of what precisely is the relation of a religion to the society in which it is practised.

Can religious beliefs play a major part in giving rise to an economic system (Weber) or does the economic system give rise to religion as a kind of by-product (Lenin)? Did Christianity initiate a social movement

---

[1] *Contributions of Science to Religion*, p. 414.

(Gladden, Rauschenbusch) or did it arise out of social movements (Kalthoff, Kautsky)? We should notice that these questions do not imply an absolute disjunction. It could be the case that religion, economics, and other social factors besides act and react upon each other, each in various ways moulding the others and being moulded by them. Or it could be the case that in any given society, religion and economics, for instance, each reflects a single underlying attitude. This is the kind of view which we met in Spengler when discussing the philosophies of culture, and on the face of it, it has more plausibility than the one-sided accounts of Weber or Lenin.

Again, are we to follow Kalthoff when he advocates the secularizing of religion, or Gladden when he urges us to make all life religious? These look like diametrically opposite points of view, but it is doubtful if they are. Both of them aim to wipe out the dividing line between the sacred and the secular, and when this distinction is obliterated, it seems to make little practical difference whether we talk about secularizing religion or hallowing all life. At any rate, the difference would seem to lie outside the scope of sociology.

This brings us to the question of the adequacy of sociological interpretations of religion. Only some of the views which we have considered go so far as to claim that religion is nothing but a social phenomenon, and that the sociological account of religion is a complete one. We found the best statement of this view in Durkheim's sociological positivism, which identifies the ideas of divinity and society. What degree of probability attaches to his account?

In recognizing religion as a social activity, Durkheim certainly supplements a deficiency in some of the earlier anthropological accounts, which had concentrated on religious beliefs. But Durkheim's general thesis derives its plausibility from the key place which he gives to totemism as the type of religion, and totemism simply will not fulfil this role. In the first place, totemism is not, as Durkheim supposed, really primitive—it has, as Freud recognized, a history of more primitive ideas behind it. In the second place, totemism is much less universal than religion, and cannot serve as the type of all religion. And it is significant that it is precisely among some of the most backward people, such as Bushmen, that totemism is absent. In the third place, most investigators now recognize totemism as being primarily not a religious phenomenon but—as Durkheim showed—a social one. But when the foundation-stone of totemism is withdrawn, Durkheim's argument for the identity of the ideas of divinity and society collapses.

We conclude that religion has its important social aspects, but that no good case has been made out for the view that religion is entirely explicable as a social phenomenon. In the course of this chapter, from Durkheim to Mathews, we have repeatedly met with the idea that the essence of religion is activity rather than belief, and we turn now to philosophies of life and action.

XI

PRAGMATISM AND ALLIED VIEWS

49. Thought and Action

WHILE twentieth-century schools of thought have in general shown a reaction against the imposing metaphysical systems of the past, this has in some cases become a reaction against all intellectualism. The philosopher, it is maintained, gets his best clue not in the abstract conceptions of thought but in living, striving and willing, and sometimes in instinct and intuition. We have already noted the increasing stress upon action in some of the historical and sociological thinkers whom we have been examining. Earlier, we have met scattered pointers in the same direction among such diverse thinkers as Royce, Eucken, Ward and Vaihinger. Back in the nineteenth century, Schopenhauer and Nietzsche upheld the primacy of the will. Now we turn to some twentieth-century philosophers who base their case on life and action.

Various names are applied to such philosophies. 'Vitalism' takes 'life' as its central idea, and understands 'life' as something *sui generis*, wider than 'thought' and not, on the other hand, explicable in terms of physics and chemistry. 'Activism' takes 'action' as its central idea, and assigns to this idea a very broad meaning. 'Pragmatism' and the related 'instrumentalism' apply the notion of practical utility to the problems of truth and logic themselves.

All of these views have certain basic features in common. They unite in subordinating theory to practice, or thought to action, and in attacking what they call 'intellectualism'. They are radically empiricist in outlook, and found their views not upon *a priori* conceptions but upon lived experience. They reject equally the idealist and mechanistic pictures of the world as abstract and intellectualized conceptions which distort the dynamic reality. We may, if we wish, call some of these philosophies 'naturalistic', but their naturalism is not the mechanistic variety current in the nineteenth century, but a view of nature as a flux of becoming. The key natural science is biology. Although there are differences of emphasis, the biological approach is fundamental. Comparing Bergson's vitalism and James' pragmatism, R. B. Perry has well said that 'the difference between Bergson and James is the difference between a psychological biology and a biological psychology'.[1]

Religion, according to the philosophers whom we have in view, is to be understood primarily in terms of activity, and its justification, if it has one, must be practical rather than theoretical. It is not a matter of mere belief, if by 'belief' we mean intellectual assent to a view of the universe. Yet we must notice also that some of these philosophers, in spite of their opposition to intellectualism, permitted themselves such speculations about God and ultimate reality as they believed compatible with their empiricist principles, and they were not positivists as was, let us say, Vaihinger, whose philosophy had a good deal in common with pragmatism and vitalism. Indeed, the views of religion entertained by vitalists and pragmatists had considerable attraction for theologians, and we find theological counterparts for the philosophers, especially in the 'Modernist' movement which arose in the Roman Catholic Church and provoked a crisis towards the end of the first decade of the century.

The present chapter will take account of the vitalism of Bergson (Section 50); the activism of Blondel (Section 51); the pragmatism of some American philosophers (Section 52); the influence of these views on Roman Catholic Modernism (Section 53) and on Protestant theology (Section 54). Some critical remarks will follow (Section 55).

50. VITALISM
H. Bergson

Henri Bergson[2] (1859–1941) achieved fame through a philosophy which, though naturalistic in its approach and appealing to science for its evidence, utterly rejected the mechanistic and deterministic interpretation of the world, which had customarily been given by naturalistic philosophies in the nineteenth century. Such philosophies illustrate a mistaken intellectualism. They have conceptualized reality, and in so doing, they have killed it and made it static. Bergson asks us to look instead at what is immediately given in experience. The characteristic mark of consciousness is *duration*. Whereas the time of physical science has been, as Bergson expresses it, 'spatialized', that is to say, broken up into a series of discreet points or instants, the duration which we immediately

---

[1] *Philosophy of the Recent Past*, p. 186.
[2] Professor at the Collège de France, 1900–24.

apprehend in consciousness is a continuous indivisible becoming. To quote one of Bergson's favourite comparisons, 'the mechanism of our ordinary knowledge is of a cinematographical kind'.[1] This means that in the spatialized time apprehended by the intellect, the world is represented as a rapid series of static pictures, and this in turn conduces to a deterministic view. On the other hand, the time of duration, apprehended by the immediate intuition of consciousness, has genuine unbroken movement, and since this implies an element of novelty and creativity, it makes possible free-will and spontaneity.

The distinction between *intellect* and *intuition* is fundamental in Bergson's thought. The intellect is practical in its nature, and enables us to handle experience. It breaks up experience into fragmentary elements which it conceptualizes, fixes, isolates, quantifies, measures. This procedure helps us to solve our practical problems, but it does not give us a true picture of the world, but rather 'a translation in terms of inertia'.[2] Intuition, on the other hand, is connected with instinct, and the essence of instinct is sympathy. Whereas the intellect looks at life from the outside, instinct shares in life. In the animal kingdom, the two principal lines of development have culminated in the instinct of arthropods and the intelligence of vertebrates. For practical purposes, the intellect has proved itself to be the more flexible instrument, but it would be the sympathy of instinct that could take us into the inwardness of life. 'If this sympathy could extend its object and also reflect upon itself, it would give us the key to vital operations.'[3] In man, a kind of nebulous fringe of instinct surrounds the luminous centre of intelligence, and because of the development of intellect, this fringe of instinct is no longer riveted to practical interests. It can become intuition, by which is meant 'instinct that has become disinterested, self-conscious, capable of reflecting upon its object and of enlarging it indefinitely'. This intuition gives access to the living reality which the intellect has broken up and made static, and 'by the sympathetic communication which it establishes between us and the rest of the living, by the expansion of our consciousness which it brings about, it introduces us into life's own domain, which is reciprocal interpenetration, endlessly continued creation'.[4]

The reality thus disclosed to us is a dynamic, creative, continuous becoming, a vital impetus (*élan vital*). In the evolutionary process we see the positive striving of the vital impetus. Sometimes it becomes petrified in torpor, as in species that have played for safety and remained static for long ages. Sometimes it sweeps forward. Always it is striving to overcome

[1] *Creative Evolution*, p. 323.   [2] *Op. cit.*, p. 186.
[3] *Op. cit.*, p. 186.   [4] *Op. cit.*, pp. 186–7.

the drag of inert matter. This may sound like dualism, but matter itself is regarded as a kind of by-product of the vital impetus. This creative life-force is the God of Bergson's philosophy. 'God, thus defined, has nothing of the already made; he is unceasing life, action, freedom. Creation, so conceived, is not a mystery; we experience it in ourselves when we act freely.'[1]

Bergson thinks that we act most freely and creatively in such spiritual activities as morality and religion. In his special study of these topics,[2] he again employs the distinction, by now familiar to us, between the static and the dynamic. He begins with morality, and finds that there are two types. One type is *closed* or static morality, and this is the morality of social obligation, arising from one's station within a given society. It is the morality of habit and custom and follows a set pattern. Yet one cannot look around the world without seeing that as well as the morality of social pressure, there is a morality of aspiration. This is *open* or dynamic morality. It is not dictated by social requirements but is a spontaneous striving for an ideal good. We see it, for instance, when someone performs a good action which goes beyond what is required of him by the moral code of his society. Such have been the moral heroes of humanity—men who have entered the very stream of the vital impetus and drawn from it a creative energy by which they have passed beyond the confines of a closed morality. Ordinary men may seek to follow the moral geniuses, but there is no compulsion here—only an appeal to which men may freely respond. Yet inertia operates at this level also, and in course of time the free, open morality, which originated in the vision of a gifted individual, may be reduced to a set of rules and become a new static morality.

Closed morality belongs to a particular society, while open morality broadens out to embrace all mankind. How is this possible? Bergson points out the gulf which lies between even the largest social group and all mankind, and he turns to religion to find a way of bridging it.

There are two types of religion also. *Closed* religion, the religion of myth and ritual, is a defensive social mechanism. With intelligence, there arise egoistic tendencies which might lead to the disruption of society. The religion of the group is there to prevent this. The gods of the city forbid, threaten and punish, and so maintain the social fabric. There is also, however, an *open* or dynamic type of religion. The religious genius breaks away from the mythical cults and enters the vital impetus, the absolute energy of creation, the spring of life and love which is God. This he does not through the intellect but through that aura of intuition, which, as we have seen, is supposed to remain with man. Open religion may fall back

[1] *Op. cit.*, p. 262.   [2] See his book, *The Two Sources of Morality and Religion*.

into the closed type and be tied down in dogma and legalism, but ideally it is free and spontaneous, and culminates in the mystical union of the soul with God. This supreme religious insight enables us to apprehend 'the essential function of the universe, which is a machine for the making of gods'.[1]

51. ACTIVISM
M. Blondel

Like Baron von Hügel, Maurice Blondel[2] (1861–1949) was a distinguished lay philosopher of the Roman Catholic Church, associated with the Modernist movement. Yet although his writings undoubtedly influenced this movement, he himself, like the baron, remained essentially loyal to Catholic teaching. He still has his followers in Catholic circles among those who pursue a neo-Augustinian rather than a neo-Thomist tendency.

Blondel agrees with Bergson in conceiving the real in dynamic terms, but his philosophy does not have the naturalistic flavour that belongs to Bergson's. Blondel's central conception is not 'life' but 'action', and for this reason his thought may be conveniently designated 'activism'. It should, however, be noted that it is not the *idea* of action which is the starting-point of Blondel's philosophy, but action itself in its concreteness. The philosopher does not cease to be human, and his speculations cannot replace direct experience of life. 'It is a question of the whole man, and it is not only in thought that one must look for man. We must transport the centre of philosophy to action, for there we also find the centre of life.'[3]

Action itself gives rise to the philosophical quest, for we cannot avoid the question about the meaning of our action. In language which anticipates the existentialists of a later time, Blondel points out that we are always in the midst of action and that we cannot help engaging ourselves in action, although we do not know who we are or even whether we are, and although we have not chosen to live. He rejects any negative solution to the problem of action on the grounds that to affirm nothing is at the same time to affirm being. To conceive 'nothing', one must begin by affirming something positive and then denying it; and to aspire to 'nothing', one must find in this idea a peculiar satisfaction which gives it a

---

[1] *Op. cit.*, p. 275.
[2] After holding academic posts at Montauban and Lille, he was professor at Aix-en-Provence from 1896 until retirement.
[3] *L'Action*, p. xxiii.

positive character. Nihilists and pessimists get involved in insoluble contradictions, and cannot prevent positive ideas and desires from coming to the surface. The nothing is their all. 'What they deny reveals the greatness of what they wish.'[1] Thus it is maintained that the problem of action cannot have anything but a positive solution.

Blondel seeks this solution by means of a dialectic, the terms of which are drawn not from thought but from action itself. The basis of the dialectic is the contrast between action and its realization. This contrast constitutes the permanent dissatisfaction of human life, and provides the incentive to further action. In the endeavour to close the gap, as it were, action may be seen as expanding in ever-widening circles, from self-regarding action through various forms of social action to the highest moral action which has regard to all humanity. In this process, we see the partial solution of the contrast of action and realization, and its incessant reappearance at each stage, and it becomes clear that the contrast cannot be overcome within the natural order. Thus man is directed from the natural to the supernatural by the demands of action itself. Here we may note the affinity between Blondel's views and St Augustine's reflections on man's restless quest for God. In a sense, therefore, God is already immanent in us. 'To will all that we will is to place the being and action of God within us.'[2] Yet God is also transcendent. There is a discontinuity between the natural and the supernatural orders. We do not produce God but receive him, the tendency of action towards God is met by God's movement towards us, and human action is supplemented by grace and revelation.

We apprehend God not by thought but by action. 'At the moment when we seem to touch God by a stroke of thought, he escapes, unless we hold him and seek him in action. Wherever we stop, he is not; wherever we move, he is. To think of God is an action.'[3] Yet it is clear that for Blondel 'action' is not mere will or a blind urge. It is, as he says himself, the activity of the whole man, and includes thought. The kind of thought which he criticizes is an abstract intellectualism. In his later writings he makes more room for thought, but maintains that rational arguments for theism are possible only on the basis of a positive affirmation of God which belongs to our nature as active beings. Thus action is the key to the understanding of ourselves, the world, and God.

[1] *Op. cit.*, p. 34.   [2] *Op. cit.*, p. 491.   [3] *Op. cit.*, p. 352.

52. PRAGMATISM
C. S. Peirce, W. James, J. Dewey

Charles Sanders Peirce[1] (1839–1914) was one of those philosophers who get neglected for most of their lives and only subsequently attain to fame. He is nowadays chiefly esteemed for his work in logic, but William James hailed him as the father of pragmatism. Peirce was not unduly flattered by this compliment, and later, to differentiate his position from that of James, he called his own views 'pragmaticism'.

In a subsequently famous paper entitled 'How to Make our Ideas Clear', Peirce sets out his pragmatic view of meaning, and shows how it can be used for the clarification of our thought. 'The whole function of thought', he tells us, 'is to produce habits of action.' Thus 'it is absurd to say that thought has any meaning unrelated to its only function'. Again, he says: 'We come down to what is conceivably practical, as the root of every real distinction of thought, no matter how subtle it may be; and there is no distinction of meaning so fine as to consist in anything but a possible difference of practice.' Hence, if we want to get our meanings clear, we are advised to 'consider what effects, that might conceivably have practical bearings, we conceive the object of our conception to have'.[2]

A belief, according to Peirce, is a rule for action, and its essence is the establishment of a habit. It follows that 'different beliefs are distinguished by the different modes of action to which they give rise'.[3] If we find two persons arguing about beliefs between which there is no difference that can be practically determined, we must conclude that such persons, although they do not recognize it, are really in agreement about their beliefs, and differ only in the manner in which they express the same belief, or in their emotional relation to a particular expression. Peirce illustrates what he has in mind from the dispute between Catholics and Protestants over transubstantiation. What practical difference is there between wine and something which has all the sensible effects of wine but is said to be really blood? 'It is foolish for Catholics and Protestants to fancy themselves in disagreement about the elements of the sacrament, if they agree in regard to all their sensible effects, here and hereafter.'[4]

This pragmatic theory of meaning might seem to cut away the ground

---

[1] He spent most of his life in government service, and only once for a short time held an academic post.

[2] *The Philosophy of Peirce: Selected Writings*, pp. 30–1.

[3] *Op. cit.*, p. 29.   [4] *Op. cit.*, p. 31.

for all metaphysical inquiry, and Peirce did indeed believe that many metaphysical controversies have been mere sophistry. 'Metaphysics is a subject more curious than useful, the knowledge of which, like that of a sunken reef, serves chiefly to enable us to keep clear of it.'[1] Yet Peirce was no positivist, and he believed it possible to construct a purified metaphysic consonant with his pragmatic method.

This metaphysic is an evolutionary one, and, like Bergson's, it opposes a deterministic or materialistic interpretation of nature. In Peirce's view, there are three modes of evolution. First, there is an element of chance, the *tychastic* element. There is an element of spontaneity and variability in nature, which is never quite precise in its operations and may in the beginning have been completely chaotic. Secondly, there is the element of mechanical necessity, the *anancastic* element. Nature tends to become law-abiding. It forms habits, but its regularity is not evidence for a purely mechanical view of nature but rather suggests an affinity with the habit-forming tendency of minds. The third element is love, the *agapastic* element. Attraction, sympathy and purpose appear in the evolutionary process, and these may point us to the goal, just as chance may point us to the beginning.

As we might expect, Peirce has no sympathy for any merely academic theology. The only theology which would interest him would be one which advanced the gospel of love, and most theology has not done this, but busied itself with abstract and frequently meaningless questions. Yet Peirce thinks that his doctrine of evolutionary love is in agreement with the teaching of the great religions. 'The gospel of Christ says that progress comes from every individual merging his individuality in sympathy with his neighbors.'[2] The agapastic doctrine is not held as a mere theory about the world, but as a passionate belief which is a rule for action.

What of the idea of God? Can it be given meaning by the pragmatic method? 'If a pragmaticist is asked what he means by the word "God" ', says Peirce, 'he can only say that just as long acquaintance with a man of great character may deeply influence one's whole manner of conduct, so if contemplation and study of the psycho-physical universe can imbue a man with principles of conduct analogous to the influence of a great man's works or conversation, then that analogue of a mind—for it is impossible to say that *any* human attribute is *literally* applicable—is what he means by "God".'[3]

Peirce's ideas, as we have already noted, were taken up and given a broader scope by William James[4] (1842–1910). Of course, other influences

[1] *Op. cit.*, p. 40.   [2] *Op. cit.*, p. 364.
[3] *Op. cit.*, p. 376.   [4] Professor at Harvard, 1885–1910.

too contributed to James' thought, notably his work in psychology and the ideas of the British empiricists. A brilliant writer, he puts across the pragmatic method in persuasive language. 'It is astonishing to see', he writes, 'how many philosophical disputes collapse into insignificance the moment you subject them to the test of tracing a concrete consequence. There can *be* no difference anywhere that does not *make* a difference elsewhere—no difference in abstract truth that does not express itself in a difference in concrete fact and in conduct consequent upon that fact, imposed on somebody, somehow, somewhere, and somewhen.'[1] Or again: 'You must bring out of each word its practical cash-value, set it at work within the stream of your experience. Theories thus become instruments, not answers to enigmas, in which we can rest.'[2] To sum up, pragmatism means a new attitude in philosophy—'the attitude of looking away from first things, principles, categories, supposed necessities; and of looking towards last things, fruits, consequences, facts'.[3]

So far, this is simply a restatement of Peirce's teaching, and indeed James says that the pragmatic approach is not something new but something with a very long history in philosophy. But we find that pragmatism now gets extended from a method of determining meaning into a theory of truth. 'Any idea upon which we can ride, so to speak; any idea that will carry us prosperously from any one part of our experience to any other part, linking things satisfactorily, working securely, simplifying, saving labor, is true for just so much.'[4] The pragmatic philosophy's 'only test of probable truth is what works best in the way of leading us, what fits every part of life best and combines with the collectivity of life's demands, nothing being omitted'.[5] On this radically empiricist view, truth is not a separate value accessible to the intellect alone, but rather a species of the good which guides our conduct. Truth is, moreover, not something eternal and absolute, but a matter of degree—our ideas become true just in so far as they help us to organize our experience successfully.

While James opposes intellectualist systems of metaphysics, he also opposes positivism. Since our beliefs are so closely related to action, we must take a risk in our beliefs. He argues that in cases where conclusive evidence is not available, we may sometimes be entitled to adopt a hypothesis suggested to us by the demands of our volitional nature, and by acting upon such a hypothesis, we may prove that it works and is so far true. In his famous essay, 'The Will to Believe',[6] James applies this argument to the case of religious belief. If religious belief, or faith, were

---

[1] 'What Pragmatism Means', in *Selected Papers in Philosophy*, p. 201.
[2] *Loc. cit.*, p. 203.   [3] *Loc. cit.*, p. 204.   [4] *Loc. cit.*, p. 206.
[5] *Loc. cit.*, p. 217.   [6] *Selected Papers*, pp. 99–124.

merely a matter of the intellect, one might be entitled to suspend judgment about it until conclusive evidence is forthcoming. But such faith is far more than an intellectual belief, and to suspend judgment about it means in fact to act as if the religious hypothesis is untrue. One has to choose in such a case between the *fear* of falling into error and the *hope* of embracing a truth. We are therefore entitled to commit ourselves to the religious belief in the hope that it will prove itself in experience—and indeed, only if we do take this risk can the belief be tested. 'When I look at the religious question, then the command that we shall put a stopper on our heart, instincts and courage, and *wait*—acting of course meanwhile as if religion were *not* true—till doomsday, or till such time as our intellect and senses working together may have raked in evidence enough—this command, I say, seems to me the queerest idol ever manufactured in the philosophic cave.'[1]

The truth of religion, then, does not depend on abstract and unconvincing metaphysical arguments for theism, but hinges on the answer to the question of whether religious belief turns out to have value in concrete life. Can this be shown? In his Gifford Lectures, which still remain a classic in their own field, James investigates the manifold forms of religious experience from an empirical and psychological standpoint. While he believes that psychology can go far towards explaining in natural terms many features of the religious life which have in the past been deemed supernatural, and while he notes that the religious person has a tendency to adopt 'over-beliefs' which go beyond the empirical data, he nevertheless thinks that the observable effects of religious experience in regenerating human nature and in influencing conduct provide empirical confirmation for the religious hypothesis—the hypothesis that our lives are continuous with a larger spiritual world from which help comes to us. Just as the pet cat sitting on the study carpet surrounded by books and papers takes part in the scenes of a larger human life of which he has presumably hardly an inkling, so we may touch upon a larger unseen life which we cannot comprehend but which makes itself felt in religious and mystical experience.

James thinks that the unconscious reaches of the self, in which so many religious experiences originate, may form the link with the spiritual world. 'The further limits of our being plunge, it seems to me, into an altogether other dimension of existence from the sensible and merely "understandable" world. Name it the mystical region, or the supernatural region, whichever you choose. The unseen region in question is not merely ideal, for it produces effects in this world. But that which

[1] *Loc. cit.*, p. 123.

produces effects within another reality must be termed a reality itself. "God" is the natural appellation for the supreme reality, so I will call this higher part of the universe by the name of "God".[1] Thus James thinks of our human life as touching a wider, unseen, higher, spiritual region of the universe, of which we have evidence in the visible fruits of religious experience.

Can we, however, call this wider life 'God'? James agrees that strictly speaking, his empirical study of religion supports only the belief in *something* larger than ourselves. This 'something' need not be an all-embracing absolute Spirit. Indeed, while James thinks that some form of theism is the most 'practically rational' solution, he prefers to think of God as finite rather than as sovereign, and of the universe as incomplete and pluralistic rather than as a perfect unity. These ideas may seem to take us far into the region of speculation, but James insists that the distinction between monism and pluralism has its practical bearing. A monistic universe with an omnipotent God would be a dead static world, where everything is already settled. A pluralistic universe with a finite God accords with the sort of reality given to us in experience—'that distributed and strung-along and flowing sort of reality which we finite beings swim in'[2]—and moreover leaves room for genuine freedom, striving, and action, which were of such importance to James.

Whereas the pragmatism of James starts off by repudiating intellectualism and abstract metaphysics but goes on to the defence of religion and ends up by proposing a new spiritualistic metaphysic, the pragmatism of John Dewey[3] (1859–1952) takes a more naturalistic and positivistic turn. Dewey's naturalism, however, is not of the mechanistic variety. It accepts the distinctively human, without trying to explain it in terms of something lower, but it studies the human in this world, as its natural home and environment. Man is accepted as man, not as an angel who has strayed into this world of space and time from some empyrean region beyond, nor yet as a mere machine of unusually complicated structure. Hence the concepts of this naturalism are drawn from biology, psychology and sociology.

The idea of evolution played a large part in Dewey's thinking. Just as the various organs of the body are adapted for dealing with the environment, so the function of mind is to provide us with ideal tools or instruments for coping with the situations in which we find ourselves. This is

---

[1] *The Varieties of Religious Experience*, pp. 506–7.

[2] *A Pluralistic Universe*, p. 213.

[3] After various appointments, he was professor at Chicago, 1894–1904, then at Columbia, 1905–30.

Dewey's 'instrumentalism'. The aim of thought is not to gain knowledge of the world, as if we were spectators at a show, but to attain control of the environment for beings who have to live their lives in it.

If ideas have this instrumental character, then what is to be said of philosophy? Clearly, Dewey could have no interest in a philosophy which regarded its task as disinterested speculation on ultimate questions. His own philosophy renounces any inquiry after absolute beginnings or absolute finalities, or any guardianship of eternal values. As he sees it, philosophy has a much more practical function. Its business is to resolve the conflicts and to co-ordinate the values that arise in any human society. This is partly a critical function, since it involves the continual testing in the light of their consequences of accepted ideas, values and institutions; and it is partly a creative function, since it involves pointing to new possibilities which emerge with advancing knowledge, for our values are always changing. 'A philosophy which abandoned its guardianship of fixed realities, values and ideals, would find a new career for itself. To abandon the search for absolute and immutable reality and value may seem like a sacrifice. But this renunciation is the condition of entering upon a vocation of greater vitality.'[1]

Since our own study is directed to the subject of religion, we are chiefly interested to note what Dewey's philosophy has to say about resolving the conflict, found in any modern industrial democracy, between religious and secular values. As we might have anticipated, Dewey is highly critical of traditional religion, with its appeal to the supernatural, its fixed values and dogmas, and its belief in a God in whom the union of the actual and the ideal is eternally realized. Yet he recognizes a 'religious attitude' which can be extricated from what he regards as its unfortunate entanglements. This religious attitude is 'a sense of the possibilities of existence and devotion to the cause of these possibilities'. Such an attitude must 'surrender once for all commitment to beliefs about matters of fact, whether physical, social or metaphysical'. This purified religious attitude would no longer be in conflict with other elements in a modern society, and it would take the form of a kind of natural piety. 'Nature, including humanity, with all its defects and imperfections, may evoke heartfelt piety as the source of ideals, of possibilities, of aspirations in their behalf, and as the eventual abode of all attained goods and excellencies.'[2]

The gulf between Dewey's 'religious attitude' and what we ordinarily call 'religion' is, however, so great, that it is hard to see why he should want to go on talking about religion at all. Yet obviously he attaches considerable importance to the idea. He says: 'The opposition between

[1] *The Quest for Certainty*, p. 295.   [2] *Op. cit.*, pp. 288–9 and 291.

religious values as I conceive them and religions is not to be bridged. Just because the release of these values is so important, their identification with the creeds and cults of religions must be dissolved.'[1] He is even ready to reinstate the word 'God', provided that it is purged of its traditional metaphysical connotations, and understood to mean an imaginative unification of ideal values, a projected union of the ideal and the actual. The function of a religious faith which has been separated from supernatural, cosmological and static ideas is to unite men in a sense of common effort and shared destiny. Dewey believes that the idea of God, in the sense explained, can be a powerful help towards unifying interests and energies, and towards stimulating action. But perhaps both the theist and the thoroughgoing secularist would object to the proposed function for God. Dewey is essentially a humanist, and for him the way forward lies not through religious insight but through science, intelligence and education.

53. CATHOLIC MODERNISM
A. F. Loisy, L. Laberthonnière, E. Le Roy, G. Tyrrell

The influence of the philosophers whom we have surveyed upon theological thinking is most strikingly seen in the Modernist Movement, which caused a considerable stir in the Roman Catholic Church in the first decade of this century. The Modernist Movement had many aspects, and for this reason it was described by Pope Pius X, in a well-known phrase, as 'the compendium of all heresies'. With some of these aspects, such as the exercise of freedom in the field of biblical criticism, we are not directly concerned. Our attention must be directed rather to the philosophical side of the movement, and its ideas about the nature of religion. Confronted with the task of reconciling the Catholic faith with modern thought, the Modernists in general believed that traditional theology had been too intellectualist in its approach, and they believed that the desired reconciliation might be achieved by abandoning intellectualism and by applying to the religious problem the new philosophies of life and action. Revelation, they maintained, is not an imperfectible deposit of truth, descended from heaven, as it were, and expressible in propositions to which intellectual assent may be given. Such assent would, in any case, fall short of a genuinely religious faith. Religious truth is the kind of truth that must be lived. It is immanent in religious experience, and is therefore always incomplete and in process of development. At the same time, the Modernists believed that the Catholic Church is the *locus* within which

[1] *A Common Faith*, p. 28.

this truth develops, so that their radical theology was usually combined with a sincere love of the Church.

The leading Modernist, Alfred Firmin Loisy[1] (1857–1940), was primarily a biblical scholar, but his investigation of the historical problem of Christianity led him towards the typical Modernist philosophy of religion. His most famous book, *L'Evangile et l'Eglise*, is a shattering criticism of the view of Christianity held by Harnack.[2] The German scholar had left no room for life, growth or movement in his conception of Christianity, but had tried to strip away all accretions so as to isolate a fixed original content as the essence of Christianity. As over against this static conception, Loisy asks: 'Why not find the essence of Christianity in the fulness and totality of its life, which shows movement and vitality just because it is life?'[3] The truth of Christianity develops as Christianity affirms itself in the life of the Church. 'The gospel has not entered the world as an unconditioned absolute doctrine, summed up in a unique and stedfast truth, but as a living faith, concrete and complex.'[4]

Loisy often writes as if there is indeed an absolute and eternal truth, a kind of Platonic essence laid up in the heavens, as it were, so that what changes and develops would be only our way of grasping and expressing the truth. This remaining element of static truth is, however, hard to reconcile with some of Loisy's more forthright pronouncements, which suggest that truth itself is in the making, and that reality is a process of creation and development. In *Autour d'un petit livre*, a sequel to the earlier book which has been quoted, he says: 'Truth does not enter our brains ready-made; it makes itself slowly, and we cannot say that it is ever complete. The human spirit is always in travail. Truth is no more immutable than man himself. It evolves with him, in him, by him; and this does not prevent it from being the truth for him, but is even the only condition on which it is truth.'[5]

The whole tendency of these ideas of Loisy is away from the view that religious truths afford any knowledge of a transcendent and eternal order. These truths are rather imperfect symbols forged by experience, and they have an immanent origin in life and action. At a later period of his life, Loisy could write concerning the rise of Christianity: 'In the whole course of this remarkable evolution, nothing happened which cannot be explained by the laws that govern human life.'[6] By this time, in Loisy's

---

[1] Ordained priest, 1879; excommunicated, 1908; professor at the Collège de France, 1909-32.

[2] See above, pp. 88–9.   [3] *Op. cit.*, (English translation), p. 16.

[4] *Op. cit.*, p. 87.   [5] *Op. cit.*, pp. 191–2.

[6] *The Birth of the Christian Religion*, p. 358.

thinking, religion had become almost entirely merged into moral action. Religion is the spirit which animates morality and gives to duty its sacred character.

While Loisy comes to the problem of religion as a biblical critic and historian, we find among the Modernists men like Lucien Laberthonnière[1] (1860–1932) whose interests were primarily philosophical. Some early notes, printed at the beginning of the posthumous edition of his works, show us very clearly that Laberthonnière's conception of philosophy was a pragmatic one—or perhaps we would nowadays say, an existential one. 'The aim of every philosophical doctrine', he declares, 'is to give sense to life, to human existence, so that every such doctrine is a *moral work*. It gets worked out by living, and it is not, as people seem so often to believe, a collection of abstract propositions linked together and derived from certain axioms or fundamental principles.' Thus the truth of such a doctrine 'cannot be an abstract truth. Its truth is *to be viable*.'[2]

Some philosophical doctrines are, of course, more obviously geared to life than others. In one of his writings, *Le Réalisme chrétien et l'Idéalisme grec*, Laberthonnière draws a contrast between what he takes to be extreme cases. Greek philosophy is said to deal in abstract eternal essences, and its God is a static ideal, the object of thought and contemplation. Christian realism, on the other hand, is concerned with the concrete active inwardness of life, and it brings the activity of God into the human spirit. Its truth is not something external to be reached by intellectual contemplation, but something intrinsic to be grasped in living. Religious truths are of no value to us if they are merely external; they must be recreated in ourselves. The external formulations of belief are to be taken into experience and their truth lived out there. The truth of the fall of Adam, for instance, is not the objective truth of a remote and unverifiable event, postulated as an abstract explanation of the origin of sin. It is the truth of an event which we experience—an event which has lasted till our time and will continue to last as long as there is history.[3] Similarly, Laberthonnière thinks of Christ not as a fact or a problem of past history, but as a present reality whom the believer experiences as the truth and the life.

These reflections may seem once again to drive us in the direction of pure immanence, and up to a point this is true. But Laberthonnière certainly does not intend to reduce the divine to the natural. Rather, he would say that the natural is already penetrated by divine grace. The supernatural is not added on to the natural, nor is it merely above and

---

[1] Ordained priest, 1886; his writings were condemned, and in 1913 he was prohibited from further publication.

[2] *Œuvres*, vol. I, pp. 1–2.   [3] *Essais de philosophie religieuse*, p. 288.

beyond. It is in the inmost being of the natural, it is 'the prolongation of the divine life into the life of man'.[1]

Perhaps the most radical pragmatist among the Modernists was Edouard Le Roy[2] (1870–   ), disciple and successor of Bergson. As a lay professor, he made one of the clearest contributions to the Modernist controversy.

Le Roy poses the question, 'What is a dogma?' He notes that a dogma is held to have a binding or obligatory character for the faithful, but he rightly sees the difficulty in ascribing such an obligatory character if a dogma is held to be a proposition to which one gives intellectual assent. For surely we are obliged to believe something only if there is a logical obligation to do so, that is to say, if some valid proof has been adduced; and in the case of dogmas, no such proof is available. Moreover, Le Roy confronts us with a dilemma. If a dogma formulates absolute truth in adequate terms—supposing for the moment that such a thing were possible—then we could not understand it; while if a dogma formulates truth in imperfect and relative terms, it cannot be unconditionally binding. Thus the intellectualist interpretation of dogma is rejected.

Le Roy suggests that a dogma is to be understood in two senses. First, it has a negative sense. It safeguards us against possible errors, without defining the positive truth of the matter. There is, of course, nothing new in what Le Roy says here. St Athanasius said something rather similar about the Nicene formula, which he called a 'bulwark against irreligious notions'.[3] To say that the Son is consubstantial with the Father is not positively very enlightening, as subsequent disputes in the Church show us, but at least it does rule out Arianism and other errors. But much more important than this negative sense is the second sense which Le Roy assigns to a dogma. A dogma, he tells us, is prescriptive; it is a 'rule of practical conduct'.[4] This explains the obligatory character of dogma. The obligation is not an obligation to give intellectual assent to something —which would be in any case a very difficult conception—but an obligation to act in a certain way.

Let us take, for instance, the statement that God is personal. This is not to be understood as giving us metaphysical information about God, though presumably it rules out subpersonal conceptions of him. Primarily, however, it is an injunction to treat personal relations as of ultimate value. Or again, let us take the statement that Christ is risen. This does not assert a past event, according to Le Roy, who specifically rejected the miraculous

---

[1] *Essais*, p. xxvi.
[2] Professor at the Collège de France, 1924–45.
[3] *De Synodis*, III, 45.   [4] *Dogme et Critique*, p. 25.

stories of the empty tomb,[1] but is a command to live as a contemporary of Christ.

Such views may seem to have brought us back to something very like Vaihinger's philosophy of 'as if'. Le Roy, however, does not agree that his pragmatic interpretation of dogma lands us in positivism or agnosticism. Here we must remember the Bergsonian influence in his thinking. Discursive reasoning, according to Le Roy, never gives us a true picture of reality, but only an abstract scheme which we find useful for some of our practical purposes. Reality itself is a continuous flowing process which we can grasp intuitively in the life of action. Hence the existence of God can never be proved by intellectual means, but his reality can be intuited in action, and above all in moral action. 'The affirmation of God is the affirmation of the moral reality, as a reality which is autonomous, independent, irreducible, and also the primary reality.'[2]

Thus once again religion is brought into the closest connection with moral action. To believe in God and to act morally are, at bottom, one and the same, while the dogmatic formulations of religious belief are symbols of the needs and aspirations of the moral life.

Before leaving the subject of Catholic Modernism, we may glance at the principal representative of the movement in the British Isles, George Tyrrell[3] (1861–1909). It is to him that we owe the definition of a 'Modernist' as 'a churchman of any sort who believes in the possibility of a synthesis between the essential truth of his religion and the essential truth of modernity'.[4] Yet Tyrrell makes it clear that the truth of his religion weighed more with him than the truth of modernity, and he says that his concessions to modernity are reluctant. There is indeed no mistaking his profound religious temperament, and his sincere attachment to the Catholic Church, in spite of the freedom with which he criticized what he took to be its abuses and imperfections.

Tyrrell has left us no systematic account of his views, for his short life

---

[1] Le Roy devotes to the resurrection a very long and detailed discussion in *Dogme et Critique*. He begins by declaring: 'I believe without restriction or reserve that the resurrection of Jesus is an objectively real fact.' He then points out that no Council has defined what is an objectively real fact, or to what order of facts the resurrection belongs. He soon makes it clear that for him the reality of the resurrection has nothing to do with the 'vulgar notion' of the 'reanimation of a corpse'. The real, for Le Roy, is to be recognized by the presence of two characteristics: it can be put to the test of use without breaking down; and it is inexhaustibly fertile for life. Judged by these criteria, the resurrection possesses reality of the highest order, though this can be known only to the life of faith within the Church, which is Christ's body.

[2] *Le Problème de Dieu*, p. 105.

[3] Originally an Anglican, he became a Jesuit priest in 1891; virtually excommunicated in 1907, he continued to regard himself as a Catholic, and received the last rites.

[4] *Christianity at the Crossroads*, p. 5.

was largely taken up in controversy. In his writings, however, we may distinguish two important ideas which are typical of the Modernist Movement as a whole and are also in line with the teaching of the philosophies considered earlier in this chapter.

The first idea arises from the distinction between a static, abstract, intellectualized theology which formulates a fixed deposit of unchanging truth, and, on the other hand, the living, dynamic experience of religion itself. Tyrrell declares himself in favour of an evolving theology which is continually tested by living experience. Such a theology 'has for its subject-matter a certain ever-present department of human experience which it endeavours progressively to formulate and understand, and which is ever at hand to furnish a criterion of such endeavours'.[1]

The second idea is the pragmatic one—a belief is to be tested by its fruits. Here, however, we may notice Tyrrell's specifically religious interest, for the test of the fruitfulness of a belief is to consider not only its moral but also its devotional and spiritual consequences. He writes: 'Beliefs that have been found by continuous and invariable experience to foster and promote the spiritual life of the soul must so far be in accord with the nature and the laws of that will-world with which it is the aim of religion to bring us into harmony.'[2] But while Tyrrell holds that right religious beliefs are determined by the needs of the soul rather than by metaphysical considerations, he is far from being a positivist. Beliefs which prove fruitful, he maintains, do in some way represent to us the realities of the spiritual world.

The Modernist Movement was condemned by Pope Pius X in 1907. The decree *Lamentabili* listed the errors of the Modernists, and among the propositions which are condemned we find the view that 'the dogmas of faith are to be held only according to their practical sense, that is to say, as norms which prescribe action, not as norms of belief'.[3] Our survey, however, makes it clear that although some of the Modernists came near to such a view, they mostly stopped short of holding that a dogma has *only* a practical sense.

54. PROTESTANT EMPIRICAL MODERNISM
H. N. Wieman, H. E. Fosdick

While the word 'modernism' has a fairly restricted denotation in the Roman Catholic Church, it is used much more loosely in the non-Roman churches. In the Church of England, it would most probably refer to the

---

[1] *Through Scylla and Charybdis*, p. 136.   [2] *Lex Orandi*, p. 57.
[3] See H. Denzinger, *Enchiridion Symbolorum*, p. 566.

adherents of the Modern Churchmen's Union.[1] In America, 'modernism' is usually contrasted with 'fundamentalism'. Here modernism designates an attitude to the Bible, such as we find expounded in H. E. Fosdick's *The Modern Use of the Bible*. This attitude takes the Bible to be rather the record of a developing experience of God than a static once-for-all authoritative deliverance of divine truth, equally true in all its parts. But the mention of development here links this attitude with evolutionary ideas. Shailer Mathews, whose evolutionary theology we have already noticed,[2] called one of his books *The Faith of a Modernist*. Thus 'modernism' comes to mean a type of theology which employs evolutionary, empiricist and pragmatist ways of thinking; and the Protestant empirical modernism of America has much in common with the Roman Catholic Modernist Movement.

This American modernism is well represented by Henry Nelson Wieman[3] (1884–   ). He has much in common with Dewey, with whom he would agree that knowledge must be gained by empirical methods requiring observation of predicted consequences, and that therefore we must look not to some alleged region of transcendent being, but to what actually goes on in our temporal experience of the world.[4] Wieman, however, parts company from Dewey's humanistic conception of 'God' as simply the name for an imaginary unity of man's ideal possibilities.[5] According to Wieman, there is discoverable to empirical investigation a structure of increasing value, not created by man but rather providing the test for human aspirations. There operates in human life something which transforms man as he cannot transform himself, and this we may call 'God'. So God is 'that behavior of the universe which preserves and increases to the maximum the total good of all human living',[6] or, alternatively, 'what saves man from evil, as he cannot save himself, is properly called "God", no matter how different it may be from traditional conceptions of God. The operative reality is more important than any cherished belief about it.'[7] Thus Wieman's conception of God is in terms not of static being but of dynamic process.

'Unabashed naturalism' is how one conservative theologian[8] describes Wieman's views. Wieman would cheerfully agree that this is naturalism, but he would claim that it is Christian naturalism. Man can give himself to the transforming power, of which Wieman speaks, with that wholeness

---

[1] See below, p. 250.   [2] See above, p. 165.

[3] Like Mathews, he was a member of the Chicago school, being professor in the university 1927–47.

[4] See Wieman's essay, 'Naturalism', in *A Handbook of Christian Theology*, p. 246.

[5] See above, p. 181.   [6] *The Wrestle of Religion with Truth*, p. 62.

[7] 'Naturalism', *ibid*.   [8] Carl F. H. Henry in *Christian Personal Ethics*, p. 189.

of the self which is religious faith. And if the bare propositions of natural theology seem abstract, we have to remember that human experience is something richer than knowledge, and that concrete symbols can bring awareness of a depth and fullness which escape abstract propositions. 'Worship is the only possible way to form those most subtle and complex habits of the heart and mind which organize and mobilize the total personality.'[1]

But while Wieman's empiricism conduces to a religious attitude, can it find room for distinctively Christian belief? Wieman believes that it can, and he tries to show this in *The Source of Human Good*. We are to think of Jesus too in terms of an operative relationship to his followers. Jesus sacrificed himself to the creative good of God, so pointing beyond himself to the divine activity which breaks up the old in order to bring in new life and greater good. The relationship of the believer to Jesus is that he too participates in the crucified life, surrendering all created goods for commitment to the new good opened up by Jesus.

In accordance with our practice of introducing into this survey a few writers of a more popular sort, we may notice here the tremendous influence which modernism exercised through the preaching and writing of Harry Emerson Fosdick[2] (1878–1969). We have already noted his empirical and evolutionary approach to the Bible. 'The Bible is the record of an amazing spiritual development'—the view usually called 'progressive revelation'; and 'the strength of the Bible has always been its appeal to the deep and abiding realm of man's basic experiences, for out of that realm the Bible came'.[3] In his general thinking about religion, Fosdick reflects chiefly the empiricist and pragmatist tradition from James to Wieman. But like most popularizers, he is also something of an eclectic, and draws widely on contemporary ideas. He speaks with enthusiasm of Royce's ideal of loyalty; he is at one with the personalists in the high place he assigns to personality; when he tells us that religion is good for the health, and that he has found God as well in the worship of Buddhists, Muslims and Catholics as of Protestants, we seem to hear echoes of R. W. Trine.[4]

Religion, Fosdick repeatedly says, is a psychological experience. Moreover, it is an experience that makes a difference, for the kind of religion

---

[1] *The Wrestle of Religion with Truth*, pp. 69–70.

[2] He became a Baptist minister in 1903, and was minister of Riverside Church, New York, 1926–46.

[3] *The Modern Use of the Bible*, pp. 12, 59.

[4] Fosdick has indeed a kind word for 'New Thought' as 'translating religion into terms of power available for daily use', though, of course he explicitly rejects its metaphysics. See *As I See Religion*, p. 22.

that matters is the kind that saves, that is to say, the kind that integrates, strengthens and enriches the personal lives of those who engage in it. Prayer, to instance a common religious practice, is not a matter of reminding God to do something that he might otherwise have forgotten, or to confer a benefit that he might otherwise have withheld. Prayer is 'fulfilling inward conditions of attitude and receptivity, and getting appropriate results in heightened insight, stability, peace and self-control'.[1]

This practical kind of religion, while it is not interested in the traditional ecclesiastical and theological disputes, is not indifferent to theology. It requires an appropriate theology for its support, and such a theology is in turn supported by experience. Fosdick's idea of God adds nothing to the ideas of such modernists as Mathews and Wieman. 'There is a creative factor in the universe favorable to personality, or else personality never would have arrived. A cosmic power is operative here, propitious to enlarging truth, creative beauty, and expanding goodness, or else they never would have existed. If by the term "God" one means this, then one does most certainly mean something real and efficient in this universe whereof the picture-thinking of our religious symbolism is only one partial representation.'[2]

What is distinctive in the Christian religion is reverence for personality, though this is not exclusive to Christianity. The primacy of personality means that God is to be thought of in personal terms, though admittedly these are symbolic. And 'the gist of what the Church has meant by the divinity of Jesus lies in the idea that, if God is to be symbolized by personal life, he should be symbolized by the best personal life we know'.[3] To be a Christian does not depend on the acceptance of an orthodox creed, but on the acceptance of Jesus' attitude towards personality.

This practical undogmatic version of Christianity leaves many questions unanswered, but at least it puts little strain on our credulity, and there is no question that Fosdick's teaching has been of great help to very many people.

55. CRITICAL REMARKS ON THE PRAGMATIC VIEW OF RELIGION

It is undeniable that the philosophies of life and action have in them something strongly attractive. They bring us down to earth, make us look at the facts of experience, and remind us that in the study it is possible to construct finely spun theories which just will not bear confrontation

---

[1] *As I See Religion*, p. 23. [2] *Op. cit.*, p. 30. [3] *Op. cit.*, p. 58.

with the world which encounters us when we come out of the study door. There is surely point in asking about any theory, or at least, about any theory that claims to have to do with the real world in which we live: 'How does it work out in practice?' C. D. Broad talked in one place about 'silly' theories, by which he meant the kind 'which may be held at the time when one is talking or writing professionally', but which no sane person would think of carrying into daily life. As instances of what he had in mind, Broad mentioned some forms of behaviourism and idealism. Such theories may be very clever—'only very acute and learned men could have thought of anything so odd or defended anything so preposterous'—but the point is that even those who hold them in the study give the lie to them in their daily actions.[1] There is force in Laberthonnière's contention that a philosophical doctrine has got to be viable.

Furthermore, the pragmatic defence of religion is an impressive one. Religion is not just a matter of holding intellectual opinions about the nature of the universe, though most naturalistic criticisms of religion have treated it as if it were. Religion cannot be judged apart from the action which is integral to it. There is profound insight in James' contention that one cannot pronounce about a religious belief in detachment, but must have committed oneself to it and lived by it; and in Tyrrell's view that the doctrines of the Church have been shaped more by religious needs than by metaphysical considerations.

But just how far does this line of thought take us? Is religion merely a human activity, a kind of adjunct or spur to moral action? Dewey and the later, post-Catholic Loisy perhaps think of religion in this way, but they have really abolished religion and become humanists. Dewey goes on talking about religious values which have nothing to do with traditional religion and Loisy talks of religion as the spirit of morality, but the ordinary religious person would not recognize these things as 'religion' at all. Admittedly, this 'ordinary religious person' is something of a convenient fiction, and he certainly cannot be set up as the judge of the truth of a philosophy of religion. But anyone who sets out to construct a philosophy of religion is bound to have regard to what is meant by 'religion' among those who practise religion; and while the 'ordinary religious person' would agree that religion involves action, he would usually claim that it also affords insight into some transhuman (though not necessarily 'supernatural') reality. If religion is merely an immanent human activity, a kind of booster for morality, as it were, then it is not 'religion' in the standard usage of the word. The Catholic Church could scarcely do anything else than condemn Modernism if that movement really taught

[1] *The Mind and Its Place in Nature*, pp. 5–6.

that dogmas have *only* a practical sense. And if Modernism meant this, then Santayana was right in saying that it is suicide for religion. 'It concedes everything; for it concedes that everything in Christianity, *as Christians hold it*, is an illusion.'[1] But we have seen that few Catholic Modernists went so far; and neither did their Protestant counterparts, such as Wieman.

Are we to say on the other hand that the practical efficacy of religion establishes the truth of its belief in a transhuman order? Most of the philosophers who begin by telling us that religious beliefs have to do with action, end up by assuring us, 'Of course, there *really is* a God corresponding to your beliefs.' James persuades himself that there is such a God, albeit a finite one. Blondel finds his way from action to the supernatural. Le Roy starts off from a radically pragmatic interpretation of dogma, but hastens to tell us that this is not agnosticism; there is a God, and though we cannot prove that he is there, we can know him intuitively. How is this transhuman reality established?

Could it not be the case that a false belief might turn out to be practically efficacious? This is the thesis of Vaihinger's fictionalism, and also the point where his philosophy differs radically from pragmatism. Vaihinger tries to show that a false or contradictory notion may nevertheless be a fruitful one. If Vaihinger is right, a belief does not become true merely by proving itself fruitful. The pragmatist might reply that although a false belief may be efficacious for a time, it will be caught out in the long run, and will come into conflict with other beliefs. James, for instance, insists that fruitful beliefs are not isolated but carry us from one area of experience to another. But when the pragmatist takes this line, how does his view of truth differ from the coherence theory, as held by Bradley and other 'intellectualists' whom the pragmatists are so fond of attacking?

All the pragmatists, in fact, have their metaphysics—Peirce has his evolutionary theory, James has his pluralism, and even Dewey has his metaphysic—he believes in an active process of which nature and experience are different aspects, though he does not make a deity out of the process. It can hardly be denied that speculative elements enter into these metaphysics. James, for instance, backs up his case for the existence of God with a speculation that the unconscious may be our channel of communciation with the spiritual world. If Freud is right, however, the unconscious is more of a jungle than a gateway to God. Jung might be more sympathetic, but the God who dwells in his unconscious is no more than a psychological reality.

[1] 'Modernism and Christianity', in *Winds of Doctrine*, p. 57.

All the philosophies considered in this chapter fall back on a metaphysical view of reality as activity or process, as opposed to any static view of reality. Such metaphysical views must be subjected to critical scrutiny like any others, and appeals to 'intuition' can make us only more distrustful. Take, for instance, Bergson's metaphysic, as perhaps the most impressive of these which we have surveyed. In the series, matter—life— mind, Bergson takes the middle term as the clue to reality, whereas the materialist takes the first term and the idealist the last. Bergson's choice is no more self-evident than the others, especially since the 'life' of which he speaks is not the kind of life with which the biochemist deals but a much more mysterious entity. Bergson may be right or he may be wrong, but the point is that his philosophy issues in a metaphysic which has to be intellectually criticized, and compared with alternative views.

The philosophies of life and action, then, in spite of their anti-intellectualism, do not escape intellectual problems. The pragmatic method and the metaphysics of process keep slipping apart. Perhaps because of these interior strains and stresses, pragmatism and vitalism have both declined, and their more valuable insights have passed into existentialism on the one hand and the newer process philosophies on the other.

XII

PHILOSOPHIES OF PERSONAL BEING

56. PRECURSORS OF EXISTENTIALISM

WE turn now to some philosophers and theologians who push even further the anti-intellectualist tendencies noted in the philosophies of life and action. Again we find an insistence that man is more than a cognitive being, that philosophy has to take account of the whole experience of being a person, and that truth is to be sought not so much in ideas as in life. But in the thinkers whom we are about to consider—perhaps some of them should be called 'prophets' rather than 'thinkers' in the narrower sense of the term—we find a more subjectivist strain than we have so far encountered. Not only striving and willing, but also suffering, guilt, finitude and all the pathos of human life are brought into the foreground. Not the progress and success of life, which appeared in pragmatism and vitalism, but rather life's fragmentariness and tensions are now presented as irreducible facts. At the same time God, whom the philosophies of life and action tended to regard as immanent, now appears in a transcendent role as he stands over against the contradictions of finite life. One of the prophets of this way of thinking, Nicolas Berdyaev, says explicitly that his philosophy 'must be distinguished both from the philosophy of life and from pragmatic philosophy. It is associated with the experience of tragic conflict. There is in it no cult of life as the highest criterion; it is not biological in character. What is important is not the quantitative maximum of life, not its flourishing condition in the world, nor its power, but the quality of it, its intensity, its moving and pathetic character.'[1]

We have called such thinkers as Berdyaev 'philosophers of personal being', and this seems to be a broad enough designation to cover the philosophers and theologians reviewed in this chapter, for with all of them the experience of being a person is central to their philosophizing. They might have been called 'personalists', except that this term might imply too close an affinity with the personalism of Bowne and his followers

[1] *The Beginning and the End*, p. 48.

in America. There is indeed an affinity, since personal categories are primary in each case, but whereas Bowne retains the framework of an idealist metaphysic, the thinkers whom we are now considering are not happy with metaphysical systems, which, they think, distort the lived reality of personal being. Again, they might have been called 'existentialists', and some of them often are. But this term is less appropriate to some than to others, and it is perhaps better to regard this group of thinkers as precursors of the later, full-blown existentialism. Most of them, in any case, belong to an older age-group than the outstanding existentialist philosophers.

The philosophers of personal being represent a type of thinking which has a long history, and which has been also very widespread. We can trace its various strands back into Jewish and Hebrew reflection; or in Western thinkers like Pascal and St Augustine; or in the novels of Dostoyevsky and some of the ideas of Russian religion. The most immediate influence with which we have to reckon, however, was the rediscovery in the present century of the thought of Kierkegaard. As he died in 1855, he falls outside the scope of our present study. But at the time of his death and for long afterwards, he attracted little notice beyond his native Denmark. He did indeed win some appreciation. For instance, in 1883, Otto Pfleiderer, after summarizing Kierkegaard's teaching, remarks that 'there is something refreshing, something commanding in this resolute consistency, when we contrast it with the half measures and the ambiguities of our neo-Kantian theologians'.[1] Yet Kierkegaard has really come into his own only in the twentieth century, and it would be difficult to overestimate his influence on the religious thought of our time. Rejecting Hegel's attempt to construct a rational system of reality, Kierkegaard maintained that the reality which we subjectively experience is incapable of rational synthesis. Abstract forms of thought cannot grasp the concrete act of existing, which by its very nature is fragmentary, paradoxical and incomplete. In particular, there is no route to Christianity through rational thought or through a stereotyped institutional religion. The way lies only through passionate, inward, subjective appropriation. God stands over against our finite existence as qualitatively different, and discontinuous with it; and the Christian religion, with its assertion that the transcendent and eternal God has appeared in the flesh in a particular moment of time, so far from being explicable or defensible in terms of a speculative philosophy, remains essentially paradoxical and calls for a radical decision of faith.

The thinkers whom we are about to survey vary much among themselves

[1] *The Philosophy of Religion*, vol. II, p. 212.

in stressing different aspects of personal being, but in each case it is this irreducible, personal being which lies at the centre of their philosophies. Some make more and some less of the elements of conflict and tragedy; some tend towards individualism while others are chiefly concerned with the community of personal being; some stand close to the philosophies of life and action while others are further removed from them; some seem impenitently irrationalist while others seek a logic appropriate to personal being. We shall consider them in four groups. The first group stresses the uniqueness and importance of interpersonal relations, and is represented by the Jewish philosopher Martin Buber, and the Christian theologian Karl Heim (Section 57). The second group comprises the Spanish philosophers Miguel de Unamuno and José Ortega y Gasset, who may be said to stand halfway between the philosophies of life and existentialism (Section 58). The third group takes in the Russians, Nicolas Berdyaev and Sergius Bulgakov, who draw upon the religious insights of their country as well as on the ideas of modern Western philosophy (Section 59). Standing somewhat apart is the British philosopher, John Macmurray (Section 60). A brief discussion and evaluation follows (Section 61).

57. THE LIFE OF DIALOGUE
M. Buber, K. Heim

In his prefatory remarks to a collection of his essays written between the years 1909 and 1954, Martin Buber[1] (1878–1965) has summarized for us the development of his thought. In his first phase, he was attracted by the kind of mysticism which aims at the absorption of the finite self into the Infinite. But he soon became dissatisfied with this kind of mysticism. Since the experience of mystical union is one which can be had only from time to time, the intervals between such experiences—and these intervals, of course, take up by far the greater part of our lives—come to be regarded as preparations for the higher moments. And in the higher moments themselves, we cease to be the persons that we really are, for we know of nothing standing over against us, and our distinct selves have been merged in the all-inclusive self. So Buber thinks of this kind of mysticism as an escape from the reality of life, for it regards everyday life as an obscuring of the true life. The mystic 'turns away from his existence as a man, the existence into which he has been set, through conception and birth, for life and death in this unique personal form'. Yet Buber

[1] Professor at Frankfurt, 1923–33; Hebrew University of Jerusalem, 1938–51. He has had a long association with the cultural side of the Zionist Movement.

considers that it was necessary for him to pass through this mystical phase before he could reach his own distinctive position, which consists in a frank acceptance of that personal form of being for which man is destined, a being which lives in dialogue or in person-to-person relations with that which stands over against it. 'Being true to the being in which and before which I am placed is the one thing that is needful.'[1]

According to Buber, there are two primary attitudes which man may take up to the world, and these attitudes express themselves in two primary words, or rather, combinations of words: 'I-It' and 'I-Thou'. There is no 'I' taken in itself, apart from combination with an 'It' or a 'Thou'. The 'I' which is present in the speaking of the two primary word-combinations is, moreover, different in each case. 'The primary word "I-Thou" can only be spoken with the whole being. The primary word "I-It" can never be spoken with the whole being.'[2]

The 'I-It' attitude is associated by Buber with what he calls 'experience' —a term which he uses in a rather special sense for those activities which have some thing for their object, as when we perceive something, imagine something, will something, think something, and the like. Experience objectifies, and it implies a certain detachment from its object. As we have already seen, the 'I-It' language is never spoken with the whole being. It is, of course, a primary language, and obviously we cannot do without our objectifying experience and the science that develops out of it if we are to find our way around the world. But if anyone were to live purely on the level of this attitude, he would be less than a man.

The 'I-Thou' attitude, on the other hand, is associated with what Buber calls the world of 'relation', another term which he uses in a restricted sense. The relation is described as 'meeting' or 'encounter'. It is a relation not of subject to object, but of subject to subject. Such a relation is direct, and it is also mutual, as involving a response which is absent in the detached objective attitude which may be taken up in experience. It is, furthermore, a relation of the whole person.

The most obvious case of an 'I-Thou' relation is the relation between two persons, expressing itself in dialogical speech. Buber believes, however, that below the level of speech there is also possible an 'I-Thou' relation with nature. A tree, for instance, can be considered objectively in a number of more or less abstract ways, but Buber thinks it is also possible to encounter the tree as a whole, to 'become bound up in relation to it'.[3] The tree ceases to be an 'It' and the relation to it is mutual, though Buber does not claim that the tree has a life similar to ours. In a similar way, the artist is said to be bound in relation to the spiritual forms which he seeks

[1] See *Pointing the Way*, pp. ix–x. [2] *I and Thou* (Second Edition), p. 3. [3] *Op. cit.*, p. 7.

to bring to expression in his creative works. Thus the 'I-Thou' attitude may extend its range beyond other persons, and every 'It' is a kind of chrysalis which may from time to time metamorphose into a 'Thou'.

The various 'Thous' with which we come into relation may be thought of as constituting a perspective, the extended lines of which meet in the eternal 'Thou' or God. 'Every particular "Thou" is a glimpse through to the eternal "Thou".'[1] Is God then also a person? Buber clarifies this point in a postscript to the new edition of his book. Whatever else God may be, it is claimed that he is a person in the sense that 'he enters into a direct relation with us men in creative, revealing and redeeming acts, and thus makes it possible for us to enter into a direct relation with him'.[2]

The more tragic side of human life is brought out by Buber in what he calls 'the exalted melancholy of our fate'. Just as every 'It' is potentially a 'Thou', so every 'Thou' can and indeed must sink back to an 'It'. Even other persons and God himself become 'Its' as we cease to address them and transform them into objects among other objects. As Buber sees it, the ills of the contemporary world spring from the injury that has been done to the essentially personal nature of man, not only as between man and man but also as between man and God. So he becomes the prophet who proclaims that 'the hope for this hour depends upon the renewal of dialogical immediacy'.[3]

Although himself a Jew, Buber has had an important influence on recent Christian theology, and we may take as an example of this the work of Karl Heim[4] (1874–1959). In a lesser degree, Buber's influence may also be traced in theologians so diverse as Barth, Brunner and Tillich, but Heim, who belongs to the same older generation as Buber himself, is particularly close to the Jewish philosopher in his thinking.

Heim is primarily an apologist, and the belief which he considers it most important to defend is belief in a transcendent God. 'Between the man who is bound to a God in heaven, and another who knows nothing of this bond, there is a contrast deeper than all other contrasts which separate man from man.'[5] At various periods in his life, Heim has had to defend his belief against different rival creeds. Sometimes he has had to defend it against the secularism of our scientifically-minded age, and for twelve years he had also to defend it against the Nazi idea of a God who is purely immanent in the spirit of the race, as taught by Rosenberg and others. Heim saw clearly that talk of God as 'above' or 'beyond' has, in any literal interpretation, been rendered meaningless by modern cosmology. He saw equally that a mere biblicism or neo-orthodoxy which

---

[1] *Op. cit.*, p. 75.   [2] *Op. cit.*, p. 135.   [3] *Pointing the Way*, p. 228.
[4] Professor at Münster, 1914–20; at Tübingen from 1920.   [5] *God Transcendent*, p. 26.

has no interest in coming to terms with modern secular thought does poor service to the cause of religion. So he sets out to restate the belief in a transcendent God in a way which shall be intelligible and convincing to contemporary minds.

Heim thinks that religious belief must be put on a foundation which lies outside of the reach of science, and he finds such a foundation in personal being, the world of 'I-Thou' relations as described by Buber. Science takes the 'I-It' attitude and shows us a world of objects. It shows us therefore only one side of the world, for we live at the same time in a world of interpersonal relations which cannot be objectivized. Buber supposes that it is possible to have an 'I-Thou' relation to nature, but Heim goes further and maintains a doctrine of panpsychism. Everything is animate, and so in everything there is an element which cannot be grasped objectively.

Heim's distinctive contribution to the philosophy of personal being comes with his introduction of the notion of spaces. It is well-known nowadays that Euclidean space is not the only kind. Heim uses the term 'space' in a wide sense for a framework of relationships, and speaks of spaces which have structures of a different order from geometrical spaces. Thus the worlds of 'I-It' and 'I-Thou' are represented as two distinct spaces. We ourselves are in both spaces.

This suggests a way of reconciling the scientific and spiritual attitudes to the world, for what is impossible in one kind of space may become possible in a space which discloses new dimensions. For instance, in two-dimensional space, through any point outside of a given straight line, there is only one straight line that can be drawn such that it will never intersect the first line; but in three-dimensional space, any number of lines can be drawn which will not intersect the first line. 'That which in the space hitherto known was the excluded third is in the new space not excluded. It is included in the extended range of dimensional possibilities which this new space contains within itself.'[1]

Heim now takes the further step of maintaining that physical space and interpersonal space are alike embraced in an archetypal space. This archetypal space is said to be the suprapolar space, since in it the polarities which characterize both physical and interpersonal space are overcome. The presence of God is found in the suprapolar space, and in this conception Heim claims to find a meaning for the idea of transcendence. God is not literally 'above' in a three-dimensional physical space but is found in the new dimension of the suprapolar space. That there is such a suprapolar space cannot indeed be proved. It is rather disclosed or

---

[1] *Christian Faith and Natural Science*, p. 150.

revealed in the life of faith, which may be understood as a fuller life, opening up hitherto unknown dimensions of being. The God who meets us in the suprapolar space is a 'Thou', or rather, he is 'the eternal "Thou" of all beings',[1] the suprapolar 'Thou', who has with us a personal relation free from the limitations which attend our relations with finite exclusive 'Thous' in the polar 'I-Thou' space.

58. Two Spanish Activists
M. de Unamuno, J. Ortega y Gasset

Of Miguel de Unamuno[2] (1864–1936), John A. Mackay, who knew him well, has said that in a sense he 'is the frankest and most thoroughgoing of existentialists' and also that 'he incarnated Spain in much the same way as the soul of Russia was incarnated in Dostoyevsky'.[3] As regards Mackay's first point, if we understand an 'existentialist' in the sense of one who regards truth as a concern of the whole person and not of the intellect alone, then Unamuno is certainly thoroughly committed to this point of view. But it is worth noting that some recent historians of philosophy, including Bochenski and Abbagnano, prefer to group Unamuno with the philosophers of life and action rather than with the existentialists, and, as we have suggested,[4] he is perhaps best regarded as intermediate between the activist philosophies and the later developments of existentialism. As regards Mackay's second point, Unamuno's inspiration derives primarily from the Spanish tradition, and he thought of himself as a kind of modern Don Quixote. Yet here we may notice that Unamuno was familiar with Kierkegaard and had written about him long before the name of the Danish thinker had acquired anything like its present vogue, and perhaps we may see some parallel between the image of Don Quixote and Kierkegaard's 'knight of faith' who seems crazy to the uncomprehending.[5]

It is in a discussion of Don Quixote that we find the following passage, in which Unamuno gives uncompromising expression to his anti-intellectualist and activist position: 'Not the intelligence, but the will makes our world. All is truth in so far as it feeds generous longings and bears fruitful works; all is falsehood that smothers noble impulses and aborts sterile

[1] *Op. cit.*, p. 216.

[2] Professor at Salamanca, 1892–1921, and rector, 1901–14; exiled for political reasons, 1921–30.

[3] 'Miguel de Unamuno' in *Christianity and the Existentialists*, ed. Carl Michalson, p. 47.

[4] See above, p. 195.

[5] See *Fear and Trembling*, p. 115.

monsters. Every creed that leads to living works is a true creed, as that one is false that conducts to deeds of death. Life is the criterion of truth, logic is but the criterion of reason. If my faith leads me to create life or to increase it, what further proof of my faith would you have? When mathematics kills, it is a lie. If, trudging half dead with thirst, you see a vision of what we call water, and, rushing to it, you drink, slake your thirst, and revive, that vision was genuine and the water true water.'[1]

This is a kind of pragmatism, but not the kind which sifts and criticizes beliefs in the light of their practical consequences. It is a much more subjective kind in which the will to believe is extravagantly emphasized and the distinction between dream and reality is blurred. Philosophy is not a disinterested intellectual quest for objective truth, but at bottom expresses the vital yearnings and feelings of the men who philosophize—concrete men of flesh and bone who cannot help philosophizing 'not with the reason only, but with the will, with the feelings, with the flesh and with the bones, with the whole soul and with the whole body'.[2] Philosophy has irrational roots in our feeling for life itself.

But life has its tragic character, for the reason is unable to confirm the beliefs of the heart, and may even contradict them. We cannot, however, abandon these beliefs, for without them life would be insupportable, and moreover they are based on the whole life itself, which is wider than reason. We must therefore continue to assert them and to live by them even when they are irrational or run counter to reason. 'Against values of the heart, reasons do not avail. For reasons are only reasons—that is to say, they are not even truths.'[3] Like Tertullian and Kierkegaard, Unamuno thinks that faith, so far from being supported by reason, must maintain itself in the face of reason. Faith is quixotic.

Central in Unamuno's conception of faith is the individual's belief in his own immortality. Though continually placed in doubt by the sceptical conclusions of reason, this belief keeps asserting itself in action—we must live so as to deserve immortality, and if there is only annihilation, then at least the universe will have been shown to be unjust. Thus faith maintains itself in suffering and struggle. 'Suffering', says Unamuno, 'is the substance of life and the root of personality.'[4] Through suffering, the individualistic faith in immortality expands to sympathy and love for all that lives and seeks to survive. It reaches out to God, as the universal life or consciousness which suffers in and with each individual life. The universe, Unamuno persuades himself, has a conscience; it is a personality that environs me, living, suffering, loving and asking for love.

---

[1] *Don Quixote Expounded with Comment*, pp. 114–15.   [2] *The Tragic Sense of Life*, p. 28.
[3] *Op. cit.*, p. 14.   [4] *Op. cit.*, p. 205.

Unamuno's faith is therefore a religious one. His religion is not a religion of peace and submission, but of struggle and action, maintaining itself amid doubt and uncertainty; and his God is a suffering striving God, symbolized above all in the suffering Christ.

José Ortega y Gasset[1] (1883–1955) stands, like Unamuno, between pragmatism and existentialism. Once again we are told that intellect is subordinate to life: 'Intelligence, science, culture have no other reality than that which accrues to them as tools for life.'[2] To believe otherwise is 'intellectualist folly', which destroys intelligence itself. Even our knowledge of things is not a disinterested knowledge of the things themselves—if one can talk of things 'themselves'—but a personally centred knowledge. Projected into an environment of things, 'man feels lost among them, stranded among them, and has no choice but to create a being for them, to invent one for their sake and for his own'.[3] He must do this because he has to get along with them, to find out what he can do with them and what he can expect from them.

The subordination of intelligence to life does not mean, however, that intelligence is to be despised. If intellectualism leads to a useless pedantry, sheer voluntarism is equally dangerous, for it means that man, instead of directing his environment, becomes enslaved to it and is made other than himself. Life is lived on a precipitous edge, and one may slip down on one side or the other. We think in order to live, but if we do not think well, we cannot live well and we suffer alteration from our genuine humanity. To live in harmony with ourselves, we need convictions that we can hold with a sense of personal and intimate veracity.

In history there are times of crisis when such convictions seem to fade away. At such times, man must withdraw into himself and undergo a radical and even paradoxical change of mind. 'He must abandon the false positions he occupied and come to himself, return to his own intimate truth, which is the only firm base.'[4] A classic instance is afforded by the breakdown of Roman civilization and its supersession by Christianity. According to Ortega y Gasset, the primitive Christian message may be expressed: 'Deny what you were up to this very moment and affirm your truth, recognize that you are lost. Out of this negation comes the new man who is to be constructed.'[5] Ortega y Gasset thinks that we too may be living in a time of crisis when the modern world that has lasted since the Renaissance may be giving way to something else. And he counsels us to make a new change of mind, to withdraw within ourselves, to take a

---

[1] Professor at Madrid, he went abroad after the Spanish Civil War, and taught in South America and Portugal. He returned to Spain in 1946.

[2] *Man and Crisis*, p. 112.   [3] *Op. cit.*, p. 107.   [4] *Op. cit.*, p. 151.   [5] *Op. cit.*, p. 151.

stand on the truth that is within us. In this way the convictions of the post-modern age will take shape.

But what shape? Ortega criticizes Christianity for looking beyond life to eternal beatitude as the justification for life; and likewise he criticizes secular doctrines of culture for supposing that life exists for the sake of producing cultural values. On the contrary, he maintains, life is valuable for its own sake, and vitality itself needs to be reinstated as a value. 'Is it not a theme worthy of a generation which stands at the most radical crisis of modern history, if an attempt be made to oppose the tradition, and see what happens if instead of saying, "Life for the sake of culture", we say, "Culture for the sake of life"?'[1]

Thus Ortega's 'existentialism', if we may so call it, has a strong bio-logical flavour. God himself would seem to be the sum total of that life which particularizes itself in individual existences, each with its own perspective on the world. He does not possess some transcendent universal viewpoint of his own, but 'enjoys the use of every point of view, resuming and harmonizing in his own unlimited vitality all our horizons'. He is 'the symbol of the vital torrent through whose infinite nets the universe gradually passes, being thus continuously steeped in and consecrated by life, that is to say, seen, loved, hated, painfully endured and pleasurably enjoyed by life'.[2]

59. The Russian Tradition
N. Berdyaev, S. Bulgakov

Nicolas Berdyaev[3] (1874–1948) was for a time a Marxist before he returned to the fold of the Russian Orthodox Church. Although his philosophy draws freely on Western thought, he claims that it is rooted in currents of Russian religious thought which have flowed for a long time in the history of his people. For Russian Christianity, he claims that 'there is to be found in it more freedom, more feeling of the brotherhood of man, more kindliness, more true humility and less love of power than in the Christianity of the West. Behind their external hierarchical system the Russians in their ultimate depth have always been anti-hierarchical, almost anarchist. There is something which does not belong to the realm of determinism in the life of the Russians, something which is too little grasped by the more rationally determined life of the men of the West.'[4]

---

[1] *The Modern Theme*, p. 70.
[2] *Op. cit.*, p. 95.
[3] Appointed professor at Moscow after the Russian Revolution, he was exiled in 1922 and lived mostly in France.
[4] *The Russian Idea*, pp. 253-5.

'Cognition', according to Berdyaev, 'is emotional and passionate in character. It is a spiritual struggle for meaning.'[1] Hence, like Unamuno, Berdyaev thinks of philosophy as an activity of the whole man, and as consciously or unconsciously shaped by the will and emotions of the philosopher. Or, to put it in another way, philosophy is concerned with concrete wisdom rather than abstract knowledge. 'Philosophy is the love of wisdom and the unfolding of wisdom in man, a creative effort to break through to the meaning of existence.'[2] It is even said that the choice of a philosophy will depend on the spirit of the philosopher himself, and will be settled by decision and emotion rather than by intellect. 'I define my own philosophy', says Berdyaev, 'as being of the subject, of spirit, of freedom; as being dualistically pluralist, creatively dynamic, personalist and eschatological.'[3] We shall briefly consider these distinguishing marks.

Like the other thinkers considered in this chapter, Berdyaev gives primacy to the subject over the object. Reality is, so to speak, behind us in the life of the subject rather than spread out before us in the objective world. 'There is no greater mistake than to confuse objectivity and reality. The objective is that which is least real.'[4] Like Ortega y Gasset, Berdyaev thinks that the danger to man is that he may become other than himself by being enslaved to the objective world which he creates, but Berdyaev goes further than any thinkers whom we have hitherto considered in his antipathy to objectification, which he identifies with the fall of man. In the quest for truth and reality, therefore, we must turn away from objects to the life of the subject.

The life of the subject is spirit, and spirit is characterized by freedom, as opposed to the determinism of the objective world. It is on the level of spirit that we have knowledge of God. As spirit, God is not like anything objective, and we cannot prove his existence by the discursive reasoning which is employed in relation to objects. God is not even creator of the objectified world. He is known intuitively in the depths of personal existence. Here we may notice a difference between Berdyaev's idea of God and the idea held by Kierkegaard and the Barthian theologians. Although there is a place for discontinuity in Berdyaev's philosophy, this is not a discontinuity between God and man, and God is not wholly other or qualitatively different from man. On the contrary, it is insisted that man has in him an indelible godlike element. 'The one and only reason for belief in God is the existence of the divine element in man. The very idea of revelation is made meaningless if he to whom God reveals himself is a creature of worthless insignificance who in no respect

---

[1] *The Beginning and the End*, p. 37. [2] *The Destiny of Man*, p. 5.
[3] *The Beginning and the End*, p. 51. [4] *Op. cit.*, p. 53.

corresponds to the One who reveals himself.'[1] The idea of the divine element in man is, of course, again one which is typical of eastern Christianity.

We can now see the dualistic character of Berdyaev's philosophy, the element of discontinuity which leads him to reject any monistic point of view. Standing over against one another in sharp distinction are the realm of spirit, which is the reality, subjectively grasped, free, creative and dynamic; and the objective world, the realm of being as it is sometimes called, a kind of congealed world which is phenomenal only. But we are not left with this blank opposition, for now the eschatological element in Berdyaev's thinking has to be taken into account. Russian philosophy, he tells us, looks to the end rather than to the beginning. Popular eschatology has objectified and distorted the profound spiritual truth in the idea. As Berdyaev understands it, what is meant is the redemption of the objectified order and its transformation into the spiritual order. This is not an automatic process, but one in which we can freely and creatively play a part; it is not a steady advance or progress, but may be subject to interruptions and reversals; it does not belong only to the end, but goes on continuously. 'At each moment of one's living, what is needed is to put an end to the old world and to begin the new.'[2]

While we have noted some parallels between Berdyaev and the two Spanish thinkers considered in the preceding section, we should notice also that Berdyaev's approach is much less individualistic than theirs. Berdyaev stands closer to Buber in respect of asserting the essential community of personal existence; and again he would claim that this is a Russian characteristic. 'Philosophical knowledge', he says, 'is personal in character, and the more personal it is, the more important it is. But the personal character of knowledge does not mean the isolation of personality, which gets to know things in communion and in community with the world and with men. Knowledge is at the same time personal and social.'[3]

Since Berdyaev claims that his ideas are rooted in the Russian religious tradition, we may conclude this section by glancing at a Russian theologian Sergius Bulgakov (1870–1944).[4] His career was similar to that of his friend Berdyaev—that is to say, he was for a time a Marxist, then returned to the Orthodox Church and spent much of his life in exile. How far his ideas can be taken as representative of the Russian Church is doubtful, since his writings were condemned by the Patriarch of

[1] *Op. cit.*, p. 234.   [2] *Op. cit.*, p. 254.   [3] *Op. cit.*, pp. 39–40.
[4] After lecturing in Moscow and Simferopol', he left Russia in 1923. In 1925 he founded the Institute of Orthodox Theology in Paris, and directed it till his death.

Moscow in 1935. The condemnation, however, may have been motivated more by political than by theological considerations.

Eastern Orthodox Christianity, Bulgakov assures us, is not the rigid petrified survival that the rationalistic mind of the West so often imagines it to be. Speaking of the Church, he says that it is to be regarded not as an institution but as a life; and similarly, speaking of the beliefs of his Church, he says that it gets along with a minimum of indispensable dogma, and that faith is not a doctrine but life itself. In both cases he illustrates his position by introducing conceptions which are unfamiliar in Western theology.

One is the conception of *sobornost*, which he defines as 'the state of being together'. This is said to be a distinctive mark of the Orthodox Church, differentiating it both from the authoritarianism of Roman Catholicism and from the individualism of Protestantism. In its outward sense, *sobornost* designates a conciliar Church, that is to say, a Church of ecumenical councils, as opposed to either a monarchical institution or a collection of individuals; in its inward sense, *sobornost* expresses 'the liberty in love which unites believers'.[1] This union, living and immediate, is said to be the very soul of Orthodoxy, and, like Berdyaev, Bulgakov holds that truth is accessible only within such a community of persons.

The other conception is *sophia* or wisdom. This is the principle which is common to God and man, the divine element in man which makes possible God's revelation. The truth which is revealed to wisdom is 'life in the truth, and not an abstract and theoretical knowledge'.[2] Revelation is said to be dialogue, colloquy, communion, conversation. 'Revelation is a *personal* act which takes place "face to face".'[3] Yet, as we might expect from Bulgakov's insistence on community, revelation, though personal, is not individualistic but is accumulated and integrated in corporate experience.

Of course, Bulgakov is no anarchist, and he believes both in the hierarchical ordering of the Church and in its basic dogmatic formulations. Yet the way in which he interprets the inward meaning of the Church and her beliefs indicates that personal and existential categories are by no means strange to the theology of the Russian Church.

[1] *The Orthodox Church*, p. 75.
[2] *Op. cit.*, p. 77.
[3] See Bulgakov's contribution to the symposium *Revelation*, ed. J. Baillie and H. Martin, p. 127.

60. The Form of the Personal
J. Macmurray

Just as he stands apart from the main stream of British philosophy, so in some respects John Macmurray[1] (1891–   ) stands somewhat apart from the writers hitherto considered in this chapter. He joins with them in agreeing that new ways of thinking must be sought, after the breakdown of established philosophical traditions, and he agrees further that it is to personal being that the philosopher must look. 'The cultural crisis of the present is a crisis of the personal',[2] and it is the personal that constitutes the emergent problem for philosophy. But whereas some of the writers expounded above might best be described as prophets, Macmurray is determined to remain a philosopher. Poetry, drama and paradox may have their uses, but they are not philosophy. Faced with the crisis of the personal, the philosopher's business is to discover the *form* of the personal.

In the past, Western philosophy has tried to conceive the self either as a substance, where the analogy is that of material thinghood, or as an organism, where the analogy is that of the living structure of a plant or animal. Such conceptions have broken down under criticism, and Macmurray thinks that we can never arrive at an adequate understanding of selfhood by such analogies. We must consider the self directly as a person, for to be personal is the distinctive characteristic of selfhood. Macmurray claims that we have indeed come to form an understanding of the substantial and the organic only by abstracting from the more inclusive conception of personal selfhood.

The error of traditional philosophy, Macmurray believes, was to take as its starting-point 'I think'—the self as subject. Macmurray proposes to substitute, as a new and more adequate starting-point, 'I do'—the self as agent. Thought is derivative from action, and when we recognize the primacy of the practical, then, Macmurray claims, it is possible to overcome the dualisms which are intractable for theoretical thinking. For when we set out from the standpoint of action, a new logical form emerges —the form of the personal, a unity in which the positive contains its own negative as a necessary constituent. Action itself contains mere process as its negative, for if we abstract from action its intentional character, it presents itself as a process of events. From the standpoint of action, it is argued, we must postulate that the world itself is not just a process, but one action, and so 'the argument which starts from the primacy of the practical moves steadily in the direction of a belief in God'.[3]

---

[1] Professor in London, 1928–44; Edinburgh, 1944–58.
[2] *The Self as Agent*, p. 29.   [3] *Op. cit.*, p. 221.

The sequel to *The Self as Agent* is *Persons in Relation*, for, like Buber, Macmurray thinks that an isolated self is an unreal abstraction. It is in the consideration of the community of personal selves that he states his view of the function of religion, already foreshadowed in the idea of the world as one action. Religion is distinctive of personal life, and there is no parallel to it among the animals. It celebrates and expresses the unity of persons in fellowship, and this in turn is possible only in a world informed by the unifying intention of God as the supreme Agent.

61. REMARKS ON THE PHILOSOPHERS OF PERSONAL BEING

One cannot read men like Buber, Unamuno and Berdyaev without being profoundly impressed by their wisdom of life. On almost every page of their writings, there are illuminating insights into the genuinely human problems which concretely confront every one of us in the daily business of living. A whole new world is opened up with sympathy and understanding—the world of personal relations. In an age like our own, which has been so largely preoccupied with things and their abstract relations, these writers have done a great service in bringing us back to our essentially personal nature. Even the individualism of some of them is excusable as a protest against the dehumanized mass-existence of our times. The great truth which these writers teach us is that we must take account of the personal realm, and that we cannot understand it in terms of anything but the personal itself, that is to say, in terms of our own personal existence.

Yet at the same time we have found confirmation of the suggestion made in the introductory section of this chapter that most of the writers considered are perhaps better described as 'prophets' than 'philosophers'. Or possibly we should call them 'seers', men of vision. From both philosophy and theology, it is right that we should expect some formal structure, for these are reflective disciplines, differing from poetry or devotional literature. Unamuno himself says that 'philosophy answers to our need of forming a complete and unitary conception of the world and of life'.[1] Wise and solid insights fall short of a philosophy or a theology unless they are given some formal unity. John Macmurray complains about philosophers of the kind whom we have been considering that while they get to grips with the genuine problems, they 'find no formal analysis that is equal to the task'.[2] There is some justice in this complaint, and it is for

---

[1] *The Tragic Sense of Life*, p. 2.   [2] *The Self as Agent*, pp. 27–8.

this reason that we have called these philosophers 'precursors of existential-ism' rather than 'existentialists', for none of them achieve the detailed existential analyses that we find in Heidegger and Sartre. There is, for instance, an aura of vagueness surrounding the existential elements in the thought of Ortega y Gasset, and this may be set down to his lack of existential analysis.

Of course, some philosophers of personal being might reply that the kind of analysis which we have in mind kills the living personal reality with which they desire to confront us. This is in fact the charge that has been brought against Heim, who would be least affected by the line of criticism stated in the preceding paragraph. Heim, by his theory of spaces, does try to provide some kind of formal framework for Buber's 'I-Thou' philosophy. But the adherents of Buber's philosophy claim that Heim has distorted it. Maurice Friedman, for instance, alleges that Heim has 'systematized the "I-Thou" philosophy to the point where it bears un-mistakable traces of that reliance on the reality of abstraction which characterizes the "I-It"'.[1] The real criticism of Heim, however, is not that he has tried to provide a formal structure for the philosophy of personal being but that he has chosen a singularly unfortunate way of going about it. It is surely impossible to explicate the structures of personal existence in terms of something so impersonal as space. If we want to know about space, we go to the mathematician and the physicist, not to the theologian; and if Heim tells us that there are 'spaces' of a different order from those which geometry studies, this can be only metaphor or analogy, useful perhaps up to a point, but certainly not having the value that Heim wants to assign to it. Yet the failure of Heim's attempt does not rule out the possibility of a formal analysis of the structures of personal existence in more adequate terms.

One must also be critical of some exaggerations among the thinkers we have been considering. They are right in upholding the importance and the irreducibility of personal being, but they sometimes go to extremes in their defence of it. An obvious example is Berdyaev's polemic against objectification and his identification of it with the fall of man. More serious, perhaps, is the irrationalism or even contrarationalism which is especially noticeable in Unamuno. It is justifiable to criticize an abstract intellectualism, to remind us that man is more than a cognitive being, and even to hold that some things which are veiled from the intellect may be disclosed in feeling or in striving. But it is going far beyond this when one begins to decry reason, or to claim that when reason contradicts our personal desires, it is a liar. Reason is admittedly not the whole of man

[1] *Martin Buber*, p. 271.

and its pretensions need sometimes to be held in check, but on the other hand it is an integral element in personal life which would be less than personal without a rational element to sift, guide and criticize our feelings and desires. A philosophy of personal being need not and ought not to fly in the face of reason, but unfortunately this tendency appears in some of the adherents of this kind of philosophy. In the concrete, life undoubtedly has its contradiction, its paradoxes and its discontinuities, and we can appreciate the fear that these features may be glossed over in an abstract rationalism; but the fear of a misuse of reason becomes a phobia when it attacks reason itself.

The philosophies of personal being are obviously of importance for religious thought. Like the philosophies of life and action, they make it clear that religion is an affair of the whole man, and that religious faith is not the same as intellectual belief. But the philosophies of personal being employ spiritual rather than biological categories and make personality rather than life or action central to their thought. In claiming a distinctive sphere for personal being, these philosophies opened up new ways of understanding religion as essentially a personal activity. Already we have seen that the insights of the philosophies of being can take different directions in their application to religion. Faith may be regarded as quixotic and paradoxical, discontinuous with reason and to be maintained in the face of it (Unamuno); or faith may be made possible by a divine element in man (Berdyaev); or it may be considered important to reconcile faith with the pronouncements of natural science (Heim). How these insights have developed further will be seen in later chapters on the Barthian type of theology and on existentialism.

XIII

THE RELIGIOUS CONSCIOUSNESS AND PHENOMENOLOGY

62. The Exploration of the Religious Consciousness

I N the present chapter we shall consider a group of thinkers who are only very loosely related among themselves. It is however convenient to bring them together, because all of them, in their several ways, employ an approach to the religious problem of a basically *descriptive* character. They set out to explore and describe the main features of the religious consciousness as found in the experience of religious persons. Such an approach might seem to be similar to that of the psychologies of religion already considered, but it differs from them in leaving aside their naturalistic presuppositions and in interesting itself more in the description of religious attitudes than in the genesis of religious beliefs. This approach is differentiated, on the other hand, by its contemplative attitude from the pragmatist and activist accounts of religion.

Many people would agree in naming Schleiermacher as the greatest theologian of the nineteenth century, and the views which we are about to consider may to some extent be regarded as continuing and developing the tradition which Schleiermacher initiated. Reacting against both the orthodoxy and the rationalism which prevailed at the beginning of the nineteenth century, Schleiermacher found the essence of religion in what he called a 'sense and taste for the Infinite',[1] or again, in a later and more famous phrase, a 'feeling of absolute dependence'.[2] The words 'sense', 'taste', 'feeling', could be misleading, since what Schleiermacher had in mind is not just a blind stirring, but an emotionally coloured attitude or state of mind which nevertheless carries in itself some kind of implicit understanding. Doctrine, for Schleiermacher, is not religion itself, but rather the making explicit through reflection of the understanding which is implicit in the religious affections. His theology is often called, therefore, a 'theology of consciousness' (*Bewusstseinstheologie*). Karl Barth sums

[1] *On Religion*, p. 39.   [2] *The Christian Faith*, p. 12.

up very neatly when he says that in Schleiermacher's theology 'Christian pious self-awareness contemplates and describes itself'.[1]

Somewhat parallel to the theological tradition stemming from Schleiermacher, there has arisen in the twentieth century a type of philosophy which takes as its task the precise description of the experiences of the conscious self, and which has worked out a definite method for accomplishing its purpose. This is the phenomenology of Edmund Husserl and his followers. While Husserl himself was interested primarily in logic and in the technical problems of philosophy, his disciples soon began to apply his method to the investigation of special problems in particular fields of expcreince. Among these was the field of religion, and phenomenology as a method of investigation has continued to be influential in theology down to the present time.

In what follows, we shall begin by examining the description of the primitive religious consciousness as given by the British anthropologist, R. R. Marett (Section 63). Then we shall turn to Rudolf Otto's classic exposition of man's experience of the holy—an exposition which, it should be noted, Husserl himself regarded as a masterly application of the phenomenological method to religion, although Otto, despite the fact that he and Husserl were colleagues at Göttingen, seems to have worked independently, and makes no explicit reference to Husserl's method (Section 64). We shall then leave aside the specifically religious problem to make an excursus into the field of philosophy, so that we can grasp some of the principles in Husserl's phenomenology that have been significant for later theology and philosophy of religion (Section 65). Coming back to the religious problem, we shall see how the phenomenological method is explicitly applied to it by Max Scheler and others (Section 66). A concluding section will gather together the results of our several surveys, and will indicate the lines of further development (Section 67).

63. THE PRIMITIVE RELIGIOUS CONSCIOUSNESS
R. R. Marett

In the English anthropologist, Robert Ranulph Marett[2] (1866–1943), we find that a new direction is given to the study of primitive religion. In 1902 Marett had been a contributor to the symposium, *Personal Idealism*,[3] and like his collaborators, he declared his opposition both to naturalism and to speculative idealism. Hence, what Marett offers us is neither a naturalistic nor a metaphysical explanation of the origin of

---

[1] [*Protestant Thought:*] *From Rousseau to Ritschl*, p. 338.   [2] Professor at Oxford.
[3] See above, p. 54. Marett's essay was entitled 'Origin and Validity in Ethics'.

religion. He says that he has sought 'not so much to explain as to describe', that he has concentrated his attention on 'the psychological analysis of rudimentary religion', and that his aim has been 'to translate a type of religious experience remote from our own into such terms of our consciousness as may best enable the nature of that which is so translated to appear for what it is in itself'.[1]

Central in Marett's account is the idea of '*mana*'. This word comes from the Pacific regions, but the idea for which it stands is said to be widespread among primitive peoples, and so the word itself has come to be generally applied to a certain type of religious experience, represented also in the *orenda* and *wakanda* of North American tribes, the *mulungu* of African tribes, and so on. What then is *mana*? Marett quotes the English missionary, Bishop R. H. Codrington, who describes *mana* as 'a force altogether distinct from physical power, which acts in all kinds of ways for good and evil'.[2] This occult force is supposed to attach to a wide range of natural objects, artefacts, and even persons, and to it are attributed success in war, prosperity in agriculture, prowess in hunting, and so on. The negative aspect of *mana* is *tabu*. That which possesses *mana* is *tabu*, that is to say, it is not to be lightly approached, lest its power break forth in a harmful and destructive fashion.

What does *mana* tell us about the mentality of the people among whom it is found? According to Marett, what lies behind *mana* is not so much an idea as an emotional attitude—though no doubt such an attitude contains elements which may become eventually conceptualized. 'Savage religion', he says, 'is something not so much thought out as danced out; it develops under conditions which favour emotional and motor processes, whereas ideation remains relatively in abeyance.'[3] It is on this point that Marett takes issue with the theory of primitive animism—he thinks that Tylor, for instance, gives far too intellectual an account of the matter, treating primitive religion as if it were primarily a matter of belief. It should be remembered, however, that Tylor deliberately set out to examine the intellectual side of primitive religion, and he was fully aware that its beliefs are closely associated with powerful affective states. However this may be, Marett thinks that in *mana* we have evidence of a pre-animistic phase of religion—a phase in which feeling predominates over thought, or in which thought and reflection have not yet emerged from feeling.

'Of all English words', says Marett, ' "awe" is the one that expresses the fundamental religious feeling most nearly.'[4] It is awe, then, that constitutes the core of the primitive religious consciousness, and is man's

[1] *The Threshold of Religion*, pp. xxiii-xxviii.   [2] *Op. cit.*, p. 104.
[3] *Op. cit.*, p. xxxi.   [4] *Op. cit.*, p. 13.

reaction to the hidden mysterious forces of his environment. By 'awe', Marett tells us, he understands something much more than merely fear. Religion does not originate just in fear of the unknown, and Marett is not subscribing to the view expressed in the well-known line of Petronius: *Primus in orbe deos fecit timor*. According to Marett, we must admit 'wonder, admiration, interest, respect, even love perhaps, to be, no less than fear, essential constituents of the elemental mood of awe'.[1] Humility too belongs to the complex.

Mana, as we have learned from Codrington's description, can act for good and evil, and is in itself non-moral. It is, in Marett's view, a kind of undifferentiated magico-religious matrix, from which both religion and magic take their rise. Marett thus rejects Frazer's view of the relation of magic to religion.[2] The line of religious development consists in the moralizing and spiritualizing of the primitive experience which, as we have seen, already contains in itself the seeds of more refined feelings—reverence, love, humility and the like—as well as the possibility for intellectual development through reflection. Religion, in Marett's view, is a permanent possibility of the human spirit, but in its many variations it will retain as its basic structure something akin to that attitude of awe which is disclosed in the study of *mana*. And indeed it is not difficult to see the lines of connection between the Melanesian's experience of *mana* and, let us say, Schleiermacher's more sophisticated 'sense and taste for the Infinite'.

64. THE EXPERIENCE OF THE HOLY
R. Otto, J. W. Oman

In this chapter of our survey a central position is occupied by Rudolf Otto[3] (1869–1937) because he links together the somewhat scattered topics that have been included in the chapter. He was an admirer of Schleiermacher, whom he credited with a 'rediscovery of religion'.[4] He had a high regard for the anthropological work of Marett, and believed that the views of the English scholar 'came within a hair's breadth' of his own.[5] On the other hand, as we have noted, Otto himself was praised by Husserl for having made a masterly phenomenological analysis of the religious consciousness. But apart altogether from the fact that he illumines the connections among the different approaches to the description

[1] *Ibid.* [2] See above, p. 103.
[3] Professor at Göttingen, 1904–14; Breslau, 1914–17; Marburg, 1917–29.
[4] See his essay, 'How Schleiermacher Rediscovered the *Sensus Numinis*', in *Religious Essays*, pp. 68-77.
[5] *The Idea of the Holy*, p. 15, n. 1.

of the religious consciousness, Otto is in his own right a religious thinker of first-class importance. My own teacher, Professor C. A. Campbell, has stated that to him Otto is 'by a wide margin the most illuminating religious thinker of modern times'; and even those who might hesitate to subscribe to so decisive a judgment would agree with Professor Campbell's further remark that acquaintance with Otto is 'among the most rewarding experiences that anyone with a concern for religious understanding is likely to enjoy in a lifetime'.[1]

Otto's analysis of the structure of the religious consciousness is based on an elucidation of the key-word of all religion—the word 'holy'. This word stands for a composite group of characteristics. Some of these characteristics are rational, in the sense that they can be thought conceptually. For instance, 'holiness' commonly includes the notion of 'moral goodness', and we have some conception of what goodness is. But these rational characteristics do not exhaust the meaning of the word 'holy', and indeed, in Otto's view, they are derivative. In its most fundamental sense, the word 'holy' stands for a non-rational character, that is to say, a character which cannot be thought conceptually. For this fundamental signification of the 'holy', taken in isolation from such derivative meanings as 'moral goodness', Otto employs the term 'numinous'— a term derived from the Latin *numen*, which may be fairly said to have had originally the same kind of semantic range as Marett's '*mana*' and similar words in other languages. The numinous is inconceivable, but it can be pointed to, and it *is* pointed to in the word 'holy'.

From this preliminary examination of its key-word, we see then that religion is compounded of rational and non-rational elements. The Christian thinks of God in terms of goodness, personality, purpose, and so on, and although—as Otto recognizes—these ideas are applied to God analogically, they are nevertheless rational characteristics in the sense that we have definite concepts of them. This rational side of religion, Otto believes, is an indispensable element in it, but it has tended to over-shadow the deeper non-rational core. God is not exhausted in his rational attributes. He is the 'holy' God, and the adjective points to his deeper, inconceivable, suprarational nature. Otto wishes to stress this non-rational side of religion, for traditional theology has, in his view, lost sight of it and given an excessively intellectualistic interpretation.

But if the numinous core of religion is inconceivable, how can we talk about it or describe it? Otto holds that although it is inconceivable, it is somehow within our grasp. We apprehend it in feeling, in the *sensus numinis*—and by 'feeling', as we shall see, is intended not mere emotion

[1] *On Selfhood and Godhood*, pp. 327, 331.

but an affective state of mind which involves some kind of valuation and preconceptual cognition. The most valuable part of Otto's study consists of his careful analysis of the feeling-states which constitute the numinous experience. There is on the one side what is called 'creature-feeling'—the feeling of the nothingness of finite being. On the other side is the feeling of the presence of an overwhelming Being—the numinous Being which strikes dumb with amazement. Otto's analysis is summarized in the expression '*mysterium tremendum et fascinans*'. *Mysterium* points to what is called the 'wholly other' character of the numinous Being, which, as suprarational, utterly transcends the grasp of conceptual thought. The element of *tremendum* points to the awe or even the dread experienced in face of the majesty, overpoweringness and dynamic energy of the numinous Presence. The element of *fascinans* points to the captivating attraction of the numinous Being, evoking rapture and love.

So far, Otto's description of the numinous state of mind may look like a more detailed version of Schleiermacher's 'feeling of absolute dependence'. But Otto differentiates his own position from Schleiermacher's, and this becomes important when we are led on from the description of the numinous experience to the question of its validity. According to Otto, Schleiermacher, while indeed stressing the distinctiveness of the feeling of religious dependence, makes the distinction between the feeling of absolute dependence and feelings of relative dependence one of degree, rather than of kind. Perhaps the point is debatable, for it may be that a feeling of *absolute* dependence would necessarily imply qualitative distinctness. In any case, Otto himself insists that the feelings revealed in the analysis of the numinous experience, while analogous to natural feelings, have a *unique quality*. The *sensus numinis* is something *sui generis*. He firmly maintains that it cannot be compounded out of merely natural feelings, nor can it even, on account of its qualitative distinctness, be regarded as evolved from natural feelings. It is connected by Otto with what he calls the 'faculty of divination'—a 'faculty, of whatever sort it may be, of *genuinely* cognizing and recognizing the holy in its appearance'.[1]

These speculations prepare the way for Otto's assertion that the holy is an *a priori* category. Its non-rational or numinous element is said to arise 'from the deepest foundation of cognitive apprehension that the soul possesses'.[2] The idea of a non-rational category may surprise us, and when we find Otto talking also of 'a hidden predisposition of the human spirit'[3] we may think that what he has in mind is more like one of Jung's archetypes[4] than like one of Kant's categories. But Otto would reject the naturalistic flavour of Jung's thought, and in any case, he has an

[1] *The Idea of the Holy*, p. 148.   [2] *Op. cit.*, p. 117.   [3] *Op. cit.*, p. 119.   [4] See above, p. 110.

additional reason for turning to Kant. For Otto has still to show how the rational and non-rational elements in religion are connected, and in order to do this he invokes Kant's theory of the schematism of the categories. This is one of the most difficult doctrines in the *Critique of Pure Reason*. It seeks to show how the pure categories of the understanding become applicable to the phenomena of experience, intuited under the forms of space and time. Otto similarly seeks to show that the originally non-moral and non-rational category of the 'numinous' undergoes schematization in human experience so as to acquire those moral and rational characteristics which transform it into the idea of the 'holy'.

Whatever we may think of the more speculative elements in Otto's thought—and they will be criticized in due course—we must acknowledge that in his analysis of the numinous he has led us into the innermost sanctuary of religion, and described it with extraordinary power.

It is interesting to compare with Otto's account of the holy the quite independent researches of the Scottish theologian, John Wood Oman[1] (1860–1939). An early interest in Schleiermacher led him to make the English translation of *On Religion*, from which we have quoted above;[2] while a reading of Windelband's essay on the holy[3] was another important influence in determining the direction of Oman's thought.

Oman makes a fourfold analysis of our experience in the face of any environment. There is '(1) the unique character of the feeling it creates; (2) the unique value it has for us; (3) the immediate conviction of a special kind of objective reality, which is inseparable from this valuation; and (4) the necessity of thinking it in relation to the rest of experience and the rest of experience in relation to it'.[4] This formal scheme is then applied to the concrete case of religious experience. Here the unique feeling is the sense of the holy. This feeling is inseparable from a valuation—the judgment of the sacred. 'The "sacred", as here used, just means absoluteness of value, that which is of incomparable worth, and incomparable is not merely super-excellent, but what may not be brought down and compared with other goods.'[5] The sacred, in turn, is not a free-floating value, but attaches to an objective reality in the environment—the supernatural. The supernatural is the special concern of religion. The supernatural is not to be inferred from the natural as something standing behind it. The two are given together, 'so constantly interwoven that nothing may be wholly natural or wholly supernatural'.[6] The distinction is that the natural is known by sensation and its varied comparative values, while the

---

[1] Professor at Westminster (Presbyterian) College, Cambridge, from 1907, and Principal, 1925–35.
[2] See above p. 210.   [3] In *Präludien*, p. 357.   [4] *The Natural and the Supernatural*, p. 58.
[5] *Op. cit.*, p. 65.   [6] *Op. cit.*, p. 72.

supernatural is known by the sense of the holy and its sacred or absolute value. The last element in this fourfold analysis of religious experience is theology—the attempt to think the experience as a coherent whole.

Here we must pause to notice Oman's sharp criticism of Otto's idea of the numinous. Oman complains that this idea separates feeling from valuation, and puts at the centre of religion a 'mere impression of an awe-inspiring something, the mightier for stirring intense feeling the vaguer it is'.[1] Against this, he maintains that the sense of the holy 'may also be the calmest of all responses to a reality in which we find our true independence'.[2] No one would wish to quarrel with this last sentence, but we may well feel that the criticism of Otto has missed the mark. The one-sidedness of Oman's censure has been effectively exposed by Professor Campbell. Oman has dwelt on only one major aspect—the *tremendum*—in Otto's analysis of the numinous. 'But surely it is the merest caricature of Otto's position to put forward this *one* major aspect as sufficiently defining what Otto means by the numinous? What of the *other* major element or factor, the other of what Otto expressly calls the "two poles" of the numinous consciousness—the *fascinans*? The *fascinans* aspect is that in virtue of which the numinous consciousness is enraptured and entranced by the transcendent *worth* or *value* of the *numen*.'[3]

But leaving aside this controversy, let us go on to see how Oman elucidates the character of the supernatural. Recognizing that historically the supernatural has been conceived in many ways, Oman refers these differences to different ways of conceiving the relation of the supernatural to the natural, and on the basis of this he sets forth a classification of religious types.[4] Where the supernatural is conceived as a vague force diffused through the natural, we have *primitive animism*. The attempt to manage the natural by faith in individual supernatural spirits believed to rule over various parts of the natural is *polytheism*. The *mystical* type of religion is usually associated with the pantheistic acceptance of the natural in its wholeness as the supernatural. *Legalistic* religion is associated with a dualism which sharply distinguishes the sacred from the profane. Finally, there is 'reconciliation to the natural by faith in one personal Supernatural, who gives meaning to the natural and has a purpose beyond it'.[5] This last type is *prophetic* religion and true monotheism. Oman rightly points out that every classification of this kind must be made from the writer's own point of view, and he will have adopted this point of view because he regards it as the most adequate. Oman believes that the

[1] *Op. cit.*, p. 61.   [2] *Ibid.*   [3] *On Selfhood and Godhood*, p. 343.
[4] This may be compared with the phenomenological types listed by G. van der Leeuw. See below, p. 221.
[5] *The Natural and the Supernatural*, p. 370.

supernatural is most truly conceived in prophetic religion, for here it is conceived under the highest terms available to us—ethical and personal terms.[1]

65. THE METHOD OF PHENOMENOLOGY
E. Husserl

We have seen that Otto's description of the religious consciousness was hailed as a masterly piece of phenomenological analysis by Edmund Husserl[2] (1859–1938), and we must now take a closer look at the phenomenological method of investigation which Husserl worked out. No attempt can be made here to give anything like an adequate account of the difficult and wide-ranging thought of this important thinker, but in a book devoted to the problems of religion we are under no obligation to do so. Husserl himself was primarily a technical philosopher, interested in problems of logic and methodology. Yet his influence has been so widespread, and has made itself felt in so many fields, including those of theology and the philosophy of religion, that we are bound to take at least a barely adequate notice of him if we are hoping to understand properly some later writers who will fall within our purview, and we shall immediately go on in the next section to the explicit application of the phenomenological method to the study of religion, as found in one of Husserl's disciples.

Husserl's aim is to make philosophy a strict science, different in kind from the empirical sciences whose results are always provisional and subject to revision. Phenomenology is the method which Husserl has devised for the accomplishment of his aim, and he repeatedly states that phenomenology is a 'descriptive science'. It describes and distinguishes the phenomena given in consciousness without introducing doubtful presuppositions or fallible deductions. But it is extremely difficult to attain to this phenomenological standpoint, or even to understand precisely what it is. Husserl complained that more often than not he got misunderstood, and he warns us frankly that 'to move freely along this new way without ever reverting to the old viewpoints, to learn to see what stands before our eyes, to distinguish, to describe, calls for exacting and laborious studies'.[3]

Perhaps the easiest way of getting some grasp of what phenomenology is, is to begin by clearly recognizing *what it is not*. Husserl emphatically

[1] H. H. Farmer makes the interesting point that although personal categories were usually regulative of Oman's thought, he introduces them rather late and somewhat grudgingly into *The Natural and the Supernatural*. See *Revelation and Religion*, p. 28, n. 1.

[2] He was appointed to academic posts successively at Halle (1887), Göttingen (1900) and Freiburg (1916).

[3] *Ideas: General Introduction to Pure Phenomenology*, p. 43.

insists that phenomenology *is not* psychology. For although both psychology and phenomenology are concerned to describe the experiences of the self, their approaches are quite different. The distinction is twofold. Firstly, psychology, as an empirical science, deals with 'facts', whereas phenomenology, as a science of a different order, is concerned not with 'facts' but with 'essences'; secondly, psychology is a science of 'realities', understood as events which have a place in the spatio-temporal world, whereas phenomenology is said to 'purify' the phenomena from what lends them 'reality', and to consider them apart from their setting in the 'real world'.[1]

These distinctions enable us to grasp two of the leading characteristics of phenomenology. It is, in the first place, what Husserl calls an 'eidetic' science, that is to say, it is a knowledge of universal essences. The eidetic character of phenomenology reminds us of Plato's theory of ideas, and presumably it is to universal essences that we must look if we are to achieve that certainty and that precision which are unattainable in the realm of individual empirical facts. In the second place—and here we come to the most characteristic and also the most difficult element in the phenomenological method—the intuition of the essence is to be attained by an '*epoche*', that is to say, by a suspension of judgment. This is the phenomenological 'reduction', whereby an object which is present to consciousness is reduced to the pure phenomenon by 'putting in brackets' or excluding from further interest those elements which do not belong to the universal essence. For instance, the existence of the individual object is to be bracketed. Again, one must seek to exclude from the mind any presuppositions derived from previous philosophy—this is the 'philosophic epoche'. Other bracketings too are to be carried out, and if the procedure is followed, one is said to come to 'the things themselves', to the pure phenomena which can then be described in their essence free from distorting factors.

Phenomenology thus becomes a fundamental investigation into the basic structures of consciousness, and into the conditions under which any kind of experience is possible. Husserl himself came round to an idealist metaphysic in a way which is reminiscent of Descartes' procedure of doubt. When everything else has been bracketed, one cannot bracket consciousness itself, save by a conscious act, so that consciousness remains as the sole Absolute. Some of his followers, however, do not think that idealism is a necessary consequence of his doctrines, and they have seen the chief value of his work as providing a method for obtaining clear descriptions of the basic structures which belong to the various fields of conscious experience.

[1] *Op. cit.*, pp. 44–5.

66. THE PHENOMENOLOGICAL INVESTIGATION OF RELIGION
M. Scheler, G. van der Leeuw, M. Eliade

While we have seen that Otto's account of the religious consciousness may be called 'phenomenological', we must turn to one of Husserl's most famous disciples, Max Scheler[1] (1874–1928), for an explicit application of phenomenology to the problems of religion. Scheler had been a student under Eucken, from whom he gained an interest in the philosophy of the spiritual life, and he saw Husserl's phenomenology as affording a way of investigating man's spiritual experience.

Like Husserl, Scheler distinguished sharply between the empirical knowledge of facts and the *a priori* knowledge of essences, but whereas Husserl had been interested primarily in logical essences, Scheler directs phenomenology upon the practical and affective life of man. For even feelings have their *a priori* structure; they carry with them their own kind of understanding and have their own 'logic of the heart', in Pascal's phrase. This *a priori* structure is grounded on values, which are the objects of feeling. Scheler recognizes four classes of values, which he arranges in a hierarchical scheme. Lowest in the scheme stand *sensible* values—the pleasant and the unpleasant; then there are *vital* values, such as the noble and the common; next come *spiritual* values, such as the beautiful and the ugly; at the top of the scale stand the *religious* values, the holy and the unholy. Moral values do not appear in this list because Scheler, following St Augustine, for whom he had a great admiration, thinks that morality has to do with preferring the higher goods to the lower goods.

From our point of view, the interesting feature of Scheler's scheme is the distinctive place given to religious values. This sharply differentiates his scheme from that of Windelband,[2] and brings him close to Otto. For, like Otto, Scheler considers the religious value to be *sui generis*. It has a distinct irreducible essence which cannot be explained in terms of anything other than itself. This essence is identical in all manifestations of the holy, from the most primitive to the most advanced, so that it does not evolve, though of course the intuition of the essence may develop.

Since he thus rejects any naturalistic account of religion, Scheler is committed to the point of view which is already indicated in the title of the volume containing his religious writings—*On the Eternal in Man*. 'The veritable eternal does not exclude time, or stand alongside time, but embraces in timeless fashion the content and fullness of the times, and penetrates their every moment.'[3] The eternal in man is his permanent

---

[1] Professor at Cologne, 1919–28.   [2] See above, p. 79.   [3] *Op. cit.*, p. 7.

possibility for the religious experience, and this he has in virtue of the very structure of his being. The analysis of this structure shows man to be more than a merely natural phenomenon. He is a person, and in so far as he is a person, he is theomorphic, seeking God and capable of responding to him. The religious experience culminates in love, which, as more than a feeling, does not have a value for its object, but always a person. God is the Person of persons, and the source of love.

The systematic application of phenomenology to religion in all its manifestations, primitive and modern, eastern and western, is carried out by Gerardus van der Leeuw[1] (1890–1950). In his notable book, *Religion in Essence and Manifestation*, He seeks neither a naturalistic account of the origin and evolution of religion, nor a metaphysical account of its ultimate nature. His aim is to explore the structure of the religious pheno- menon as it offers itself in experience. But religions cannot be laid out on a table, as it were, and studied objectively like pieces of rock. The pheno- menon is neither purely subjective nor purely objective.

Man not only lives, but seeks power for his life. Religion arises at the point where man's own power is met by another power, such as the *mana* of primitive religion. 'A strange, wholly other power obtrudes into life.'[2] Phenomenology, of course, cannot grasp this power in itself, but only in the phenomena in which it is experienced.

Van der Leeuw goes on to describe the types of religion in which man is encountered by this wholly other power. The religion of *remoteness*, exemplified by Confucianism and eighteenth-century deism, is one in which the power is at a distance. This type of religion is characterized by man's flight from the power, and its limiting case is atheism. 'There is no historical religion quite devoid of atheism.'[3] The religion of *struggle* is dualistic. Zoroastrianism is the classic example, and in this type man participates in the cosmic conflict. The religion of *repose* has no particular historical exemplar, but describes the mystical type that is found in all traditions. Greek religion is a religion of *form*, manifesting itself alike in the statues of the gods and the ideas of Plato. Hinduism shows the religion of *infinity* and Buddhism the religion of *nothingness*. There is a religion of *will*, correlated with obedience on the part of the worshipper, and a religion of *majesty* correlated with humility. These types are illustrated respectively in Israel and Islam. Finally, there is the religion of *love*— 'the typology of Christianity needs only one word—love'.[4]

Van der Leeuw does not conceal his belief that Christianity is the central form of historical religion. This does not mean that other religions are to be dismissed as spurious or illusory, but he maintains that an unprejudiced

[1] Professor at Groningen, 1918–50.　[2] *Op. cit.*, p. 681.　[3] *Op. cit.*, p. 601.　[4] *Op. cit.*, p. 646.

or neutral attitude is impossible. This follows from what has been said already, that religions cannot be laid out on the table and examined like so many natural objects. Comparison implies a standard of comparison, and this standard will be the investigator's own religion, to which he stands in a peculiar relation. This will be true even if his religion is atheism, which, as we have seen, is a limiting case of a special religious attitude, the avoidance of God.

Phenomenology plays a large part also in the studies of religion made by the Roumanian scholar, Mircea Eliade[1] (1907–   ). His interest has been directed primarily towards myth and symbol. His aim is not to disentangle the genesis or evolution of these, but, as he tells us, 'our ambition is to understand their meaning, to endeavor to see what they show us'.[2]

The symbols of ancient mythology integrated the experience of archaic man. When anything was used as a symbol, it was transformed from what it seems to be in profane experience into a cosmic principle, embodying a whole system in itself. Archaic peoples did not have words like 'being', 'reality', 'becoming' and the like, but they nevertheless had their ontology, implicit in their myths. Eliade's comparative study of the archaic myths leads him to see these as embodying 'archetypes', a word which he uses in a different sense from Jung. Eliade's 'archetypes' are exemplary acts performed by gods or heroes in the beginning, or rather in mythical time, and all subsequent human actions repeat these. The first battle, the first marriage, the first dance—these become the timeless models for imitation. The myths and rituals of archaic religion bring again the moment of creation when everything was given and revealed. Archaic man, in other words, had no understanding of history as we understand it—as an irreversible unrepeatable happening for which man is responsible and in which he makes himself. Archaic man did not have to tolerate the weight of history, for it was concealed from him by his myth of the ever-recurring events. 'This eternal return reveals an ontology uncontaminated by time or becoming.'[3]

Biblical religion broke out of the cyclical framework, and revelation became not cosmic but historical. The God of the Hebrew people is not one who creates archetypal gestures, but one who constantly acts irreversibly in history. This idea is carried on and enriched in Christianity, with its recognition of the unique event of Jesus Christ. In popular Christianity, it is true, the archetypes tend to return, and men take shelter in them from the terror of history. But for the individual, Judaeo-Christian religion

---

[1] Professor at Bucharest, 1933–9. After teaching in France, he became professor at Chicago, 1958.
[2] *Cosmos and History*, p. 74.   [3] *Op. cit.*, p. 89.

makes possible the attitude of faith, of which Abraham is the first example. By 'faith' is understood a creative freedom, subject to no natural laws and having its source and support in God. Christianity thus becomes the religion of fallen man, that is to say, of man who is irremediably identified with history and who has been driven out of the paradise of eternally recurring archetypes.

67. REMARKS ON THE DESCRIPTIVE APPROACH TO RELIGION

A descriptive approach to religion, whether it takes the form of a strict phenomenological analysis in Husserl's sense, or proceeds in a more general way, does seem to have much to commend it. It sets plainly before us what the basic elements in religious experience are, without distorting the picture by introducing doubtful speculations about the possible genesis or ultimate significance of such experience; or at least it defers speculative constructions until after the descriptive work has been carried out, as is the case with Otto. Of course, it is questionable whether the kind of 'philosophic *epoche*' of which Husserl speaks is possible. Husserl certainly agrees that it is a most difficult exercise to purify the mind of presuppositions. Oman and van der Leeuw frankly say that their descriptions are made from a definite point of view, though this does not mean that they are being grossly partisan. Presumably one can aim at presenting the thing itself, the essence of the phenomenon which appears in the religious consciousness. And in such thinkers as Marett, Otto and Scheler, we do seem to get the essence of the phenomenon, that which is genuinely religion, for these thinkers have penetrated to the affective states of mind which lie at the heart of religion, and which are so often overlooked both in intellectualist accounts which understand religion as a kind of world-view, and in pragmatic accounts which tend to assimilate religion to morality.

By any reckoning, an accurate description of the typical experiences of the religious person, and a description which is, moreover, as far as possible free from presuppositions, naturalistic or otherwise, would seem to provide at least a firm starting-point for an investigation into religion. But would something more be required? Perhaps the answer to this question depends on whether or not the religious experience can be regarded as *sui generis*, qualitatively unique and irreducible. Otto, Oman and Scheler take this view, but Marett is more cautious, and suggests that the awe which he considers basic to religion may be compounded of natural feelings like fear, love, reverence and the like.

Now if religion is a distinct and autonomous region of experience, it might be claimed that its deliverances are entitled to the same respect as we accord to those of any other region of experience. In that case, it might be sufficient to describe this religious experience in its pure essence, and assert for its intimations equal rights as over against other fields of experience. On the other hand, if religious experience is compounded out of 'ordinary' feelings, the question of its validity would be much more difficult to answer. It could be the case that in the experience of the holy, natural feelings have been switched from their normal objects and projected upon an imaginary object, and have been so subtly compounded that the resultant combination looks like a new and unique kind of feeling.

Both Otto and Scheler think it important to maintain the unique quality of the religious experience, but when they seek to do this by talking of a faculty of divination or of the theomorphic structure in man, they seem to have left the relatively firm ground of description and receded into a more speculative realm. To take Otto as an example, it will be recalled that he adopts Kantian terminology and speaks of the 'numinous' as an *a priori* category which undergoes schematization into the idea of the 'holy'. Kantian scholars, however, have had no difficulty in showing that the comparison with Kant is a specious one. For instance, H. J. Paton points out that apart from the difficulty of knowing what a non-rational category might be, Otto first of all confuses Kant's Ideas of Reason with the categories of understanding, and then reverses what Kant means by schematism—in Kant this is the incorporation of a non-rational element into a rational concept, whereas in Otto it is the addition of a rational element to what was originally non-rational.[1] It would seem therefore that the analogy between Otto's schematism and Kant's is pretty remote. This merely shows, however, that Otto misuses Kant, and it may not be the case that his general position is a mistaken one. But one is bound to say that he has not made out his case decisively.

However searching and accurate the descriptions of religious experience that are offered to us may be, it seems that they cannot establish the validity of such experience. As Bochenski has said of phenomenology, 'What it lacks is a capacity to grasp concrete being; it is a philosophy of essence and not of being.'[2] Yet on the other hand a clear description of religious experience must be the first step towards its assessment. Perhaps there is no way at all in which the validity of religious experience can be *established*, and one can only be pointed to the kind of experiences which Otto and the others describe, and be left to decide about it in the light of the most honest discrimination of one's experience that can be made.

---

[1] *The Modern Predicament*, pp. 137–9. [2] *Contemporary European Philosophy*, p. 153.

From a different angle, the descriptive approach to religion has been criticized by some theologians. Barth and his school have turned away from the tradition of Schleiermacher and from *Bewusstseinstheologie* on the grounds that we should look to revelation and to the Bible rather than to religious experience. Yet to this it might be replied that revelation and the teaching of the Bible must be appropriated in experience, and certainly both Otto and Scheler attached great importance to revelation.

In any case, we shall find that phenomenology continues to exercise a powerful influence which extends into the religious thought of our own day. Paul Tillich states that 'theology must apply the phenomenological approach to all its basic concepts', though he regards this as a preliminary to 'discussing their truth and actuality'.[1] Among philosophers, we shall meet again with phenomenology in Hartmann and Heidegger, adapted to their needs. But already we can recognize the value of phenomenology and allied methods as a way of getting light on our subject-matter and coming to grips with its genuine problems.

---

[1] *Systematic Theology*, vol. I, p. 118.

XIV

THE NEW REALISM

68. The Revolt against Idealism

I F this book aimed at giving a general account of philosophy in the
twentieth century, then the present chapter on the movement called
the 'New Realism' would need to be a very long one, because this
movement is one of the most important philosophical developments in
recent times—certainly *the* most important in the English-speaking
countries. But since our aim is the much more restricted one of tracing
the story of religious thought in the twentieth century, the present chapter
will in fact turn out to be a fairly short one. The reason for this is that
many of the leading spirits of the new movement were either indifferent
or hostile to religion, and so made little contribution to religious thought.
The movement itself marks a widening of the gulf between philosophy and
theology, and a loosening of their traditional ties. Yet if we are to give a
fair survey of modern religious thought, we must take account of hostile
evaluations as well as friendly ones, and even when we find a philosopher
who is almost silent on the subject of religion, we must inquire whether
this silence may be due to a conviction that the traditional problems of
religion are not a fit subject for philosophical discussion.

The word 'realism' has borne various meanings in the history of
philosophy, but nowadays it may be taken to stand for the view that we
have knowledge of a real world which exists quite independently of our
cognition of it. Realism is regarded as opposed to idealism, for which the
world is in some sense mind-dependent. The so-called 'New Realism'
emerged at the turn of the century as a revolt against the dominance of
idealism, and as a kind of third force between idealism and the materialistic naturalisms of the nineteenth century. The pragmatists too were
realists and opponents of idealism, but the new realist movement was
intellectualist in character, and so just as much opposed to pragmatism as
to idealism, and it was the new realism which eventually became the
spearhead of the revolt against the declining idealist tradition.

While we have said that the new realist movement made little positive contribution towards religious thought, it should be added that there is in realism no inherent predisposition against religion. After all, the largest of the Christian Churches has as its official philosophy Thomism, which is a moderate realism. One of the most influential pioneers of modern realism, Franz Brentano, was a lifelong theist and for a time a Roman Catholic priest. Other noted realists have had a high appreciation for religion. On the other side, it has to be remembered that in asserting the primacy of spirit, idealism had given a privileged place to spiritual activities such as religion. For realism, mind is only one factor among others in the world. Spiritual activities lose their privileged position, and have to readjust themselves to a conception of the world in which facts count for more than values. In addition to this, the new realist movement contained strong analytical and anti-metaphysical tendencies which militated against traditional theology and philosophy of religion.

In this chapter we consider only the beginnings of the movement and its general character. Both the metaphysics and the analytical philosophy which came out of the New Realism will be discussed at a later stage. Here we look first at the beginnings of contemporary realism on the continent of Europe, as seen in the thought of Brentano (Section 69). Then we consider some representatives of British neo-realism, especially Moore and Russell, who succeeded that equally famous pair, Bradley and Bosanquet, in the hegemony of British philosophy (Section 70). Realism in the United States will next be considered, and illustrated from two of its best-known exponents, Perry and Santayana (Section 71). As usual, the chapter is rounded off with some concluding remarks (Section 72).

69. CONTINENTAL REALISM
F. Brentano

Directly or indirectly, much of our modern thought has been influenced by a remarkable man whom John Laird called the 'Austrian Socrates'—Franz Brentano[1] (1838–1917), clergyman, psychologist, philosopher, and a nephew of the famous German poet, Clemens Brentano. The influence of this Austrian thinker has flowed through his disciple Meinong into the whole neo-realist movement, while in other directions he touches upon phenomenology and neo-Thomism.

Schooled in Aristotle and the medieval philosophers, Brentano sought to go back beyond Kant and the idealist tradition to an empirical and realistic standpoint. The essence of mental activity, as he saw it, is to refer

[1] Priest, 1864–73; professor at Vienna, 1874–80; later lived in Florence and Zürich.

beyond itself to real things. To express this realistic outlook, Brentano discovered—or better, rediscovered in the Aristotelian and scholastic tradition—a principle which has been of considerable importance in recent philosophy: 'intentionality'. Every mental act, whether it is the entertaining of an idea, or the making of a judgment, or the taking up of an emotional attitude such as love or hate—these are the three basic classes of mental phenomena, in Brentano's view—has an 'intentional' character. That is to say, mental life is not shut up in itself but has a directed character, and refers beyond itself. As Brentano expresses it, 'there is no hearing without the heard, no believing without the believed, no hoping without the hoped for, no striving without the striven for, no joy without the enjoyed, and so with other mental phenomena'.[1] This idea provides the basis for detailed arguments to show that the intent of minds is always to refer to real things.

Brentano's realism was decidedly theistic. He seems to have resigned from the priesthood largely because he could not accept the dogma of papal infallibility, promulgated in 1870, but he continued to champion the Christian ethic and to maintain a form of theism which, however, deviates from the orthodox view. Brentano indeed thought that his greatest work was a defence of theism, published posthumously as *Von Dasein Gottes*. Here he rehabilitates the cosmological and other traditional arguments for God's existence, and maintains that theism is intellectually the most satisfying hypothesis. But what is of interest is the kind of God whom Brentano envisages. This is not the immutable God whom traditional theology conceives as dwelling in eternity, but a God who has been brought into the temporal process and is subject to change. The imperfection of the world points to a God whose works are advancing towards perfection, and who must in some sense be himself developing. Already in this conception we have a foreshadowing of the ideas of later realist metaphysics.

70. Realism in England
G. E. Moore, B. A. W. Russell, C. D. Broad, H. H. Price

George Edward Moore[2] (1873–1958) is one of those philosophers whose importance depends not so much on what has been written by them—Moore's literary output was relatively slender—as on the influence which they have exerted on contemporary thinkers. It would be universally agreed that Moore was one of the major influences in changing the course

---

[1] *The Origin of the Knowledge of Right and Wrong*, pp. 12–13.
[2] Lecturer, 1911–25, and professor, 1925–39, at Cambridge.

of British philosophy in the present century. The change has expressed itself in tendencies away from idealism towards realism, and away from system-building towards analysis, and both of these tendencies owe much to Moore.

Moore regarded himself as the defender of common-sense, and was one of the leaders in the revolt against the dominance of idealism in Britain. His 'Refutation of Idealism', published in 1903, marks a turning-point in British philosophy. Rather like Brentano, he asks us to distinguish between the object of which one is aware—for instance, a sense-datum such as 'yellow'—and the act of awareness. The act is mental, but the object of which we are aware is not. In the case of such an act of awareness, it is claimed that 'its object, when we are aware of it, is precisely what it would be, if we were not aware'.[1] Moore experienced many difficulties in trying to work out his realist thesis, but the essential point that our knowing does not constitute reality but discovers it soon came to be widely accepted.

Realism tends towards pluralism, and in this respect also Moore attacked idealism. On the idealist view, reality is an organic whole in which any particular thing is constituted by its relations to the totality. Moore, on the contrary, held that any particular thing has its own nature which is not affected by its relations to other things. Hence, it is not necessary, as some of the Hegelians had implied, to know everything before one can know anything. Thus Moore directed British philosophy away from metaphysics to analysis and the clarification of specific problems. John Wisdom tells how he went to Moore's lectures on the soul, in the hope of getting some light on the religious and metaphysical question. Instead, he found that such questions were avoided, and he was offered 'a game of logic'—the minute analysis of ordinary statements, an analysis in which Moore excelled.[2]

While he was an opponent of idealism, Moore shows us in his ethical teaching that he did not favour the traditional naturalism either. ' "Good" ', he says, 'is a simple notion, just as "yellow" is a simple notion.'[3] Attempts to explain 'good' in naturalistic terms, such as Spencer's evolutionary ethics, are criticized and rejected. 'Good' is said to be a 'non-natural' quality, and this quality belongs intrinsically to certain things, such as aesthetic enjoyment or relations with one's fellows. But if the naturalistic explanation of 'good' is rejected, so is any attempt to explain it in terms of some alleged supersensible reality. It may fairly be

[1] *Loc. cit.*, in *Philosophical Studies*, p. 29.
[2] *The Philosophy of G. E. Moore*, ed. P. A. Schilpp, pp. 423–4.
[3] *Principia Ethica*, p. 7.

said that Moore's ethic is a humanistic one: and to sum up the direction
of his thought, one may say that the impulse which he has given to
contemporary philosophy has pointed it towards realism, pluralism,
analysis and humanism.

Closely associated with Moore in the rise of the neo-realist movement in
Britain was Bertrand Arthur William Russell[1] (1872–1970), the best-known
British philosopher of recent times. In many ways, Russell offers a striking
contrast to Moore. Whereas Moore wrote but little, Russell has to his
name a staggering literary output which has flowed for more than
sixty years. Moore's writings are miniatures, devoted to limited problems,
but Russell has not shrunk from broad canvases, such as *An Outline of
Philosophy* or his *History of Western Philosophy*. Moore wrote for professional
philosophers, but Russell, as well as doing technical philosophical work,
has a gift for popular exposition, and has come to be regarded as a kind of
apostle of the modern scientific and secular world. Moore was at home in
academic circles, but Russell has always interested himself in public
affairs, and has passionately championed various social and political
ideals—some of them, it must be said, a little eccentric. Finally, from the
point of view of our own study, we note that while Moore is almost silent
on the problems of religion, Russell has frequently written about them,
and has expressed himself in no uncertain fashion.

Since Russell has been active over the whole period covered by our
survey, and since his thought has undergone many changes during that
time, he is not the kind of philosopher whose teachings can be neatly
summarized. For the limited purpose of our inquiry, however, we are
helped by the fact that his views on religion have remained constant
over the whole period.

In an early and often reprinted essay, 'A Free Man's Worship',[2] Russell
states a frankly materialistic view of the world, and rejects the religious
interpretation with impressive rhetoric and more than a little dogmatism.
'That man is the product of causes which had no prevision of the end they
were achieving; that his origin, his growth, his hopes and fears, his loves
and his beliefs, are but the outcome of accidental collocations of atoms;
that no fire, no heroism, no intensity of thought and feeling, can preserve
an individual life beyond the grave; that all the labours of the ages, all
the devotion, all the inspiration, all the noonday brightness of human
genius, are destined to extinction in the vast death of the solar system—

[1] Fellow of Trinity College, Cambridge, 1910–16. Owing to his pacifist views, he lost
his fellowship during World War I, but was re-elected in World War II. His life has
been mostly spent in writing and lecturing. In 1931 he succeeded to the peerage as the
third Earl Russell.

[2] In *Mysticism and Logic*, pp. 46–57.

all these things, if not quite beyond dispute, are yet so nearly certain, that no philosophy which rejects them can hope to stand.'[1] In this essay, Russell's rejection of the religious understanding of the world is grounded mainly in an appeal to the facts. Religion represents the cosmic powers as good, but 'the world of fact, after all, is not good'.[2] Not the cosmic powers are worthy of man's worship. Man's own ideals are alone worthy of his reverence, and he has to recognize that he must strive for these ideals on his own in a world which is indifferent or even hostile to them. Such a view stands at the opposite extreme from that expressed by idealists like Jones.[3]

As is well known, Russell's most significant philosophical work has been done in the field of logic. While his logical investigations are of a highly technical character, they are determinative for his whole philosophical outlook, including his negative attitude to religion. Our knowledge of the world must be obtained by valid logical procedures, and while science is able to point to such procedures, religion is not. Russell maintains that philosophical knowledge itself does not essentially differ from scientific knowledge, though it is more critical and more general. Philosophy 'examines the various parts of our supposed knowledge to see whether they are mutually consistent, and whether the inferences employed are such as to seem valid to a careful scrutiny'.[4] Philosophy on the other hand claims no special source of wisdom that is closed off from science.

These considerations prove fatal for religion, or, more strictly, for the religious world-view. In his essay 'Mysticism and Logic', Russell asks whether there are two ways of knowing—the mystical way and the scientific way. While acknowledging that mysticism, considered as an emotional attitude to life, may have something to commend it, he denies that there is any mystical insight that can properly be called 'knowledge'. 'Insight, untested and unsupported, is an insufficient guarantee of truth.'[5] No valid logical procedure can be pointed out, and the beliefs to which mysticism leads are examined and rejected—belief in a supersensible reality, belief that the world is not a plurality but a unity, and so on. Even if the findings of science attain at best to probability, we are left with science as the only sure way of knowing; and science must be our guide even in the field of moral conduct, which has been traditionally dominated by religious conceptions. A similar statement is made in a passage in Russell's *History of Western Philosophy*: 'Ever since Plato, most philosophers have considered it part of their business to produce "proofs"

---

[1] *Loc. cit.*, pp. 47–8. [2] *Loc. cit.*, p. 49. [3] See above, p. 20.
[4] *An Outline of Philosophy*, p. 308. [5] *Mysticism and Logic*, p. 12.

of immortality and the existence of God. In order to make their proofs seem valid, they have had to falsify logic, to make mathematics mystical, and to pretend that deep-seated prejudices were heaven-sent intuitions. All this is rejected by the philosophers who make logical analysis the main business of philosophy. They confess frankly that the human intellect is unable to find conclusive answers to many questions of profound importance to mankind, but they refuse to believe that there is some "higher" way of knowing, by which we can discover truths hidden from science and the intellect.'[1]

Russell often speaks like a materialist, and indeed there is a strong materialistic flavour in his thought. He has usually preferred, however, to call his view 'neutralism'. The raw material of the world is neither mental nor physical, or rather, there is one raw material for minds and bodies. These are alike 'logical constructions' built out of 'events' which themselves belong to a neutral order. This view is obviously akin to that of Mach[2] or, to go further back in the history of philosophy, to the views of David Hume.

But however we may label it, Russell's philosophy is essentially scientific in outlook and secular in spirit. Since science lends no support to a belief in God or in immortality, these beliefs must be discarded as survivals from the immature thought of earlier times, but we are compensated by the prospects which science itself holds out to us; and Russell sees in the scientific spirit, if its powers can be rightly directed, the chief hope for mankind. To quote his own estimate of his philosophy: 'In the welter of conflicting fanaticisms, one of the few unifying forces is scientific truthfulness. To have insisted on the introduction of this virtue into philosophy, and to have invented a powerful method by which it can be rendered fruitful, are the chief merits of the philosophical school of which I am a member.'[3]

A further interesting example of the New Realism is provided by the thought of Charles Dunbar Broad[4] (1887–   ). Broad considers that the best method for philosophy is to begin with limited problems and to explore these thoroughly; but then one may go on to wider unities, and we shall see that Broad permits himself a measure of speculation, though this falls far short of the construction of a metaphysical system. In *The Mind and its Place in Nature* he takes up the problem of mind, and we see how in realism the mind, when deprived of the privileged position that it enjoyed in idealism, is given a humbler and more problematical status in the scheme of things. Of the various possible theories on the relation of

[1] *Op. cit.*, pp. 863–4.   [2] See above, p. 97.
[3] *History of Western Philosophy*, p. 864.   [4] Professor at Cambridge, 1933–53.

mind and body, Broad is inclined to favour the view that mind is an 'emergent characteristic' of matter.

But his discussion is complicated by the introduction of an unusual element into philosophy; he takes seriously the findings of psychical research. That some 'supernormal' phenomena occur, Broad takes to be well established. The question is whether psychical research affords empirical evidence for a mind's surviving its body. Broad does not think that the evidence proves *survival*, but it does point to the *persistence* of some element in mental life after death. Broad calls this element a 'psychic factor'. This is not a mind, but in association with a nervous system it goes to constitute a mind. It would be capable of persisting after death, and would retain some traces of the experiences which belonged to the mind it once helped to constitute. The psychic factor may itself be constituted of a subtle form of matter, in which case only a slight modification of the theory of emergent materialism is required to accommodate it. Broad also points out that if such psychic factors exist, they would make probable a theory of metempsychosis or transmigration of souls, the psychic factors associating with mediums during the intervals in which they are dissociated from bodies of their own.

What has this to do with religion? Broad thinks we have no good reasons for believing in a personal God such as Christianity envisages. But he does think that psychical research, though its findings are ambiguous, offers some possibility of support for the belief in survival. And it is clear that for Broad survival is the primary article of religious belief. He regards it as 'almost a *sine qua non* of any religious view of the world that some men at least should survive bodily death', and points out that Bishop Butler, for whom he has considerable admiration, begins his defence of religion by considering arguments for a future life, 'which he rightly holds to be an absolutely essential doctrine of religion'.[1]

The stress on survival rather than God as the centre of religious belief may remind us of McTaggart; and this is not accidental, since Broad wrote a major work on McTaggart's philosophy. It is true that the two are very different: one an idealist who thought matter unreal, the other with leanings to materialism; one a speculative metaphysician, the other interested in critical analysis, science and empiricism; one a believer in immortal souls, the other in the possibility of somewhat vague psychic factors, persisting after death; one in indestructible minds which go through a series of lives, the other in possibly fragile factors which might possibly constitute with different bodies a series of minds. But it is not fanciful to see in Broad's views a fragmentary and somewhat ghostly

[1] *Religion, Philosophy and Psychical Research*, pp. 234, 207.

reflection of McTaggart's metaphysic, transposed on to a realist basis.

Broad's attitude to religion is not entirely negative. He rejects as far-fetched the suggestion that the whole religious experience of mankind is illusory. He recognizes that there has been development of depth and insight in religious beliefs. And just as he is prepared to recognize telepathy and clairvoyance, so he is willing to give *prima facie* recognition to mystical experience, though he does not think that this is experience of a personal God. Such a religion as Buddhism, he thinks, stands up to criticism better than Christianity. The latter is made vulnerable by some of its special beliefs, and Broad takes a gloomy view of its prospects. But this gives him no pleasure, since he fears that its place will be taken by less desirable ideologies.

In addition to the three Cambridge philosophers just considered, we may mention a representative of Oxford realism, Henry Habberley Price[1] (1899–   ). His philosophical work has been mainly concerned with such themes as perception and thinking, but he has also written on religion, and like Broad he directs our attention in this connection to the findings of psychical research.

Price thinks it ludicrously one-sided to represent religion purely as a practical activity, and to interpret religious assertions as veiled moral assertions, in the manner of R. B. Braithwaite.[2] Of course, every religion recommends a way of life, and perhaps the teaching of Confucius does little more. But with Christianity the case is different. 'A Christian teacher's recommendations', says Price, 'make no sense at all apart from his theistic theory of the universe.'[3] So the religious man cannot escape the task of trying to show that theism is true, and that his statements refer to some facts beyond the world of sense.

But how is he to do this? The evidence seems to be against him. The traditional proofs of God's existence are not really proofs, but rather 'analyses of clarifications of propositions which religious persons antecedently believe'.[4] Nor is it of any avail to appeal to some inward, private, unverifiable religious experience—an alleged 'mystical' way of knowing, as Russell would call it. Science, for its part, cannot disprove religious beliefs, but it does not support them, and we can hardly be content to hold them as mere assertions.

It is when confronted with this seeming *impasse* that Price sees a possible way out by an appeal to the findings of parapsychology or psychical research. He regards it as an indisputable fact that such phenomena as telepathy and clairvoyance do occur, and he suggests that they may

---

[1] Professor at Oxford, 1935–59.   [2] See below, p. 312.
[3] *Some Aspects of the Conflict between Science and Religion*, p. 6.   [4] *Op. cit.*, p. 18.

operate through the unconscious reaches of the mind. Telepathy, of course, as a relation between finite minds, is different from the sense of the divine, but it does show that there are empirical evidences apart from those provided by the senses, and so it removes the chief obstacle to religious belief, which was the lack of any empirical evidence susceptible to scientific investigation. Similarly, psychical research may provide evidence for the survival of death, and although survival is something less than immortality, nevertheless the chief obstacle to belief in immortality will have been removed if empirical evidence is forthcoming that souls can endure after the dissolution of their bodies. There is thus the possibility that religious assertions could be regarded as empirically verifiable, and that they might be placed on a scientific footing, if we are prepared to extend the notion of 'experience' from the senses to such extra-sensory experiences as could establish the claim to be open to some kind of inter-subjective testing. Thus Price invites us to think again about human personality and the range of its experiences in the real world.

71. REALISM IN AMERICA
R. B. Perry, G. Santayana

Those American philosophers who were thinking along similar lines to those of Moore and Russell issued in 1912 as a kind of manifesto a symposium entitled *The New Realism*, and we select as an exemplar one of the most distinguished contributors to this manifesto, Ralph Barton Perry[1] (1876–1957). The philosophy which he developed incorporates the empiricism and pluralism of his teacher, William James, and also has many points of resemblance to the views of Russell.

'The human mind', says Perry, 'is instinctively and habitually realistic, so that realism does not so much need to be proved as to be defended against criticism.'[2] In his Gifford Lectures,[3] he summarizes the characteristics of the philosophy which he builds on this common-sense basis of realism. As well as being *realist*, his philosophy is also *neutralist*—that is to say, it rejects the dualism of mind and body, which can both be regarded in Hume's manner as different organizations of neutrals; again, his philosophy is *empiricist*—that is to say, it must submit to being tested by observed facts; further, it is *naturalistic*—that is to say, it confines its attention to the spatio-temporal world which is accessible to the natural

---

[1] Professor at Harvard, 1913–46.
[2] *Philosophy of the Recent Past*, p. 201.
[3] See *Realms of Value*, pp. 444ff.

sciences, though it finds within this world human nature itself, with its higher faculties; finally, it is *pluralistic*—that is to say, it finds no unifying cause or purpose in the world, but only limited unities together with residual pluralities.

Man, then, is immersed in a natural order in which he seeks to realize his values. These values are generated by man's own interests, and reality itself is neither good nor bad apart from these human interests. It is in connection with this notion of the pursuit of values in a neutral world that Perry introduces his view of religion. In its widest sense, religion is said to be 'man's *deepest solicitude*, his concern for the fate of that which he accounts most valuable'.[1] This religion of which Perry speaks is, like Dewey's, a humanistic faith. 'There is a ship on which all men are embarked, and which is launched upon the high seas of existence laden with all their painfully acquired treasure. Religion speaks for this perilous but hopeful voyage. It declares that this community of interest in interests makes all men, otherwise differently interested, partners in the great enterprise of replacing evil with good and good with better, so as to achieve the best possible. It is the office of religion to proclaim this proud purpose and to hearten men in its pursuit.'[2]

In a later book, *Puritanism and Democracy*, Perry turns to the specific contributions of Christianity to the values of a democratic society. What can still be affirmed in America's puritan heritage? Perry's interest lies chiefly in the moral values of Christianity, but this does not mean that religion is simply absorbed into the democratic ideal or reduced to its lowest common denominator. Religion needs its diverse and concrete manifestations, and a democratic society will encourage such faiths as Christianity, as enriching the range of human values and possibilities.

For our other exemplar of American realism, we take George San-tayana[3] (1863–1952). Born in Spain, he went when a child to the United States, though he never became an American citizen and regarded himself as a sojourner in the country. But since he was educated in America, taught in an American university, published his writings in the English language, and now enjoys a philosophical reputation which seems to stand higher in the United States than elsewhere, he can hardly escape being counted an American philosopher. For these reasons we are justified in taking his work as an illustration of realism in America. It should be added, however, that his view of religion is peculiar to himself, and cannot be taken as typical. Perhaps because of his Catholic European

[1] *Op. cit.*, p. 463.
[2] *Op. cit.*, p. 492.
[3] He taught at Harvard, 1889–1912; thereafter he lived mostly in Italy.

heritage, he was able to combine a frank materialism with a fine perception and appreciation of the spirit of Christianity, as may be seen from many passages in his writings.[1]

Santayana was a poet, and his literary style does not always make for the clearest presentation of his philosophical ideas. These ideas belong to a type of view called 'critical realism'. Not individually existent objects, but general essences are what we directly grasp in intuition—colours, odours and the like. But by an act of prephilosophical 'animal faith', as he calls it, we refer these essences to things which exist independently of us. Just as Moore defends common-sense, so Santayana defends this animal faith in the reality of the external world. German philosophers—whom Santayana does not take too seriously—may persuade us of the truth of idealism when we are reading their books, but when we go back to daily living, we revert to our animal faith. 'I should be ashamed', says Santayana, 'to countenance opinions which, when not arguing, I did not believe.'[2] Our guide must indeed be reason, but reason in turn must go hand in hand with our deepest instincts, for if it is divorced from the instincts, reason loses itself in idle speculation. Santayana's ideal is thus a life of reason which frankly accepts science and the intellect as the only reliable ways to knowledge but which at the same time remains firmly down to earth. The philosophy of the life of reason, while guided by the intellect, does not fall into the idealist error of taking the intellect itself as its foundation, but looks rather to the world of nature whose real independent existence is accepted as a primary article of animal faith.

What then is nature? Nature is not a self, and there is no point in calling it 'God'. Santayana's view of nature is frankly materialistic and mechanistic. Even the workings of the soul are presumably at bottom those of a refined mechanism. It is true that we do not know what matter is, and Santayana is willing to distinguish in nature realms of essence, of truth, and even of spirit, in addition to the realm of matter itself. But these other realms are, so to speak, superstructures on the material basis. However important and precious the realm of spirit appears to man, it is not the basic reality but rather a fragile epiphenomenon of material nature. A fall of a few degrees in the temperature of the solar system would destroy spirit.

It is against this realist and materialist background that Santayana develops his view of religion, and the importance which he attaches to the subject is shown by the fact that he devoted to it a whole book, considered by many to be his best—*Reason in Religion*. Santayana believes that

[1] See, *e.g.*, *The Realm of Spirit*, pp. 203–12.
[2] *Scepticism and Animal Faith*, p. 305.

religion originates in the experience of adversity, and the beliefs which it engenders—belief in God, belief in the goodness of the world, belief in the immortality of the soul—are, of course, not true in any literal sense. But religion should not be taken literally. Santayana has only scorn for the shallow sceptic who points to the literal falsity of religious beliefs and thinks he has thereby disposed of the subject. Such a sceptic has not begun to understand religion—if he did understand it, Santayana thinks, he would also 'understand why religion is so profoundly moving and in a sense so profoundly just'.[1] Santayana has no time for what he calls a 'sour irreligion', and despite his scepticism finds much to love in the 'splendid error' of the Catholic faith.

The criticism of myths goes through two stages. 'The first stage treats them angrily as superstitions; the second treats them smilingly as poetry.'[2] Religious beliefs and the wisdom which they contain are understood when they are removed from the sphere of literal truth and even of controversy to the sphere of poetry, where they rightly belong. 'What is the whole phenomenon of religion but human experience interpreted by human imagination?'[3] Embodied in the myths and fables of religion are the qualities of piety and spirituality, and we must honour both. These two qualities, indeed, constitute rational religion—piety as 'loyalty to necessary conditions' and spirituality as 'devotion to ideal ends'.[4]

72. REMARKS ON THE NEW REALISM

Enough has been said to make clear the general character of the neo-realist movement, and also to indicate its possible bearings on the problems of religious thought. As over against idealism, the new movement introduces a kind of Copernican revolution. Mind ceases to be the source and centre of things and becomes one factor among others in a world which exists independently of our knowing it. Hence come the realist appeal to matters of fact rather than to judgments of value, and the insistence on the fragmentary character of our minds in the world—points which are frequently made by both Russell and Santayana. If the realist thesis is true, it means that the place of mind in the scheme of things needs to be re-assessed; this in turn means that the significance of spiritual activities, such as religion, needs to be re-assessed.

Russell and Santayana tend to make their re-assessment in materialistic terms, and in so far as this is the case, the new realism tends to slip

---

[1] *Reason in Religion*, p. 4.   [2] *Scepticism and Animal Faith*, p. 247.
[3] *Winds of Doctrine*, p. 46.   [4] *Reason in Religion*, p. 276.

back into the old naturalism, and becomes open to all the objections to which that older naturalism was exposed.[1] But of course, realism does not necessarily lead to materialistic and mechanistic views, and often enough it follows quite other directions. Already, however, it has become apparent to us that the realist estimate of religion, though far from unanimous, tends to be less favourable to traditional religious beliefs than was the usual idealist estimate. Of the writers considered in this chapter, Brentano was heterodox, Moore indifferent, Russell hostile, Perry nebulous, and Santayana nostalgic in their several attitudes to religion; more will be said later[2] about the suggestion of Broad and Price that religious assertions might find an empirical anchorage in psychical research, but obviously what is conceded here is something very tentative and even precarious.

In this chapter, we have confined ourselves to the earlier stages of the realist movement, as marking one of the transitional moments in what we have called the 'second phase' of our survey. Price too, although of a younger generation than the others, adheres to an older style of philosophizing. But it is already clear that the movement contained two distinct possibilities for further development. On the one hand, the realist thesis could be developed into realist metaphysics; on the other hand, the strong analytical tendencies in Moore and Russell could be developed into an analytical philosophy. At a later stage, we shall see what form these developments have taken, and how they have impinged on contemporary religious thought.

[1] See above, p. 111ff.   [2] See below, p. 314.

XV

THE NEW PHYSICS, PHILOSOPHY
AND THEOLOGY

73. The Changing Scientific Picture

No account of recent religious thought would be complete without some mention of the impact upon it of the new scientific conceptions developed in the present century. Yet this topic must be approached with considerable caution. Partly, caution is demanded because the layman has great difficulty in getting even a general understanding of the complex ideas of contemporary science. Yet to this it might be replied that in this scientific age every educated person has a duty to acquaint himself with what scientists are saying, and he has no excuse for doing otherwise since many scientists with a gift for lucid expression have written popular accounts of their ideas. Partly—and this is more important—caution is demanded because ideas which are well established in a scientific realm of discourse are sometimes rashly generalized and applied to other realms of discourse where their relevance is very doubtful. One occasionally hears, for instance, naïve arguments from relativity in physics to relativity in morals, or from the principle of indeterminacy to the reality of free-will. Even worse is the appeal to great names. Because the scientist enjoys so much prestige in the contemporary world, all shades of opinion want to claim his authority. Churchmen, for instance, are apt to quote anything that Einstein may have said favourable to religion, such as his famous remark that the German churches stood up better than the universities and scientists to the Nazis, while on the other hand agnostics eagerly claim Einstein as one of themselves. This vulgar appeal to the great name proves nothing, except that those who make it are so unsure of their beliefs that they need to bolster them up.

The relations of science to philosophy and theology are very complex, and we must be on our guard against all rash and premature generalizations from scientific findings. There have, indeed, been many philosopher-scientists in recent times who have come forward with what they believed to be the philosophical implications of their scientific studies. On the whole, they have been coldly received by professional philosophers, who are inclined to regard their approach to philosophical problems as amateurish. There is considerable justification for this attitude on the part of the philosophers, but perhaps there is also an element of professional jealousy here, and a resentment of the scientist who invades the philosopher's domain and offers to solve his problems for him. Thus if we have to avoid the danger of making rash philosophical inferences from science, we have also to avoid the danger of thinking that the scientist can have nothing worthwhile to say on philosophical problems. We ought to be willing to give a critical and yet respectful hearing to those scientists who believe that from their special studies they have gained insights which shed light on more general philosophical problems, or even on the problems of God and religion.

At the beginning of the century, biology with its theory of evolution was the science which exerted the most obvious influence on philosophical and religious thought. We have already seen this influence clearly exemplified in thinkers so diverse as Caird, Ward, Haeckel, Tylor and others. But after two or three decades, physics began to exert the chief influence from the scientific side, for physics was undergoing a kind of revolution and was presenting a picture of nature different in many ways from the picture which had been current in the nineteenth century. To mention some of the major stages in the revolution, Planck formulated his quantum theory in 1900; Einstein put forward his special and general theories of relativity respectively in 1905 and 1916; Heisenberg announced the uncertainty principle in 1927. The nineteenth-century picture had been of solid indestructible atoms of matter existing in an infinite Euclidean space and an absolute time, and rigidly conforming to the laws of mechanics. This was the universe of Haeckel and the older naturalists. But the new physics asks us to think instead of a space-time continuum which is non-Euclidean in its properties, probably finite in its extent, and in which there is no absolute size, rest, motion or even simultaneity. Matter ceases to be conceived in terms of solid atoms, and instead the atom is thought of as a complex rhythmical pattern of energy. When thought of in this way, the atom obviously needs a minimal time as well as a minimal space in which to exist—that is to say, it is conceived as a process. Furthermore, in the new physics, it appears to be impossible to give a complete description of the behaviour of elementary physical entities in the way that would be necessary for causal explanation. Hence the new physics introduces some radical changes into the understanding of nature, and calls for a fairly drastic revision of the older picture.

There is of course division of opinion as to just how radical the revolution in physics has been. Some prefer to stress the continuity of the new physics with the old, and point out that what has occurred has been a reconstruction·rather than a revolution; they deny that the principle of uncertainty means the abandonment of determinism; and they rightly remind us that to think of atoms in terms of energy does not make them any less physical. On the other hand, it is argued that if matter is process rather than an inert substance, it has more in common with life and mind, which are obviously processes; that if the physical world, vast though it is, and expanding, is nevertheless not infinite in space or eternal in time, it is less likely to be the ultimate reality; and that if universal mechanistic determinism is even brought into doubt, there is more room to believe in the free creative life of spirit. We have already warned against any rash inferences from contemporary scientific findings to philosophical generalizations, but *prima facie* one would say that the world as conceived by the new physics seems more amenable—or at least less intractable—to a religious interpretation than was the world of the older physics. When we turn to those physicists who have indulged in philosophical speculation, we find that on the whole their attitude towards religion is more hospitable than the attitude of scientists a generation before them. Around 1934, R. G. Collingwood was noting that 'modern scientific leaders talk about God in a way that would have scandalized most scientists of fifty years ago'.[1] On the other side, those Christian theologians who took an interest in science were not slow to recognize the apologetic possibilities of the new physics, and began to seek new correlations between science and religion.

Since the number of philosopher-scientists in recent times has been very great, we can here consider only a few of the most eminent, and hope that they fairly represent the kind of things that have been said by physicists themselves about the nature of scientific knowledge and its significance for philosophical and religious questions (Section 74). Then we shall see how some science-conscious theologians have striven to reconcile the new physics with Christian thought (Section 75). The chapter ends with an attempt to assess the value of these various points of view (Section 76).

[1] *The Idea of Nature*, p. 156.

74. SOME PHYSICISTS' VIEWS ON PHILOSOPHY AND RELIGION
M. Planck, A. Einstein, W. K. Heisenberg, A. S. Eddington

We may begin by considering Max Planck[1] (1858–1947), the founder of quantum theory and considerably senior in years to most of the other leaders of the new physics.

At first sight, Planck's view of the nature of scientific knowledge seems a complicated one. He asks us to distinguish three worlds. Firstly, there is the world of sense-perception, the world as *man* perceives it. All ideas in physics are said to be derived from this world, and physical laws refer ultimately to events in it. Secondly, though we cannot prove it by logical argument, we are 'compelled to assume the existence of another world of reality behind the world of the senses'.[2] This real world is independent of man, and cannot be directly apprehended. We can, however, have some apprehension of the real world, and we get it in two ways. We apprehend the real world *indirectly* through the senses, though we do not know how the medium of the senses distorts or transforms the real world; and we also apprehend the real world 'by means of certain symbols', themselves derived from sense-experience. Such a symbol, presumably, is Planck's own quantum of action, which he picturesquely describes as 'like a new and mysterious messenger from the real world'.[3] Thirdly, there is the world of physics. This world differs from the other two in being a deliberate creation of the human mind. It is a world which continually changes as science progresses, and Planck laid great stress on the continuity of scientific development and on the relation of the new physics to the old. The direction of this development may be expressed by saying that the physical world keeps receding from the world of the senses and keeps approaching—though this cannot be proved—to the real world.

Though less subtly expressed, Planck's views are obviously akin to those of Cassirer.[4] The world of physical science is a symbolical form which the mind constructs out of its experience. The real world, however, is richer than the physical world which, as we have seen, sets out from sense-perception. 'Modern physics impresses us with the truth that there are realities existing apart from our sense-perceptions, and that there are problems and conflicts where these realities are of greater value for us than the richest treasures of the world of experience.'[5]

In particular, Planck finds that both moral and religious experience is

---

[1] Professor at Kiel, 1885–89; Berlin, 1889–1926. His son was executed by the Nazis.
[2] *The Universe in the Light of Modern Physics*, p. 8.
[3] *Op. cit.*, p. 20.   [4] See above, p. 126.   [5] *Op. cit.*, p. 107.

compatible with the physicist's view of the world. Planck does not think that modern physics implies any abandonment of universal determinism, but he claims that such determinism is quite compatible with human free-will. The point about a conscious person is that he is aware of the connections of his experience, and that such awareness itself becomes a determining factor in his experience, introducing new motives and so making it possible for him to act from ethical rather than causal laws.

As far as religion is concerned, Planck admits the religious interpretation of the world alongside the scientific one, and stresses that both have their right in a balanced development of the human spirit. 'There can', he says, 'never be any real opposition between religion and science, for the one is the complement of the other. Every serious and reflective person realizes, I think, that the religious element in his nature must be recognized and cultivated if all the powers of the human soul are to act together in perfect balance and harmony. Science enhances the moral values of life because it furthers a love of truth and reverence—love of truth displaying itself in a constant endeavour to arrive at a more exact knowledge of the world of mind and matter around us, and reverence, because every advance in knowledge brings us face to face with the mystery of our own being.'[1]

Turning to Albert Einstein[2] (1879–1955), probably the most famous of modern physicists on account of his relativity theory, we may note the following statement: 'The belief in an external world independent of the perceiving subject is the basis of all natural science. Since, however, sense-perception gives information of this external world indirectly, we can only grasp the latter by speculative means. It follows from this that our notions of physical reality can never be final. We must always be ready to change these notions in order to do justice to perceived facts in the most logically perfect way.'[3] Here we find the same threefold scheme as in Planck—the real world, the perceived world, and our notions somewhere between. It would seem that Einstein was no positivist. His aim was to know reality. 'Behind the tireless efforts of the investigator there lurks a stronger, more mysterious drive: it is existence and reality that one wishes to comprehend.'[4]

It is in this quest to know the real world that Einstein finds the meaning of religion. We invent from our own minds notions of mathematical

[1] *Where is Science Going?*, p. 168.

[2] Professor successively at Zürich, Prague and Berlin. He left Germany after the Nazis came to power, and in 1941 became professor at the Institute for Advanced Study, Princeton.

[3] *Albert Enstein: Philosopher Scientist*, ed. P. A. Schlipp, p. 248.

[4] *Op. cit.*, p. 249.

elegance, we submit them to the test of experience, and they turn out to be true! 'The most incomprehensible thing about the world is that it is comprehensible.'[1] The faith that the world is rationally ordered is what Einstein calls 'cosmic religion', and he regards it as an important inspiration to the creative power of the scientist.

But has this 'cosmic religion' anything to do with religion as we ordinarily understand it? Is it not perhaps rather an aesthetic feeling, of the kind which Bertrand Russell says he experiences when he contemplates the austere beauty of mathematics? It seems clear that Einstein means more than this. Probably generalizing from his own experience as recorded in his autobiography,[2] he distinguishes three stages in religious development: these are, the anthropomorphic stage, the moral stage, and then the stage of 'cosmic religion'. This last stage is purged of all anthropomorphic conceptions, but it is religious rather than aesthetic in its accompanying feelings of awe, wonder, humility. The God of cosmic religion is quite impersonal. 'I believe', says Einstein, 'in Spinoza's God who reveals himself in the orderly harmony of what exists, not in a God who concerns himself with the destinies and actions of human beings.'[3]

These views of Einstein on the nature of religion may seem like a compromise, disappointing both to the orthodox and to the irreligious. Yet there is no doubt that they represent a positive faith—strongly coloured, of course, by the preoccupations of a physicist—and that this faith stands in recognizable relation with the historic faiths of mankind. This last point is borne out by what Einstein has to say of the faith of his own people, the Jews. As he interprets it, Judaism appears as a kind of foreshadowing of his cosmic religion. 'Judaism', he says, 'is no transcendent religion'; its God is 'the negation of superstition'—presumably an overcoming of all anthropomorphic imaginings.[4]

After Einstein and Planck, perhaps the best-known name among modern physicists is that of Werner Karl Heisenberg[5] (1901–   ). His principle of uncertainty states that there is an inherent uncertainty in describing the motion of elementary particles. For instance, if the position of an electron is determined, there is a measure of uncertainty about its momentum. But both properties would need to be accurately determined for a completely causal description. Hence Heisenberg's principle seems to strike at rigid determinism, or at least to introduce a weaker kind of

[1] *Op. cit.*, p. 284.
[2] See *op. cit.*, p. 3.
[3] *Op. cit.*, pp. 659-60.
[4] *Ibid.*
[5] Professor at Leipzig, 1927-41; Director of the Max Planck Institute from 1941.

determinism. As far as phenomena on the very small scale are concerned, physical laws would appear to be statistical averages, and not rigidly applicable in individual cases.

Opinions have been sharply divided over the significance of Heisenberg's principle, and we may turn to his own Gifford Lectures to see what he himself has to say about its implications. While he speaks with great modesty and reserve, Heisenberg clearly thinks that the break with the old physics is more radical than it appeared to Planck or Einstein. 'The nineteenth century', he says, 'developed an extremely rigid frame for natural science, which formed not only science but also the general outlook of great masses of people.'[1] This frame was constituted by the fundamental concepts of 'space', 'time', 'matter' and 'causality'. Whatever is real had to find a place within the frame, and 'the frame was so narrow and rigid that it was difficult to find a place in it for many concepts of our language that had always belonged to its very substance, for instance, the concepts of "mind", of the human "soul", or of "life".'[2] Hence arose, among other things, the hostility of science to religion.

In Heisenberg's view, however, this rigid nineteenth-century framework has been dissolved, for science itself has profoundly modified its fundamental concepts. The error of materialistic naturalism was to take the language applicable to the kind of existence that we see around us, and its ordinary conceptions of 'matter', 'causality', and the like, and to think that these can be extrapolated into the atomic range. But modern physics shows us that we cannot speak about the atoms in ordinary language. If we would speak about the atoms, we need a peculiar kind of language suited to a world of potentialities rather than to one of facts. If this is so, however, our ordinary conceptions of 'matter', 'causality', and so on, lose the privileged position that was accorded to them in the old framework, and 'our attitude towards concepts like "mind" or the human "soul" or "God" will be different from that of the nineteenth century'.[3] Heisenberg's conclusion is that 'modern physics has perhaps opened the door to a wider outlook on the relation between the human mind and reality',[4] and this conclusion, though modest enough, nevertheless implies a radical change of attitude from that of the older naturalism.

To conclude this survey of the physicist-philosophers, we turn to the one who is perhaps most widely known in the English-speaking countries—Arthur Stanley Eddington[5] (1882–1944). He indeed ventures much further into philosophical territory than do most of his scientific colleagues.

Eddington develops a point which is already familiar to us from the

[1] *Physics and Philosophy*, p. 169.   [2] *Op. cit.*, p. 169.   [3] *Op. cit.*, p. 172.
[4] *Op. cit.*, p. 173.   [5] Professor at Cambridge, 1913-44.

remarks of the other physicists considered here—namely, that the world of physical science is a symbolic world, far removed from the world of sense-experience. The physicist begins by abstracting from the world of sense-experience those aspects which are measurable, and he ignores the rest. His business is therefore to correlate and interpret what Eddington calls 'pointer-readings'. In the course of making his interpretation, the physicist formerly maintained a closer linkage with the familiar world of sense, and borrowed his raw material from that familiar world, but now he does so no longer. He introduces such symbols as 'electrons', 'quanta', 'potentials', for which there are no analogues in the familiar everyday world of sense. Hence the world of physical science becomes increasingly an abstract symbolical world, and Eddington can even call it a 'world of shadows', deprived of the richness and substantiality of the world of sense.

While depriving sensible objects of the substantiality which we normally attribute to them, the symbolic world of physics remains itself a construction of mind. It is constituted by thought, and we must attach our pointer-readings to a background of mental activity. So Eddington argues that the ultimate reality is spiritual. 'Recognizing that the physical world is entirely abstract and without "actuality" apart from its linkage to consciousness, we restore consciousness to the fundamental position, instead of representing it as an inessential complication occasionally found in the midst of inorganic nature at a late stage of evolutionary history.'[1] Carrying his speculation further, he states that 'the idea of a universal Mind or Logos would be a fairly plausible inference from the present state of scientific theory'.[2]

But Eddington does not try to base a religious view of the world on scientific findings alone. He recognizes that even if, as he claims, science makes plausible the idea of a universal Mind, such a Mind would be only a pale replica of the God of religion. Further, he understands the danger of building a theology on the constantly changing concepts of science. 'The religious reader', he says, 'may well be content that I have not offered him a God revealed by the quantum theory, and therefore liable to be swept away in the next scientific revolution.'[3] The positive evidence for religion, Eddington thinks, comes from mystical experience, and this experience deserves our respect, for, as we have already seen, physical science is abstract and therefore limited in its approach to reality, so that plenty of room is left for other approaches. Modern science does not offer a 'proof' of religion which could be substituted for the mystical experience,

---

[1] *The Nature of the Physical World*, p. 332.
[2] *Op. cit.*, p. 338.
[3] *Op. cit.*, p. 353.

but by abolishing the notion of an inert material substance and—as Eddington believes—the notion of strict universal determinism, it encourages a spiritual view of the world and lends its support to the mystical insight.

75. THE NEW PHYSICS AND CHRISTIAN APOLOGETICS
B. H. Streeter, E. W. Barnes

One of the first theologians to recognize the apologetic possibilities of the new physics was Burnett Hillman Streeter[1] (1874–1937). Though primarily a New Testament scholar, Streeter was keenly interested in the problem of solving the conflicts between Christianity and modern thought. Like most other theologians of his generation in England, he had at first found a way of reconciliation through idealist philosophy, but becoming dissatisfied with this, he looked for a new approach which would be less speculative and more firmly based in experience. Such an approach he found by setting out from a frank acceptance of the findings of the empirical sciences, and by endeavouring to reach a correlation between these findings and the theistic world-view which is taught by the Christian religion.

Streeter divides world-views into two major types, which he calls respectively the 'mechanomorphic' and the 'anthropomorphic'. The mechanomorphic type of world-view conceives the world as a machine, and offers an explanation of its workings in terms of such categories as matter, force, cause and effect. Streeter acknowledges that from Newton to Darwin the mechanistic hypothesis was a fruitful one for scientific research, and that by the nineteenth century mechanistic materialism looked like a highly plausible world-view. Yet it had always contained in itself unexplained problems and paradoxes, and now with the revolution in fundamental physical concepts, the old picture of solid atoms pushing and pulling each other in mechanistically determined ways has become quite inadequate. 'That beautiful clear-cut simplicity which was once the main attraction of mechanistic materialism has today completely disappeared.'[2]

Streeter argues that in place of the discarded mechanistic model, life and the peculiar organization which goes with it can supply us with an analogy on which to interpret the dynamic processes of nature. The influence of Bergson's philosophy is obvious in Streeter's description of the

[1] Fellow, 1905-33, and Provost, 1933-7, of The Queen's College, Oxford.
[2] *Reality*, p. 16.

world as a scene of creative strife—a process which brings forth new and higher values, culminating in the manifestation of love. But Streeter will not be content with a mere 'life-force', if by this is understood something less than the God of Christian theism. If we are to take life as our clue, then we must take life at its highest as we know it in the mind and spirit of man. It is in this sense that Streeter's view is 'anthropomorphic'—that is to say, he is not championing a crude anthropomorphism which pictures God in the image of man, but is maintaining that the highest activities of human life afford us our best clue to the nature of ultimate reality.

From this point the link with Christian theology is easily made. Reality, or God, though in itself transcending our comprehension, has its most adequate symbol or analogue in the ideal of human life. The ideal man, in turn, would be the man whose life most fully manifested creative love. Such a man, Streeter claims, was Jesus Christ. Hence the Church sees in him the image and revelation of God, and 'if life instinct with love is the dynamic essence of reality, then to describe him we shall find no words more true than "Son of God"'.[1]

Contemporary with Streeter lived a much more controversial figure who likewise devoted himself to reconciling Christianity with the new scientific theories—Ernest William Barnes[2] (1874–1953). Barnes was on the one hand a brilliant mathematician and a Fellow of the Royal Society, and on the other hand a churchman and bishop for nearly thirty years of a great urban diocese.

His twofold interest finds clear expression in his Gifford Lectures. There Barnes maintains that religious beliefs cannot be accepted merely on intuition or authority, but must be submitted to rational testing. He proposes to begin with the information provided about the world by the sciences, and then to ask whether in the light of this a theistic world-view seems plausible. Most of his lectures are taken up with a comprehensive review of the state of the sciences around the year 1927, and his conclusion is that their findings point to a spiritual rather than a materialist interpretation of reality. 'An increased recognition of the important place which mental constructs occupy in physical theory, coupled with an understanding that thought, will and feeling cannot be wholly sundered from one another, has produced a widespread conviction that theism and science will in the end form a harmonious unity.'[3]

If this were all that Barnes had to say, there would not be much point

---

[1] *Op. cit.*, p. 215.

[2] Master of the Temple, 1915-19; Canon of Westminster, 1919-24; Bishop of Birmingham, 1924-52.

[3] *Scientific Theory and Religion*, pp. 593-4.

in mentioning him in our survey, since the philosophical side of his argument is not particularly coherent or original. But he deserves mention because he understood more clearly than many theologians have done that the work of the apologist is not merely to interpret the scientific understanding of the world in a way which leaves room for Christian faith, but also to reformulate that faith itself in a way which will not conflict with the presuppositions which we all hold in a scientific era. Barnes saw that Christian theology has been wedded to an outmoded cosmology, involving in particular a crude supernaturalism which he believed to be quite incompatible with the presuppositions of scientific inquiry.

He therefore attacked the miraculous elements in the Christian tradition, including the miracles of the virgin birth and bodily resurrection of Jesus. 'Ignore the miracles of the New Testament', he says, 'and Christianity remains that same way of life, lived in accordance with Christ's revelation of God, which through the centuries men have been drawn to follow.'[1] On the resurrection, he remarks that it is a great essential truth of Christianity, but one 'which is quite independent of the question as to whether the body of Jesus was reanimated after his death. What matters is that Christians shall feel a spiritual power in their lives, which they can rightly interpret as that of the spirit of Jesus revealing, as in his teaching in Galilee, the wisdom and righteousness of God.'[2] Such views brought upon Barnes the censure of his fellow bishops. But surely one of the chief glories of the Church of England is her comprehensiveness, and it is to her credit that Barnes continued in his office as a chief pastor of the flock.

It may be added that both Streeter and Barnes—as likewise Rashdall and Inge—were prominent members of the Modern Churchmen's Union, a society founded with the aim of bringing Christian life and thought into relation with the trends of the modern world. Its journal, *The Modern Churchman*, has been published since 1911 and has served as a forum for liberal theological thinking.

76. REMARKS ON THE NEW SCIENTIFIC THEORIES AND RELIGION

What results can we draw from our survey of the impact of the new physics on philosophical and religious problems? It would seem that little has been forthcoming in the way of securely based *positive* results. There is no unanimity among the physicists themselves about the significance of their scientific findings for the wider philosophical problems. Are we to

---

[1] *The Rise of Christianity.* p. 67.　　　[2] *Op. cit.,* p. 166.

follow Planck or Einstein, Heisenberg or Eddington? Or are we perhaps to look to one of the dozens of other lesser-known philosopher-scientists? As we noted earlier[1] in criticizing some philosopher-scientists of an earlier generation, as soon as scientists forsake their special territories to pronounce on the wider questions, their views diverge and one speculation has to be judged against another not on scientific but on philosophical grounds. There is good justification for John Passmore's remark that 'like a great many other revolutions, the revolution in physics raised no new philosophical problems and settled no old ones, for all the dust and fury'.[2]

Yet on the *negative* side, it may be claimed that one result has emerged. The older naturalism—the mechanistic materialism of the nineteenth century—has been more than ever discredited by the revolution in the fundamental physical concepts which lay at its basis. If the atoms of which material bodies are composed are not solid particles but rhythmical processes, then, as Streeter was quick to see, they may in their nature be akin to the processes of life and mind. Again, if the physical universe is finite, it may not be the ultimate reality which the older naturalism supposed it to be. Carl von Weizsacker mentions the violent emotional reaction of a physicist of the older school against the suggestion of a finite universe—a suggestion which strikes at mechanistic materialism's central and almost deified notion of the infinite eternal cosmos.[3] But these pointers are mainly negative. They discredit the older naturalism, but they do not positively point to theism—perhaps they call only for a more refined naturalism. Christian apologists have possibly tried to make too much of the revolution in physics. Here the work of Barnes has its value, for although his positive philosophy of religion is a thing of shreds and patches, he was quite clear that even if the new physics encourages us to think of a measure of indeterminacy on the level of very minute phenomena, it leaves the determination of large-scale phenomena untouched, and lends no support to ideas of miracle or divine interventions in nature.

The most subtle interpretations of the new physics are probably to be found in the process philosophies of realist metaphysicians, to whom we shall be turning shortly.[4] But in the meantime, we have completed our survey of the second or transitional phase of twentieth-century religious thought, and we must pause to see what stage we have now reached and what still lies ahead of us.

---

[1] See above, p. 111.   [2] *A Hundred Years of Philosophy*, p. 334.
[3] In a Gifford Lecture at Glasgow, 1960.   [4] See below, pp. 258ff.

XVI

MORE COMMENTS BY THE WAY

77. From the Second to the Third Phase

Now that we have reached the end of our survey of the second phase of our story, and can pause to look around us once more, we see at once how great is the change that has come over the pattern of religious thought. We are already among the distinctive themes of the twentieth century, and those ways of thinking which were the legacy of the preceding century—ways which still seem firmly established in the first phase of our story—already begin to look like somewhat ghostly figures in the distance. We have seen the idealist philosophies and theologies wilt away in face of the rise of realism; we have seen idealism's old enemy, the nineteenth-century naturalism, discredited by the very sciences on which it had claimed to base itself; we have seen the liberal anti-metaphysical theology of men like Herrmann and Harnack rendered untenable by the researches of new scholars like Weiss, Schweitzer and Loisy. At the same time we have seen that an extravagant optimism—whether based on the perfection of the Absolute or on the coming millennium of science—gives way to more sober attitudes; while there is a growing distrust of metaphysics, and even in some quarters a distrust of reason itself, as witness the rise of such anti-intellectualist views as pragmatism, Catholic Modernism, and the various philosophies of life and personal being.

At this stage, however, the picture which confronts us is still a very confused one. We have seen the old landmarks crumble and the old dividing lines rubbed out, but new ones have not as yet got firmly established. New orientations and new techniques have indeed appeared, but we have seen that there were many of them, and of those that we have described, few remain today as they were originally formulated. They have now had time to intersect, collide, coalesce, and sort themselves out, and it is from this process that the stable currents of mid-century thought will be seen to emerge. The movements which we have considered in the second phase had a transitional character. We may think of them as providing the matrix of ideas out of which or against which arise those major forms of religious thought which have come to dominate the scene in the middle of our century.

These major forms of mid-century thought afford the theme for the third phase of our story. We shall find that they introduce little that is really novel; they rather crystallize and carry still further the ideas that have already appeared in the second phase, and bring these ideas to definitive form as typical expressions of twentieth-century thinking. This is not to be wondered at when we recall that the historical, sociological and psychological conditions which were operative in the second phase have been continued and even intensified in the third. If we concede that such conditions are at least in part determinative for the philosophical and theological beliefs of any society—and it would be difficult to suppose otherwise—then the mid-century trends of religious thought reflect the outlook of a culture that has sailed into increasingly stormy weather as the century has proceeded, and that has become less and less sure of itself. To the First World War succeeded the Second World War, and to that the 'cold war' and the age of the nuclear deterrent. Meanwhile the nations of Asia and Africa rise up to end white supremacy. The future of Western culture is put in question—as perhaps it ought to be. Indeed, the future of mankind is in question—is his fate to be that of the trilobites or the reptiles, and is it reserved for some species other than *Homo sapiens* to exploit the future of the planet? In such an age of anxiety, it will not surprise us to find philosophers who make the phenomenon of anxiety itself one of their leading themes.[1] Nor will it surprise us to find theologians who forsake almost entirely God's immanence to stress his overwhelming trans-cendence, and whose theology in consequence takes on a distinctly eschatological tone.[2]

We must now go on to characterize briefly the specific types of thought which we shall encounter in our survey of the third phase.

78. SOME CHARACTERISTICS OF THE THIRD PHASE

We have already noted the anti-metaphysical temper of twentieth-century thought, and perhaps the most obvious dividing line among the mid-century schools is that which separates the surviving metaphysicians from those who declare metaphysics to be impossible or nonsensical. It must be observed that here the term 'metaphysics' is being used in the strict sense of an intellectual discipline, a rational speculation about

[1] See below, p. 354.   [2] See below, pp. 323-4.

ultimate reality, and not in the looser sense of knowledge about God and the supersensible. We shall find that some of those who are most forward in their denunciation of metaphysics can nevertheless talk freely about God and the supersensible, but they claim the right to do this not on the basis of metaphysical speculation but on the ground of an alleged 'encounter' with God, or something of the sort. Yet in spite of the unpopularity of metaphysics, we find two major metaphysical schools still flourishing in mid-century, and both of them very important for religious thought.

The first of these schools is that which comprises realist metaphysics. In our concluding remarks on the movement known as the 'New Realism', we pointed out that it contained two possibilities for further development.[1] The more conservative of these possibilities was to construct a realist metaphysic to take the place of the rejected idealist metaphysic. Such a possibility had already been adumbrated by Brentano.[2] In England a powerful school of realist metaphysics arose, combining the realist thesis with the findings of the new physics. This school was perhaps short-lived in England itself, where probably most philosophers and theologians today would consign it to what we have called the second phase of our story, but in the United States, where Whitehead went to spend the last years of his life, realist metaphysics is still a powerful influence and has notable advocates. A metaphysical type of realism arose also in Germany, allied there to some extent with phenomenology, and this too is still an unspent force. Hence we are justified in counting these metaphysical types of realism, together with their repercussions in theology, among the mid-century trends of religious thought to be studied in the third phase of our survey.

The other metaphysical school is neo-scholasticism, and more particularly neo-Thomism. As well as having a common interest in metaphysics, neo-Thomism and the metaphysical school of realism are related in certain ways—neo-Thomism is itself usually described as a 'moderate realism', while it will be remembered that Brentano, the father of contemporary realism, found his point of departure in the medieval conception of 'intentionality'.[3] The origin of contemporary neo-Thomism is, however, quite distinct from that of the current realism. Back at the end of the nineteenth century, it became part of the policy of the Roman Catholic Church to revive the study of St Thomas Aquinas and the other great medieval thinkers. Of course, a philosophy cannot be revived overnight, and moreover Catholic Modernism attracted some of the best thinkers of the Roman communion in the early years of the present century. Thus it has only been as the twentieth century has advanced that

[1] See above, p. 239   [2] See above, p. 228.   [3] See above, p. 228.

the fruits of Pope Leo XIII's far-reaching policy have begun to appear. By mid-century, neo-Thomism has become one of the major intellectual forces of our time, with a whole galaxy of first-class thinkers among its adherents. This philosophy is, of course, closely allied with Roman Catholic theology.

When we turn to the anti-metaphysical schools of mid-century thought, perhaps we can best divide them in a way that has been suggested by John Macmurray. He notes that these schools are all agreed about one thing— that 'the traditional method of philosophy is incapable of solving its traditional problems'.[1] They diverge, however, in that some stick to the method and give up the traditional problems, while others still wrestle with the substantial problems but have relinquished the traditional methods. As far as the problem of religious thought is concerned, there are three schools whose views we shall have to consider here.

First, there is logical empiricism. This represents the second possible line of development from the New Realism—the line which follows up the analytical tendencies in the thought of Moore and Russell.[2] From Macmurray's point of view, it illustrates the retention of the method accompanied by the relinquishment of the problems. In its earlier stages, the movement was called 'logical positivism', and in this iconoclastic phase it consigned not only metaphysics but also ethics and theology to the limbo of the meaningless. As time has gone on, however, the movement has become less aggressively positivist, though it is still anti-metaphysical and concerns itself with the logical analysis of language. But now the problems of religious language get more serious and patient consideration than they once did, and there are even theologians who look to logical empiricism and its techniques for a way of attacking their problems. Generally speaking, however, logical empiricism has had little interest in religion or theology, and on the philosophical side this movement represents the furthest remove from the once intimate associations of philosophy and theology.

Next, there is kerygmatic theology, associated above all with the name of Karl Barth. So far this has been the most influential movement in the Protestant theology of the present century. It has shown itself no less sceptical than logical positivism about the powers of human understanding in face of the ultimate problems, but it belongs to the other side of Macmurray's classification—that is to say, it continues to wrestle with the ultimate issues of God and of the life of the spirit, but it abandons traditional methods. It expects no confirmation of its beliefs from philosophy or from any department of human knowledge, but bases these

[1] *The Self as Agent*, p. 27.   [2] See above, p. 227.

beliefs solely on what it takes to be a unique act of God. It is true that at least in its early stages the movement looked to Kierkegaard and had affinity with some of the philosophies of personal being described above,[1] but these philosophies themselves were protests against the competence of reason to decide in matters of faith. In general, however, kerygmatic theology has endeavoured to make itself independent of all philosophy. But in thus breaking with an immediate tradition, it has claimed to rediscover an older tradition—the tradition of the Reformation and ultimately of the New Testament itself. In this respect one may notice that there is something in common between Protestant kerygmatic theology and Catholic neo-Thomism, for in the face of the conflicts of modern philosophies, both have withdrawn to the security of a classic Christian tradition. This resemblance, however, changes to a sharp divergence when it comes to assessing the relation of theology to our natural human knowledge, and kerygmatic theology represents, on the theological side, the furthest remove in the twentieth-century divorce between theology and philosophy.

Thirdly, there is existentialism. Macmurray would classify it with the schools which have discarded form in order to retain the substance of philosophy's traditional problems. But while it is true that the existentialists derive some of their leading insights not from reason but from such states of mind as are found in the 'limit-situations' of anxiety, guilt and death, we must beware of exaggeration, and remember that the earlier Heidegger made a careful formal analysis of the structures of human existence, while Jaspers has come to lay increasing stress on the place of reason. Existentialism is perhaps the most typical product of our century, and gathers up in itself not only the insights of the earlier philosophies of personal being but also elements derived from Dilthey's historicism, Husserl's phenomenology, and the philosophies of life and action. Moreover, the emergence of a powerful school of existentialist theology, springing from the side of kerygmatic theology itself, gives reason to hope that the divorce between theology and philosophy is ending, and that fruitful relations are being resumed, though no doubt on a different basis from before.

So far there has been no mention of Marxism, which has also vastly extended its hold by mid-century. But since Marxism has become a rigid orthodoxy from which no substantial deviations are tolerated, there is nothing to add to what was already said on this subject in the course of our survey of the second phase.[2]

The remainder of the book will therefore be divided in the following

---

[1] See above, pp. 193ff.   [2] See above, pp. 159–62.

manner. First, we shall consider realist metaphysics and theology (Chapter XVII). Then we pass on to neo-scholasticism and Roman Catholic theology (Chapter XVIII). Leaving the metaphysical schools, we then turn to logical empiricism (Chapter XIX), kerygmatic theology (Chapter XX), post-liberal theologies in the English-speaking countries (Chapter XXI), and existentialism (Chapter XXII). In a final chapter, we shall attempt to state such conclusions as seem justified in the light of our whole survey (Chapter XXIII).

XVII

REALIST METAPHYSICS AND THEOLOGY

79. METAPHYSICS ON A REALIST BASIS

REALIST metaphysics, like idealist metaphysics or indeed any kind of metaphysics, sets out to give a comprehensive account of reality. Whitehead remarks of his own philosophy that to some extent it represents 'a transformation of some main doctrines of absolute idealism on to a realistic basis'.[1] Some of the chief distinguishing marks of most realist metaphysics may be summarized as follows. 1) The reality of the world in space and time is recognized, whereas in idealist metaphysics the spatio-temporal world was taken to be the appearance of a reality which is itself timeless. 2) Mind, or the act of knowing, is taken to be one factor in reality among others, whereas in idealism mind is constitutive for reality. 3) There is a much closer connection with the natural sciences than there was in idealism, and indeed some of the leading realist metaphysicians were originally scientists. 4) The three distinguishing marks so far mentioned suggest a comparison with naturalistic philosophies. Realist metaphysics could be regarded as a new kind of naturalism, but a kind which is very different from the old. Realist metaphysics incorporates the findings of the new physical theories which, as we have seen, undermine the older naturalism. In particular, realist metaphysics generally make much of the notion of 'process', and recognize distinct 'levels' in nature, reaching up to the levels of spirit and even of deity. Thus the realist conception of nature is a much richer and more differentiated one than that of the old naturalism, where the tendency was to reduce everything to an ultimate substratum of solid atoms and their interactions. 5) Theologically, the tendency of realist metaphysics is to bring God into time, to make him a natural rather than a supernatural God, perhaps a finite and evolving God, as in the idea of God which we have already met in William James.[2] Such a view eases the theological problem of evil, and is perhaps more consonant with the spirit of the twentieth century than the notion of a God

---

[1] *Process and Reality*, p. vii.   [2] See above, pp. 178-9.

dwelling apart in timeless perfection, such as he was conceived in idealism and, for that matter, in most traditional theism.

In England and America, realist metaphysics represent a development in a conservative direction of the ideas of the New Realism. While continuing to lean towards mathematics and the sciences, the realist metaphysicians aim at synthesis rather than analysis. Alexander, for instance, acknowledging that his work belongs to the movement initiated by Moore and Russell, says that he can see no good reason for being suspicious of system in philosophy, and that the fault which he finds with his own work 'is not that it is systematic, but that it is not systematic enough'.[1] In similar fashion, Whitehead repudiates 'the distrust of speculative philosophy'.[2] Another important influence with the realist metaphysicians is found in the philosophies of Bergson, James and Dewey[3]—not, indeed, as regards the anti-intellectualist elements in these philosophies, but in their insistence on process and becoming. In German realism, which stands rather apart from the Anglo-American brand, the influence of phenomenology[4] is noticeable.

Our survey begins with realist metaphysics in the English-speaking countries (Section 80), goes on to realist metaphysics in Germany (Section 81), considers examples of the influence of such metaphysics in theological writers (Section 82) and philosophers of religion (Section 83), and ends with an evaluation (Section 84).

80. Realist Metaphysics in the English-speaking Countries
C. L. Morgan, S. Alexander, A. N. Whitehead, C. E. M. Joad

A good introduction to some of the leading ideas of realist metaphysics is found in the writings of Conwy Lloyd Morgan[5] (1852-1936), whose long academic career was divided between the chairs of zoology and philosophy. His philosophy likewise falls into two parts—a naturalistic basis drawn from the sciences, and a metaphysical superstructure which attempts to answer the questions which the sciences leave untouched.

The basic scientific part of Morgan's philosophy is a theory of emergent evolution. This was not a discovery on Morgan's part, but an idea which he himself traces back at least as far as John Stuart Mill. Morgan distinguishes between an 'emergent' and a mere 'resultant'. A resultant is

---

[1] *Space, Time, and Deity*, p. vi.   [2] *Process and Reality*, p. viii.
[3] See above, pp. 170ff.   [4] See above, pp. 218ff.
[5] Professor at Bristol, 1887-1919.

something which can be predicted from the factors already at work in a process and which is no more than a regrouping of these factors. For instance, to quote one of Morgan's own illustrations, if we know that carbon and sulphur combine in certain proportions, then we can tell in advance the weight of the compound simply by adding together the weights of the components. On the other hand, an emergent introduces novelty, and cannot be predicted from the antecedent factors. When carbon and sulphur combine, the properties of the compound are not merely the addition of the properties of the components. New properties have appeared which are not the properties either of carbon or of sulphur, and which could not have been predicted unless we had already had experience of what happens in such a chemical reaction.

The application of the idea of emergence to the evolutionary process implies that in that process there are certain critical stages at which something genuinely new comes into being. This may be expressed in a different way by saying that the process is not a continuous one but involves leaps on to new levels of being. The novelties which thus emerge cannot be interpreted as mere regroupings of pre-existent factors. They involve new modes of relatedness, which cannot be interpreted in terms of the factors which operate on a level lower than their own. Hence Morgan's view, though thoroughly naturalistic so far, is entirely different from the old mechanistic naturalism. 'The whole doctrine of emergence is a continued protest against mechanical interpretation, and the very antithesis to one that is mechanistic. It does not interpret life in terms of physics and chemistry. It does not interpret mind in terms of receptor-patterns and neuron-routes.'[1]

Morgan recognizes three distinct levels in the evolutionary process: at the bottom, the physico-chemical level; above it, the vital level; and at the top, the mental level. Each has its own distinct kind of relatedness, and defies interpretation in terms of the lower level from which it has emerged.

This completes the naturalistic part of Morgan's scheme, firmly founded, as he believed, on the evidence of the natural sciences. But he claims that we cannot rest here, but must go on to face more ultimate questions. We must construct an entire philosophy which will not indeed conflict with the findings of science but which will lead us beyond them.

The metaphysical part of Morgan's philosophy involves us in three hypotheses. The first of these is the realist hypothesis: although the world as we know it is to some extent shaped by our minds in the very act of knowing, we assume that there is nevertheless a real world existing in space and time in its own right and independently of our knowing it.

[1] *Emergent Evolution*, pp. 7-8.

Next, there is the hypothesis of concomitance: it is claimed that the mental and the physical never exist apart from each other, and that the world is characterized through and through by both—though it is not easy to see how this hypothesis squares with the doctrine of emergence. Finally, there is the theistic hypothesis: the orderly process of emergents points to God as its author. God is spirit, and spirit, in turn, is not another emergent character of the evolutionary process but rather the creative power which manifests itself in the whole process. These speculative conclusions may seem to hang rather loosely together with the much more compact doctrine of emergent evolution. But Morgan was no positivist, and believed that we must go on from the scientific picture to draw such metaphysical conclusions as are most consonant with it. He says of himself: 'I, for one, can and do accept the most thoroughgoing naturalism. I, for one, still retain, and am confirmed in, my belief in God.'[1]

The type of philosophy which we have met in Morgan is developed with greater rigour and consistency in the thought of Samuel Alexander[2] (1859-1938). Born in Australia, he studied and taught in England, and his philosophy is reckoned one of the greatest efforts in recent times towards a comprehensive metaphysical system. The main strands in his thinking are well summarized by Rudolf Metz: 'Alexander takes over Hume's empirical philosophy, but not his scepticism; Spencer's evolutionary philosophy, but not his agnosticism; the theory of knowledge of New Realism without halting at it; and the physical theory of relativity, but not without a speculative evaluation and a subordination of it to his own system.'[3]

The groundwork of Alexander's metaphysic is an all-embracing scheme of emergent evolution—a scheme which is more comprehensive than Morgan's, and extends beyond it at both ends. Alexander reaches down below the level of the physico-chemical to find the foundation of his scheme in *space-time* itself. In the manner of modern physics, space and time are taken together, and we do not have one without the other. Space-time is therefore already dynamic in its character, and is constituted by a multiplicity of point-instants. This space-time is the primal stuff or matrix out of which everything that is arises. The next level in Alexander's scheme is *matter*, which emerges from the dynamic matrix of space-time. In Alexander, the breaks between levels are less sharp than in Morgan, and there is more stress on continuity and on intermediate stages—levels within levels, so to speak. But it would seem that when a certain degree of complexity is reached, something qualitatively new appears. He says:

[1] *Life, Mind, and Spirit*, p. 1.
[2] Professor at Manchester, 1893-1925.
[3] *A Hundred Years of British Philosophy*, p. 624.

'Ascent takes place, it would seem, through complexity. But at each change of quality the complexity as it were gathers itself together and is expressed in a new simplicity. The emergent quality is the summing together in a new totality of the component materials.'[1] From matter there emerges *life*, not as a mere epiphenomenon but as a qualitatively new level of complexity which nevertheless stands in a relation of continuity with thé old level. There are various levels of life itself, and with the evolution of organisms having a highly developed nervous system we come to the next level, that of *mind*. This was the highest level in Morgan's scheme, and it is indeed the highest of which we have experience. But Alexander carries his own scheme a stage further. The next level after mind is *deity*. This is the goal towards which the *nisus* of the evolutionary process presses—a goal which always lies ahead, but towards which conscious mind is able to look. Thus, God, who stood outside of emergent evolution in Morgan's scheme, is boldly brought by Alexander into the evolutionary process itself, as its highest goal.

Alexander's philosophy is consistently realist. The cognitive relation is said to be one of 'compresence' between two entities, and what we know is not contributed by the subject but belongs to the object which is present to that subject. The very categories of our thinking—identity, substance, causality and the like—are universal not because they are due to mind but because they are pervasive fundamental characteristics of space-time. Qualities also—not only the so-called 'primary' qualities like shape but also the so-called 'secondary' qualities like colour—really belong to objects in the spatio-temporal world. It is true that what Alexander calls the 'tertiary' qualities—values such as beauty and goodness—occur only when there is an evaluating subject, but nevertheless Alexander's world is one in which qualitative distinctions are real, and it is such qualitative distinction that differentiate the various levels in his emergent scheme.

Thus although we have to do here with an entirely naturalistic philosophy, it is clearly a naturalism of a different kind from the older varieties. Everything is indeed generated out of the matrix of space-time and so has a physical basis—mind has its neural basis and even God has his spatio-temporal aspect. But each emergent introduces a qualitative difference which places it on its higher and distinctive level. Quality is associated with the time-aspect of entities, while their physical side is associated with the space-aspect. Thus the suggestion is introduced that just as everything that is has its physical side, so too it has its mental side. 'Time is the mind of space and any quality the mind of its body.'[2] This is a difficult doctrine, and the suggestion that the mental and the physical are

[1] *Space, Time, and Deity*, vol. II, p. 70.   [2] *Op. cit.*, vol. II, p. 428.

somehow correlated throughout reality is not easily harmonized with the notion of emergence. But it is clear in Alexander's case, as in Morgan's, that this naturalism works with a conception of nature which is far richer and more diversified than the conception held by the nineteenth-century naturalists.

From the religious point of view, the most interesting feature in Alexander's metaphysic is, of course, his revolutionary idea of God. As we have seen, God is himself brought within the scheme of emergent evolution, so that he arises out of the primal space-time. Here the usual conception of God has been turned around, for God is commonly regarded as the author or creator of the world, the *terminus a quo* of the universal process, while in Alexander's thought God appears as the *terminus ad quem*. But Alexander thinks that such a God may well satisfy the religious consciousness, and draw men towards him. Alexander will not even allow that his conception of God is a pantheistic one, though to many of his critics it has seemed that to think of God as so thoroughly immersed in the natural order is a thoroughgoing pantheism. To this Alexander replies that 'God is immanent in respect of his body, but transcendent in respect of his deity.'[1] For God, like everything else in space-time, has both his physical aspect and his mental aspect. His body is the whole of space-time, so that he includes all finite existents. In this respect God is immanent and the doctrine is pantheistic. But he is transcendent in respect of his deity, which is carried by only a portion of the universe—that region of space-time which always lies ahead and to which, at any actual stage of the evolutionary process, one looks forward and upward, so to speak. And since deity is the distinctive quality of God, this whole conception of God is claimed to be theistic rather than pantheistic.

No less comprehensive than Alexander's metaphysic, and perhaps even more celebrated, is the philosophy of Alfred North Whitehead[2] (1861-1947). Closely associated with Russell in the development of modern mathematical logic, Whitehead later diverged widely from his erstwhile collaborator. As against Russell's positivist and analytical tendencies, Whitehead believed the time to be ripe for a new comprehensive synthesis of knowledge. And while Russell remained close to materialistic views, Whitehead developed a philosophy that is far removed from materialism, though one which keeps closely in touch with the natural sciences. The contrast between the two men perhaps comes out most strongly in their respective accounts of religion. Russell, as we have seen, thinks of religion

---

[1] *Op. cit.*, vol. II, p. 396.

[2] Fellow of Trinity College, Cambridge, 1880-1910; thereafter held appointments in London University, 1911-24, and Harvard University, 1924-37.

as a useless survival which is now to be superseded by scientific humanism, and it is in science that he places his hopes for the future. Whitehead, on the other hand, thinks that the religious vision is 'the one element in human experience which persistently shows an upward trend. The fact of the religious vision, and its history of persistent expansion, is our one ground for optimism. Apart from it, human life is a flash of occasional enjoyments lighting up a mass of pain and misery.'[1]

The philosophy which lies behind this estimate of religion is called by Whitehead a 'philosophy of organism', where the word 'organism' is used not in a narrowly biological sense but for a conception of reality in which all aspects of experience are interconnected—aesthetic, moral and religious interests as well as those ideas of the world which have their origin in the natural sciences. Like Morgan and Alexander, Whitehead conceives the world in dynamic terms. We are not to think of a static 'substance' underlying the things of the world, still less are we to think dualistically of two such substances, mind and matter. We are to think rather in terms of 'process'. In working out his philosophy, Whitehead introduces many novel terms, and sometimes uses traditional terms in new senses. Here we can offer only an outline of some of his more important ideas.

'The final real things of which the world is made up' are called by Whitehead 'actual entities'. [2] There are many such actual entities, ranging from God at the top of the scale down to the most trivial 'puff of existence'. The world-process consists in the becoming of these actual entities, and we cannot go behind them to find anything more real. As we have already noted, we cannot posit some underlying substance. Descartes thought of body and mind as two ultimate substances which can somehow act on each other, but Whitehead rejects all bifurcation of nature. His own view is that every actual entity is bipolar; it has both a physical pole and a mental pole, though here the word 'mental' does not necessarily imply consciousness.

Since God is an actual entity, he is to be conceived as himself bipolar. His mental or conceptual pole, called by Whitehead his 'primordial nature', is unchanging, complete, the source of all ideals and new possibilities. But God has also his physical pole, his 'consequent nature', which shares in the creative advance of the world. On these two sides of the divine being, Whitehead says that the conceptual side is 'free, complete, primordial, eternal, actually deficient, and unconscious. The other side originates with physical experience derived from the temporal world, and then acquires integration with the primordial side. It is determined,

---

[1] *Science and the Modern World*, p. 275.   [2] *Process and Reality*, p. 24.

incomplete, consequent, everlasting, fully actual, and conscious.'[1] According to Whitehead, while conceptual experience can be infinite, physical experience is necessarily finite, so that in regard to his consequent nature God is limited and is involved in becoming. He is engaged in the battle to overcome evil, and is 'the great companion, the fellow-sufferer who understands'.[2]

At the other end of the range of actual entities, the 'puff of existence' also is bipolar. It has its mental pole—though of course this is not conscious—as well as its more obvious physical pole. Thus in Whitehead's metaphysic we meet once again a kind of panpsychism.

All actual entities participate in what Whitehead calls 'eternal objects'. These are not unlike the 'ideas' of Plato. They are universal qualities, but they do not exist independently and are realized only in the concrescences of actual entities in the world-process. Apart from that, they are mere potentialities in the primordial nature of God. The creativity of God consists in his being the source of these eternal objects, that is to say, of all possibilities. They flow from God and are realized in actual entities. Thus while actual entities are always becoming and producing novelty, the eternal objects are fixed in their being; they are eternally present in God, awaiting realization.

Actual entities involve one another and enter into relations, and it is this involvement that Whitehead designates by the important term 'prehension'. Whitehead's rejection of dualism and his recognition of the bipolar character of actual entities is reflected in his doctrine of prehensions, which are both physical and mental. And just as he rejects dualism, so too he rejects any faculty-psychology, and denies that there is any mere awareness, mere emotion or mere volition. Thus a prehension involves causation, emotion, purpose and valuation. There is no process that is devoid of value, and Whitehead's realism, like that of Morgan and Alexander, presents us with a far richer picture of the world than did mechanistic naturalism.

In virtue of their prehensional involvements with each other, actual entities constitute webs of togetherness, and such a web is called by Whitehead a *'nexus'*. Thus the idea of prehension enables him to pass from pluralism of the multiplicity of actual entities towards the conception of an organic universe.

Against the background of this complex and difficult metaphysic, we can now perhaps understand Whitehead's high estimate of religion, from which our exposition of his ideas set out. 'Religion', he says, 'is the vision of something which stands beyond, behind, and within, the passing flux of immediate things; something which is real, and yet waiting to be realized; something which is a remote possibility, and yet the greatest of present facts; something whose possession is the final good, and yet is beyond all reach.'[1]

How does this estimate of religion touch upon Christianity? Institutional Christianity has fallen into decay, yet the religious spirit still remains effective.[2] Whitehead sees the key to this situation in three phases of historical development. First, there was Plato's insight that the divine persuasion is foundational to the order of the world, an insight which anticipates a doctrine of grace. Next, there was the life of Christ which revealed in act what Plato had divined in theory. Thirdly, there was the attempted synthesis in theology of Plato's intellectual insight with practical Christianity. But this attempt at synthesis failed. Theology lapsed into dogmatic finality, and clung to outmoded ideas which turn the notion of divine persuasion into the doctrine of a despotic God who stands over against the world as a coercive Power. The persuasive eternal ideals, as taught by Plato and actualized by Christ, still stand; but theology needs a new reformation if it is to point us to them effectually.

After the massive systems of Whitehead and Alexander, it may seem something of an anticlimax to allude to Cyril Edwin Mitchinson Joad[3] (1891-1953). This younger member of the realist school, however, deserves mention for the same reason as men like Trine and Haeckel—that is to say, as the popularizer of philosophical ideas among hundreds of thousands of people who would never dream of reading the philosophical giants, and who perhaps have scarcely as much as heard their names. Joad has the further interest of illustrating the progression from an agnostic to a theistic type of realism. For however eclectic and superficial some of his writings may have been, he was at least consistent in his realism, and never ceased to insist that what we know is an object which is quite independent of the fact that we know it.

In what is probably the best of his many books, *Matter, Life, and Value*, Joad sets out a threefold metaphysical scheme. There are three distinct realms of being, these are matter, life, and value, and no one of them can be explained in terms of the others. At first glance, this looks like the emergent schemes of Morgan and Alexander, but although Joad had at one time been strongly attracted by evolutionary philosophies, his stress is on the distinctness of the three realms. In particular, the realm of values cannot be derived from the lower levels. Values are objectively real, and constitute a transcendent realm of their own.

---

[1] *Science and the Modern World*, p. 275.   [2] See *Adventures of Ideas*, pp. 205ff.
[3] He taught at Birkbeck College, London, 1930-53.

In his subsequent writings, Joad increasingly emphasizes the transcendence of the realm of values, which is also the realm of God. He criticizes as humanistic, philosophies like that of Alexander, which bring God and values into the natural order entirely. Humanism is regarded by Joad as the symptom of a decadent society. The recurrent pattern of such societies is represented by a threefold scheme: *hubris*—man seeks to go beyond his place in the order of things; *nemesis*—justice catches up with him; *ate*—the wrath of the gods descends upon him, or, to speak less mythologically, he suffers the disintegration that results from his infringement of the right order of things. The fundamental error is a false view of man's status in the universe and 'a failure to acknowledge the non-human elements of value and deity'.[1] But Joad can also express this in terms of his realist philosophy as a failure to acknowledge the reality and independence of the object, and he connects decadence with subjectivism.

These tendencies in Joad's thought reach their culmination in his last book, *The Recovery of Belief*. Here, like a modern Justin Martyr, he finds the most satisfying answer to his philosophical quest in the Christian faith.

81. REALIST METAPHYSICS IN GERMANY
N. Hartmann

In Germany, the metaphysical developments of realism have been represented above all in the work of Nicolai Hartmann[2] (1882-1950), several of whose books are well-known in translation in the English-speaking countries. Beginning in the Marburg school of neo-Kantianism, Hartmann abandoned idealism for realism. The object of knowledge is not constructed by thought but is given to thought and exists independently of thought. Thus Hartmann's philosophy envisages a world in which mind and its activities constitute only one factor among others.

While we have included Hartmann among the realist metaphysicians, we should note that he himself prefers to speak of ontology. He can indeed claim that 'no philosophy can stand without a fundamental view of being',[3] but he distinguishes sharply between his kind of ontology and the older style of metaphysics. The latter looked for a universal principle in terms of which it could give a rational account of all being. Hartmann's ontology is less ambitious. He says that it gleans its categories step by step from an observation of existing realities. Moreover, it does not offer a

---

[1] *Decadence: a Philosophical Inquiry*, p. 15.
[2] Professor at Berlin, 1931-45; Göttingen, 1945-50.
[3] *New Ways of Ontology*, p. 4.

complete account of reality, for Hartmann believes that there is an unknowable element in the world. Some problems are insoluble, and lead to an *aporia* or impassable perplexity. His own ontology contents itself with the analysis, description and clarification of the intelligible aspects of being in ways that are somewhat reminiscent of the phenomenological method, here applied to the ontological problem. But if Hartmann's ontology does not offer a complete system, at least it aims at cutting down the areas of unintelligibility.

We find a point of contact between Hartmann and the English realists in his doctrine of levels or layers of being. He does not use the emergent evolutionary scheme, preferring not to speculate on the genesis of one level from another, but speaks instead of the 'stratification' of reality. Four such *strata* are recognized: in ascending order, they are matter, life, consciousness (which is found both in animals and men), and spirit (which is found only in the higher activities of man). Each *stratum* has its own peculiar categories of being. Some categories of the lower *strata* penetrate to greater or lesser extents in the higher ones—for instance, space characterizes life as well as matter, while time is common to all four *strata*—but the peculiar categories of the higher levels do not penetrate down to the lower ones. The higher *strata* are thus rooted in the lower ones and are not found apart from them, so that these lower *strata* are described as the stronger, because they support the whole structure of being. On the other hand, the higher *strata* are not wholly determined by the lower ones, but have autonomy in the face of them, and may make use of them. The relation may be likened to that of a rider on a horse. Man, for instance, is free in a natural world which is determined, and only in such a world could he be free, for his purposive behaviour requires that he should be able to predict how things will happen.

This world-view is far removed from any materialistic naturalism, yet it turns out to be equally far from theism. The world, though stratified and heterogeneous, is nevertheless one world, but the modest aims which Hartmann has assigned to ontology forbid us to come to any hasty conclusion about the principle of unity in the world. In particular, the explanation of this unity in terms of a personal God seems to Hartmann a piece of anthropocentric megalomania.

He has, moreover, ethical reasons for rejecting theism. He praises Christianity for commanding brotherly love, but thinks that the ethical value of this command is vitiated by the other command to love God, for this introduces a metaphysic of the beyond and supplies a prudential motive for brotherly love. Yet Hartmann himself recommends as well as brotherly love what he calls 'love of the remotest'. This is said to involve 'faith of a unique kind, differing from trust between man and man; a faith which reaches out to the whole of things'.[1] Moral passion is said to spring 'from reverence for the unbounded abundance of the things that are of worth; it is knowledge filled with gratitude, and, where knowledge fails, it is the presentiment that the values of existence are inexhaustible'.[2] Thus in Hartmann the religious sentiments of love, faith, reverence and gratitude are directed not to a personal and transcendent God but to the enigmatic sum of being. Yet the sentiments he mentions are so thoroughly personal that it may be doubted whether he escapes the anthropomorphism which he dreads.

82. REALIST METAPHYSICS IN THEOLOGICAL AND RELIGIOUS WRITERS
W. Temple, L. S. Thornton, P. Teilhard de Chardin

The impact upon theology of the realist metaphysics already described in this chapter has been considerable, and of course in some instances it has been much more thoroughgoing than in others.

We begin with one of the more moderate instances, as found in the thought of William Temple[3] (1881-1944). His death two years after his appointment as Archbishop of Canterbury deprived the Church of England of an outstanding leader, one who was not only an ecclesiastic and theologian, but who kept in close touch with the social problems of the contemporary world. While Temple's theology centres in the Christian revelation, he believed, in the tradition of Anglican theology, that this revelation must find its confirmation in reason and conscience. Thus he looked for a philosophical framework for his theology. At first he found this in idealism, and indeed he never ceased to acknowledge his indebtedness to his teacher Caird, and the British idealist school. But by the time he published his Gifford Lectures in 1934, he had joined in the general migration from idealism to realism.

Descartes is blamed by Temple for having misled modern philosophy into the belief that what we know are our own ideas; what we know, Temple asserts, is a world that stands over against us. Following the British realist metaphysicians, Temple conceives this world as a process in which there have emerged distinct levels of being. In his scheme, there are four such levels: matter, life, intelligence, spirit. Among them, 'the

---

[1] *Ethics*, vol. III, p. 330.   [2] *Op. cit.*, vol. I, p. 210.

[3] Canon of Westminster, 1919-21; Bishop of Manchester, 1921-9; Archbishop of York, 1929-42; Archbishop of Canterbury, 1942-4.

higher can only exist by means of the lower; but, far from being controlled by that lower, takes control of it'.[1] Here Temple comes very close to Hartmann, though probably the two reached their ideas independently.

But Temple insists that it is the highest stage in the evolutionary process which makes the whole process intelligible as a unity. In man, for instance, we can discern all four levels of being—we can consider him as a material object, as a living organism, as an animal intelligence, or as a spirit; but it is his spirit that makes him a unity, and gives him his distinctive humanity. In the same way, it is argued, we must consider the universe as a whole. We began with natural process, but when we have traced this to the emergence of its highest level, spirit, we must turn back and interpret the unity of the whole process in terms of spirit. Because of this procedure, Temple calls his philosophy 'dialectical realism'.

The spiritual interpretation of the universal process leads to theism, for the spirit which emerges within the process has a transcendent character which points to God as the unifying principle who controls and indeed creates the whole process. We discover the 'transcendence of the immanent', but this, in turn, leads us to view the world in terms of the 'immanence of the transcendent'. Thus understood, the world has a sacramental character, manifesting in its natural processes the values which have their source in the transcendent God. And with this idea of a sacramental universe we are pointed to the completion of natural theology in the Christian revelation and its central doctrine of the incarnation.

The philosophical ideas of process, organism and emergence are prominent in the theology of another Anglican scholar, Lionel Spencer Thornton[2] (1884-1960). A somewhat diffuse writer, Thornton belongs to the Anglo-Catholic or traditionalist school of thought, so that it may seem surprising to find in him this interest in contemporary realist metaphysics. Yet it is precisely in his exploration of the traditional patterns of biblical and patristic theology that Thornton discovers an analogy between these and modern process philosophies, so that these philosophies can be used to elucidate the Christian revelation in terms intelligible to the contemporary mind; though it should at once be added that the Christian revelation on its side is held to elucidate the process philosophies.

Thornton reverts to a method of biblical exegesis widely practised among the early fathers of the Church, and usually called 'typology'. This method interprets the Bible in terms of recurring images or patterns and, for instance, regards the persons and events of the Old Testament as prefiguring and finding their fulfilment in the New Testament. The

[1] *Nature, Man and God*, p. 478.
[2] He taught at Mirfield, 1914-44.

method is, of course, occasionally used in the Bible itself, as when St Paul speaks of Christ as a second Adam.[1]

In particular, Thornton is interested in the parallel between the ideas of 'creation' and 'incarnation'. This line of thought is, of course, found in the New Testament, and it becomes very important in patristic theology. St Irenaeus interprets it in terms of 'recapitulation'; the divine *Logos*, who was the creative agent in the beginning, becomes incarnate to restore and sum up his work in a new creation.

Thornton sees in this traditional teaching about the incarnation a link between the order of creation and the order of redemption, and so between the philosophy of nature and the Christian revelation. Drawing on Morgan, Alexander and Whitehead, he sees the universal process as an ascent from one level to another, such that on each new level the earlier levels are gathered up into a new unity. Man is a kind of microcosm who includes in himself all the levels but sums them up in the new unity of his spiritual being. But man is not the end of the process. 'As the series is taken up into the human organism, so in Christ the human organism is taken up on to the level of deity.'[2] Thus from man we go on to God, and the 'deification' of man is again a common patristic idea, to which St Athanasius gives expression in his well-known statement about Christ: 'He was made man that we might be made God.'[3] Thornton says that 'Christ sanctified and deified all human nature',[4] and sees the emergence of a new kind of society in the 'Body of Christ'.

Thus Thornton boldly places the incarnation at the centre of the universal process. But we should notice that he certainly does not think of Christ as a product of the process. God is not only the end towards which the process moves, but also its beginning. There is a transcendent order over against the created order, and it is to this transcendent order that Christ belongs in his creative and redemptive work.

Another interesting example of the combination of a dynamic worldview with the central teachings of Christian theology is found in the French Roman Catholic writer, Pierre Teilhard de Chardin[5] (1881-1955). He was both a Jesuit priest and a scientist of high distinction, with a special interest in the problems of evolution.

Teilhard's starting-point is scientific and naturalistic. He sets out not to explain but to see and to describe the phenomena, and what he sees is a vast evolutionary process in which the simpler elements build up into ever more complex unities—elemental particles into atoms, atoms into

---

[1] I Cor. 15.45ff.   [2] *The Incarnate Lord*, p. 255.
[3] *De Incarnatione*, 54, 3.   [4] *Revelation and the Modern World*, p. 129.
[5] Joined the Society of Jesus in 1899; spent most of his life abroad in teaching and scientific research.

molecules, molecules into living cells, cells into multicellular organisms. The law of this process appears to be that with increasing complexity of physical organisation there goes an increase in the direction of life and consciousness. On the one hand, Teilhard recognizes critical points in the process, when complexity reaches such a stage that some new condition appears. On the other hand, he holds that 'nothing could ever burst forth as final across the different thresholds successively traversed by evolution (however critical they may be) which has not already existed in an obscure and primordial way'.[1] Thus both the notion of emergence and the notion of a kind of panpsychism find a place in his scheme of thought.

The details of this evolutionary process are fully observable only upon our planet, though Teilhard believes that an evolutionary interpretation is to be placed on the universe as a whole. On the earth, the great critical moments in the process have been, first, the appearance of life when molecules of sufficient complexity had been built up, and next, the appearance of man as the bearer of reflective thought. This second event is called 'hominization', and with it the evolutionary process becomes conscious of itself, and man becomes its spearhead. The appearance of life and then of thought have, as it were, added two new envelopes to the earth in addition to its physical layers—the 'biosphere' or connected film of life which covers the earth's surface, and the 'noosphere' or mental envelope, which includes not only men themselves but also their works—their fields and factories, cities and communications, and so on.

Without forsaking his phenomenal starting-point, Teilhard now becomes more speculative, and seeks to extrapolate the evolutionary process into the future. The law which relates complexity and consciousness will continue to operate, and Teilhard sees the process converging upon what he calls the 'omega-point', a suprapersonal unity of all things in God. In this view, God is the final rather than the efficient cause of the universe, drawing all things towards perfection in himself. While Teilhard wishes to speak of God as transcendent, it is not clear that his argument does not rather tend towards the kind of God whom we met in Alexander's philosophy. It may have been because of this and other ambiguities that the Roman Catholic authorities forbade the publication of his writings during his lifetime.

Like Thornton, Teilhard thinks of Christ as at the centre of the evolutionary process. Christ is, so to speak, the reflection into the heart of the process of the omega-point which stands at its end. Christ assures us of its reality by actualizing it in our midst, and in the Christian society of self-transcending love the end is already being realized.

[1] *The Phenomenon of Man*, p. 71.

We may think that in the illustrations which have been set before us in this section, theologians have been somewhat half-hearted in their reactions to the realist philosophers. Temple, Thornton and Teilhard go some way towards meeting process philosophies, and perhaps gain some valuable theological insights in so doing, but they end up by sticking to traditional theism. God is conceived as standing beyond the world-process, eternally complete in his unchanging perfection—though it must be said that Teilhard comes very near to bringing God into the process.

83. REALISM, THEISM AND CHRISTIANITY
C. Hartshorne, A. C. Garnett

For less inhibited theological applications of the realist philosophies, we turn to the United States. We have already seen something of the influence of realist metaphysics in the ideas of some American thinkers, though they have been introduced in other connections. For instance, the personalist Brightman, who conceived of a finite God taking in time and struggling in the evolutionary process, owed something both to Brentano and Whitehead; while Wieman of the Chicago school, though we noticed him in connection with Dewey, was also influenced by Whitehead.[1] Here we consider two younger thinkers who look for a form of theism that will be compatible both with realist philosophy and with the Christian religion.

Belonging to the Chicago school itself is Charles Hartshorne[2] (1897-). In his book *Beyond Humanism,* he argues that a genuine humanism must be based on the recognition of a reality that is more than human. At the same time, he rejects the claim that traditional theism can provide the kind of basis that is required. Traditional theism presented us with a supernatural God, but the notion of the 'supernatural' is one that has been discredited and is no longer tenable. We must look for God in the world-process itself, and, following Whitehead, Hartshorne thinks that this process has its psychical as well as its physical aspect throughout.

What, then, is the new kind of theism which he prefers to the old? In his subsequent book, *Man's Vision of God,* Hartshorne holds that the disjunction between the traditional theism and atheism is not an exclusive one. Between these extremes lies a third possibility. The three possibilities—which can be further subdivided—are expressed as follows: '1. There is a Being in *all* respects absolutely perfect or unsurpassable.

[1] For Brightman, see above, pp. 67-8; for Wieman, pp. 187-8.
[2] Professor at Chicago, 1928-55; Emory University, Georgia, from 1955.

2. There is no Being in all respects absolutely perfect; but there is a Being in *some* respects perfect, and in some respects not so. . . . It is not excluded that the Being may be relatively perfect in all the respects in which it is not absolutely perfect. 3. There is no Being in *any* respect absolutely perfect.'[1] The first and third of these possibilities, in the traditional forms of theism and atheism, have for long contended with each other. Both are unsatisfactory, and the debate between them has been so stubborn only because the remaining possibility—the second on Hartshorne's list—was overlooked. But this is the possibility which Hartshorne chooses as the true one—'panentheism',[2] he calls it—the doctrine of a God who has indeed an unchanging essence but who completes himself in an advancing experience.

Hartshorne goes on to argue that this doctrine is religiously as well as intellectually the most satisfying. It is indeed something of an accident that Christianity has been historically associated with the doctrine of a static supernatural God. If we take the teaching that God is love seriously, then we must believe that he is really involved with his creatures, acting upon them and being himself acted upon in turn. Divinity is not the privilege of standing beyond all suffering, but rather of sharing in it. God and his creatures are together in a dynamic society, and Hartshorne believes that his revolutionary and social conception of theism is truer to the essence of biblical religion than the old theism was.

Arthur Campbell Garnett[3] (1894-   ) remarks that in the early part of the century religion seemed to many to be in rapid decline. By mid-century, both religion and theological studies had undergone a remarkable revival in the United States. Garnett sees clearly enough that there may be many motives for this revival—such as patriotic feeling, the need of a tranquillizer, and the like—but he claims that the basic motive is man's need of a supreme object of love and loyalty that can lift him above his divisive loyalties. 'Nothing can do this so effectively as the concept of a God of love who is equally the God and Father of us all and who equally loves us all.'[4] But if contemporary man's need is to be met, theology must present him with a concept of God that is intellectually tenable, and for Garnett this means a concept that will not fly in the face of contemporary empiricism.

He takes an unfavourable view of most of the current theologies.

---

[1] *Op. cit.*, pp. 11-12.

[2] This term originated with K. C. F. Krause (1781-1832).

[3] Born in Australia, he lectured in Adelaide before proceeding to the United States, where he has been professor in the University of Wisconsin from 1937.

[4] *Contemporary Thought and the Return to Religion*, p. 14.

Barthianism is rejected for its adherence to a revelation which is untested and unsupported by reason. Neo-Thomism claims to be rational, but its language of analogy breaks down, for it is impossible to use terms drawn from temporal experience of a God who is supposed to be eternal. Tillich, who, with Bultmann, is regarded by Garnett as among the more 'sober and enlightened' of contemporary theologians, is also dismissed. For Tillich tries to find a philosophical basis for his theology by claiming that God is 'being itself', where 'being' is taken to be some mysterious 'power to be'. If Tillich had taken an elementary course in linguistic analysis, he would have seen that his argument rests on a failure to understand the logic of the verb 'to be'—a verb which has, according to Garnett, a purely logical function, and refers to nothing even when used existentially.

The basic error of all these theologies is their attempt to talk about an eternal God. Such a God would lie beyond any possible experience, which is always temporal. The remedy is to abandon this notion of the eternal God, and to recognize his temporal character. Then it becomes possible to talk analogically about God, his personality, his love, and so on. 'Just as we conceive by analogy an infrahuman experience of animals, so we can conceive by analogy the suprahuman experience of God.'[1] Analogy is legitimate here, because all three forms of experience—animal, human and divine—have a temporal character. Of course, the existence of such a God is not empirically demonstrable, but there is no *logical* obstacle in the way of conceiving such a God, and some of the realist and process philosophies show us that good reasons can be adduced for believing that there is such a God. And like Hartshorne, Garnett believes that a God of this type accords better with the living God of the Bible than does a God who is supposed to be timelessly perfect.

84. Remarks on the Realist Philosophies and Theologies

To those who think that the business of philosophy is solely analysis, the realist metaphysics must look like sorry perversions and betrayals of the spirit of the New Realism. But no one has ever shown that philosophy should take analysis as its exclusive concern. It could even be the case that when it does so, it shirks its greatest tasks. The claim to have the right to construct a system, made by Alexander and Whitehead, is a claim that no one can gainsay; but, naturally enough, once the systems have been constructed, their authors must expect them to be submitted to the most careful and critical scrutiny.

[1] *Op. cit.*, p. 73. See also *A Realistic Philosophy of Religion.*

Certainly the realist metaphysics of men like Alexander, Whitehead and Hartmann must be regarded as remarkable and even monumental examples of sustained philosophical thinking, and this can hardly be denied by those who think that these men were mistaken in their endeavours. Again, although their attempts to construct a grand system seem out of touch with the general temper of our times, this does not mean that such attempts are merely out of date. 'This grand manner', says R. G. Collingwood, 'is not the mark of a period; it is the mark of a mind which has its philosophical material properly controlled and digested.'[1] This observation could well be true.

Furthermore, the philosophies in question avoid many of the pitfalls which attended traditional metaphysics. They are much more down to earth than idealist metaphysics, and by keeping in close touch with experience and the natural sciences they escape the temptation to weave a world-system from the speculations of one's own mind. At the same time, they avoid the errors of the old-fashioned naturalism. They turn away from its false abstraction to a concrete understanding of the world, and instead of trying to reduce everything to the lowest common denominator, they give due weight to all the varied aspects of experience. Finally, they avoid the danger of anti-intellectualism, such as showed itself in the so-called 'life-philosophies'.

Can religious thought get along without some kind of metaphysics? We have already met, and we shall meet again, some thinkers who believe that it can. Either they claim that their knowledge of God comes not through metaphysics but exclusively through some revelation; or else they claim that religion is entirely a practical matter, little differentiated from morality and having nothing to do with the question of what kind of a universe we live in. In considering the Ritschlians, we have already seen reason to judge that the exclusive appeal to a revelation which gets no confirmation from our ordinary thought and experience is quite unsatisfactory.[2] On the other hand, while religion undoubtedly has its practical side and this is of very great importance, it also has its beliefs, and most people would not recognize as 'religion' a way of life which disclaimed any belief about God or the nature of the universe. Dorothy Emmet has a relevant comment: 'Religion loses its nerve when it ceases to believe that it expresses in some way truth about our relation to a reality beyond ourselves which ultimately concerns us.'[3] Those who still believe that religion is interested in the problem of God, and who further believe that any faith based on some special revelation should expect

[1] *The Idea of Nature*, p. 158.   [2] See above, pp. 92ff.
[3] *The Nature of Metaphysical Thinking*, p. 4.

to find some general confirmation in our experience of the world, can scarcely ignore what the realist metaphysicians have to say. Indeed, as we have seen, many theologians have shown an interest in these metaphysicians.

But here a difficulty arises. From our survey of realist metaphysics and theology, it is obvious that two different conceptions of God are current in this field. The more thoroughgoing and consistent realists—Alexander, Whitehead, Hartshorne—bring God into time so that he becomes to some extent a God who is 'on his way', so to speak, a God who in one way or another is not yet complete in his perfection, a natural God rather than a supernatural God. Others—Morgan and Joad among the philosophers, Temple and Thornton among the theologians—definitely put God beyond the spatiotemporal world, making him the eternally perfect supernatural God of traditional theism. And this difference of opinion about God seems to lead us into a dilemma; for there is no doubt that the first of these two conceptions of God is the more satisfying *intellectually*, and the one that is most consistent with the realist approach to metaphysics; but at first glance the second conception is more satisfying *religiously*, though by placing God beyond space and time in some superempirical realm it throws away those virtues of realist metaphysics already noted and reverts to the old-style metaphysics of the supernatural.

A God who is not or who is not yet completely perfect may indeed stir in us genuinely religious feelings of love and aspiration, but can he evoke that deep awe and reverence of which Otto speaks, and which is surely at the heart of religion? This question, however, is not easily answered. We must remember that Whitehead recognizes a primordial as well as a consequent nature in God; that his disciple, Hartshorne, has argued that the idea of God who completes himself is more consonant with the 'living' God of biblical revelation than the idea of a static perfection; that the notion of a God who is in some manner still 'on his way' goes far towards easing the problem of evil, so intractable for traditional theism; and that such a notion also gives fuller meaning to the moral life of men by taking seriously their responsibility as 'co-workers' with God. At least, it cannot be lightly said that such an idea of God is not religiously satisfying, or that it does not accord with the Christian idea of God, freed, perhaps, from some of its patristic and medieval accretions.

We now turn to the second type of metaphysical religious thought which flourishes in mid-century—to neo-Thomism and Roman Catholic theology.

XVIII

NEO-THOMISM AND ROMAN CATHOLIC THEOLOGY

85. The Revival of Scholastic Studies

THE term 'neo-Thomism' is commonly used for the contemporary revival of philosophical and theological ways of thinking which have their basis in the thought of St Thomas Aquinas. This revival has taken place above all in the Roman Catholic Church, but we should notice that there are some neo-Thomists who are not Catholics, and that on the other hand there are Catholic thinkers who are not neo-Thomists. Among Catholic thinkers of recent times, Maurice Blondel would be better described as 'neo-Augustinian'; and the neo-Thomist label would not be applicable to men like Baron von Hügel, Pierre Teilhard de Chardin, and Louis Lavelle, to say nothing of the Modernists.

But 'neo-Thomism' may be too narrow a term even for the contemporary movement which derives its inspiration from the Christian thought of the Middle Ages; for St Thomas was surrounded by a whole constellation of Christian doctors, all of whom made their contributions to the philosophy of the time. One is therefore tempted to speak of 'neo-scholasticism'; but unfortunately this term is often used not for the contemporary movement but for the continuation of scholasticism in the period following the Reformation, and so it is misleading. Moreover, since the influence of St Thomas is the dominant one in the patrimony of medieval Christian thought, it is not far wrong to speak of the contemporary movement as 'neo-Thomism'.

The origins of the present movement go back to 1879, when Pope Leo XIII, in his encyclical *Aeterni Patris*, commended to the Church the study of philosophy, and especially the work of St Thomas Aquinas. Since the origin of neo-Thomism goes back into the nineteenth century, it may seem surprising that we have deferred consideration of it until this late stage in our survey. It must be remembered, however, that it took time before the effects of Leo's recommendation began fully to show themselves. It was indeed only after the First World War that neo-Thomism had established itself as one of the major strands in contemporary thought, and counted among its representatives thinkers of the first rank. By mid-century it had fully emerged as an intellectual force of the first magnitude, and it is said that at the present time more scholars are engaged in the study of Thomist and scholastic philosophy than ever before in history.

Neo-Thomism connects with the philosophies described in the last chapter in so far as it is, in the expression commonly employed by its adherents, a 'moderate realism', and also in its recognition of the possibility of metaphysics, for the neo-Thomist holds that the business of philosophy is synthesis as well as analysis. What distinguishes neo-Thomism are the basic ideas which it inherits from St Thomas and scholastic philosophy—and many of them ultimately from Aristotle. It has indeed at its disposal an extraordinarily subtle and adaptable conceptual framework. Among these basic ideas we may notice the distinction between 'act' or 'actuality' and 'potency' or 'potentiality'. With the exception of God, who is 'pure act', that is to say, completely actualized in his being, everything is made up both of act and of potency. Corresponding to the distinction of act and potency are other distinctions—'existence' and 'essence', 'substance' and 'accident', 'form' and 'matter'. Among other elements in the heritage which neo-Thomism has received we may note the doctrine of causes—material, formal, efficient and final; the proofs for the existence of God; the doctrine of analogy; and a kind of gentleman's agreement with theology, whereby the fields of philosophy and theology are demarcated. Philosophy does not contradict the revealed truths of theology, but it is autonomous in its own sphere; and furthermore it is believed that reason correctly applied will lead to results which support the assertions of revelation. Of course, these various ideas are not simply reasserted by neo-Thomism. Its task is rather to apply them anew to the problems of our own time. The bald summary given here will become clearer when we see how these ideas are applied in concrete instances by contemporary neo-Thomists.

We shall consider first some pioneers of the movement (Section 86), then its flowering in some of the major neo-Thomist thinkers (Section 87), we shall then look at some leading Roman Catholic theologians of the present time (Section 88), before passing on to an assessment (Section 89).

86. Some Pioneers of Neo-Thomism
D. J. Mercier, M. de Wulf, P. Coffey

Désiré Joseph Mercier[1] (1851-1926) is perhaps best known to the wider public as the heroic Belgian primate who championed the interests of his people during the German occupation of their country in the First World War. He is known also as the leading figure on the Roman Catholic side in the conversations about reunion which took place with representatives of the Church of England. But from the point of view of our survey, his importance lies in the outstanding work which he did for the revival of scholastic studies, especially in building up at Louvain a major centre of neo-Thomist philosophy in the decades following the encyclical of Leo XIII.

Alarmed at the isolation of the Catholic faith from the scientific temper of modern times, Mercier urges Catholics to join in the disinterested scientific quest for truth, and is at the same time inspired by the hope that science and faith can be reconciled through the mediation of the Church's traditional philosophy. In a report on his philosophical institute at Louvain in 1891, he says: 'The particular sciences do not give us a complete representation of reality. They *abstract*; but the relations which they isolate in thought *lie together in reality*, and that is why the special sciences demand and give rise to a science of sciences, to a general synthesis, in a word, to philosophy. Sound philosophy sets out from analysis and terminates in synthesis.' The conviction is expressed that 'undoubtedly this final synthesis will harmonize with the dogmas of our *Credo*', and St Thomas Aquinas is claimed to be the 'striking incarnation of the spirit of observation united with the spirit of synthesis'.[2] This frank acceptance of the special sciences as the starting-point for philosophy aroused suspicion among the more conservative circles of the Church, but Mercier's own unshakable and most characteristic conviction, as we have already seen it expressed in the sentences quoted above, was that reason will in the long run lead to the same conclusions as faith.

What has so far been said about Mercier, however, might suggest that he was a more adventurous spirit than he actually was. His own philosophical teaching, expounded in a lengthy manual, is a fairly conservative Thomism. 'One system of philosophy alone', he declares, 'amidst the incessant endeavours of the many systems through three centuries to

[1] Professor at Louvain, 1882-1906; Archbishop of Malines, 1906-26, and cardinal from 1907.

[2] The report quoted here is to be found in the appendix to Maurice de Wulf's *An Introduction to Scholastic Philosophy*, pp. 263ff.

investigate the inmost mysteries of reality, has been able to stand without modification in its fundamental tenets, and this is the philosophy of Saint Thomas.'[1] Mercier's close adherence to St Thomas is evident in his natural theology, where, rejecting St Anselm's ontological argument for God's existence, he relies on the *a posteriori* proofs of St Thomas. Rational philosophy thus provides a firm basis for religion and the superstructure of revelation. If indeed reason should sometimes come into conflict with revealed truth, then we must trace back our argument and look for the flaw. But an ultimate clash between the two is unthinkable.

Mercier's essential conservatism is clearly expressed in a famous pastoral letter of 1907, in which he attacks Modernism, and in particular the teaching of Tyrrell. Since both the cardinal and the Modernists were seeking to bring together the scientific temper and the Catholic faith, one might have expected some sympathy between them. But as Mercier understood it, Modernism did not genuinely represent 'that science of which we are so justly proud, or its methods which Catholic scientists rightly regard it an honour to put into practice and to teach'. Mercier sees Modernism as a kind of subjectivism: it 'consists essentially in maintaining that the devout soul should draw the object and motive of its faith from itself, and itself alone'.[2] Its radical error is said to be an individualism, and the cardinal makes it clear that in spite of his sincere love of science and philosophy, the individual's autonomy of thought must be governed by the authoritative teaching of the Church.

Next to the cardinal, we may mention among the pioneers of the movement his colleague at Louvain, Maurice de Wulf[3] (1867-1947). He was the historical scholar of the movement. His *History of Medieval Philosophy* is the standard work in its field, and he edited many medieval writings. The study of the history of thought has a broadening influence —as indeed it is part of the purpose of this survey to show—and we can see this clearly in what de Wulf says about the new scholasticism. Though profoundly convinced of its value and importance, he avoids extravagant claims.

He much prefers to talk of 'neo-scholasticism' than of 'neo-Thomism', for the latter title, he thinks, 'labours under the obvious disadvantage that it likens the new philosophy too exclusively to the thought-system of *some particular individual*, whereas in reality this new philosophy is sufficiently large and comprehensive to pass beyond the doctrinal limitations of

---

[1] *Manual of Modern Scholastic Philosophy*, vol. I, p. 30.

[2] The pastoral letter quoted is reprinted at the beginning of G. Tyrrell's *Medievalism: A Reply to Cardinal Mercier*.

[3] Professor at Louvain from 1894.

any individual thinker and to draw its inspiration from the whole field of scholastic philosophy'.[1] Moreover, while of course Mercier was well aware that the traditional philosophy calls for revision and restatement, de Wulf is more forthcoming about the drastic changes required. He is guided by two principles—'respect for the fundamental doctrines of 'tradition' and 'adaptation to modern intellectual needs and conditions'.[2] Many ideas of the old scholasticism must be simply *abandoned*, especially in such fields as cosmology and natural philosophy. The ideas that are retained must be *tested* and *enriched* through confrontation with other philosophical systems. De Wulf rightly sees that the strength of the new scholasticism lies in the constitutive principles or basic categories which it inherits from its medieval predecessor. These can pass the test, so to speak, and de Wulf believes that in such fields as metaphysics and theodicy the scholastic ideas can prove as fruitful to-day as they did in the Middle Ages.

De Wulf shows great tolerance towards other philosophical systems. Referring to the 'voluntarism' prevalent at the beginning of the twentieth century among some French Catholics, de Wulf makes it clear that he himself does not share their 'theoretical subjectivism', but their views do not provoke from him the sharp reaction which, as we have seen, Modernism drew from the cardinal. De Wulf says rather: 'Let us freely accept the conclusion that a Catholic may, in good faith, give his allegiance to systems other than the new scholasticism. This being so, it is clear that there can be no such thing as a *Catholic philosophy* any more than there can be a *Catholic science*.'[3] This opinion drew upon de Wulf the criticisms of some of his fellow Catholics, but the very moderation of his views makes all the more impressive his persuasive defence of the new scholasticism, a defence backed by his comprehensive erudition.

Neo-Thomism speedily took root in many countries, and among its most notable pioneers in the English-speaking world the name of Peter Coffey[4] (1876-1943) deserves mention. As well as translating important continental works into English, he himself produced an extensive treatise on scholastic philosophy, embracing logic, epistemology and ontology. He leans, like Mercier, to the conservative side, and there is an interesting illustration of this in his translation of de Wulf's book on scholastic philosophy, quoted above; for here Coffey has added some cautious footnotes to those passages in which de Wulf maintains that the Catholic faith may be held along with philosophical systems other than the traditional one of the Church. Coffey thinks that although in fact Catholics may have given their allegiance in good faith to various philosophical systems,

---

[1] *An Introduction to Scholastic Philosophy*, p. 159.   [2] *Op. cit.*, p. 163.
[3] *Op. cit.*, p. 194.   [4] Professor at Maynooth, Ireland, 1902-43.

this does not deliver these systems from any errors which they contain. He believes that de Wulf does not make it sufficiently clear that there can be only one *true* philosophy, even if its expressions vary. This one true philosophy is 'that philosophy which embraces and harmonizes natural and revealed truth'. We are told that 'the man who loves truth and seeks it will embrace a philosophy that makes room for revelation and recognizes on earth an infallible exponent of that divine message to mankind'.[1]

The metaphysical system which is most in accord with the Christian religion is the one embodied in scholastic philosophy, and Coffey further maintains that 'the greatest intellect of the Middle Ages, Saint Thomas Aquinas, gave to this philosophy an expression which is rightly regarded by the modern scholastic as his intellectual charter and the most worthy starting-point of his philosophical investigations.'[2]

Coffey's own philosophical writings are for the most part a careful exposition of the ideas of scholastic philosophy, but his avowed aim is to transpose these ideas from their medieval setting into the context of contemporary philosophy, and so we find that as each major idea is expounded, an attempt is made to vindicate it as against rival theories. For instance, the notion of 'substance' is defended against phenomenalism, and a 'moderate realism' is upheld against idealism. If Coffey's writings seem somewhat unadventurous, we must remember that perhaps little more should be looked for among these pioneers of neo-Thomism. The achievement of Coffey and the others was to bring back the ideas of the scholastic philosophy on to the philosophical map, and to win respect for them, while the more original developments and applications of these ideas were left to a younger generation of neo-Thomist thinkers.

87. THE FLOWERING OF NEO-THOMISM
J. Maritain, E. Gilson, F. C. Copleston, A. M. Farrer

The labours of the earlier neo-Thomists have led to the flowering of a richly diversified and influential philosophical movement. The diversification has come about partly through the application of scholastic ideas to a wider range of problems and partly through the contacts of the movement with other philosophical trends, such as phenomenology, personalism and existentialism. Yet it would seem to be the case that the most outstanding figures in the movement are those who have remained close to the teachings of St Thomas.

[1] Translator's notes to pp. 192-8 of M. de Wulf's *An Introduction to Scholastic Philosophy*.
[2] *Ontology*, p. 26.

The acknowledged leader among them is Jacques Maritain[1] (1882-   ). He began as a follower of Bergson, but in 1906 was converted to the Catholic faith, and eventually became one of the Church's most outstanding intellectual leaders of recent times. He now came to attack the philosophy to which he had formerly subscribed. 'By replacing intelligence by his intuition, and being by duration, by becoming or pure change, Bergson annihilates the being of things and destroys the principle of identity.'[2] For in Bergson's dynamic philosophy sameness engenders otherness, entities can yield more than they have, and so we are landed in contradictions. Maritain likewise rejects anything that savours of idealism and subjectivism. It is to the realism of the neo-Thomist philosophy that we must turn for the solution to the intellectual and cultural problems of our time.

'Thomistic realism', says Maritain, 'in preserving according to a truly critical method the value of the knowledge of things, opens the way to an exploration of the world of reflection in its very inwardness, and to the establishment of its metaphysical topology, so to speak.'[3] St Thomas Aquinas is said to have been, like Aristotle, supremely docile to the lessons of the real. Maritain announces his intention of rigorously maintaining the formal line of Thomistic metaphysics, though at the same time he acknowledges that Thomism is essentially a progressive and assimilative doctrine.

His exploration of the world of reflection leads him to a recognition of three major degrees of knowledge. These are, in ascending order, scientific knowledge, metaphysical knowledge, and the suprarational knowledge which belongs to mystical experience. The reader will notice that this scheme turns precisely upside down the positivist scheme of Comte, which recognized three stages in human understanding, and supposed that it ascends from the theological through the metaphysical to the positive or scientific level.[4] There is of course the further difference that whereas Comte thought of successive stages, Maritain thinks of degrees which subsist alongside one another, each type of knowledge having its own place and its own rights within the grand synthesis. Maritain's aim is to 'show the organic diversity and the essential compatibility of those zones of knowledge through which the mind passes in its great movement in quest of being'.[5] It is held that the Thomistic scheme best safeguards the claim of each zone to a knowledge of the real.

---

[1] Professor at Paris, 1913-40; Toronto, 1940-44; French ambassador to the Vatican, 1945-48.

[2] *La philosophie bergsonienne*, p. 149.   [3] *The Degrees of Knowledge*, p. ix.

[4] See above, p. 94.   [5] *Op. cit.*, p. xi.

The first zone, that of the sciences, concerns itself with objects which can be realized only in sensible or empirical existence. While we spoke above of three degrees of knowledge, the details of Maritain's scheme are much more subtle, and he recognizes further degrees within the major zones. Thus some sciences, especially physics, lend themselves to quantitative treatment and employ mathematical methods of investigation; while others, such as biology, deal with objects which are less amenable to these methods. Again, in addition to the special sciences, Maritain recognizes a philosophy of nature, which has for its objects such general notions as number, space, time, life and so on. Thus 'there can be two complementary knowledges of one and the same reality which is the world of sensible nature and of movement: the sciences of nature and the philosophy of nature'.[1] But the mind cannot rest even with these complementary knowledges, and presses on to the higher synthesis of metaphysics.

Metaphysics rises above the degrees of knowledge so far considered, and has as its object being as such. The notion of 'being' is indeed the first object grasped by the intellect; for instance, if I know that this sensible object is a diamond, I already know it as *something which is*. But it is extremely remarkable that being, the first object attained by our mind in things, bears within itself the sign that beings of another order than the sensible are thinkable and possible'.[2] Metaphysics leads the mind beyond the sensible manifestations of being to a realm of being which does not require matter for its realization; or, to put it in another way, it leads us beyond the sensible proximate causes of things to their ultimate cause in the uncreated self-subsistent being of God. Of course, language is not being used univocally in this line of thought. When we speak of a first 'cause', for example, this cause is of a different order from the second and from the whole subsequent series. 'To demonstrate the existence of God is neither to subject him to our grasp, nor to define him, nor to seize him, nor to manipulate anything except ideas which are inadequate to such an object. The procedure by which reason demonstrates that God exists puts reason itself in an attitude of natural adoration and of intellectual admiration.'[3] Rational metaphysics can indeed know God—his existence and his perfections—and so it represents a higher degree of knowledge than that which we met in the sciences. But this metaphysical knowledge, as we have seen, proceeds by concepts which are inadequate to their object. It is an analogical knowledge—'a knowledge refracted in the prism of creatures, yet veracious for all that'.[4] Are there still higher degrees of knowledge? Maritain believes that there are.

[1] *Op. cit.*, p. 202.   [2] *Op. cit.*, p. 214.
[3] *Op. cit.*, p. 225.   [4] *Op. cit.*, p. 248.

These higher degrees are suprarational, for reason is in them illuminated by divine revelation. They culminate in the beatific vision in which God is known by and in his very essence, without the mediation of any analogy or concept. Theology rises above metaphysics, for theology has the light of revelation, but theology still moves in the discursive mode of thought. Above theology rises the infused wisdom of mystical experience, which Maritain illustrates especially from the writings of St John of the Cross, thus going beyond St Thomas' estimate of mysticism. Such experience brings the soul into a loving and intimate union with God, and 'thus it brings the human being to the highest degree of knowledge accessible here below'.[1]

We have endeavoured here to sketch out some of Maritain's central doctrines, but from this centre he extends his thought into many fields, and makes his neo-Thomism the basis for the ideals of a Christian humanism and a democratic order. In all this, Maritain powerfully demonstrates the capacity for renewal which belongs to the *philosophia perennis*, and the scope of its application to contemporary problems.

Like Maritain, Etienne Gilson[2] (1884-   ) adheres to neo-Thomism not because of any youthful indoctrination but by conviction, after having studied various types of philosophy. His interests have lain mainly in the field of the history of philosophy, but he rightly observes that when one has examined the several historical systems of thought, one comes to the problem of philosophy itself—the task of judging among these systems to find the one that is most adequate and most capable of further development. This privileged position Gilson assigns to the Christian philosophy of the Middle Ages, and by a 'Christian philosophy' he understands one which 'considers the Christian revelation an indispensable auxiliary to reason, although distinguishing formally between the two orders'.[3]

Not Descartes but Kant is regarded by Gilson as the true inaugurator of modern philosophy; for Descartes, even if unconsciously, still worked within the framework of scholastic ideas, but Kant, by his onslaught on the possibility of metaphysics, marks a real breach with the past. With this, we enter the age of positivism. But in Gilson's view, the metaphysical problem is inescapable, and we cannot help giving some answer to it, even if we do so only implicitly. If, however, we wish to give the correct answer, then we must go back beyond Kant to St Thomas Aquinas, and study his solution of the problem.

[1] *Op. cit.*, p. 383.
[2] Appointed professor successively at Lille, 1913; Strasbourg, 1919; the Sorbonne, 1921; the Collège de France, 1932.
[3] *L'esprit de la philosophie médiévale*, vol. I, p. 39.

The question of metaphysics is the question of being. It is the question of why anything exists, a question which science cannot answer and may even deem senseless. 'To this supreme question', says Gilson, 'the only conceivable answer is that each and every particular existential energy, each and every particular existing thing, depends for its existence on a pure Act of existence.'[1] This is of course the standard answer of scholastic philosophy, but what is perhaps distinctive in Gilson's formulation of it is his stress on the notion of 'existence'. In this formulation we see an answer to those existentialists who complain that Thomism is a philosophy of *essences*, and that it neglects *existence*. But such is not Gilson's reading of neo-Thomism. 'True metaphysics', he claims, 'does not culminate in a concept, be it that of "thought" or "good" or "one" or "substance". It does not even culminate in an essence, be it that of "being" itself. Its last word is not *ens* but *esse*; not *being* but *is*.'[2] God is the supreme Act of existing, HE WHO IS, in St Thomas' expression.

Here metaphysics comes to an end, for we cannot comprehend this Act of existing, whose very essence is to be. But again we can learn from Christian medieval philosophy, and this time the lesson is that where metaphysics ends, religion begins. The existent God of metaphysics is the same as the God who revealed his name to Moses as I AM, and the truths which lie beyond the reach of unaided reason are illuminated by the biblical and Christian revelation.

An outstanding representative of neo-Thomism in the English-speaking countries is Frederick Charles Copleston[3] (1907-   ). In Copleston we again meet a thinker who has devoted much attention to the history of philosophy; his massive work, *A History of Philosophy*, must indeed be reckoned a major contemporary achievement in its field. Copleston's claims for the Christian philosophy of the Middle Ages are sane and moderate. 'An unprejudiced mind should avoid the two extremes of thinking that nothing worth saying or doing has been said or done in philosophy since the Middle Ages, and of ruling out medieval philosophy without more ado as intellectual obscurantism.'[4] It would be absurd to uphold what Copleston calls the 'diehard' view that philosophy is to be identified with the system of some medieval thinker; but it would be equally absurd to ignore an important period in European thinking, and if we approach scholasticism in a sympathetic way, we may well find that it has important insights to offer for our contemporary philosophical problems.

[1] *God and Philosophy*, p. 139.   [2] *Op. cit.*, p. 143.
[3] Professor at Heythrop College, Oxford, from 1939.
[4] *Medieval Philosophy*, p. 3.

We noticed that Gilson, confronted with the challenge of continental existentialism, tends to develop the existential element in Thomism. In a similar fashion, Copleston tends to stress in his writings on contemporary philosophical problems those elements in Thomistic philosophy which can be developed in response to the pretensions of English logical empiricism. Perhaps most contemporary British philosophers regard metaphysics as impossible, and many of them think that all talk of God or of the supersensible is senseless. What response can neo-Thomism make to this challenge which strikes at its very roots?

Copleston suggests that a distinction between 'seeing' and 'noticing' may throw light on the possibility of metaphysics.[1] Everyone knows that several people will *see* the same thing, but each may *notice* something about it which the others fail to notice. The metaphysician, who takes 'being' as his problem, does not *see* any more than other people see, for being is not another *thing* in addition to railways, sheep, trees and so on, nor is it another *characteristic* in addition to whiteness, weight, cheapness and the like. Being is rather the condition that there should be any such things or characteristics at all. As such, being, which is the first object to be grasped by the intellect, is so familiar to us that we scarcely ever *notice* it. But when someone does notice it, being can become a problem— the problem of metaphysics.

Neo-Thomism answers this problem in terms of the self-subsistent being of God. But now another problem arises, for how can we talk meaningfully of God in a language that is tied to finite experience? Copleston here brings into play the scholastic doctrine of analogy. 'It is certainly no part of the Christian religion', he declares, 'to say that God in himself can be adequately comprehended by the human mind.'[2] Yet if one has found reasons for believing in the existence of God, one can also find terms drawn from finite experience—for instance, the term 'intelligence'— which are more adequate to the description of what such a God must be than other terms. These terms, moreover, are to be understood within the universe of discourse in which they are used. This may suggest that the metaphysical description of God is very shadowy, but Copleston would say that it is a matter for joy that the reality of God so far exceeds our analogical concepts. Like Gilson, he would also say that where metaphysics ends, religion begins, but enough has been said to show how he presents neo-Thomism in the face of current empiricist and positivist philosophies.

In the introductory section of the present chapter, it was mentioned that neo-Thomism is not confined to the Roman Catholic Church. We

[1] *Contemporary Philosophy*, pp. 77ff.   [2] *Op. cit.*, p. 101.

may recall that some of the thinkers considered in earlier chapters—such as A. E. Taylor, W. G. de Burgh, and W. M. Urban—showed a deep respect for the teachings of St Thomas, though since these teachings were with them only one influence among others, such philosophers could hardly be reckoned neo-Thomists. There are, however, especially in the Anglo-Catholic wing of the Church of England, several notable thinkers who make Thomism the basis for their philosophizing, and these thinkers should be noticed here along with the Roman Catholic neo-Thomists.

As an example, we take Austin Farrer[1] (1904–1968), though there are other equally distinguished representatives, such as E. L. Mascall.[2] Like Copleston, Farrer undertakes his philosophizing in an environment dominated by Oxford analytical philosophy, and thus much of his endeavour is directed towards demonstrating the possibility of metaphysical thinking, and towards explaining the logic of our talk about God and the supersensible. On the other hand, he has an eye on the many contemporary Protestant theologians who declare that the knowledge of God is possible only through some kind of direct revelatory personal encounter with him. Against this point of view also, Farrer has to justify metaphysics and rational theology, for he believes that 'if we surrender metaphysical inquiry, we shall vainly invoke supernatural revelation to make up for our metaphysical loss of nerve'.[3]

The complex argument of *Finite and Infinite* is a sustained attempt to show that when we examine finite substance—including man himself—and attend to some of its universal characteristics, we are led to the apprehension of the infinite creative act in virtue of which any finite substance is. 'All finites, in being themselves and expressing their natures in their acts, are expressing also the creativity of God.'[4] But Farrer also insists on the limitation of the knowledge which we attain of God in this way. In the first place, it is an oblique knowledge. God, as it were, casts his shadow upon finite substances, so that we apprehend him through analogues which may be more or less adequate. In the second place, the knowledge of God to which rational theology conduces shows him as creator, but does not establish his providence or his grace, though these are left as open possibilities.

[1] Fellow and Chaplain of Trinity College, Oxford, 1935-1960; Warden of Keble College, Oxford from 1960. His philosophical writings include *Finite and Infinite, The Glass of Vision, The Freedom of the Will* (Gifford Lectures). He has also written a number of books on biblical theology.

[2] Author of *He Who Is, Existence and Analogy, Words and Images*, etc.

[3] *The Glass of Vision*, p. 78.

[4] *Finite and Infinite*, p. 299.

This natural knowledge of God is, however, the bridgehead into the supernatural knowledge of God. 'Get a man to see the mysterious depth and seriousness of the act by which he and his neighbour exist, and he will have his eyes turned upon the bush in which the supernatural fire appears.'[1] Our natural knowledge is continuous with the supernatural knowledge bestowed by God when the finite is open to the infinite. Natural and supernatural knowledge constitute one universe of sense. The difference between the two levels, as Farrer sees it, lies in the fact that rational theology works with natural analogues which can at best afford a somewhat meagre apprehension of God as creator, while at the supernatural level God himself communicates revealed analogues or images which lead to the fuller apprehension of God in his providence and grace. The revealed images set forth the supernatural revelation. We should notice however that the images are associated with the events of the Christian revelation, and that it is said to be the interplay of events and images that constitutes the revelation. The images by themselves would be mere shadows, while the events would not be revelatory without the interpretative images.

The revealed images are compared not only with the analogues of metaphysics but also with the language of poetry, which affords another example of how words may be stretched beyond their everyday usage so as to become evocative symbols. Poetic language has a power to move and shape the lives of men; and the comparison with poetry helps us to understand how the revealed images are living images, possessing a creative and supernaturalizing power.

Farrer has pursued these lines of thought into the exploration and elucidation of the great image-patterns of the Bible. But we shall not follow him into these fields, since our interest here is not in his biblical theology but in his philosophical ideas.

88. SOME ROMAN CATHOLIC THEOLOGIANS
K. Adam, K. Rahner, H. U. von Balthasar, E. Przywara, J. Daniélou, F. J. Sheen

If anyone takes up one of the many manuals of Roman Catholic theology, he might easily come to conclude, firstly, that this theology is a propositional one, and that faith consists in giving intellectual assent to the dogmatic propositions; and secondly, that this theology is an utterly monolithic and rigid structure, in the sense that every Catholic theologian

---

[1] *The Glass of Vision*, p. 78.

simply says the same things in slightly different words. Both conclusions would be unjust.

On the first charge of an arid intellectualism, it is of course true that the Roman Catholic Church more than any other precisely defines its dogmas in propositional form. We may recall that the Modernists complained that faith was made a matter of giving intellectual assent to propositions.[1] Even so eminent a Protestant theologian as Brunner equates the Catholic conception of faith with 'doctrinal belief',[2] though he at once acknowledges that the same holds for many phases of Protestant thought. No doubt many Catholics have identified and do identify faith with mere intellectual assent, yet here is what a leading Catholic theologian, Karl Adam, says of those who hold their faith in an intellectualist way only: 'Their faith often is reduced to a purely intellectual and therefore shallow awareness of the teaching of the Church, and to a mere assent of the mind. And yet every *Credo*, if said in the spirit of the Church, ought to be an act of completest dedication of the entire man to God, an assent springing from the great and ineffable distress of our finite nature and our sin.'[3] Such a statement makes it clear that the Catholic conception of faith is a richer one than some of its critics will allow it to be, and that it is indeed inseparable from the wider life of the Church.

As to the second charge of a dreary uniformity, there are no doubt some grounds for this also. If the *magisterium* of the Church has pronounced on a theological dispute, a Catholic theologian will not proceed to discuss the issue as if it were still an open question. Again, the encyclical *Humani Generis* of Pope Pius XII in 1950 reasserted the basic place of Thomistic philosophy in Roman Catholic thought. But just as we found diversity among the Catholic philosophers considered in the last section, so too we find diversity among the theologians with their different emphases and varying reactions to the contemporary world. A massive collection of contemporary essays, *Modern Catholic Thinkers*,[4] was recently published to show the variety of thought that is possible within the unity of the Catholic faith. Hans Urs von Balthasar has recently distinguished three major movements in contemporary Catholic theology—the biblical movement, the liturgical movement and the personalist movement. The first two movements are said to be 'efforts within the Church to make up for things that have long been neglected by going back to the sources', and the third movement is described as 'the organic reaction to, and the complement of, neo-Scholasticism'.[5] It is clear that Catholic theology does not have the dull monotony sometimes mistakenly ascribed to it.

[1] See above, pp. 181-2.   [2] *Revelation and Reason*, p. 37.   [3] *Two Essays*, p. 41.
[4] Edited A. R. Caponigri.   [5] *Science, Religion and Christianity*, p. 112.

In what follows, we may hope to glimpse something of the spirit which animates contemporary Catholic theology by passing in review some of the leading theologians of the Roman Catholic Church. Our selection must of necessity be a very restricted one, and will take account only of those thinkers who have acquired reputations extending beyond their own countries and their own communion.

We may conveniently begin with a book which has already become something of a classic—*The Spirit of Catholicism*, by Karl Adam[1] (1876-   ). Since the Renaissance Western man, according to Adam, has been increasingly afflicted by a shallow rationalism which cuts him off from God and by a disruptive individualism which cuts him off from his fellow-men. These rationalistic and individualistic tendencies have infected even our understanding of religion, and may be seen in an extreme form in liberal Protestant theology. Adam may well have Harnack in mind when he writes of this theology that it 'behaves as though Christianity is and must be a mere object of knowledge, a mere subject for scientific investigation, as though the living Christian faith could be resolved into a series of ideas and notions which might be examined, considered, and classified according to their provenance and according to their relation to a supposed primitive Christianity'.[2] Such an approach misses the full living reality of Christianity, and as against the bias of this approach towards rationalism and individualism, Catholicism insists on the supernatural dimension of the Christian life and on the unity of mankind within that life.

Catholicism has three focal points: God, Christ, Church. Its teaching may be summed up in the sentence: 'I experience the action of the living God through Christ realizing himself in his Church.'[3]

God, the first of these three focal points, may be known by the natural light of reason. But Adam is careful to point out that even natural theology is different from any profane inquiry. Natural theology does not have God for its object in the same way as, let us say, entomology has insects for its object. The religious inquiry arises out of our finite, conditioned human nature, so that we never stand on a level with that which we are seeking and our inquiry must be characterized by humility and reverence. Natural reason shows us God as existing, as omnipotent, wise and good, and so it conduces to a natural worship of God. It stops short, however, of a supernatural commerce of life and love with this God. Such a commerce is made possible only by grace and revelation, a movement from God towards us. So we come to the second focal point—Christ, the incarnate word in which the divine life condescends to us. But how do we know Christ as the revealer of God? Not primarily through the scriptural

---

[1] Professor at Tübingen, 1919-49.   [2] *Op. cit.*, p. 69.   [3] *Op. cit.*, p. 53.

records, says Adam, but through incorporation into the living Church as the Body of Christ. Here we come to the third focal point, and the important place assigned to the Church is perhaps the most distinctive characteristic of Catholicism.

We may therefore dwell a little longer on what is said about the Church. The Church is not separated from Christ, but related to him as the Body to its Head. Christ is the new humanity, and with the incarnation the Church itself was born, and continues to manifest the supernatural life that comes from God through Christ. Her dogmas set forth this life in all its dimensions; her morals aim at conforming mankind to the image of Christ; her worship, and especially the sacrament of the altar, make present the divine grace and make possible a continual participation in Christ. The man whose life is rooted in supernatural grace has ceased to be the autonomous man, the self-sufficient individualist. He belongs to the community, a community which ideally embraces all mankind. But this is not to say that the individual is simply submerged in the community. Personality itself can be deepened only through the life of the community which 'compels the individual to love and sacrifice, to humility and simplicity'.[1] As regards its visible organization, the community is aristocratically structured under the papacy and the episcopate. But this structure follows from the fact that the life of the community flows from above downward, and the papacy itself serves the life of the community.

This summary does little justice to Adam's high conception of Catholicism as the permeation of all human life by divine supernatural grace. Though he does not close his eyes to the historical lapses of the Church, he presents an impressive picture of Catholicism at its best. If this is error, then at least, in Santayana's words, it is a 'splendid error'.

That faith is more than mere doctrinal belief is explicitly stated by Karl Rahner[2] (1904-   ), who describes faith as 'the assent of the whole man to the message of God'.[3] Theology, which cannot proceed without faith, is the methodical effort to achieve a reflective understanding of what faith accepts. The Catholic theologian, says Rahner, will always set out from the solid ground of Church doctrine as it is proposed to the faithful by the *magisterium* of the Church. But from this basis the theologian will go on to elaborate the concepts which he has taken over, to compare them among themselves and with other concepts, and to seek a more precise

[1] *Op. cit.*, p. 263.

[2] Lecturer from 1937 and professor from 1949 at Innsbruck. Some of his principal writings have been translated in a volume entitled *Theological Investigations*.

[3] *Modern Catholic Thinkers*, p. 138.

understanding of what is already accepted on faith. In doing this, he will, explicitly or implicitly, make use of philosophical ideas that are extrinsic to theology itself.

We shall briefly consider two essays in which Rahner puts this method into practice, and shows that the Catholic theologian, while working within the framework of the Church's traditional faith, is nevertheless able to come to grips with the problems of the modern world in a thoroughly contemporary manner. The absence of God from the world, and the dark phenomenon of death—these are two bleak features of such contemporary philosophies as that of Heidegger, and it is on these themes that Rahner has something to say in his essays.[1]

In the world as we have now come to conceive it, God is silent, withdrawn, absent. Science has taught us to regard the world as a self-regulating mechanism with impersonally objective laws which extend even to man himself. It seems that we need no longer posit divine interventions. The world has been secularized, and to many people the conclusion to be drawn is atheism. But this conclusion is drawn because we have accustomed ourselves to look for God in the wrong places and in the wrong way. The secularized world of science challenges the Christian to rethink what he has always theoretically but perhaps unreflectingly believed—that God is above all else that we can conceive. He is not one object among others, not a concluding hypothesis, not a bit of the world, not a sporadic force operating at certain observable points. God is rather the world's presupposition, and only as a whole does the world point to him.

If modern man's autonomous life is lived in a secular world, his equally autonomous death has become for him the symbol of nothingness and emptiness. Rahner's analysis of death is a profound one. Death is not merely a natural phenomenon, but an event of the whole man, the final confrontation of the self; and death is already being enacted through all the deeds of life. Death can be considered in two ways: as a blow from without which disintegrates a man, or as an act from within which consummates his life. The Church's teaching connects death with sin, and because of sin, death is experienced as loss. If there were no sin, life would still come to its end, but the end would be consummation. Death, however must be faced in a sinful world, and its dark side cannot be removed. Christ's death is depicted as moving through the absence of God to the advent of God. The whole Christian life, especially the sacramental life, is a sharing in this death of Christ, so that for the Christian death can become the highest act of believing, hoping and loving.

The interpretation of Christianity in a world that has been secularized

[1] 'Wissenschaft als Konfession' and 'Zur Theologie des Todes'.

by science is likewise the concern of Hans Urs von Balthasar[1] (1905-   ). 'Modern man', he writes, 'has had the frightful misfortune that God in nature has died for him. Where religion once flowered like a blooming meadow, there is nothing left now but dry clay.'[2] The last vestiges of animism have been stripped from our understanding of nature, and the gods have been driven from their ancient haunts. Even the desert, the last refuge of romantic nature-worshippers, is now covered with oil-wells and pipelines. We cannot halt the secularization of nature. Von Balthasar has little sympathy for those misguided apologists who look for God in the interstices of the scientific picture—those, for instance, who posit him in the initial explosion of the expanding universe, or who try to bolster free-will on the principle of indeterminacy. God has disappeared into his transcendence, and man has emerged from the shelter of nature into his lonely responsibility which sets him over against nature. Hence contemporary philosophy has become anthropology, man's quest for an understanding of himself.

Von Balthasar himself puts forward three theses concerning man. The first is that the norm of all knowledge is to be found in the meeting of persons. In such encounter, the whole man is involved, whereas a merely theoretical knowledge of things is abstract and its elucidation must be sought in recognizing that at its root there is something of that personal openness which is fully seen in a meeting of persons. The category of 'meeting' or 'encounter' remained rudimentary in medieval philosophy, which needs here to be enriched and supplemented in the light of such contemporary teaching as that of Buber. The second thesis is that although man emerges from nature and takes over responsibility for it, he nevertheless remains tied to nature in his corporeal being. He is the serving rather than the absolute monarch of the world. 'This predicament', claims von Balthasar, 'will teach him to pray and to look for God.'[3] The third thesis is that the human spirit is the *locus* of openness to being. Man can listen for a word from God, he can be the recipient of grace and revelation. The secularization of the world does not lead to atheism but to a new awareness of the ineffable transcendence of God, of whom even personality can be predicated only analogically.

The claim of the Catholic Church, however offensive it may be to some philosophers, is that God has indeed spoken his absolute revelatory word of love in Christ. It is of the nature of this love which flows from God that it does not remain a mutual love within the Church, but goes beyond

---

[1] Swiss Catholic theologian, author of works on contemporary literature, philosophy and theology, including notable studies of Barth and Buber.
[2] *Science, Religion and Christianity*, pp. 100-1.   [3] *Op. cit.*, p. 27.

the frontiers of the Church and surrenders itself to non-love. The Church must be radically open to the world, which is the potential Church. The Christian loves God in his brother, and finds him in the sacrament of the neighbour.

Yet another aspect of contemporary Catholic thought is found in the work of Erich Przywara[1] (1889-   ). His writings remind us that the influence of St Augustine lives on alongside and as a complement to the influence of St Thomas. *An Augustine Synthesis* is much more than a mere anthology or compilation from the writings of St Augustine. In this book Przywara presents the integral sweep of St Augustine's thought, from the quest for truth which turns the inquirer away from the sensible to the intelligible world, to the consummation of the quest—man's life in God.

Przywara's presentation of St Augustine's thought suggests the basic characteristics of the Augustinian view—the restless striving of the creation towards God, and the ascent through the grades of created things to the God in whom they participate. By contrast, the Thomistic view thinks of the creatures as external to God, and proceeding from him as from their first cause. But as Przywara understands it, these two classic streams of Catholic thought supplement each other. Their difference is one of 'varied rhythms'; 'there stand opposed two forms which can unify the totality of creation'.[2]

The unifying principle is found by Przywara in the fundamental Catholic idea of the analogy of being (*analogia entis*) between God and the creature. We may say indeed that the unifying principle is the Catholic conception of God himself. God and the creatures alike have existence and essence; but in God, existence and essence are identical, whereas in creatures they are held together in a 'tension-in-synthesis'. Augustinianism sets out from the restless tension of the creature; Thomism thinks rather of the creature as proceeding from and external to the self-existent God. But the two are reconciled by the *analogia entis*, which permits us to say that 'the view *towards* God is already essentially the view *from* God *hitherward*'.[3]

Besides the tension between Augustinianism and Thomism, there are many other tensions and seeming paradoxes in theology and the interpretation of religion. God is sometimes represented as purely immanent, sometimes as starkly transcendent; religion is sometimes regarded entirely as a work of God, sometimes as a merely human act; on the practical side there is the tension between the individual and the community. When we fly to extremes in any of these matters, we destroy religion. We must find a *via media* which will permit legitimate expression to both poles within

[1] German Jesuit scholar.   [2] *Polarity*, p. 128.   [3] *Op. cit.*, p. 75.

these antitheses, and it is Przywara's conviction that the Catholic conception of God, expressed in the doctrine of the *analogia entis*, is able to reconcile in a satisfying way not only the Augustinian and Thomist traditions but all the major tensions of theological thought.

Among French Catholic theologians, one of the best-known is the Jesuit, Jean Daniélou[1] (1905-   ). His most distinguished work has been done in the field of biblical theology, and in exploring the great images, symbols and analogues of the scriptural writers. But Daniélou is no narrow biblicist. While recognizing that the Bible and tradition are regulative for theology, he sees that contemporary philosophical terms are needed to interpret the realities of revelation. The revelation transcends every culture and is expressible in every language, so that it is a mistake to try, as some biblical scholars do, to confine oneself to the Semitic categories of the Bible. 'Hebrew', remarks Daniélou, 'was not part of the revelation.'[2]

Daniélou's conception of theology may be seen in what he has to say about the central Christian doctrine of God. Dissociating himself from those Protestant biblical theologians who would deny that there is any genuine knowledge of God apart from the biblical revelation, he follows the Catholic tradition in maintaining that there is such a knowledge in philosophy and the pagan religions. There is 'a revelation of God that speaks to every human soul through the cosmos, the conscience, and the spirit'.[3] But this natural knowledge of God is imperfect, and man requires a more positive revelation.

This revelation is given in the Bible and in the life of the Church. The Old Testament depicts God in terms of truth, justice, love and holiness. The New Testament unfolds the mystery of the Trinity. And the knowledge of God is developed in the sacramental life of the Church, and in mystical experience.

Throughout his exposition, Daniélou presents not just an idea of God but rather the reality itself of a holy and living God who must be approached with reverence. The reading of his pages is one of the best correctives to the popular error that for the Roman Catholic, faith is equated with doctrinal belief and theology with the intellectualist elaboration of propositions. 'Theology', says Daniélou, 'is inadequate if it does not end in mysticism'—and he immediately defines this 'mysticism' as 'a living encounter with the living God'.[4] Sometimes indeed theologians talk about their subject with as much detachment as one might talk about any secular subject, but this is wrong. Though theology is an intellectual inquiry, it must be characterized by a spirit of reverence, since it is a

---

[1] Professor at Paris from 1944.   [2] *God and Us*, p. 165.
[3] *Op. cit.*, p. 41.   [4] *Op. cit.*, p. 162.

question of the living God. 'The true science of God is that which leads us to love God.'[1]

We end this section on Roman Catholic theology with a mention of Fulton John Sheen[2] (1895-   ). He is a popularizer of the same type as Joad, and perhaps with rather similar merits and defects. His numerous writings put across theological and philosophical ideas to vast numbers of people who would never read the more demanding literature on these subjects. In one of his more substantial works, *Philosophy of Religion*, he expounds his reading of the present religious situation.

The true age of reason, according to Sheen, was also the age of faith— the thirteenth century. The classical reason of that period was the reason which discovers ends and is an activity of the whole man. The kind of reason which has supplanted it in modern times is a thin, abstract, technical reason, and the irony of modern rationalism is that it has led into irrationalism. It has denatured man, who no longer appears as a rational being, but, for instance, as the plaything of economic forces (Marx) or the victim of his own unconscious (Freud). The fact that our age has plunged into irrationalism does not, of course, invalidate reason, and Sheen thinks that rational reflection still leads us to belief in God. The proofs of God offered by St Thomas Aquinas were not tied to medieval cosmology, and can be restated in modern terms. In the first of St Thomas' five ways, for instance—the proof which begins from the notion of 'movement'—Sheen boldly equates 'movement' with 'evolution', and argues valiantly for a theistic conclusion.

But although he thus defends the classical style of reason, and holds that these arguments still provide the best approach to the problem of God, he acknowledges frankly that 'classical philosophers might just as well face the unpalatable fact that modern man is no longer interested in metaphysics'.[3] What then? Sheen, like so many other contemporary writers, suggests an anthropological approach to religion. Contemporary denatured man is told by astronomy of his insignificance, by biology of his animality, and by psychoanalysis that he is not even master in his own house. The course of events itself has destroyed his belief in progress. He has become frustrated man, the man who groans for deliverance. This is indeed how he is depicted in contemporary literature, and Sheen thinks that this picture comes closer to the Christian understanding of man than did the liberal understanding of man in the nineteenth

---

[1] *Op. cit.*, p. 171.

[2] Professor at the Catholic University of America, 1926-50; Auxiliary Bishop of New York from 1951.

[3] *Op. cit.*, p. 381.

century. From the theological point of view, the malaise of frustrated man is original sin, and indeed this frustrated man is already described in St Thomas and in classical Christian theology. It is through the development of this traditional teaching of the Church about man that Christianity can be made meaningful to the men of our time who are alienated both from God and from themselves.

89. Remarks on Neo-Thomism and Roman Catholic Theology

In the preceding pages we have seen something of the scope of Catholic philosophy and theology in the mid-century. It is an impressive picture, and we have seen good reasons for rejecting some of the common superficial accusations against Catholic thought. It has become clear, for instance, that neo-Thomism is not to be dismissed as merely a retreat into medievalism. In the hands of its best exponents, such as Maritain, Gilson and Copleston, its categories are deployed so as to tackle contemporary problems in a contemporary way, while at the same time drawing on the wisdom of the past. The strength of Catholic philosophy may be seen by glancing at France, where not only neo-Thomism but also the philosophies of such Catholic thinkers as Blondel, Marcel and Lavelle have drawn to themselves many of the best minds, so that Catholic philosophy flourishes with remarkable vigour amid the deserts of an effete and sterile secularism. It has become clear also that Catholic theology is not, as it is sometimes represented, an intellectualist game played with abstract concepts, for in the theologians whom we have considered we have found that there is plenty of room both for personal values and for the living religious experience. And further, although there is naturally a family likeness among Catholic theologians, there is no dreary uniformity, and the *magisterium* of the Church does not rule out a rich diversity of theological thought.

Welcome, too, is the recognition which Catholic thought accords to reason and to natural theology—a recognition frequently withheld by contemporary Protestant theologians who would find in revelation alone any genuine knowledge of God. But it is just in connection with the place of reason in Catholic thought that the non-Catholic will have most difficulty in coming to terms. According to Mercier, reason will not contradict revelation—if it seems to do so, we have made a mistake in our reasoning. Coffey states more forthrightly that the true philosopher makes room for revelation and moreover recognizes that there is an infallible exponent on earth of that revelation. Now the sympathetic student of religion might reply that he would indeed be overjoyed to find that reason and revelation converge upon a single truth. But he would also have to say that this is not something that can be assumed at the beginning, but only a conclusion that can be reached at the end of a free inquiry. Here we see a limitation of neo-Thomism. However valuable many of its insights may be, it excludes certain possibilities from the beginning, and in particular the unpalatable possibility that after all reason may not coincide with revelation. In so far as both neo-Thomism and Catholic theology accept a certain core of doctrine from the beginning, they would seem to lack a radical openness to the discovery of truth. Of course, the rejoinder might be made that it would be foolish in any subject to begin from scratch and to ignore what is already known. With this one must agree, but even so one is not absolved from a critical attitude even towards the most sacred convictions that are held. This is not, as some would imply, an attempt to sit in judgment on God, for such an attempt would be both absurd and blasphemous, a supreme act of *hubris*. But what is asserted, and surely must be asserted, is the right to judge and criticize every human claim to be in possession of a divine revelation, whether the claim is made by Catholic or Protestant, by Christian or non-Christian.

XIX

LOGICAL EMPIRICISM

90. PHILOSOPHY AS ANALYSIS

WE have already seen how one branch of the neo-realist movement issued in the construction, from a realist standpoint, of metaphysical systems on just as grand a scale as the systems of idealism, and how these systems gave their own account of the theistic problem, and had their repercussions in theology. But this metaphysical development of realism has not been the most typical one. Philosophy has tended rather to follow the analytical direction indicated for it by Moore and Russell, and has become more and more equated with the techniques of logical analysis. The investigation of empirical fact has been handed over to the various special sciences; the investigation of a transcendent realm of allegedly transempirical fact has been abandoned as a fruitless and probably illusory undertaking; and so the task remaining to philosophy has been seen as that of analysing and clarifying the logical procedures involved in what we say about the world. Thus the philosopher ceases to be the man who pronounces on the ultimate questions about God and the universe. Indeed, he gives us no information about the world at all, leaving that to the special sciences and confining himself to his own technical problems of analysis. This revolution in the conception of philosophy has, as Gilbert Ryle points out,[1] coincided with the laicizing of our culture, so that, unlike many of his predecessors, the contemporary philosopher may find plenty of problems to occupy his attention without touching on the problems of the philosophy of religion. As likely as not, he may regard these as merely pseudo-problems, and if he has anything to say about them, it may be simply to point out that such traditional problems as that of the existence of God can neither be answered nor even properly formulated.

The most obvious characteristic of this new style of philosophizing is its interest in language. It is in words and sentences that our thought about the world becomes publicly accessible. Language, however, is by

[1] *The Revolution in Philosophy*, pp. 2-4.

no means a perfect instrument and can be very misleading. Sentences which have the same grammatical form may perform very different logical functions. For instance, the two sentences, 'The French novels are on the top shelf' and 'The souls of the righteous are in the hand of God', have a similar grammatical form, but whereas the first sentence bears a fairly obvious meaning which stands in some kind of relation to facts observable by sense experience, the meaning of the second sentence is much less obvious, and if it has a meaning at all, this would seem to have nothing to do with observable facts. Thus we soon learn the need for a logical analysis of language. The philosophical movement of which we are speaking is usually called 'logical empiricism', and in this compound expression the adjective indicates both the concern with the problem of meaning and the debt of the movement to the logical investigations of men like Russell and Frege, while the noun indicates that the meaning of factually informative propositions—as distinct from definitions and the like—stands in some kind of relation to sense-experience.

The contemporary movement originated in England and in Austria, and has since spread to the United States, though it appears to have made little headway in France and Germany. In its early phase, the movement was usually known as 'logical positivism'. Scientific language was taken as the norm of what may be said meaningfully about the world, and any kind of language—such as theological language—which did not satisfy the criteria laid down for science was dismissed as factually meaningless. Logical empiricism has since entered a somewhat milder phase, when the criteria of meaningfulness are no longer laid down in advance and various kinds of language are analysed on their own merits, so to speak. As far as the problem of religion is concerned, this means that the philosophy of logical analysis has shifted attention from the question of truth to what is, after all, the prior question of meaning. The religious philosopher who would formerly have set out to prove the existence of God is now much more likely to begin by discussing what is meant by the 'existence of God'. The anti-religious philosopher on his side is making a more radical attack upon religion than his predecessors, for he tries to show not that assertions about God's existence are false but that they are not even meaningful, and so are incapable of either truth or falsity.

In the remainder of this chapter, we shall first of all consider the most eminent representative of the movement, Ludwig Wittgenstein, whose thought passed through both of the phases which were mentioned (Section 91). Next we shall look at some analysts who take scientific language as their norm and who, though not all positivists, give an account of language which is hostile to the claim of religious statements to be informative

(Section 92). Thereafter we turn to those analysts who do not lay down criteria in advance but examine the claims of each kind of language as we find it in use; it is not to be supposed that the philosophers in this group are all friendly to the claims of religious language, for some of them are at best neutral and all of those whom we shall consider would resist the claim that religious statements can be informative about metaphysical entities beyond space and time; yet either directly or indirectly, they indicate ways in which meaning can be attached to religious assertions (Section 93). The chapter ends with a critical review (Section 94).

91. THE LIMITS AND FUNCTIONS OF LANGUAGE
L. Wittgenstein

Perhaps the most eminent representative of the movement which we are considering is Ludwig Wittgenstein[1] (1889-1951). By birth an Austrian and by training an engineer, he eventually settled in England, and his influence as a teacher was so remarkable that something like a cult has sprung up around him.

He first attacted attention by his short but very difficult book, *Tractatus Logico-Philosophicus*, published in 1922. The aim of this book is to show the limits of meaningful language, to show what can be said and what cannot be said at all. Its teaching is summed up in the often quoted but usually ungrammatically translated concluding sentence: 'Whereof one cannot speak, thereon one must be silent.'[2]

On Wittgenstein's view, the world consists of an indefinite number of 'atomic facts'. Corresponding to these are simple propositions which 'picture' the facts. More complex propositions are 'truth-functions' of the simple propositions. All propositions which picture the world, that is to say, all propositions which say something meaningful and can be informative, belong to the natural sciences. All other propositions are either tautologies or nonsense. Among the tautologies are the propositions of logic and mathematics, while to the area of nonsense are consigned most of the traditional questions and discussions of the philosophers—the metaphysical questions which arose from a failure to understand the logic of language.

Properly understood, philosophy is itself quite uninformative. 'The right method of philosophy would be this: to say nothing except what can be said, that is, the propositions of natural science, something that has nothing to do with philosophy; and then always when someone else wished to say

---

[1] Professor at Cambridge, 1939-47.   [2] *Op. cit.*, p. 189.

something metaphysical, to demonstrate to him that he had given no meaning to certain signs in his propositions.'[1] Wittgenstein compares his own book to a ladder, which is to be kicked away after one has climbed up it.

The bearing of this work on the question of religion emerges in what he has to say about the 'mystical'. Although Wittgenstein is said to have been a careful student of St Augustine, the word 'mystical' should not be understood here in the strict sense that would be given to it by a theologian. 'Not *how* the world is, is the mystical, but *that* it is.'[2] The 'how' of the world is described by the sciences, and God is not revealed *in* the world; the 'that' of the world is a problem that we may feel, but can neither answer nor even formulate. We may *feel* that when all the questions of science have been answered, the problems of life still remain untouched. But if we have understood the limits of language, we shall see the solution of the problem of life in the vanishing of the problem. This may be interpreted as a thoroughgoing positivism, or it may be taken to mean—as some of Wittgenstein's followers have taken it—that religion is inexpressible. This would indeed accord with what some of the great mystics have said, and also with Otto's conception of the numinous as beyond conception. Wittgenstein does say: 'There is indeed the inexpressible. This *shows* itself; it is the mystical.'[3] But however one may interpret this cryptic aphorism, it is plain that he places an embargo on theological talk.

Having thus pronounced on the limits of language, and believing at the time that he had done so in a definitive way, Wittgenstein seems to have given up philosophy for some years. But around 1930 he returned to philosophical problems, and worked his way to new and very different ideas, which find expression in his posthumous book, *Philosophical Investigations*. With commendable candour, he writes: 'It is interesting to compare the multiplicity of the tools in language and of the ways they are used, the multiplicity of kinds of word and sentence, with what logicians have said about the structure of language—including the author of the *Tractatus Logico-Philosophicus*.'[4] The point of this sentence is that we may not take one language—the language which conveys factual information—and make it the norm by which all other kinds of language are to be judged. There are many 'language-games', as Wittgenstein calls them, such as giving orders, making up stories, guessing riddles, thanking, cursing, greeting, praying. The business of analysis is to discover the various rules which hold in each particular game. 'We remain unconscious of the prodigious diversity of all the everyday language-games because the

[1] *Op. cit.*, pp. 187-9.   [2] *Op. cit.*, p. 187.
   Op. cit., p. 187.   [4] *Philosophical Investigations*, p. 12e.

clothing of our language makes everything alike.'[1] Of course, some games are more serious than others, and some have more coherent rules than others. But we can find out about them only by considering how each is actually played.

This new approach to language at least gives religious language a reprieve. And although Wittgenstein himself does not undertake its analysis, we shall see later how some other logical empiricists have tried to provide intelligible rules for this particular language-game.

92. THE LANGUAGE OF SCIENCE AS A NORM
R. Carnap, H. Reichenbach, K. R. Popper, A. J. Ayer

In this section we shall consider a number of philosophers who, though not all positivists, are agreed in taking the language of science as their norm. They all offer criteria by which scientific language can be recognized, and although the criteria vary, the point about scientific language is that it is always in principle testable with reference to some sense-experience. Language which fails to satisfy these criteria is either dismissed as factually meaningless, or as at least suspect and of an inferior kind. Religious and theological language fares badly at the hands of these thinkers. Such language is usually taken to be merely an emotive utterance, logically meaningless and quite uninformative. These philosophers raise one of the most acute questions for the contemporary philosophy o religion, the question of what meaning, if any, attaches to the religious man's talk of God.

Rudolf Carnap[2] (1891-), a leading representative of the Vienna Circle which formed the core of the new philosophical movement in its early days, insisted on the unity of science. However diverse may be the contents of the many fields investigated by the special sciences, there is one science in so far as there is one language of science. Philosophy is simply the logic of science, and its business is to clarify the concepts and propositions of science, so that it becomes essentially an analysis of language. Like Wittgenstein, Carnap would say that philosophy tells us nothing about the world. It cannot speak of objects or objective relations, but only about the meanings of propositions and the significations of words. Unlike Wittgenstein, however, Carnap does not think that the philosophical ladder is to be kicked away once one has surmounted it,

---

[1] *Op. cit.*, p. 224e.

[2] A German by birth, he taught in Vienna and Prague, and since 1936 he has taught in Chicago and Los Angeles.

for he believes that philosophy can devise what he calls a 'metalanguage' in which to discuss the language of science.

Any language is characterized by its vocabulary and its syntax. The *vocabulary* is the list of words which possess significations; the *syntax* is the body of rules which indicate how sentences are to be constructed from the different kinds of words. When we fail to pay attention to these two characteristics, we may get two kinds of 'pseudo-propositions': those in which there appear words erroneously thought to signify something; and those in which individually significant words have been put together without regard to syntax so that the resulting sentences are devoid of sense. These two kinds of pseudo-propositions are what we meet in metaphysics, both ancient and modern. Heidegger, for instance, has a good deal to say about 'nothing', and according to Carnap he has mistakenly assumed that the word 'nothing' is the name of an object, and by treating it as such, he has produced sentences that are senseless. Metaphysics, ethics, theology and the like deal in pseudo-propositions which 'have no logical content, but are only expressions of feeling, which in their turn stimulate feelings and volitional tendencies on the part of the hearer'.[1]

The propositions of science are distinguishable by the fact that they can be verified in experience, and this makes them meaningful and informative. Verification is said to take place by way of 'protocol sentences' which refer immediately to what is given. They describe the content of immediate sense-experience and also the simpler kinds of relations. Whether the given consists of elemental *sensations*, as Mach held, or of *things* immediately perceived as three-dimensional bodies, is left unsettled, though Carnap seems attracted to the latter alternative because of the findings of *Gestalt* psychology, which suggests that sensations are not the original elements of sense-experience but rather the products of analysis and abstraction.

How do we get from these protocol-sentences which admit of immediate verification to the general hypotheses of science? Protocol-sentences, after all, are private to the individuals who have the immediate experiences. We can break out of subjectivism only by agreeing on an intersubjective language which will be universally valid. The language which meets this requirement is the language of physics which, by observation and measurement, reconciles the different opinions of different subjects. What cannot be expressed in the language of physics cannot claim universal or intersubjective validity. Even sciences like psychology and sociology, if they claim to be authentic sciences, must be able to speak in the language of physics. This doctrine of 'physicalism' is materialistic in its

[1] *Logical Syntax of Language*, p. 278.

method, but differs from classical materialism in neither affirming nor denying the existence of matter or spirit. It simply expresses the necessities of translating into physical terms all kinds of protocols, so as to contruct a truly intersubjective and universally valid language.

A less dogmatic line is taken by Hans Reichenbach[1] (1891-1953), who indeed came to accuse the thoroughgoing physicalists of erecting a new religion of science. He thinks that the attempt to find a basis of certain truth by appealing to the verification of protocol-sentences is a mistaken one. Truth is unattainable, and we have to content ourselves with probability.

A favourite metaphor with Reichenbach is that of the gambler, and A. N. Prior has pointed out[2] that Reichenbach's argument for scientific induction bears an astonishing resemblance to Pascal's wager argument for religion. As Reichenbach sees it, 'there is no certainty in any knowledge about the world, because knowledge of the world involves predictions of the future'.[3] Now 'any statement concerning the future is uttered in the sense of a wager. We wager on the sun's rising to-morrow, on there being food to nourish us to-morrow, on the validity of physical laws to-morrow; we are all of us gamblers– the man of science, and the business man, and the man who throws dice; and, if there is any difference in favor of the scientific gambler, it is only that he does not content himself with weights as low as accepted by the gambler with dice.'[4]

The allusion to 'weights' in this quotation is to be explained with reference to Reichenbach's theory of probability. We have noted that he denies that truth is attainable. Truth and falsity are ideal limiting cases, and between these lies a range of probability. The weight of a proposition is the degree of its probability, and this in turn is something that can be statistically calculated. Indeed, the possession of a determinable degree of probability is what gives meaning to a proposition.

The religious man and the man of science may be considered as alike gamblers, but there is a big difference between their wagers, or 'posits', as Reichenbach calls them. The scientist proceeds from observed phenomena by inductive inference to posits having a determinate weight, but in the case of the religious man, it would be hard to show that his posits have any weight at all. To believe that the sun will rise to-morrow is a pretty safe bet, in the light of experience; to believe that Christ will return on the clouds has just no comparable weight. When we ask what

---

[1] After being professor in Berlin and Istanbul, he taught at Los Angeles from 1938 until his death.
[2] *New Essays in Philosophical Theology*, ed. by A. Flew and A. MacIntyre, p. 8.
[3] *Experience and Prediction*, p. 345.
[4] *Op. cit.*, p. 315.

kind of knowledge affords our best posits, 'our stake', says Reichenbach, 'is not low; all our personal existence, our life itself, is at stake'.[1] Logical analysis, he believes, points to science as our best bet. Science does not offer us truth, but it does show us our best wagers.

Reichenbach in turn is criticized by the logician and sociologist, Karl Raimund Popper[2] (1902-   ). He denies that scientific theories are constructed by inductive procedures from our observations. On the contrary, they begin as creative intuitions or bold conjectures about the world, and sometimes arise out of metaphysical speculation. What distinguishes genuine scientific theories from metaphysics and the like is that the scientific theory is subjected to empirical testing, and the relevant test, Popper thinks, is a negative one: 'it must be possible for an empirical scientific system to be refuted by experience'.[3] Our attention is shifted from verifiability to falsifiability. After all, as Popper says, 'it is easy to obtain confirmations or verifications for nearly every theory—if we look for confirmations'.[4] A theory is really tested when we look for some state of affairs that would be counted as falsifying it.

The principle of falsifiability provides a way of demarcating science from theories which look like science but are only pseudo-science. Popper mentions as examples of pseudo-science the Marxist view of history and Freudian psychoanalytic theory. Such theories can get verification, since they interpret all events in accord with their own presuppositions, and do not recognize any event as refuting them. But irrefutability is a vice rather than a virtue in theories.

Popper is not a positivist nor does he think that philosophy is confined to the analysis of language. He explicitly states that his principle of falsifiability is not a criterion of meaning, but a line of demarcation between science and pseudo-science. 'It draws a line inside meaningful language, not around it.'[5]

Nevertheless, Popper is a champion of the claims of scientific language, and his principle of falsifiability has often been used to show the vacuous character of religious assertions, which seem to suffer from the vice of irrefutability. For instance, a man enjoying health and prosperity may say, 'God cares for me.' He loses his prosperity, but he still says that God cares for him, for he retains his health. He falls ill, but now he points to the fact that his life is spared as evidence that God cares for him. He eventually dies, but his friends claim that God still cares for him in a world beyond.

---

[1] *Op. cit.*, p. 404.
[2] He taught philosophy in Austria, then after 1937 in New Zealand, and from 1945 in London.
[3] *The Logic of Scientific Discovery*, p. 41.
[4] *British Philosophy in Mid-century*, p. 159.   [5] *The Logic of Scientific Discovery*, p. 40.

Nothing is allowed to refute the assertion, but what began as a seemingly important assertion appears to have been so whittled down that by the end one may ask whether, in Antony Flew's expression, it has not died by a thousand qualifications.[1] What would need to happen to falsify the belief that 'God cares for me'? And if nothing is counted as refuting this belief, then how does it differ from the belief that 'God does not care for me'? Such are the problems raised for religious language by Popper's doctrine of falsification.

We conclude this section with a mention of Alfred Jules Ayer[2] (1910-   ), whose brilliant early book, *Language, Truth and Logic* remains a classic statement of logical positivism in its most aggressive and iconoclastic phase. The book was first published in 1936, and Ayer has since remarked that although it was written with more passion than philosophers usually allow themselves, and although it oversimplified some of the issues, he still substantially adheres to the views which it expresses.

All genuine propositions are divided into two classes. Firstly, there is the class of analytic propositions, which are necessary and certain simply because they are tautologous. They assert nothing about the empirical world, but record our determination to use symbols in certain ways. To this class belong all the propositions of logic and mathematics. Philosophy properly understood, is likewise uninformative about the world. Its business is not speculation about reality but the analysis and clarification of the propositions of science. Secondly, there is the class of synthetic propositions. These do make assertions about the world, and their characteristic is that they are in each case capable of empirical verification—not that they can always be conclusively verified, but that always some sense-experience will be relevant for determining their truth or falsity.

Any supposed propositions which fall outside of this twofold classification are not genuine propositions at all, and are strictly meaningless, incapable of being either true or false. Such are most of the sentences found in metaphysics, ethics and theology. Being incapable of verification, they are incapable of expressing meaning as synthetic propositions, and obviously they are not tautologies. They are, according to Ayer, emotive utterances, more or less sophisticated interjections which evince feeling but assert nothing.

Religious talk about a transcendent God or the immortality of the soul is declared to be senseless. As senseless, such talk cannot be contradicted, since there is no logical relation between its pseudo-propositions and the

---

[1] See *New Essays in Philosophical Theology*, p. 97.
[2] Professor at London, 1946-59; Oxford, from 1959.

genuine propositions of science. But by making the world intelligible, science, in Ayer's view, 'tends to destroy the feeling of awe with which men regard an alien world',[1] and so it takes away one of the major sources of religious feeling.

Ayer points out that his positivist estimate of theology as devoid of sense is different in an important respect from traditional criticisms of transcendent beliefs, for the positivist is no more an atheist or an agnostic than he is a theist. All unverifiable talk about a transcendent God is without logical content, and so to deny that there is such a God or to say that it is an unsettled question whether there is such a God, is just as senseless as to claim that he exists. But whether this refinement which Ayer makes is supposed to offer any comfort to the theist is, of course, very doubtful.

93. Functional Analysis of Language and Empiricist Views of Religious Belief
G. Ryle, R. B. Braithwaite, J. Wisdom

The term 'functional analysis' is one which we borrow from Frederick Ferré's useful book, *Language, Logic and God.* Whereas the analysts considered in the last section took the language of science as their norm and were inclined to dismiss as meaningless all language which does not conform to the criteria laid down for the language of science, many analysts adopt a more flexible approach. They are prepared to examine each kind of language on its own merits, so to speak, to ask what function it performs and what kind of meaning it can have. Although this approach is more open-minded, it need not of course lead to a more friendly attitude towards religious language, for the result of the analysis might well show that religious language has no legitimate function and possesses no coherent logical structure. In any case, we shall see that even those analysts who are friendly towards religion, and those empiricists whom we shall consider along with them, are unwilling to readmit the traditional metaphysical concepts of God and the soul, and look for ways of explaining how religious language can function meaningfully without the embarrasment of the old-fashioned metaphysical trappings.

We begin with Gilbert Ryle[2] (1900-   ) as an exemplar of ordinary language analysis. He is well-known for his analysis of mental concepts and his attempt to rectify their logical geography, as he would express it. In particular, he attacks Descartes' dualistic theory that man is compounded of an immaterial thinking substance, or soul, and a material

---

[1] *Op. cit.,* p. 117.   [2] Professor at Oxford from 1945.

extended substance, or body, which mysteriously interact—what Ryle calls 'the dogma of the ghost in the machine'.[1] This dualism, which leads to insuperable difficulties, rests on a category mistake. Nouns like 'mind' and 'intelligence' are taken to be the names of things, but there are no such things, and these words function as descriptions of human behaviour. So Ryle's analysis of mental concepts proceeds to drive out the ghost from its hiding places, and ends up in a kind of behaviourism. But we should notice that Ryle's behaviourism is not of the crudely materialistic or physicalist variety. Somewhat ironically, he says: 'Man need not be degraded to a machine by being denied to be a ghost in a machine. He might, after all, be a sort of animal, namely, a higher mammal. There has yet to be ventured the hazardous leap to the hypothesis that perhaps he is a man.'[2]

That Ryle, in spite of his denial of substantial souls, is not leading us into a simple materialism or physicalism, seems clear from another of his books, *Dilemmas*. Here Ryle considers the conflicts which sometimes arise between theories which are pursuing entirely different lines of business, as it were, but which seem to arrive at incompatible results. As an example, he mentions the conflicts between science and religion in the nineteenth century. Theologians and scientists began by assuming that they were dealing with the same questions. As a result, theologians produced bad science, when they tried to draw geological conclusions from theological premises, but equally, says Ryle, scientists became bad theologians when they strayed into their opponents' field. Of T. H. Huxley's theological speculation, Ryle says that 'it was not only baseless, but also somewhat cheap, where the Christian picture, whatever its basis, not only was not cheap but itself taught the distinctions between what is cheap and what is precious'.[3] Expertness in one field does not carry with it expertness in another field, and if we are to avoid the kind of trespassing which leads to pseudo-conflicts, we must clearly see what the boundaries of the various provinces of discourse are.

This does not mean, of course, that the physicist is restricted to some particular sector of the world. He takes the whole world for his province. But Ryle tries to show by an analogy that this does not imply that any other talk about the world is excluded. The analogy is that of a college auditor who shows his accounts to an undergraduate, and tells him that all the activities of the college are represented in these columns. So they are— teaching, games, entertainments, food and drink, libraries and so on. Everything is covered, yet the things for which the undergraduate cares most seem to have been left out of these precise impersonal columns. Surely other things can be said about the life of the college, and these will

[1] *The Concept of Mind*, pp. 15-16.　　[2] *Op. cit.*, p. 328.　　[3] *Op. cit.*, p. 7.

not conflict with what the auditor says, even if his accounts cover every-thing that goes on. So we are free to say things about the world which will not conflict with what the physicist says, though they are not amen-able to his kind of book-keeping.

It would of course be an over-simplification to say that the physicist, the artist and the theologian give us different, and possibly complementary pictures of the world. This would blur the differences between them, whereas these differences need to be brought out into the open, so that we can see whether the different lines of business are legitimate. Ryle himself offers no analysis of what the theologian's business is, but he at least leaves open a logical door. Presumably the theologian who wanted to follow Ryle would need to get along without a soul, but he might at least reply that the 'ghost in the machine' is not a dogma of the New Testament, which always talks of a 'resurrection of the body'—a 'spiritual body', according to St Paul—and however bristling with difficulty this language may be, it can hardly be taken as dualistic.

Richard Bevan Braithwaite[1] (1900-   ) succeeds in giving us quite a plausible analysis of religious language without introducing the conception of a substantial soul or even, it would seem, of a substantial God. Braith-waite would agree that religious assertions are neither tautologies nor empirically verifiable propositions, but he does not conclude that they are therefore nonsensical or merely emotive utterances. Moral assertions are equally unverifiable, but they have a use in guiding conduct, and so, it is argued, they have some kind of meaning. Braithwaite modifies the older verification principle by changing it into a wider principle of use: 'the meaning of any statement is given by the way in which it is used.'[2] This principle is no less empirical than the verification one, and the question is now to show how religious assertions are used.

Braithwaite's answer is that they are used primarily as moral assertions, that is to say, to announce allegiance to a set of moral principles. The sentence, 'God is love', which Braithwaite takes to epitomize the assertions of the Christian religion, declares the Christian's intention to follow an agapastic[3] way of life. This is the meaning of the assertion. On this view, religion is regarded as primarily a way of life. Religious beliefs are not assertions about supersensible realities nor are they merely emotive utterances; they have rather a *conative* character. The core of all the great religions, Braithwaite believes, is the agapastic way of life.

[1] Professor at Cambridge from 1953.
[2] *An Empiricist's View of the Nature of Religious Belief*, p. 10.
[3] Braithwaite writes 'agapeistic', but here, for the sake of uniformity, we have followed C. S. Peirce in writing 'agapastic' as the adjective corresponding to *agape*. See above, p. 176. A purist might prefer 'agapetic' as having a precedent in Greek.

How then are we to distinguish religion from plain morality, or one religion from another? The answer to both of these questions is to be found in the *stories* which belong to each religion, such as the New Testament stories about Christ, belonging to Christianity. These stories usually consist of straightforward empirical propositions, so that there is no problem about their meaning. Whether these stories are true or false is of little importance, for what matters is that they should be *entertained* in the mind of the religious person. So to entertain the stories acts as a powerful psychological aid towards carrying out the agapastic policy, and it is in this way that religion can be a moral dynamic, making us more successful in carrying out our moral intentions and less prone to the moral sloth and weakness which affects us.

Here the logical empiricist's account of religious belief seems to come near to that of the pragmatist. But it is not to William James that Braithwaite has looked for inspiration but rather to Matthew Arnold and his teaching that religion consists primarily in conduct.

A different line is taken by John Wisdom[1] (1902-   ). His interests extend beyond the technical problems of philosophy to such subjects as literature, psychoanalysis, and religion, but because of his habit in his analyses of drawing attention to certain features of the matter under discussion, and then paradoxically drawing attention to other conflicting features, his findings are somewhat indefinite, and this, we may suppose, is intentional.

On religion, he remarks that 'the existence of God is not an experimental issue in the way it was'.[2] In a world which we no longer conceive animistically and in which we look to science for the natural explication of phenomena, there seems to be no way of getting empirical verification of God's existence. We would not think nowadays of trying Elijah's method when he called down fire on his altar on Mount Carmel. Does this mean then that the question about God is not a question of fact? It might seem so. Two people come upon a long-neglected garden. One says: 'A gardener comes and looks after this place.' The other says: 'There is no gardener.' On inquiry, they find that nobody has ever seen a gardener about. But the first man says: 'A gardener comes unseen and unheard.' The second still says: 'There is no gardener.' They do not seem to be disputing about any facts, for what difference is there between a gardener who never shows himself and no gardener at all? Is it not just the case that one of the two men feels indifferently about the garden from the other—and so with the theist and the atheist in their attitudes to the world?

[1] Professor at Cambridge from 1952.   [2] *Philosophy and Psychoanalysis*, p. 149.

But now Wisdom maintains that the dispute between the two men is more than a question of different emotional attitudes. They may go on arguing, each of them retracing and emphasizing those features of the garden which favour his belief. 'We must not forthwith assume that there is no right and wrong about it, no rationality or irrationality, no appropriateness or inappropriateness, no procedure which tends to settle it, *nor even that this procedure is in no sense a discovery of new facts.*'[1] The difference as to whether there is a God is certainly one that involves our feelings more than most scientific disputes do, but it is also a question of noticing or failing to notice certain patterns in the world, and so it is in a sense a difference as to the facts, though not in the simple way that might be supposed when the question of empirical verifiability is first raised.

It would not be inappropriate to compare the situation that Wisdom has in mind with the ambiguous figures which we find in some text-books of psychology. Such a figure might appear to one man as a flight of steps; to another, as an overhanging architrave; or to one and the same man as either, at different times. In a much more complex way, the religious man notices in the world a pattern or *Gestalt* to which he draws attention in his talk about God.

In concluding this section, we may recall some writers of empiricist outlook who have been already mentioned in other connections but whose views include suggestions for justifying the logic of religious assertions. We have seen that H. H. Price[2] has recommended the religious man to take a look at the findings of psychical research to see whether there might not be available there some empirical evidences that would allow religious talk to get under way. It would seem that in spite of Ryle's logical exorcism, Price still suspects that there may be a ghost lurking in the machine, and that it is moreover a ghost which manifests itself in some objectively testable phenomena. Likewise A. C. Garnett[3] has devoted attention to the problem of the logic of religious language. On the one hand, we have seen that his criticism of contemporary theologies turns largely on the inadequacy of their respective logics: the unbridgeable gulf in Thomistic analogy; the appeal to an untestable revelation in Barthianism; and the misunderstanding of the logical function of the verb 'to be' in Tillich. On the other hand, Garnett's own thesis of a God-in-process is partly defended on the ground that the logical barrier to analogical talk about God is removed if God's experience is temporal like our own. Thus although neither Price nor Garnett would usually be classed as logical analysts, they have both dealt with the kind of problem that confronts us in this section, and it is worthwhile setting down their views alongside those of

---

[1] *Op. cit.*, p. 159.   [2] See above, p. 234.   [3] See above, p. 275.

Braithwaite and Wisdom, so that we can see the astonishing variety of answers that can be given when empiricists set out to explain the logic of religious assertions.

94. Critical Remarks on the Ideas of Religion in Logical Empiricism

The reader may well feel slightly bewildered after having gone through the preceding section. It would seem that when, from an empiricist's point of view, it is asked what the religious man can conceivably mean by his talk about God, many replies can be made, and all of them have some degree of plausibility. Yet obviously they are not all compatible with each other; and some of them seem far removed from what the unsophisticated religious person fancies that he means when he talks about God.

These various attempts to discover what religious language is about are at least an advance on the older logical positivism which dismissed religious assertions as without meaning. Like other kinds of positivism, this one did not escape involvement in some kind of metaphysical assumptions, so that we are reminded of Bradley's dictum that no one can deny the possibility of metaphysics without himself becoming a brother metaphysician. As has often been pointed out, the verification principle does not itself belong to either of the classes of meaningful propositions which the positivists allowed—it is neither a tautology nor itself an empirically verifiable proposition. 'The fact is', says John Wisdom, 'the verification principle is a metaphysical proposition—a "smashing" one if I may be permitted the expression.'[1]

What the positivists do succeed in showing pretty decisively is that assertions about God are quite different from assertions about any particular empirical facts. This, however, is not a discovery, but something that would be clear to anyone who had even a sketchy acquaintance with the history of religious thought. The theologian need not be worried when the logical positivist takes an assertion about God as if it were an assertion about some empirical fact, and proceeds to show that on the logic applicable to factual assertions, an assertion about God is senseless. The question, 'Is there a God?', is not to be settled in the same way as the question, 'Are there subatomic particles?' Yet the positivists by forcibly drawing attention to this difference in logical status make it imperative for the theologian to think out just what the difference is, and to explain to us what kind of logic is applicable to his statements about God.

[1] *Philosophy and Psychoanalysis*, p. 245.

It is when we turn to this problem that we meet so many conflicting answers. Braithwaite is right in drawing attention to the relation of religious language to conduct, and he succeeds in showing how it can be given a meaning in this context. But in entirely assimilating religious assertions to moral assertions, he has surely exaggerated his thesis beyond what is plausible. The religious man is certainly committed to a way of life, but he also believes that his religion gives him some insight into the kind of world in which he has to follow his way of life. Braithwaite seems to admit as much when he says that there enter into religion 'feelings of joy, of consolation, of being at one with the universe'.[1] For how could anyone feel 'at one with the universe' without having some belief as to what kind of universe it is? Are we then helped out by Wisdom's view that the religious man notices certain patterns in the world? Perhaps we are, but Wisdom is not very specific about the kinds of pattern he has in mind. Ayer had already pointed out, correctly, that a mere regularity in nature is much less than what the religious man intends to assert when he says that there is a God.[2] If a providential pattern is intended, then perhaps one could argue meaningfully about this, but it would seem that the argument must always remain inconclusive. The tracing of rival patterns in the world would be rather like working out rival interpretations of a play of Shakespeare. Could one ever say that this interpretation is true and another false, or does the question of truth and falsity arise in such a case? Is it perhaps the mark of a great work of art that it can yield many patterns to its interpreters?

When we turn to other suggestions that have been made for giving an empirical justification to talk about God, we must frankly say that the religious man would need to be in pretty desperate straits before he would take Price's advice and stake his case on such dubious evidence as that provided by J. B. Rhine and similar investigators in the field of psychical research. Even if he accepted their findings—and of course it would be sheer dogmatism to reject them out of hand—there would still be a long road, as Price acknowledges, from, let us say, the fact of telepathy to the existence of God. Garnett's view that religious talk makes sense when referred to a God who is temporally characterized brings us back to the question, already discussed,[3] whether such a God satisfies the demands of the religious consciousness. This question is not easily settled, and Garnett's attempt to combine his Christian faith with his empiricist philosophy is worthy of serious attention. But it may be the case that radical empiricism and traditional Christianity are just incompatible.

[1] *An Empiricist's View of the Nature of Religious Belief*, p. 15.
[2] *Language, Truth and Logic*, p. 115.   [3] See above, p. 277.

While some of the thinkers considered in the present chapter, such as Popper, Price and Garnett, do not take the view that philosophy is confined to logical analysis, this is the view of the majority of the philosophers whom we have examined, and even the exceptions have been considered primarily with regard to what they have to say on the question of whether religious language can be justified. It is obvious that a purely analytical approach can be no more than a *prolegomenon* to a philosophy of religion, since it is just as uninformative about God as it is about the physical world. It contents itself with the analysis and clarification of religious assertions, leaving to the specialist the elaboration of such assertions and the determination of their truth or falsity, if it is found relevant to speak of their truth or falsity. Leaving aside the question whether philosophy does not have a synthetic as well as an analytic function—and many philosophers would say that it does—we can still see that the purely analytical approach has its value. Ian T. Ramsey, for instance, claims that 'the contemporary philosophical interest in language, far from being soul-destroying, can be so developed as to provide a novel inroad into the problems and controversies of theology' [1] The jungle of theological verbiage stands badly in need of some cleaning up.

But what gives to so many analyses of religious language a superficial character—especially the matter-of-fact analyses offered by thinkers of positivist leanings—is a failure to remember that language is a function of human existence. All talk is *somebody's* talk in some situation. This is partly recognized in the new insistence on how language is *used*, but unfortunately many analysts seem to set up words and sentences as quasi-substantial ghostly entities that somehow get along by themselves and can be considered in complete abstraction from the people who express *themselves* in these words and sentences. No doubt some kinds of language are more closely bound up with the existence of the speaker than others —and religious language would seem to be very closely bound up. This means that the analysis of religious language, if it is to be carried out with a clear understanding of what it involves, must be correlated with an analysis of the existence of the man who expresses *himself* in religious language. In other words, linguistic analysis is preceded by existential analysis. We shall see the implications of this statement when we come to existentialism. [2]

---

[1] *Religious Language*, p. 11.

[2] See Chapter XXI, below, pp. 339ff. The reader's attention may be drawn to *The Christian Scholar*, vol. XLIII, no. 3, published in the fall of 1960. This number is devoted to the question of contemporary analytical philosophy and its relevance to Christian thought. Contributors include I. T. Ramsey (Oxford), John E. Smith (Yale) and Carl Michalson (Drew). There is an extensive bibliography, compiled by Ruel Tyson.

XX

THE THEOLOGY OF THE WORD

95. The Distinctiveness of Christianity

In the last chapter we have noticed that British philosophers are wont to speak of a 'revolution in philosophy'. Many theologians talk of a 'revolution in theology', and this theological revolution gathered momentum around the same time as the philosophical one. It is customary to date the revolution in theology from the publication of Karl Barth's *The Epistle to the Romans* in 1919. We may call this new theological orientation a 'theology of the word', for its concern is to let us hear what God has to say to men. Barth has recently written: 'The subject of theology is the "word of God". Theology is a science and a teaching which *feels itself responsible* to the living command of this specific subject and to nothing else in heaven or on earth, in the choice of its methods, its questions and answers, its concepts and language, its goals and limitations.'[1]

We may think that there is little in common between the two revolutions, since the one led to logical positivism while the other demands unquestioning obedience to a divine word. Yet there are obviously some things in common. Both the philosophical movement and the theological one are disillusioned with the pretensions of speculative reason to grasp the being of God and the supersensible, and are united in their uncompromising rejection of metaphysics. For this reason, the theological movement has sometimes been called 'theological positivism'. Again, on both sides we can see a quest for autonomy, for a distinctive field where philosophy or theology, as the case may be, can reign in undisputed freedom. Philosophers believe that in logical analysis they have found an area of investigation where philosophy may legitimately operate free from the encroachments of the special sciences. Theologians who take the 'word of God' as their subject believe that this subject is *sui generis* and sovereign, so that they are under no obligation to conform their findings to the current philosophical or scientific fashions. The inevitable result of these

[1] In the new Foreword (1959) to *Dogmatics in Outline*, p. 5.

movements towards autonomy has been a widening of the gulf between philosophy and theology.

But while there are these similarities between the two revolutions, even more striking is the difference which is visible in their consequences. Analytic philosophy, as we have seen, tends to develop in a secular humanistic way, and may even dismiss all talk of God as senseless. The theology of the word on the other hand, while it denies that there is any way from man to God, does claim that God has come to man and has spoken his word. The knowledge of God, inaccessible from man's side because of his finitude and sinfulness, is made available to faith by God's free act of grace. God's word is known in Jesus Christ, to whom the Bible bears witness and whom the Church proclaims in her preaching. Apart from this revelatory word, we can know nothing of God, but in the word God makes himself known to man by his own revelation.

Of course, the theology of the word is not immune from some philosophical influences, and probably no theology is. The disjunction between speculative reason and faith is one that goes back to Kant, and we have already met it among the Ritschlian theologians. However much the newer theology may disagree with Ritschlianism in some matters, it agrees in rejecting speculative metaphysics in favour of revelation as the *locus* for the knowledge of God. Again, the view that revealed knowledge is *sui generis* and discontinuous with the speculations and aspirations of humanity is plainly traceable to the influence of Kierkegaard. But although we may discern such influences in the theology of the word, this theology would claim that the word stands over against all human philosophies and judges them. It does not need to be justified by them, and indeed it cannot get any confirmation from them. We cannot amalgamate things that are qualitatively different. It would be equally wrong to try to use the word for the confirmation of our political and social ideals, as Harnack attempted to do.

The theology of the word stands in sharp contrast with some of the theologies which we have already surveyed. It could have nothing to do with Harnack's idea that Jesus simply fulfils the demands of our moral nature, or with the idealist judgment that the Christian revelation concretely symbolizes the understanding of the world to which reason would conduct us in any case, or with the neo-Thomist conception of revelation as a kind of superstructure which completes natural theology. In varying degrees, the adherents of the theology of the word reject any natural theology.

Other names are given to the movement which we are considering. It may be called 'kerygmatic theology', which draws attention to the content of theology as a *kerygma* or proclamation of the revelatory and saving acts of God. The term 'dialectical theology' points to the belief that one cannot characterize God in some simple formula, but may have to speak of him paradoxically, balancing each affirmation with a corresponding negation in order to do justice to a God who so infinitely transcends our finite creaturely being. The expression 'theology of crisis' does not simply mean that this is the kind of theology which emerged after the crisis of the First World War, but indicates the crisis or judgment of the divine word upon the world. The term 'neo-orthodoxy' is perhaps unfortunate, though of course it depends on what we mean by 'orthodoxy'. The theology of the word does not mean assent to orthodox propositions, nor does it mean literal assent to the words of the Bible. The theology of the word is in fact severely criticized by fundamentalists, for the word is conceived as the living incarnate Word, Jesus Christ, to whom, indeed, the human words of the Bible bear witness, but cannot express the fullness of the divine word. On the other hand, we find a theologian like Brunner dissenting from the orthodox dogma of the virgin birth. If we wish to call theologians of this school 'neo-orthodox', perhaps we should think of this term as meaning simply that they try to recapture the spirit of Reformation theology, as the classic period of Protestant thought, just as the Middle Ages were of Catholic thought. Secular critics have suggested that both the neo-orthodox in their return to the Reformation and the neo-Thomists in their return to the Middle Ages are running away from the problems of the modern world. But both groups might reply that we have the right and duty to judge modern ideas in the light of classic Christian insights of the past.

Beginning in Switzerland, the revolution in theology soon made its influence felt in most Protestant countries, and had perhaps reached its peak by the outbreak of World War II, though it still continues to be one of the major theological forces of our time. As it fanned out, however, some of its original assertions came to be modified, and conflicts developed within the movement itself, so that in this chapter we shall be confronted with a group of theologians who show considerable diversities. But they all maintain the distinctive claim of Christianity, and repel the claims of philosophy to pronounce on matters which are taken to be revealed. We shall group these theologians according to their countries, beginning with Switzerland (Section 96), then going on to look at representatives from Sweden (Section 97) and Germany (Section 98). The reader may be surprised that Germany is represented here by only one theologian, and one who, in his later thought, seems to have moved far from the more typical expositions of this kind of theology. Our procedure, however, is deliberate. While the theological revolution certainly had far-reaching effects in Germany, the most brilliant theologians associated with it in that country—Gogarten, Bultmann and Tillich—have diverged so far from thinkers like Barth and Brunner that they will have to be considered in a separate chapter; while those German theologians who have remained in many respects close to Barth do not appear to have said anything sufficiently distinctive to warrant special mention. The theological revolution has had its influence too in the English-speaking countries; but here again the differences are so considerable that a separate notice is demanded. After surveying the various groups in this chapter, we end with a critical assessment (Section 99).

96. THE THEOLOGY OF THE WORD IN SWITZERLAND
K. Barth, E. Brunner, O. Cullmann

By far the most outstanding of the theologians we have to consider, and probably the most famous Protestant theologian of the twentieth century so far, is Karl Barth[1] (1886–1968). Since he published *The Epistle to the Romans* in 1919, Barth has in many ways modified his views, and we shall try to take account of these modifications, and of the definitive statement of his theology in the massive volumes of *Die kirchliche Dogmatik*.[2] But we may begin by recalling an exchange of letters between Harnack and Barth in 1923. Harnack maintains that 'the task of theology is one with the tasks of science in general'. Barth, on the contrary, holds that the task of theology 'is one with the task of preaching; it consists in taking up and passing on the word of Christ'.[3] He adds that he has no quarrel with scientific theology and historical criticism, but these tasks are preparatory to the authentic work of theology in its concern with the word.

This word comes from God to man, that is to say, the movement is in the reverse direction to all human science and research. There is a way

---

[1] Professor at Münster, 1925-30; Bonn, 1930-5; Basel, 1935-62.
[2] E. P. Dickie seems to be right in saying that probably Barth 'will be known to the history of theology by his earlier contributions. It is one of the ironies of controversy that amendments and alterations are apparently better done by others'—*God is Light*, p. 2. The early, exaggerated writings made the decisive impact which changed the course of theological thinking. Yet it is only fair to Barth to take account of his most mature and considered work. Already in 1933 when *The Epistle to the Romans* appeared in an English translation, he wrote in his new preface: 'When I look back at the book, it seems to have been written by another man to meet a situation belonging to a past epoch.' It is instructive to compare his early commentary with the later and quite independent book, *A Shorter Commentary on Romans*. This later book tones down somewhat the insistence on the stark sovereign transcendence of God; on the other hand, it makes clear Barth's uncompromising rejection of any natural theology or natural religion.
[3] *Theologische Fragen und Antworten*, pp. 10ff.

from God to man, but no way from man to God, so that we are to hear the word, not to find it out. The word centres in Christ, and the Bible in turn bears witness to Christ, so that it is in the Bible that we hear the word and learn its unique quality and its discontinuity with all human researches. 'Within the Bible there is a strange new world, the world of God. There are no transitions, intermixings or intermediate stages. There is only crisis, finality, new insight.'[1] What we learn here is not the continuation to a higher stage of what we can learn elsewhere, but something *sui generis*. There is, in Barth's view, no natural theology forming, as it were, a propaedeutic to revealed theology. When he was invited to give the Gifford Lectures at Aberdeen University in 1935, he wrote back to the senate: 'I am an avowed opponent of all natural theology.'[2] And although he was persuaded to give a course of lectures, these very lectures make it clear that for Barth there is no possibility of a genuine knowledge of God apart from the Christian revelation.

This raises in an acute form the question of the relation of theology to philosophy, and of the Christian religion to other religions. Barth is uncompromising in his refusal to allow any true knowledge of God to any of these. Like Feuerbach, he regards man's ideas of God as projections of man's own wishes—though of course Barth makes an exception in favour of the Christian revelation, which is qualitatively unique in that it has come from God to man. Philosophical and non-Christian ideas of God are therefore idolatrous. Yet Barth is anxious not to appear completely negative in his attitude to reason and philosophy. Like St Anselm, Barth would acknowledge a *fides quaerens intellectum*, where faith leads the way and reason follows. He agrees that we are at liberty to use ideas taken from secular philosophy in the work of exegesis, and that such ideas can be 'legitimate and fruitful', always provided that they are kept subordinate to the text and follow after it.[3] But we should notice that the concession to secular thought is a pretty meagre one. The ideas drawn from secular thought are different in principle from those of the text, about which only the Holy Spirit can enlighten us. Philosophy cannot put the word in question nor can it confirm the word, but is itself always put in question by the word. Theology is an autonomous science and has no obligation to harmonize its findings with those of secular thought. 'Theology is a free science because it is based on and determined by the kingly freedom of the word of God.'[4]

The God who reveals himself by his own word is represented, as we

[1] *The Word of God and the Word of Man*, pp. 33, 91.
[2] *The Knowledge of God and the Service of God*, p. 6.
[3] See *Die kirkliche Dogmatik*, vol. I/2, pp. 815-25 [ET, pp. 727-36].
[4] *Dogmatics in Outline*, p. 5.

would expect, primarily in terms of his transcendence. He is free and sovereign, and his action is vertically from above. In reaction against the humanized God of the liberal theologies, Barth has insisted on God as the 'wholly other', the One who is qualitatively different from creaturely and fallen men. We can appreciate the need for this stress on the majesty of God as over against the somewhat sentimentalized conception of God that we find in Harnack and theologians of his type. Yet if the gulf between God and man is made absolute, how can even a divine word ever get across? We find that here too Barth has modified his teaching somewhat. He says that while in his early days it was necessary and right to stress the otherness of God, this aspect of God was exaggerated, and we have also to recognize what Barth calls the 'humanity' of God, his manward side in which he relates himself to man.[1] Barth seems therefore to have withdrawn from his extreme insistence on the otherness of God, but we should notice that this kind of modification is entirely consistent with his dialectical theological procedure, whereby one statement about God needs to be corrected by a paradoxical counterstatement. It does not imply any radical departure from his emphasis on God's transcendence, or any diminution of God's freedom and initiative.[2]

When God's transcendence and otherness are stressed, as they are in Barth, how do we talk about God? It will not surprise us that he rejects the traditional doctrine of analogy, so far as this involves an *analogia entis* and implies some kind of being that is naturally common to God and man. If we take some human idea and stretch it as far as we can in the direction of infinity, it will never give us any inkling of God. For instance, we can never reach the understanding of God as creator by extending our human knowledge of originators and causes. 'If we do know about God as the creator, it is neither wholly nor partially because we have a prior knowledge of something which resembles creation. It is only because it has been given to us by God's revelation to know him, and what we previously thought we knew about originators and causes is called in question, turned around, and transformed.'[3] The same would be true of other ideas, such as fatherhood, lordship, personality; it is divine personality that enables us to

---

[1] See *The Humanity of God.*

[2] How Barth regards the modifications that he has made in his theology may be seen from a passage in *Die kirchliche Dogmatik*, vol. II/1, p. 715 [ET, p. 635]. After quoting a one-sided statement from *The Epistle to the Romans*, he writes: 'Well roared, lion! There is nothing absolutely false in these bold words. I still think that I was right ten times over against those who then passed judgment on them and resisted them. Those who can still hear what was said then, cannot but admit that it was necessary to speak in this way. The sentences I then uttered were not hazardous (in the sense of precarious) on account of their content. They were hazardous because, to be legitimate exposition of the Bible, they needed others no less sharp and direct to compensate and therefore genuinely to substantiate their total claim. But these were lacking.'

[3] *Die kirchliche Dogmatik*, vol. II/1, p. 83 [ET, p. 77].

understand human personality, and not *vice versa*. Barth may well be correct in claiming that divine personality, divine fatherhood, and the like, are *ontologically* first, and their human analogues derivative;[1] but must not the human analogues be first *epistemologically*? Reinhold Niebuhr, for instance, maintains that Barth himself must have taken the concept of personality from man and then applied it to God.[2] But Barth has his answer to such criticisms. It is God's grace in his revelation that establishes a community between himself and man, so that we can speak of him in human words.[3] Not an analogy of being but an analogy of grace (*analogia gratiae*) makes our talk of God veracious. This view of analogy preserves both the divine initiative and the entire passivity of the human mind in our knowledge of God.

Barth's disjunction between the word of God and all human thought and aspiration rules out the traditional kind of Christian apologetic, which would be an illegitimate attempt to force a way through from man to God; and also makes it hard to see how there can be a Christian leavening of social and cultural life. The Christian has simply to witness to the truth that has been given to him. Barth's apparent indifference to secular concerns has caused critics like Niebuhr to accuse him of 'transcendental irresponsibility'. This may be exaggerated, but certainly Barth's influence has tended to encapsulate Christian thinking within the Church, and to sever its connections with the secular world.

Next after Barth, Emil Brunner[4] (1889–1966) is the most eminent representative of the theology of the word. Though his outlook is fundamentally close to Barth's, Brunner differs from him on many points. Whereas the early Barth so stressed the utter transcendence of God over man that it is difficult to see how there could be a genuinely personal relation between God and man, Brunner's style of thinking is definitely personalistic and—as is obvious from such a book as *The Divine-Human Encounter*—owes much to the 'I-Thou' philosophy of Buber.

Around 1933, Brunner and Barth were engaged in a sharp controversy, though perhaps to the outside observer the similarities of their respective positions would seem far more striking than the differences. The controversy was over the possibility of natural theology. Barth, as we have

---

[1] Heidegger seems to say something similar when he claims that his expression 'house of Being' is not got by 'transferring the image of a house to Being; rather, it is from appropriately thinking the nature of Being that we may one day be able to think what a house is'—*Über den Humanismus*, p. 43.

[2] See *The Nature and Destiny of Man*, vol. II, p. 69.

[3] See *Die kirchliche Dogmatik*, vol. II/1, p. 275 [ET, p. 243]. We may compare Heidegger's statement that before a man speaks, he must first let himself be addressed by Being—*Über den Humanismus*, p. 10.

[4] Professor at Zürich from 1924.

seen, rejects natural theology. There is no point of contact between the word of God and the natural man. Brunner, on the other hand, maintains that even fallen man retains the form of the image of God, and can attain some knowledge of God. But the form which is retained is said to be a form without a content, and is of little avail; for such knowledge as the natural man attains of God apart from the Christian revelation is said to be of no saving value. About this curious controversy, John Baillie has well said: 'Barth's position seems to me untrue to the facts but clearly argued; Brunner's position seems nearer the truth but, because it is not sufficiently advanced beyond the other, to be involved in confusion and unreal compromise.'[1] Niebuhr's comment is very similar: 'In this debate Brunner seems to me to be right and Barth wrong; but Barth seems to win the debate because Brunner accepts too many of Barth's presuppositions in his fundamental premises to be able to present his own position with plausibility and consistency.'[2] What Baillie and Niebuhr say here about Brunner's controversy with Barth may perhaps be not unfairly extended to Brunner's thought as a whole—he tries hard to be less rigid than Barth, but he is so much committed to some of Barth's fundamental theses that he is continually in danger of falling into uneasy and unclear compromises.

Brunner, then, as we have seen, allows some trace of the divine *logos* even to fallen man, and acknowledges an original divine revelation in the creation, a revelation in which even the most primitive religions participate. But all this is so perverted by human sin that Brunner maintains on the other hand that a genuine knowledge of God is to be had *only* through the Christian revelation, and he even makes this claim to exclusive saving truth an essential part of the Christian faith itself: 'A real Christian faith is impossible apart from the conviction that here and here alone is salvation.'[3] Even a philosophy of religion, he maintains, must proceed not autonomously, but within the light of the Christian revelation if it is not to go hopelessly astray.

In the face of such assertions, the apparent concessions to philosophy and the non-Christian religions do not amount to very much. In the formal sciences, like mathematics, the disturbance of our knowledge by sin is said to be zero, so that it would be senseless to talk of a 'Christian mathematics'; in the natural sciences, the disturbance is still minimal; but when we approach the centre of our existence, the questions of personal being and man's relation to God, the disturbance increases, so that we can and

---

[1] *Our Knowledge of God.* pp. 30-1.
[2] *The Nature and Destiny of Man*, vol. II, p. 66, n. 2.
[3] *The Mediator*, p. 201.

must talk about 'Christian anthropology' or 'Christian ethics'. Brunner has in fact written important books on both of these themes—on Christian anthropology, *Man in Revolt*, and on Christian ethics, *The Divine Imperative*. The use of the adjective 'Christian' in these expressions suggests the way in which rational knowledge gets corrected by faith, and by what faith has learned from the Christian revelation. But 'in the case of the idea of God, it is not merely a matter of correction but of a complete substitution of the one for the other'.[1] Thus in Brunner we seem to reach just as absolute a disjunction between the Christian faith and all philosophical or non-Christian ideas of God as we do in Barth. Brunner goes so far as to maintain that if we are going to call the non-Christian religions by the name of 'religions', then we must not call the Christian faith a 'religion', since it is qualitatively different.

Can we say more exactly what it is that makes the Christian revelation qualitatively unique? Brunner would reply to this question by pointing out firstly that, whereas the general revelation is always present, in a timeless way, the Christian revelation belongs to a decisive once-for-all act of God in history; and secondly that this revelation is personal in character, given in the divine-human encounter where God in Christ meets man. Faith, as the reception of this revelation, is a personal relationship of trustful obedience, and not, as it is often mistakenly supposed to be, the giving of assent to doctrinal propositions. 'Revelation is therefore fundamentally different from all other forms of knowledge, because it is not the knowledge of something but the meeting of the Unconditioned with the conditioned subject.'[2] Other kinds of knowledge make us masters over some object or other, but in revelation we are ourselves mastered by the divine Subject.

Brunner takes up a more positive attitude to human institutions than does Barth, and devoted his Gifford Lectures to the exploration of the relations between Christianity and civilization. He believes that Christianity has made and can make creative and constructive contributions to civilization, especially in the way of personalizing its structure, and he has many interesting and perceptive observations to make. But the distance between any civilization and the eternal kingdom of God is absolute, so that 'the first and main concern of the Christian can never be civilization and culture'.[3] The Christian's contribution will be in the nature of by-products, and are made possible because his goal lies beyond all civilization and history.

The eschatological allusions with which Brunner concludes his

[1] *Revelation and Reason*, p. 383.   [2] *Op. cit.*, p. 27.
[3] *Christianity and Civilization*, vol. II, p. 140.

reflections on civilization lead us to consider the work of another Swiss theologian, Oscar Cullmann[1] (1902-   ). Primarily a New Testament scholar, he has also made contributions to theology, and takes the line that theological thinking must employ the categories of biblical thought, to the exclusion of such Hellenistic or modern conceptions as would distort the genuine essence of biblical teaching.

Like Barth and Brunner, Cullmann holds the view that Christianity is the 'absolute divine revelation to men', and he is emboldened to ask more precisely what is the distinctive element in Christianity, 'that which it does not have in common with philosophical or religious systems'.[2] He finds this specifically Christian element in the biblical conception of time and history. This conception is at the core of primitive Christianity, and Cullmann tells us that we must set aside all other views of time and come to grips with this one which is contained in the most ancient Christian writings.

The view of history which Cullmann sets forth is that there is a sacred history which is co-extensive with general history in its duration, but very much narrower in its scope. This narrow line of sacred history has its midpoint in Jesus Christ, while its beginning and its end merge into the mythical stories—'prophetic history', Cullmann calls them—of the creation and of the last things. The claim is made that 'upon the basis of the slender Christ-line of the biblical history' it is possible 'to render a *final judgment* even on the facts of general history and on the contemporary course of events at any period'.[3] Thus all history, and indeed all time is seen as a cosmic drama, with the narrow line of biblical history as the key to the action. The offence of the gospel, according to Cullmann, is its claim that we should take this slender line of sacred history as the clue to all history and to what happens in nature as well.

That the New Testament writers conceived history in the way that Cullmann indicates is not disputed, though whether this view of history is the kernel of their message is surely more doubtful. Moreover, Cullmann could get support, if he wanted it, from such students of comparative religion as Mircea Eliade for the view that the biblical writers were peculiar in holding a 'straight-line' view of history as opposed to the 'cyclical' view which was general in ancient cultures; though one should add that the biblical view may not have been unique, since it seems that the followers of Zoroaster thought of history in a rather similar way. But what will trouble the modern reader is that the view of time and history advocated by Cullmann seems to be indissolubly linked with an

[1] Professor at Strasbourg, 1930-8; at Basel from 1938.
[2] *Christ and Time*, p. 12.   [3] *Op. cit.*, p. 20.

outmoded geocentric cosmology, with creation only a few thousand years back and the end correspondingly near in the future. When we allow half a million years or more for man on the earth, what sense does it make to talk of the sacred history as co-extensive with all history? When we think of billions of years of cosmic process, during which there probably have been and will be millions of histories analogous to terrestrial history throughout the universe, what sense does it make to talk of a mid-point of time? Perhaps Cullmann's view could be made more plausible by a process of demythologizing, but he himself will not have this. However offensive the New Testament view, we are to accept it as the kernel of absolute divine revelation. This bizarre result shows us the danger of setting up a divine revelation which may not be questioned or criticized in the light of secular knowledge.

97. Two Swedish Theologians
G. Aulén, A. Nygren

Gustaf Aulén[1] (1879-   ) sturdily maintains that theology must exclude foreign philosophical influences and understand the Christian faith from its own centre, for 'the God about whom its speaks reveals himself only to the eye of faith and is not apprehended by any human wisdom'.[2] The revelation in Christ is said to be not only quantitatively but qualitatively different from anything else that might claim to be divine revelation. Yet Aulén wishes to avoid any extreme exclusiveness. The Christian faith 'does not establish any limits around the divine revelation'[3] and indeed any attempt to do so is said to be 'extreme presumption'.

How then does Aulén understand the qualitatively unique Christian revelation? For him, the core of it is a saving act of God in Christ which may be understood in terms of conflict with and victory over the forces of evil—the 'classic' or 'dramatic' view of the atonement, as Aulén calls it. In his brilliant book, *Christus Victor*, Aulén sees in this classic idea of atonement 'the genuine, the authentic Christian faith'.[4] This understanding of Christ's atoning work was, of course, the prevailing one in the early Church, and Aulén's book may be said to have done for the patristic writers what Barth's *The Epistle to the Romans* did for the New Testament— that is to say, it went beyond merely antiquarian considerations to let us hear what the writers have to say to us.

Already in St Irenaeus, we find the view that Christ's atoning work is

---

[1] Professor at Uppsala, 1907–13; at Lund, 1913–30; Bishop of Lund, 1930–3; Bishop of Strängnäs from 1933.
[2] *The Faith of the Christian Church*, p. 11.   [3] *Op. cit.*, p. 30.   [4] *Op. cit.*, p. 176.

the act which liberates man from the forces holding them in subjection. These forces are understood partly in natural terms as sin and death, partly in mythological terms as the demonic powers, which played so large a part in the thinking of the early Church. In some of the patristic writers, such as Origen and St Gregory of Nyssa, the mythological elements were multiplied, and Christ's death was regarded as a ransom paid to the devil. But in any case, the basic idea was that of a conflict and liberating victory.

After the time of St Anselm, the classic idea of atonement was abandoned in the West in favour of a satisfaction theory, but it was revived by Luther and, according to Aulén, it most faithfully represents the thought of the New Testament itself. If it has again fallen into disfavour with modern theologians, this is because they have been misled by its mythological formulation, so that 'no serious attempt was made to penetrate behind the outward form to the underlying idea'.[1] Aulén himself acknowledges that if this way of understanding the Christian faith is to come back, it will need to be differently expressed.[2] Like Cullmann's dramatic view of history, though to a less extent, Aulén's dramatic view of atonement remains entangled with mythological ideas, but he does succeed in presenting his case very persuasively, and there is an obvious relevance in such a presentation of Christianity to an age like our own when we have to contend with vast forces that threaten to enslave or even to engulf mankind.

When we quoted Aulén's remark about 'penetrating behind the outward form to the underlying idea', we were touching on a theological method which has been developed further by another Swedish theologian, Anders Nygren[3] (1890-   ). This is the method of *motif-research*, the attempt to get beyond outward forms and expressions to the underlying *motif* of any outlook, where the word *'motif'* is used in a special sense for that factor in an outlook which gives to it its peculiar character and distinguishes it from all others. All religion, in Nygren's view, seeks to establish fellowship with the eternal, usually conceived as God. Religions are therefore to be distinguished by their underlying *motifs*, that is to say, their underlying ideas as to how this fellowship is supposed to be realized. Judaism, Hellenism and Christianity are characterized by Nygren in terms of three distinct *motifs* which he designates by the Greek words *nomos*, *eros* and *agape* respectively. About *nomos* or 'law' we need not say

---

[1] *Op. cit.*, p. 27.
[2] For an attempt to demythologize the classic idea of atonement, the reader may consult the present writer's essay 'Demonology and the Classic Idea of Atonement', *The Expository Times*, vol. LXVIII, pp. 3-6 and 60-3.
[3] Professor at Lund, 1924-49; Bishop of Lund from 1949.

much—the Jew attains fellowship with God when he fulfils the law. But what about *eros* and *agape*, two words which would normally be translated both as 'love'? What is the distinction between them? This distinction is nothing so simple as the distinction between a sensual love (*eros*) and a spiritual love (*agape*). *Eros* at its highest, as it is found in Plato and in many of the non-Christian religions, is just as spiritual as the Christian *agape*, but no amount of spiritualizing can transform *eros* into *agape*. They remain rival and incompatible *motifs*. '*Agape* stands alongside, not above the heavenly *eros*. There is no way, not even that of sublimation, which leads over from *eros* to *agape*.'[1]

The heavenly or spiritualized *eros* is essentially man's longing upwards to a higher level of being. In Plato, for instance, it means stretching up to the intelligible world of ideas, away from the world of the senses. Yet even at its highest, *eros* is a desiring and an egocentric love, aimed at some satisfaction. *Agape*, on the other hand, is something outside the range of man's natural possibilities, and we could not have known about it but for the Christian revelation. The New Testament uses a new word for 'love' because it is a new kind of love of which it speaks. This is God's love coming to man, and so, in contrast to *eros*, *agape* is theocentric and selfless, seeking not its own.

Although these two kinds of love belong to different orientations of life and represent two competing *motifs*, they have sometimes been mixed together in Christianity, and Nygren sees such a mixture especially in the thought of St Augustine. Luther, by his doctrine of justification by faith alone, is credited with having restored *agape* to its central place in Christianity. We should notice that Nygren by no means denies all value to the non-Christian religions, and he is even willing to see in them some elements of theocentric love. But 'not until Christianity does it break through decisively and claim complete supremacy'.[2]

98. A GERMAN THEOLOGIAN
D. Bonhoeffer

We have already noted that the most important German theologians who like Barth and Brunner revolted against the liberal tradition have so far diverged from the typical dialectical theology that they demand separate treatment. The new theological trends, however, and perhaps especially the insistence on the sovereignty of the divine word over all human words, was an important influence in stiffening the resistance of

[1] *Agape and Eros*, p. 52.   [2] *Op. cit.*, p. 206.

that portion of the German Church which stood out against the encroachments of the Nazi régime. It is appropriate therefore that at this point we
should take note of a young German theologian of the school who took a
leading part in the struggle, although towards the end of his life he had
become critical of the principal figures in the theological revolution, and
was obviously himself on the point of passing on to new and still more
revolutionary ideas.

We refer to Dietrich Bonhoeffer[1] (1906-45). Trained in Berlin, where the
influence of liberal theology still lingered on, he soon identified himself
with the new dialectical theology. Most of his own theologizing was done
in the midst of the Church's struggle in Germany—a struggle in which he
eventually lost his life; so it will not surprise us that his theology is no
abstract speculative affair, but one that impinges on the situations of real
life.

His principal book published in his lifetime is appropriately entitled
The Cost of Discipleship,[2] and is in its central thesis reminiscent of Kierkegaard. Bonhoeffer's protest is against what he calls 'cheap grace', the
kind of 'grace' that is purveyed by an official religion of doctrines, rites
and institutions. Against this he pleads the case for 'costly grace'. This
grace is costly because it demands genuine discipleship, in the sense of an
obedient following of Christ and an exclusive attachment to him; and it
is grace because in such obedient following man receives his true life and
becomes the 'new man'. A somewhat similar view of the Christian life is
expressed in Bonhoeffer's *Ethics* under the idea of 'conformation' to Christ.
'This is not achieved by dint of efforts "to become like Jesus", which is the
way in which we usually interpret it. It is achieved only when the form of
Jesus Christ itself works upon us in such a manner that it moulds our form
in its own likeness.'[3]

The themes expressed here—the basic importance of grace, the centrality of Christ, his lordship over life—are, of course, common to all the
dialectical theologians. But what is perhaps distinctive is the way in
which these themes are relentlessly linked to the here and now of discipleship. There is no hint of 'transcendental irresponsibility' in Bonhoeffer.
This is brought out clearly in the teaching of his *Ethics* about 'the last
things and the things before the last'.[4] Christianity is indeed rooted in and
concerned with the ultimate, the transcendent, the eschatological; but
before the ultimate comes the penultimate, before the last things the next

---

[1] His life was taken up with teaching, writing, ecumenical activities, and the German
Church struggle. Arrested by the authorities in 1943, he was executed two years later.
[2] The German title was simply *Nachfolge* ('discipleship').
[3] *Op. cit.*, p. 18.
[4] *Op. cit.*, p. 79ff.

to last things, and these are the everyday social and ethical concerns of mankind. Concern for the ultimate means that there must also be concern for the penultimate, for the sake of the ultimate.

How Bonhoeffer's ideas would eventually have developed, we cannot know with certainty, but we get hints from his fragmentary *Letters and Papers from Prison*. He frankly criticizes the continental leaders of post-liberal theology—Heim, Althaus, Tillich, Barth, Bultmann—and looks for a new way forward. As Bonhoeffer sees it, the world has come of age. In the modern secularized era, we no longer need to posit a *deus ex machina* to account for the happenings of the world. It is useless, moreover, to look for God in the gaps, and he complains that the existentialists do this when they talk of limit-situations and the like. But Bonhoeffer thinks that the disappearance of false conceptions of God makes way for the truly transcendent God of the Bible, a God who is not a hypothesis or a kind of appendage to the world, and a God who through Christ grasps men not on the boundaries but at the centre of their lives.

These thoughts have revolutionary implications for Christianity. Since the old religious language has become meaningless with the edging out of the picture of the false conception of God, the Christian faith must be communicated in a non-religious or worldly way; and this would seem to be done primarily by living for others, which again means conformation with Christ. And since the Church has usually been concerned to preserve itself, it too must lose itself for others and learn the cost of discipleship. Yet this does not mean that Christianity is reduced simply to an ethic. As we have seen, the Christian way of life is founded upon grace, and so the Christian, as he lives in the world and gives himself for the world, will also have his secret discipline in which he looks beyond the world to the transcendent and the ultimate for the nourishing of his life.

99. CRITICAL REMARKS ON THE THEOLOGY OF THE WORD

That the theologies considered in this chapter have many great merits and that they have achieved profound insights into matters that had been ignored or forgotten in much modern religious thought, is something that no one would wish to deny. What these merits are, we shall see in due course. If there were no such merits, it would be difficult to explain the extraordinary influence which the revolution in theology has exerted. On the other hand, its success has probably been partly due to the fact that by returning to a more dogmatic type of theology and by reinstating at its centre the idea of an absolute divine revelation, it has appealed to those traditionalist and obscurantist elements in the Church who are only too glad to escape the philosophical problems which contemporary thought poses for the Christian religion. Before we talk about the merits of this kind of theology, we shall criticize some of its excesses, especially as found in the views of Barth and Brunner.

1. We must first dispute the view that revelation is the *exclusive* source of theology. We do not, of course, dispute that all knowledge of God must be derived from some revelation or other, though this point is so obvious as to be scarcely worth making. For how could we know anything, whether God or man or nature, unless that which is known reveals or manifests itself to us, to some extent and in some manner? Nor would we wish to dispute the fact, well attested in religious experience, that the knowledge of God, as distinct, let us say, from the knowledge of nature, is of a peculiar kind, in that what we know—God—is active and takes the initiative, as it were, coming to us so that we experience such knowledge as a gift rather than something that we have gained by our own efforts. What we wish to dispute is that any kind of knowing can consist merely in passive acceptance of the given. Always there is discrimination, sifting, testing, questioning, appropriation, before what is given can be known.

Now Barth seems to have been consistent in maintaining that man's part in the knowledge of God is a passive one. We could, of course, agree that in any revelatory experience, man cannot be other than submissive before the numinous presence. But when man begins to reflect on such an experience—and only at this point does theology begin—he must question the revelation itself. Was it indeed a revelation or only an illusion? And this questioning must be done by the light of reason and such human wisdom as the man may possess.

We do not wish to be misunderstood here. We are certainly not pleading a case for any narrow rationalism. It has surely become abundantly clear to us in earlier chapters that no abstract intellectualism can provide a foundation for religion, and that we must take into account the whole man in the entire range of his experience, including any revelatory experiences. But it may be recalled that in discussing the philosophies of personal being—the very philosophies which stress the wholeness of man, and which, especially through Kierkegaard, have had an important formative influence with Barth—we resolutely opposed the tendency of such philosophies to *undervalue* reason;[1] for we maintained that rationality is itself an essential characteristic of the whole man, and that no experience however intense and no conviction however fervent could be exempted from critical examination. In the case of any alleged religious

---

[1] See above, p. 208.

revelation, this means that we must submit it to the scrutiny of reason, both theoretical and practical.

But this seems to be what Barth and Brunner—if we have correctly understood them—will not allow. They do indeed give a place to reason and philosophy in theology, but a lowly place which is entirely subordinate to the sovereign word of God. They likewise allow a sifting and discrimination, but such sifting and discrimination are of our human words in the light of the revelation. What they will not allow is that the revelatory word itself can be either questioned or confirmed by human thought. Their view is that the divine revelation *puts us in question*, so that our attitude must be one of *unquestioning* acceptance and obedience.[1] Bultmann seems to share the view of Barth and Brunner on this matter, and there is an instructive episode in his exchange with Jaspers. The latter asks Bultmann what are the criteria by which he recognizes a divine revelation when one is presented. Bultmann replies that God does not need to justify himself before man. 'No', responds Jaspers, 'I do not say that God has to justify himself, but that everything that appears in the world and claims to be God's word, God's act, God's revelation, has to justify itself.'[2] Jaspers seems to be plainly right here. To put it in more colloquial language, whenever any person or institution or sacred book prefaces its utterances with the formula, 'Thus saith the Lord', we have immediately to ask whether this expression may not be a veiled but impressive way of saying, 'I'm telling you.' We can do this only by testing the alleged revelation by the light of that human wisdom and philosophy which is so despised by some of our theologians.

One consequence of unquestioning acceptance of revelation and the exclusion of human wisdom is that no way remains of discriminating among the many revelations. Mohammed claimed to have divine revelations, so did Kawate Bunjiro and so did Joseph Smith. Perhaps in varying degrees they did have them. But we would want to discriminate among them. It will certainly not do for the Christian theologian to maintain arbitrarily that the biblical revelation is the only true one or the superior one. We are entitled to ask him why it is so. He can scarcely reply that it carries its authentication on its face, so to speak, for every revelation claims to do this. Nor would it be satisfactory to say that the revelation is to be accepted on the authority of the Church or the Bible, for then we would need to raise a new question about the ground of this authority. In the last resort, one is bound to say that the revelation is accepted

[1] Frederick Ferré calls this point of view the 'logic of obedience'. See his acute criticisms in *Language, Logic and God*, pp. 78ff.

[2] *Die Frage der Entmythologisierung*, pp. 42, 69, 85.

because, after it has been tested in every way, it wins the allegiance of reason and conscience. It may be recalled that the Ritschlians, like the Barthians, based our knowledge of God on the Christian revelation; but the Ritschlians also made the claim that the revelation fulfils the aspirations of the practical reason.

We do not think that there is anything in the least impious in our demand that our critical faculties should be directed upon the revelation itself. Those who stake everything on an absolute divine revelation frequently imply that those who will not unquestioningly submit to it are guilty of sin and pride, because they rely on their own powers when they ought to submit to God. It is, of course, an old ecclesiastical trick to accuse those who hold different opinions not only of error but of guilt. If, however, the question of guilt arises here at all, does guilt attach more to the man who *conscientiously* (and maybe even reluctantly) rejects, or to the man who *irresponsibly* accepts?

Someone may object that we have forgotten that man's natural reason is fallen. We would certainly acknowledge not only that our human reason is finite, so that it cannot grasp unaided the truth of God, but also that it is prone to error, and that especially when man is thinking of his own nature, powers, and status in the world, his ideas are liable to be warped by pride and self-interest. We learn this from psychoanalysis as well as from theology. But the remedy is not to forsake reason for some supposed extra-rational authority, but to be more rational, more critical, more conscientious in our thinking. For it has never been held that the very *principles* of our thinking are corrupt. Brunner says it would be senseless to talk of a 'Christian mathematics'; and it would be equally senseless to talk of a 'Christian logic'. If *p* implies *q*, this holds for believer and unbeliever alike.

We may sum up this first criticism of the theology of the word by quoting from a paragraph in the late Archbishop Temple's Gifford Lectures. Temple acknowledges the centrality of revelation, and that revelation is different from rational inference. But 'the error of the Barthian school of theology—for that it contains error when judged by the canons of either natural reason or Christian revelation I cannot doubt—is, like every other heresy, an exaggeration of truth. To deny that revelation can, and in the long run must, on pain of becoming manifest as superstition, vindicate its claim by satisfying reason and conscience, is fanatical.'[1]

2. Our second criticism of the theologians under review concerns their *arbitrary narrowing* of the field of revelation to the biblical revelation, thus

[1] *Nature, Man and God*, p. 396.

denying any genuine knowledge of God to philosophy or the non-Christian religions. Barth completely denies natural theology; philosophical and non-Christian ideas of God are simply idols, having nothing to do with the true God. Brunner allows a meagre place to natural theology, but we have seen that it is so meagre that he will not even call Christianity a 'religion' along with the others—in so far as it has become a religion, it has misunderstood its own nature. This arrogantly exclusive claim for the biblical revelation must be rejected.

Such a claim ignores completely the findings of anthropology, of comparative religion, and of the historical researches of scholars like Troeltsch, which emphasize far more the unity of religions than the differences among them. Furthermore, the assertion that in the Christian revelation the movement is from God to man whereas in philosophy and the non-Christian religions the movement is from man to God is simply not true of most religions and of some types of religious philosophy. Philosophical mystics and the adherents of non-Christian religions also know of the experiences of revelation and grace, of a divine power that breaks in from beyond themselves. How can this be denied by those who have not shared the experiences of these men? And if we are to judge from outside, should not the Christian, above all, make a judgment of charity? Is it credible that Lao-tze, the Buddha, Plato, Plotinus, Bunjiro—to mention only a few—had no inkling, or at least no worthwhile inkling, of such divine realities as there may be? If we are to employ the pragmatic test, which Niebuhr seems to sanction when he says that the proof that someone has had an encounter with the true God and not with an idol is to be seen in his repentance, charity and humility, can we deny that these qualities are to be found outside of the Christian fold—or can we assert that they are always particularly noticeable within it? One might readily believe with Barth that God has revealed himself in the Christian faith, but it is much harder to believe that he has also revealed that he has not revealed himself anywhere else. It would be hard too to say exactly what is distinctive in Christianity—we have sufficiently criticized Cullmann's curious opinion that it is a view of time, while Nygren's contrast between *agape* and *eros* is generally held to be exaggerated, though in any case he does not deny that some kind of theocentric love is found outside of Christianity.

Of course, any religion may be transformed into an idolatry, and this can happen to Christianity itself, when some symbols of our human thought about God are absolutized. Have not Christians frequently unchurched and killed one another because some dogma has been idolized? Does not the claim to exclusive truth engender all kinds of fanaticism and intolerance, especially when divine truth is in question? Some European philosophers used to teach a doctrine of the spiritual supremacy of the Germanic peoples. Perhaps the unconscious factors which produced this dangerous myth are also responsible for the theological claim to exclusive truth for Western religion. It is scarcely surprising that Asian peoples associate Christianity with the imperialism of the West. Of course, Aulén and Nygren are more realistic about this question than Barth. So is the Catholic Church. We may well feel, however, that even their views do not take us far enough, and that a more adequate statement of the relation of the Christian revelation to non-Christian religions and religious philosophies is to be sought in such writers as Hocking, Toynbee and Jaspers.

3. Our third criticism concerns the tendency *to degrade man below the level of personality and responsibility*. We shall see later how Niebuhr criticizes Barth on this point. We may recall how Clement Webb taught that if it is error to exalt man to a level with God, it is equally error to debase him so far that a personal relation with God is no longer possible. One can appreciate and applaud the reaction of theologians against optimistic views of man which neglect his finitude and sin, but if the theologian's purpose is to exalt God over man, this very purpose is defeated if man is degraded too low. The paradoxical consequence of such degradation is that God is degraded too. When Barth writes, 'We are now his property and he has the disposal of us',[1] the picture of God is that of a property-owner disposing of his possessions rather than what is surely the higher picture of a father who loves his undeserving children and makes it possible for them in turn to respond in love. This, however, is one of the points at which Barth has corrected the exaggerated emphasis of his earlier thought by compensating statements, which take cognizance of the 'humanity' of God and allow for a more definitely personal relation between God and man. He does not indeed abandon the element of 'otherness' in God, and he is right in retaining this, as was asserted when we considered the somewhat sentimental idea of God found in some of the Ritschlians.[2] But the starkness of the divine transcendence has undoubtedly been modified in a more personal direction,[3] though one may complain that Barth still makes too much of the passivity of man in his relation to God. Brunner, as we have seen, insists on the personal nature of the relation between God and man, and tells us that this relation belongs to the 'I-Thou' dimension of life; yet even he can occasionally slip into the language of property.[4]

[1] *Dogmatics in Outline*, p. 151.   [2] See above, p. 93.
[3] Maurice Freidman has pointed out that in the revision of his theology, Barth has taken over much of Buber's terminology—*Martin Buber: the Life of Dialogue*, p. 274, n. 1.
[4] See *Revelation and Reason*, p. 26.

It seems to be all a question of hitting the right balance, of recognizing the distance between man and God without exaggerating it by degrading man too far. For if this happens, God himself is degraded. He ceases to be a saviour of souls and becomes a salvager of chattels.

Some of our criticisms have been rather strongly expressed, but in every case they have been criticisms of excesses, and of exaggerations of insights which, more moderately stated, might turn out to be very valuable. It seems that both theology and philosophy move forward by violent swings of the pendulum, and that new or neglected truths can get a hearing only if they are put forward in exaggerated form. Thus when the excesses have been cut away, we can gladly recognize what is of value in the revolution in theology—its recognition of the existential character of religious knowledge, as something which differs from rational inference; its realistic appraisal of man as finite and sinful, over against the myths of human progress and perfectibility; its insistence that the distinctive content of Christianity should be heard on its own merits, and not dragged at the chariot wheels of some philosophy or other. We have seen how Barth himself has modified his views. Brunner was always more moderate. In Aulén and Nygren the more objectionable features of the revolution have largely disappeared, while in Bonhoeffer we are brought to the threshold of fresh developments. The revolution has in fact settled down to become what Daniel Day Williams has happily called 'the theological renaissance.'[1]

Yet even Aulén and Nygren leave us in an unsatisfactory position in so far as they retain that suspicion of and aloofness from philosophy, a mood so characteristic of the revolution. If theology is in some sense a science, it cannot remain content with dramatic pictures but must seek categories in which to express its insights. In a later chapter, we shall see how some theologians have carried the renaissance a stage further by looking to existentialism for the required categories. But before we do so, we have still to look at the effects of the theological revolution upon the English-speaking countries.

[1] See his book, *What Present-Day Theologians are Thinking.*

XXI

POST-LIBERAL THEOLOGY IN THE ENGLISH-SPEAKING COUNTRIES

100. The Impact of the Theological Revolution on Britain and America

IN the English-speaking countries too there has appeared a new theological orientation. This has taken the form of a reaction against the older styles of liberal theology, and themes which liberalism tended to play down, such as the sinfulness of man and the divine initiative in grace and revelation, have come back into the foreground. Partly this is due to the influence of the continental movement. The works of Kierke-gaard, Buber, Barth, Brunner and others have been translated into English and have been widely studied. Partly also one can trace native influences. For instance, the English nonconformist divine, Peter Taylor Forsyth, who died away back in 1921, had already made the transition from a typically 'liberal' position to a theology which emphasized the need for atonement. On the whole, however, we may say that Anglo-American common-sense and empiricism has restrained most of our post-liberal theologians from flying to the extremes and exaggeration which we noted in some of the continental theologians of the word.

In England itself, the continental influence has not been very great. We have already seen what Archbishop Temple thought about the theological revolution,[1] and he may be taken as typical of the native Anglican tradition in theology which looks to reasonableness and conscience as its natural allies, and would (rightly, as we have argued) distrust any exclusion of these in favour of revelation alone. Scotland, with its Calvinist inheritance, has always been much more susceptible to the winds that blow from the continent, and here the influence of Barth and Brunner has been very strong. Yet, as we shall see, the most distinguished representa-tives of post-liberal Scottish theology have tempered continental ex-travagances with native sanity. In the United States, the new theological

---

[1] See above, p. 335.

orientation has also been influential, and has produced at least one thinker who is equal in statute to Barth and Brunner themselves. We refer to Reinhold Niebuhr. But again the continental ideas undergo far-reaching transformations when they fuse with native American influences. It was Brunner who wrote about Reinhold Niebuhr that he 'has made out of the dialectical theology something quite new, something genuinely American'.[1]

In this chapter therefore we have to do with theological ideas which have certain affinities with those considered in the preceding chapter, but which diverge so much from them in some respects as to demand that we examine them independently. We turn first to post-liberal theology in Britain (Section 101), then in America (Section 102), and end with a few general remarks of appraisal (Section 103).

101. POST-LIBERAL THEOLOGY IN BRITAIN
J. Baillie, D. M. Baillie, H. H. Farmer

Probably the most outstanding Scottish theologian in the mid-century years was John Baillie[2] (1886-1960). We have already noted[3] his early interest in Ritschlianism but this soon gave way to an immersion in the new problems being raised by the theological developments on the continent of Europe. In particular, the problem of revelation and of our knowledge of God continually exercised his mind; and while he welcomed many of the insights of such theologians as Barth and Brunner, he received them critically and shunned what he considered to be excesses.

Thus, Baillie is in agreement with the theologians of the word that 'the central thing in religion is not our hold on God but God's hold on us',[4] and that such knowledge of God as we may have is imparted by God himself; but, as we have seen,[5] he thinks that both Barth and Brunner have an inadequate view of that general knowledge of God which men may have apart from the Christian revelation. Again, Baillie acknowledges that 'there was every need for our being recalled from the vagaries and excesses of nineteenth-century immanentism to a proper realization of the transcendence of God';[6] but he complains that the exaggeration of the distance between God and man obscures a genuine truth for which immanentism contended.

Baillie's own view is that all men have some knowledge of God. This

---

[1] *Reinhold Niebuhr*, ed. Kegley and Bretall, p. 29.
[2] After holding several academic posts in the United States, he was professor at Edinburgh, 1934-56.
[3] See above, p. 90.   [4] *Our Knowledge of God*, p. 62.   [5] See above, p. 325.   [6] *Op. cit.*, p. 229.

knowledge is not inferential but direct, and the so-called 'proofs' of God are simply ways of persuading men of something which at bottom they already believe. The knowledge of God is based not on argument but on his presence and self-disclosure, so that all knowledge of him is revealed knowledge. The closest analogy is that of our knowledge of other persons; we do not prove to ourselves that others exist, and there has never been a time when we did not know of their existence. But if the knowledge of God is as direct as our knowledge of our persons, why are some men atheists? Baillie replies that just as a man might be a solipsist in theory and yet is likely to live as if he believed in the reality of his neighbours, so an atheist who denies God with his mind may nevertheless implicitly acknowledge him with his heart, as when he accepts an unconditonal obligation.

Of course, Baillie's purpose is not to exalt 'natural religion', still less the unconscious faith of the atheist. His own conviction is that 'it is impossible that the spiritual life should ever flourish save in the generous atmosphere of an unabridged Christian profession and practice'.[1] Thus, although we cannot set limits to the divine revelation, Baillie goes on to maintain that while God's presence is directly experienced, it is always accompanied by other presences, so that we may speak of our knowledge of God paradoxically as a 'mediated immediacy'.[2] Both in the histories of individuals and of the race, certain events and persons are the media in which the divine presence manifests itself. This in turn points to the necessity of Christ as the focal point in history, where occurs the supreme revelatory encounter with the holy and personal God.

In Donald Macpherson Baillie[3] (1887-1954), John's younger brother, we find the same keen and sympathetic interest in continental dialectical theology, together with the same firm refusal to go to extremes. This is very evident in Donald Baillie's principal work, *God Was In Christ*, which is by common consent one of the most important British theological writings of mid-century. He says frankly in his preface that the theologians with whom he engages in controversy are also those whose contributions have mattered most to him.

Thus Baillie joins with the dialectical theologians in exposing the inadequacies of the liberals' attempt to reconstruct a picture (often sentimentalized and humanized) of the 'Jesus of history', and so to evade the christological problem. But he also criticizes the dialectical theologians' apparent tendency to minimize the Jesus of history in the interests of the Christ of dogma. We are not to follow the pendulum all the way in its swing from Harnack to Barth.[4] As Baillie sees it, belief in a historical

---

[1] *Op. cit.*, p. 68. [2] *Op. cit.*, p. 181. [3] Professor at St Andrews, 1934-54. [4] See above, p. 321.

revelation given in a genuine incarnation makes it impossible to relinquish or disparage an interest in the historical Jesus.

He shows a similar caution in his handling of paradox. He agrees with the dialectical theologians that theology has to make certain statements and then correct them by making other statements which appear to contradict them. Such paradoxes are necessary, because theology transposes a revelatory 'I-Thou' encounter into the distorting medium of objectifying words and sentences. Baillie offers the illuminating analogy of the map-maker who projects the curved surface of the globe upon the flat surface of his map. Distortion is inevitable, but the cartographer may employ two or more different kinds of projection, and although the resultant maps may seem to contradict one another, in fact they correct one another. Yet Baillie also sees the danger of 'falling back too easily upon paradox in our religious thinking'[1] and although he mentions no one by name, he may well have in mind some of the leonine roars[2] of dialectical theology. He insists that we should test every theological paradox by tracing it back to the immediate experiences which justify it, and that we should purge it of all needless contradictions.

It is by means of a paradox well attested in Christian experience that Baillie makes his own contribution to the christological problem—a contribution which is designed to hold the balance between views which either stress the humanity of Christ at the expense of his divinity, or his divinity at the expense of his humanity. It is to the paradox of grace that he appeals, to the experience of action which is truly free and personal, yet action which the Christian ascribes to God. Indeed, for the Christian the word 'God' is said to mean 'the one who at the same time makes absolute demands upon us and offers freely to *give* us all that he demands'.[3] This paradox of grace, itself mediated by Christ, reflects in fragmentary form that perfect union of God and man in the incarnation, and may be our best clue for understanding the person of Christ in a way which acknowledges both his full divinity and his true humanity.

Along with the Baillies we may consider the English theologian Herbert Henry Farmer[4] (1892-   ). He owes much to his predecessor, John Oman,[5] as well as to continental thinkers. Among the latter, Buber has an important influence, and we may say that Farmer's theology, like so many other contemporary theologies, is one of personal encounter. 'The essence of religion in all its forms is a response to the ultimate as personal.'[6] God discloses himself in a personal encounter as at once 'unconditional

---

[1] *Op. cit.*, p. 109.   [2] See above, p. 323, n.2.   [3] *Op. cit.*, p. 121.
[4] Professor at Westminster (Presbyterian) College, 1935-60; also professor in Cambridge University, 1949-60.
[5] See above, pp. 216-18.   [6] *The World and God*, p. 28.

demand' and 'final succour'; and obviously this understanding of God stands in the closest affinity with what we have just noted in Donald Baillie's teaching about the Christian use of the word 'God'.

Farmer's contention is that the interpretation of religion in terms of personal encounter must be extended to the whole range of religious experience. That is to say, we must not confine the personal mode of interpretation to experiences which readily lend themselves to it, such as prayer and worship, but carry it into areas which are often interpreted impersonally. A good illustration of the personal mode of interpretation is found in what Farmer has to say about miracle. It is, he thinks, a fatal mistake to begin the consideration of miracle from an impersonal idea like the suspension of natural law. Such a mistaken procedure leads to those superstitious and magical notions of miracle which have brought the whole idea into disrepute. Miracle is a religious category, and so must be approached from within the sphere of the personal relation to God. When approached in this way, a miracle is understood primarily as a revelatory event. At a critical moment, some event within the world takes on, as it were, a personal dimension, and mediates a personal encounter with God as final succour in the situation.[1]

The same event—let us say, the crossing of the Red Sea—may be seen from the impersonal point of view as a purely natural happening (perhaps involving a lucky coincidence for the Israelites), and from the personal point of view as miracle and God's gracious dealing with his people. The religious man, moreover, will come to believe not just in isolated miracles but in God's providence over the whole course of events. Clearly such beliefs are indemonstrable, and what the religious man is talking about must remain opaque to anyone who has not himself known the dimension of revelatory personal encounter. But Farmer holds that this very indemonstrability is a certification that we really have to do with the ultimate mystery of God.

In his Gifford Lectures, *Revelation and Religion*, Farmer turns his attention to the relation of Christianity to other religions. He disagrees with Brunner's view[2] that Christianity (unless indeed it has fallen away from

---

[1] It is perhaps unfortunate that Farmer complicates his account of miracle by going on to much more speculative considerations. Miracle does not involve a suspension of natural law, but the causal texture of events is open, so that additional factors may supervene and change the course of events from what might have been predicted. A familiar example is voluntary initiation of events, as when I throw a stone into a stream and displace the particles of water from the course which they would otherwise have followed. This analogy cannot be applied *simpliciter* to miracle, for my arm which throws the stone belongs itself within the physical world, and we do not usually think of God as having a body. But Farmer maintains that the divine initiation of events may take place on what he calls the 'underside' of the physical world, conceived, apparently, as a system of creative spiritual monads. See *The World and God*, pp. 145-79.

[2] See above, p. 326.

its genuine essence) should not be called a 'religion' and placed in the same class as other religions. Farmer does not think that Christianity has a monopoly of personal revelation. He would say that it both belongs in the general class of religions, and yet is separate. It is 'not merely one more illustration of the general class of religions, but also—and in this it stands alone—the normative concept of religion itself'.[1]

What makes Christianity unique and normative is the incarnation, and Farmer's intention is to interpret general religious ideas in the light of the normative concept of religion based on the divine self-disclosure in the incarnation. He finds that the various religious types are deficient in one or other of the essential elements of normative religion, so distorting religion as a whole; and this holds not only for the non-Christian religions but also for aberrations within Christianity itself. Into the details of Farmer's analyses we need not go, for we have cited his investigations as one more illustration of the way in which British post-liberal theologians, while willing to go much of the way with their continental colleagues, stop short of extremes. However, it is a question whether Farmer has *sufficiently* dissociated himself from Brunner. There can be no quarrel with his intention to see other religions from a Christian point of view, for we must see them from some point of view, and the idea that we can view them with Olympian detachment is sheer illusion.[2] But if one makes his own point of view absolutely normative, is there not a grave risk of distorting other religions, especially when it is remembered that we see them only from the outside? The present writer would wish to move much further from Brunner, in the direction of something like Hocking's doctrine of 'reconception'.[3]

102. Post-liberal Theology in the United States
Reinhold Niebuhr, H. R. Niebuhr

Reinhold Niebuhr[4] (1892-   ) has already been mentioned as the major figure of post-liberal theology in the English-speaking world. Brunner was quoted[5] as saying that Niebuhr had made of the dialectical theology something quite new; and the differences between Niebuhr and the continental theologians are indeed striking. Perhaps the most obvious difference is that whereas continental dialectical theology tends to be encapsulated within the Church, with Niebuhr theology turns outward upon the world. Although he is an avowed opponent of the optimistic

[1] *Op. cit.*, p. 41.   [2] See above, p. 221.   [3] See above, p. 49.
[4] Professor at Union Theological Seminary, New York, 1928-60.   [5] See above, p. 340.

liberal theology of men like Shailer Mathews, Niebuhr retains the social concern that has been a traditional feature of American religious thought, and he is sternly critical of theologians whose preoccupation with the transcendent and eschatological element in Christianity makes them, as he thinks, indifferent to what is going on in this world. His references to Barth are usually critical, and sometimes sharply so. For instance, Niebuhr writes: 'The theological movement initiated by Karl Barth has affected the thought of the Church profoundly, but only negatively; and it has not challenged the thought outside of the Church at all.'[1] In the course of our exposition, the points of difference will emerge in more detail.

Yet the differences should not blind us to the affinities between Niebuhr and continental dialectical theology. The same kind of influences have been at work—we may mention the impact on Niebuhr of such writers as Kierkegaard, Unamuno, Berdyaev and Buber, as well as the fact that he early found common ground with Brunner. These affinities become apparent if we contrast Niebuhr with the other major theological figure in mid-century America, Paul Tillich.[2] Broadly speaking, one may say that the categories of Niebuhr's thinking are biblical, personal, dramatic and historical, while Tillich's categories are those of philosophy and ontological structure. Tillich is the systematic theologian who aims at presenting his Christian faith in a comprehensive scheme of thought, while Niebuhr is unwilling to be called a theologian, and is cast rather in the role of a prophet who brings the Christian revelation to bear on our social and cultural institutions. Of course, we must be careful not to exaggerate the contrast. But in any case, though he may not be a *systematic* theologian, Niebuhr is obviously a theologian of some sort, and a major one, and we must try to give some account of his teaching.

Niebuhr's concern for society makes him specially interested in the Christian doctrine of man, and it is in the light of this doctrine that he criticizes our modern institutions and the liberal humanistic conceptions that underlie them. To the optimistic view of man, stemming from the Enlightenment and the French Revolution, Niebuhr opposes the traditional Christian doctrine of *sin*. If he takes issue with the liberal view of man, he does so not as a reactionary but as one who accepts a more radical analysis of the human situation. Sin, in Niebuhr's view, is basically pride. Man is finite and creaturely, but he constantly overestimates his powers and his status, and in the extreme case he sets himself up as an absolute, usurping the place of God. 'There is a pride of power in which the human

---

[1] *The Nature and Destiny of Man*, vol. II, p. 165.

[2] For a detailed comparison, see Will Herberg's article 'Reinhold Niebuhr and Paul Tillich', in *The Chaplain* for October, 1959 (vol. XVI, no. 5), pp. 3-9.

ego assumes its self-sufficiency and self-mastery and imagines itself secure against all vicissitudes. It does not recognize the contingent and dependent character of its life and believes itself to be the author of its own existence, the judge of its own values, and the master of its own destiny.'[1]

Niebuhr teaches not only a doctrine of sin, but a doctrine of *original sin*. This again brings Niebuhr into conflict with liberal theologians such as Tennant,[2] whose writings on sin are described by Niebuhr as 'the most elaborate of modern Pelagian treatises'.[3] Sin, Niebuhr claims, is universal in mankind, and this is not only a Christian doctrine but an empirically verifiable fact. There is a universal tendency to sin, and this makes sin *inevitable*. But quite in the manner of dialectical theology, Niebuhr tells us that although sin is inevitable, it is not *necessary*; and this paradox brings us to another aspect of his doctrine of man.

This further aspect is man's *freedom*. Man sins in freedom and is responsible for his actions. What Niebuhr is guarding against here is a view of man which regards him as totally corrupt and proceeds on the assumption that because anything is human, it must therefore be evil. Such a view makes sin the fate which accompanies the being of man, rather than the guilt for which he is historically responsible. It cuts away the ground of responsibility, and makes meaningless the relative rights and wrongs of social morality by lumping together everything human as evil. Here again Niebuhr finds himself at odds with Barth, whose position he criticizes in these words: 'The emphasis upon the difference between the holiness of God and the sinfulness of man is so absolute that man is convicted not of any particular breaches against the life of the human community but of being human and not divine.'[4] Thus Niebuhr's insistence on finitude and sin is not carried to the point at which it would make it difficult or impossible to conceive of a personal responsible existence. Man is a creature, and a sinful creature; but he is also a free spirit, able to transcend nature and to make history.

These incongruous aspects belong alike to the human *self*, which cannot be grasped in terms of rational concepts. 'The whole realm of genuine selfhood is beyond the comprehension of the various systems of philosophy.'[5] Not to the ontological structures of which philosophy speaks are we to look for an understanding of the problem of man, but to the concrete dramas and personal encounters of history, such as the Bible employs as the vehicle of its teaching.

It is in history that we meet the Christian revelation, pointing us beyond the immanent factors of history to the divine grace which can overcome

[1] *The Nature and Destiny of Man*, vol. I, p. 201.   [2] See above, p. 73.   [3] *Op. cit.*, vol. I, p. 262.   [4] *Moral Man and Immoral Society*, p. 68.   [5] *Christian Realism and Political Problems*, p. 178.

sin, complete what man cannot of himself complete, and make available new resources. The gracious personal action of God in history cannot be speculatively demonstrated nor can it be analysed in philosophical concepts. Its only proof lies in such personal encounters themselves, and, Niebuhr adds, in their consequences—a pragmatic allusion which should not be overlooked. 'The creative consequences of such encounters, the humility and charity of true repentance, the absence of pride and pretension, must be the proofs that there has been an encounter with the only true God. The encounter between God and man, as the encounters between men in history, must be by faith and love and not by the discovery of some common essence of reason or nature underlying individuals and particulars.'[1] Thus Christianity may be better understood by artists and poets who have a sense of the dramatic and the historical than by philosophers, scientists and even theologians who seek to reduce all of life to rational coherences.

Finally, we should notice that although Niebuhr writes as a Christian theologian, he does not make an *exclusive* claim for the Christian revelation. We must, he tells us, guard against the assumption that only those who know Christ in the actual historical revelation are enabled to enter into the new life of grace which Christianity offers. 'A "hidden Christ" operates in history. And there is always the possibility that those who do not know the historical revelation may achieve a more genuine repentance and humility than those who do. If this is not kept in mind, the Christian faith easily becomes a new vehicle of pride.'[2]

Scarcely less distinguished as a religious thinker than Reinhold is his younger brother, Helmut Richard Niebuhr[3] (1894-1962). He too castigates liberalism, rationalism and intellectualism in theology with trenchant words. Of American liberalism, he writes: 'A God without wrath brought men without sin into a kingdom without judgment through the ministrations of a Christ without a cross.'[4]

Niebuhr tells us that among the main influences in his thinking are the writings of Barth and Troeltsch. He admits at once that these two make a somewhat bizarre combination, but he claims that it is necessary to bring together their divergent insights.[5] We thus see clearly enough that, like the other English-speaking post-liberal theologians considered in this chapter, Richard Niebuhr is willing to accept many of the insights of continental dialectical theology, yet holds that they stand in need of considerable modification.

---

[1] 'Intellectual Autobiography' in *Reinhold Niebuhr*, pp. 20-1.
[2] *The Nature and Destiny of Man*, vol. II, pp. 113-14, n. 3.
[3] Professor at Yale, 1938-62.   [4] *The Kingdom of God in America*, p. 193.
[5] See the preface to *The Meaning of Revelation*.

The influence of Troeltsch is evident in Niebuhr's interest in the sociology of Christianity, expounded in his book *Christ and Culture*, where he analyses the various attitudes that the Christian may take up towards society, ranging from hostile rejection of cultural influences to something like a complete accommodation to them. Apart from the analyses themselves, however, the interesting point is Niebuhr's recognition that to some extent and in some ways religious attitudes are always conditioned by the historical society in which they are held. It follows then that no theology can prescribe universal conditions for the religious life, beyond its own historical point of view; nor can it posit some sole and exclusive revelation. 'We can speak of revelation only in connection with our own history, without affirming or denying its reality in the history of other communities into whose inner life we cannot penetrate without abandoning ourselves and our community.'[1]

But the acknowledgement of a relative historical point of view does not mean scepticism or subjectivism. 'To the limited point of view of historic Christian faith a reality discloses itself which invites all the trust and devotion of finite, temporal men.'[2] Thus if Niebuhr takes Troeltsch's relativism seriously, he also takes seriously Barth's insistence on the primacy of revelation.

History itself is the *locus* of revelation, but there are two ways in which we can look at history. *External history* is the course of events as viewed by a spectator from outside, and such a point of view could never discover or demonstrate anything like revelation. *Internal history* is *our* history, the kind in which we participate and are personally involved. In the Christian community, we confess the whole biblical tradition as *our* history, and find in it the luminous moments which give meaning to our lives and indeed to all history.

Theologians are always under the temptation to abstract from this history general ideas, and to attempt the construction of a rational system; but in the end, we are always driven back to the concrete history itself and its personal texture. This does not mean that we abandon the attempt to find a unitary pattern. There is such a pattern, but it is a dramatic unity, not an abstract conceptual one. The event of Christ in the fullness of time is the key to this unity, and makes intelligible all history.

[1] *The Meaning of Revelation*, p. 82.   [2] *Op. cit.*, p. 22.

103. REMARKS ON THE POST-LIBERAL
ENGLISH-SPEAKING THEOLOGIANS

After retiring from Edinburgh, John Baillie returned for a year to New York where he had taught a generation earlier, and gave his impressions of the theological developments that had taken place in the intervening period in an address entitled 'Some Reflections on the Changing Theological Scene'.[1] While paying tribute to the achievements of Barth and Brunner, Baillie made it clear that he did not consider that with them theology had reached a resting place. The work of the earlier liberal theologians cannot be ignored, and a new synthesis is clearly needed. Without identifying himself with any of them, Baillie mentioned Bultmann, Tillich and Bonhoeffer as indicating possible ways forward. The work of both John and Donald Baillie may be regarded as an attempt to combine the best insights of both dialectical and liberal theology.

The same is true of the Niebuhrs. We have seen how Richard tries to bring together Barth and Troeltsch, while Reinhold, in an article entitled 'How my Mind has Changed',[2] has expressed his anxiety about the obscurantist elements in dialectical theology, and also his regret for some of his early indiscriminate attacks on liberalism.

The general impression to be gathered from our survey of the British and American theologians considered in this chapter confirms what was said in the introductory section—that the genuine insights of dialectical theology are accepted, but that Anglo-American common-sense and empiricism has saved us from the excesses. We do not indeed wish to give the impression that Britain and America do not have their quota of obscurantists! But in those leading theologians whom we have considered here, sanity and moderation prevail.

Thus, while the place of revelation is made sure, the notion of an exclusive revelation is rejected; while man's sinfulness is fully recognized, he is not deemed to be totally corrupt; while Christianity is permitted to interpret itself, the world is not shut out; while there is stress on the divine transcendence, the distance between God and man is not made so great as to preclude a genuinely personal relation between them. Indeed, the most obvious characteristic that is common to all the theologies considered in this chapter is the central place which they give to personal encounter—and in this they would seem to stand nearest to Brunner among the continentals. In this concern with the person-to-person relation, one

[1] *Union Seminary Quarterly Review* for January, 1957 (vol. XII, no. 2), pp. 3-9.
[2] *The Christian Century* for May 11, 1960.

cannot help being impressed by the remarkable debt which Christian theology has come to owe to the Jewish philosopher Martin Buber.

But it is this very matter of personal encounter that must give us pause, and make us ask whether we can go further. Personal encounter can surely be no more than an analogue of man's relation to God. Can we analyse what is involved more precisely? The Niebuhrs in particular seem to say that we should be content with dramatic pictures. But to this we must say what we have already said in respect of Aulén and Cullmann (to the latter of whom Richard Niebuhr seems very close, though he expresses himself differently). We must say, in effect, that if theology is a science in some sense, it must go beyond the dramatic pictures to some conceptual structures. Now the Niebuhrs are surely right in saying that if we try to employ the abstract concepts that are applicable to things, we are bound to miss or distort what is most characteristic in personal existence. But are there perhaps conceptual structures which are applicable to personal existence itself, and drawn from it? And might there perhaps even be a way from here towards an understanding of the being in which both persons and things participate? Such are the questions on which some of our contemporary existentialist and ontological philosophers claim to throw light. We must now turn to them, and to the theologians who have made use of their work.[1]

---

[1] Since this chapter was written, there have been published books by two of the theologians noticed here. John Baillie's death occurred shortly before he was due to give Gifford Lectures at Edinburgh. The lectures were already complete in manuscript, and have been published as *The Sense of the Presence of God*. They restate the main thesis of *Our Knowledge of God*, taking account of developments in philosophy and theology since the appearance of the earlier book. H. R. Niebuhr published shortly before his death a book entitled *Radical Monotheism and Western Culture*, in which his thought seems to be tending in the direction of Tillich's and towards a greater ontological interest. He describes radical monotheism as 'the gift of confidence in the principle of being itself', and among the henotheistic distortions of Christianity which he castigates is the kind that makes Christ the 'absolute centre of value', forgetting that, as the one who 'reconciled us to the source of being', Christ points beyond himself to the One—see pp. 59, 89.

XXII

EXISTENTIALISM AND ONTOLOGY

104. HUMAN EXISTENCE AND ITS PROBLEMS

LIKE logical empiricism, existentialism is not a body of doctrines but a way of doing philosophy. It is the way which begins by interrogating existence, where by 'existence' is understood the kind of being that belongs to man in his concrete living, acting and deciding. This human existing is contrasted with the being of everything that has a fixed essence. The peculiarity of human existence is that any man is always on his way, he is always standing before possibilities of decision. His being is always fragmentary and incomplete, so that he has no fixed essence, or, as some would put it, his essence is to exist.

It is obvious that existentialism continues along the lines indicated by the philosophies of personal being which we surveyed in an earlier chapter.[1] As was then indicated, some of the philosophers of personal being might be called 'existentialists'. But contemporary existentialism brings the earlier ideas to a more sophisticated stage—though some might argue that in so doing it has lost the most valuable insights implicit in those ideas. In the first place, the contemporary existentialists are for the most part interested in the form and structure of existence, and try to find categories in which they may describe it. Many of them use the method of phenomenology. Some of the older thinkers, as we have seen, were prophets rather than philosophers, contenting themselves for the most part with drawing attention to the concrete realities of existing, with its discontinuities and paradoxes. The violence of their reaction against a superficial intellectualism could and sometimes did break out in the form of irrationalism. But the charge of irrationalism could scarcely be brought against men like Heidegger, Jaspers and Sartre, who, although they rightly take account of the non-rational factors in existence, do not simply retreat into paradox and poetry but endeavour to give an account in the form of a philosophical analysis of how existence is constituted. Jaspers explicitly defends reason against its denigrators; and while Sartre has used literary

[1] See above, pp. 193ff.

forms for the expression of his thought, and Heidegger has become increasingly interested in poetry, both of these thinkers have shown themselves capable of the strictest philosophical analyses. In the second place,
the older philosophers of personal being, from Kierkegaard onwards,
were wont to lay stress on subjectivity. But most contemporary existentialists are highly suspicious of the notion of 'subject', and would say that
in any case a pure subject could not 'exist', since existence is precisely the
encounter of the self with what is other than the self, whether the world, or
other selves, or God.

Contemporary existentialists, like the older philosophers of personal
being, look with disfavour on speculative metaphysics, as a kind of
philosophy which deals in rational essences and disregards concrete
existence. Yet this does not hinder some of them from becoming onto-
logists, and from trying to advance from the understanding of man's being
to an understanding of being itself. Indeed, it could be argued that one
cannot properly understand man's *being* without already having some
conception of being as a whole. Heidegger, by far the most original and
profound of the philosophers to be considered in this chapter, thinks of
himself primarily as an ontologist, and his existential analytic is simply
the route towards the wider question of being in general.

Since existentialism is, as we have said, not a body of doctrines but a
philosophical attitude, it issues in very diverse points of view, and this is
particularly noticeable when we inquire what the existentialists have to
say about religion. At one end of the scale, Sartre identifies existentialism
with atheism. At the other, we find Catholic existentialists, though it may
be noted that existentialism was one of the philosophies singled out for
unfavourable mention in the encyclical *Humani Generis* of 1950. Jaspers'
philosophy is compatible with liberal Protestantism, while Heidegger's
is definitely religious and mystical in tone, though it would not coincide
with any of the commonly accepted forms of Christianity.

It will not surprise us that existentialism has made its influence felt
very powerfully in theology. No more than the philosopher can the
theologian be content with 'telling a story', as Plato expressed it,[1] and the
categorial structures worked out by the existentialists suggest a way of
expressing in a formal manner the insights which the Bible expresses in its
concrete historical or mythical stories. Thus the theologian sees an opportunity to pass beyond the stage to which Aulén and Niebuhr had conducted us. The most famous case has been Bultmann's use of the Heideggerian *existentialia* for his project of demythologizing the New Testament,
but other theologians have worked on similar lines, while Tillich has

[1] *Sophist*, 242c.

gone on from existential to ontological analysis in his treatment of theological problems.

Existentialism, as a radical interrogation of human existence, arises when violent upheavals and deep-rooted anxieties bring the question of man's own being forcibly to his notice. It is not surprising therefore that so far existentialism has flourished chiefly on the continent of Europe, and has exerted comparatively little influence in the stable and relatively un-scathed societies of Britain and America. Our survey therefore will first consider existentialism in Germany (Section 105), and then the French varieties (Section 106). Then we shall pay attention to the influence of existentialism in theology (Section 107) before going on to a critical summary (Section 108).

105. EXISTENTIALISM IN GERMANY
M. Heidegger, K. Jaspers

Martin Heidegger[1] (1889-   ) is interested in the problem of being rather than merely in the problem of human existence. But the being of man provides a way of access to the problem of being in general, for man, as Heidegger expresses it,[2] is like a clearing in being, the *locus* where being is lit up and becomes unconcealed—and for Heidegger 'unconcealedness' is equivalent to truth, in the primordial sense of *aletheia*. Man has a way into the truth of being because he 'exists'. A rock or a river does not exist; their kind of being is called by Heidegger 'presence-at-hand'. The peculiarity of 'existence', as the term is used here, is that what exists not only has being but has some understanding of being; its being is dis-closed to it in its very mode of being. Heidegger believed that by philo-sophical analysis of the understanding of being which goes along with existence, that is to say, by making unconcealed the basic structures or *existentialia* of existence, light may be thrown on the question of being itself.

In Heidegger's analysis, human existence is exhibited as *care*, and this has a threefold structure. Firstly, it is constituted by *possibility*. Man's being gets projected ahead of itself. The entities which are encountered are transformed from being merely 'present-at-hand' to being 'ready-to-hand' to man in their serviceability, and out of them man constructs an instrumental world which is articulated on the basis of his concerns.

[1] Professor at Marburg, 1923-28; at Freiburg, 1928-45. He was suspended after the Second World War on account of his alleged sympathies with the Nazi régime.
[2] *Being and Time*, p. 133; p. 222. (Page-numbers are those of the German editions; they appear in the margins of the English translation.)

Secondly, care is constituted by *facticity*. Man is not pure possibility but factical possibility, that is to say, the possibilities open to him at any time are conditioned and limited by many circumstances which he has never chosen—his historical situation, his race, his natural endowments, and the like. Heidegger speaks of man's "thrownness"; man is thrown into a world to exist there in his situation, but his whence and his whither are concealed from him. Man's situation as a finite entity thrown into a world where he must project his possibilities is not disclosed to him by theoretical reasoning but rather in his affective states, or moods, of which the basic one is *anxiety*. The third constitutive factor in care is *fallenness*. Man flees from the disclosure of anxiety to lose himself in absorption with his instrumental world, or to bury himself in the anonymous impersonal existence of the mass, where no one is responsible. When this happens, man has fallen away from his authentic possibility into an inauthentic existence of irresponsibility and illusory security. In the mode of inauthenticity, existence is scattered and fragmentary.

The way to authenticity lies through hearing conscience, understood as the summons to take upon us our finitude and guilt. Care is understood in terms of temporality—a finite temporality which reaches its end with death. In authentic existence, death ceases to be just something that happens to us, breaking in to shatter our existence. Death is itself taken up into possibility, and an authentic existence is projected upon death as its capital potentiality for being. All possibilities are evaluated in the light of death as the capital possibility, and when one lives in the anticipation of death, one lives with a resoluteness which brings unity and wholeness to the scattered self. Eternity does not come into this picture, for wholeness is attainable within man's finite temporality itself, and he lays hold on each unique unrepeatable possibility in the light of the master possibility of death. When man ceases to run away from the disclosure of anxiety that he is thrown into death, and when he resolutely anticipates death as his supreme possibility, he reaches an unshakable joy and equanimity.

Is this, then, a kind of nihilism in which man simply accepts the nothingness of his being and of all his possibilities? At first glance, this might seem to be the case, if it were not that death plays so positive a part in Heidegger's analysis. Only by living through the nothingness of death in anticipation does one attain an authentic existence. We must look more closely at what Heidegger means by 'nothing'. We have already noted Carnap's criticism that Heidegger talks of 'nothing' as if it were some entity or other.[1] Heidegger is well aware of this danger. 'The idea of

---

[1] See above, p. 306.

"logic" itself comes undone in the whirlpool of a more primordial inquiry.'[1] The 'nothing' about which he is talking is not an abstract idea but the 'nothing' which is experienced in that mood of anxiety or malaise when the entire world of entities sinks into an undifferentiated meaninglessness. This 'nothing' is decidedly not an entity, since it encounters us precisely in the absence of all entities. 'This wholly other to all entities is the non-entity. But this nothing essentiates as being.'[2] For being itself is not another entity; we cannot say that being is, nor can we make it an object as if it were an entity among other entities. Only the confrontation with nothing can awaken in us the wonder about being, which expresses itself in the question of Leibniz: 'Why are there entities at all, and not just nothing?' This is no ordinary question, and as Heidegger interprets it, it points us away from entities to being. It is an inescapable question for man, who is confronted with the nothing in his own being. 'Each of us is grazed at least once, perhaps more than once, by the hidden power of this question.'[3]

But Heidegger now approaches the question of being more directly. He does not approach it through entities, not even through man, the existent entity, but tells us that we need another kind of thinking, a thinking which is submissive to being itself.[4] Because of his essential relation to the truth of being, man is the guardian of being, he responds to the call of being, while being graciously opens itself to him. Here we seem to have passed into a mystical region of thought, reminiscent perhaps of Meister Eckhart and the Zen Buddhists.[5] In any case, the religious dimensions of his philosophy have become apparent. Being 'is' not God, for Heidegger thinks that the God of Christianity has been conceived as an entity.[6] Yet being seems to have all the characteristics of God, even grace. Heidegger's religion, as Richard Kroner remarks, 'is not all too far from the official religion which has been confessed by Christendom for two thousand years'.[7]

But although Heidegger's ontology makes an important contribution in its own right to the philosophy of religion, his main influence on contemporary theology has come not directly from his ontology but indirectly through Bultmann from the existential analytic. Heidegger

[1] *Was ist Metaphysik?*, p. 37.
[2] *Op. cit.*, p. 45.
[3] *An Introduction to Metaphysics*, p. 1.
[4] *Was ist Metaphysik?*, p. 13.
[5] William Barrett mentions Heidegger's admiration for the works of D. T. Suzuki in his foreword to the latter's *Zen Buddhism*.
[6] But see below on Tillich, p. 367.
[7] 'Heidegger's Private Religion' in *Union Seminary Quarterly Review* for May, 1956 (vol. XI, no. 4), p. 35.

indeed says that philosophy can be no substitute for theology,[1] but he also maintains that if theology is to attain to conceptual clarity, it must have regard to those existential structures which are exhibited in *Being and Time*. For in so far as theology has to do with man in his temporal and historical existence, it treats of themes which must be studied existentially. In particular, Heidegger believes that the existential analytic provides for the investigation of history in a way which directs attention not to the reconstruction of past facts but to the elucidation of repeatable possibilities of authentic existence; and, as we shall see, it is this approach which Bultmann, in his demythologizing project, applies to the historical element in Christianity.

Karl Jaspers[2] (1883–1969) began his career as a psychiatrist, but turned to philosophy and has become one of the most eminent among the existentialists. Like Kierkegaard, he recognizes the polarities, tensions and discontinuities of experience, so that philosophy is to be understood as a continuing activity, and can never arrive at some final all-embracing system. On the other hand, Jaspers stresses the importance of reason, but a reason which takes account of the irrational factors in experience and does not try to explain them away in any one-sided manner.

Three areas of being are distinguished. There is an objectifiable realm, which includes not only physical objects but also human ideas, activities and institutions so far as these can become objects. Then there is the realm of existence, our own distinctive kind of being. This cannot be objectified or derived from objects, and we are aware of it in such activities as deciding and acting. Thirdly, there is transcendence or God. This is being in itself.

Thus man's being is, as it were, surrounded by the being of the world and by transcendence, and he can stand in relation to both of these. A merely secular existence which relates itself only to the world gets entangled in its own apparatus, while the personal character of existence is lost in the collective mass. This is 'life without existence, superstition without faith'.[3] It is significant that Jaspers considers that the axis of human history, 'the point most overwhelmingly fruitful in fashioning humanity', is to be identified with 'the spiritual process that occurred between 800 and 200 BC'.[4] This was the period of prophets, ethical teachers and religious geniuses; and marks the maturing of man as a spiritual and personal being. As such, he has a relation to transcendence. But how does this relation become known to him? Jaspers' answer is in

---

[1] *An Introduction to Metaphysics*, p. 7.
[2] Professor at Heidelberg, 1920-48; at Basel from 1948.
[3] *Man in the Modern Age*, p. 43.   [4] *The Origin and Goal of History*, pp. 1ff.

terms of his doctrine of the 'limit-situation'. In his existence, man sometimes comes, so to speak, to the end of his tether, perhaps in the face of
sickness or guilt or death. At the limit, he comes to grief, and becomes
aware of the phenomenality of his existence. This is where transcendence
reveals itself. Of course, this revelation is not automatic nor is it like the
perception of an object. The encounter with transcendence belongs to the
realm of the 'comprehensive', by which is meant 'the being that is neither
only subject nor only object, that is rather on both sides of the subject-
object split'.[1] Since transcendence is not grasped as an object, we cannot
know it or talk about it in an objective way. Indeed, it makes itself known
through events in the world, but only obliquely in 'ciphers', to use Jaspers'
term, and it recedes into depths beyond our comprehension.

It is on the basis of this understanding of human existence that Jaspers
erects his 'philosophical faith'. Such a faith is not demonstrable, it offers
us no dogmas, and it does not deal in objective truths. Yet on the other
hand it is not just something subjective, a believing state of mind. It is
rooted, as we have seen, in the comprehensive. It recognizes a transcendent God, an absolute imperative, and the dependent status of the empirical
world. It is the recognition of the command of the authentic self, of what
man is eternally in the face of the transcendent, to his empirical and
temporal existence.

Such a faith must be lived out by the individual in the face of the
revelation of the transcendent to him in the present, so that this kind of
faith cannot appeal to events of the past. But we all live in a tradition, and
as far as the Western world is concerned, we have 'our specific roots in
biblical religion'.[2] Jaspers thinks it important that this biblical religion
should be transformed and revived, so that its accumulated wisdom of
transcendence and the limit can speak to us again. We cannot, however,
shelter under it, but only renew it in our own experience.

On one point, we should notice, Jaspers is severely critical of biblical
religion. The claim has often been made for it that it mediates an *exclusive*
revelation of God to man. This cannot be the case if revelation must be
present for the faith of each individual, and can be present in any limit-
situation. Furthermore, the claim to exclusive truth is seen by Jaspers as
putting an end to that openness of communication which must be dear to
the philosopher, and as a divisive influence which makes men intolerant
and even fanatical towards each other. Hence Jaspers will have no truck
with any claim to exclusive truth, or to a once-for-all revelation at some
past date. We have got to recognize that grace and revelation are present
and universal. This, however, does not mean that all religions are to be

---

[1] *The Perennial Scope of Philosophy*, p. 14.   [2] *Op. cit.*, p. 41.

merged into a syncretistic faith, for we cannot travel on all the roads at the same time. Nor does it mean a withdrawal into private religions, for Jaspers recognizes that neither philosophy nor philosophical faith can be a substitute for a living historical religion with its cult, scriptures and community. What he does ask is that men should be loyal to their own faiths without impugning the faiths of others. If openness of communication is to be preserved, then we must 'become concerned with the historically different without becoming untrue to our own historicity'.[1]

106. Existentialism in France
J.-P. Sartre, G. Marcel, L. Lavelle

No doubt if a member of the general public having only a bowing acquaintance with philosophy were asked to name an existentialist, he would mention Jean-Paul Sartre[2] (1905-   ). This is perhaps unfortunate, since Sartre represents existentialism at its most negative and egocentric pitch, and this is the impression of the movement that has gained currency, so that it is often dismissed without serious consideration as merely a symptom of twentieth-century decadence. But no one could deny Sartre's philosophical ability, though he stands on a lower plane than the two German thinkers whom we have considered. Sartre indeed borrows the basic ideas of his philosophy from Heidegger, but he works them out entirely in his own way, and it may be added that Heidegger is not flattered by this French imitation and adaptation.[3]

In Sartre's view, existentialism is equated with atheism. When he speaks of 'God', he means the ideal or limit which man holds out as the aim of his existence. Basically, man is the desire to be God, that is to say, the desire to exist as a being which has its sufficient ground in itself, *ens sui causa*. But this idea is self-contradictory, there can be no God and so man himself, as the desire to be God, is 'a useless passion'.[4]

The idea would be self-contradictory as involving the union of the two incompatible modes of being which Sartre's philosophy recognizes—the *en-soi* or 'in-itself' and the *pour-soi* or 'for-itself'. The *en-soi* consists of material things, and is characterized by *being*—massive, uncreated, opaque being, almost nauseating in its senseless plenitude. The *pour-soi* is consciousness, which constitutes itself by an act of negation whereby it separates itself from the *en-soi*. The *pour-soi* is freedom and transcendence—freedom to order a world and to create values. But freedom is precisely

---

[1] *Op. cit.*, p. 172.   [2] French teacher, novelist, dramatist and philosopher.
[3] See his *Brief über den Humanismus*.   [4] *Being and Nothingness*, p. 615.

a *lack of being*. Sartre can say, in his famous phrase, that man is 'condemned to be free'.[1] Man is, so to speak, an existence in search of an
essence, and human existence is a failure because its fundamental desire
for a godlike being is impossible.

Further frustration is caused to the *pour-soi* by other existents. When
someone looks at me, he makes me his object, takes away my freedom, and
perhaps makes me ashamed. There is, in Sartre's view, no way of coming
to terms with the other that does not end in frustration. In the well-known
expression from his play, *No Exit*: 'Hell is other people.'

Death closes off the existence of the *pour-soi*. Sartre rejects Heidegger's
view that death is the supreme possibility of human existence. Death is
not a possibility at all, but the cancellation of possibility. It is the final
absurdity of existence.

This is undoubtedly a depressing philosophy, though of course the fact
that it is depressing does not settle the question of whether it might be
true. There can be no denying the brilliance of some of Sartre's analyses,
which strip away the superficial appearances and probe into the core of
human existence. On the other hand, since he has turned more and more
to politics, he has advocated an attitude of 'engagement' whereby the
individual, in spite of his isolation, works with others in his own situation
for common ends; while Wilfrid Desan tells us that Sartre has become less
dogmatic in his atheism and materialism.[2] Nevertheless, it is the Sartre
of *Being and Nothingness* who is likely to be remembered. If we ask what
the views which he expresses there have to do with religious thought, then
it might be replied with David E. Roberts: 'The illuminating and bracing
thing about him is that he had the courage to follow the consequences of
his atheism to the bitter end.'[3] Sartre shows us what the choice really is,
and perhaps even his despairing view of existence is closer to Christianity
than much complacent optimism.

In contrast to Sartre, Gabriel Marcel[4] (1889-) talks of a 'metaphysic
of hope'. Though he dislikes the existentialist label, Marcel, like Sartre,
philosophizes by making detailed phenomenological analyses of human
situations. But Marcel's analyses lead him to quite different conclusions.

We should first guard ourselves against any mistaken interpretation of
the expression, 'metaphysic of hope'. Marcel certainly does not think it
possible to produce a metaphysic in the sense of an all-embracing rational
system. Hope, in his terminology, is a 'mystery', and he makes an important

---

[1] *Op. cit.*, p. 439.
[2] See the new foreword (1960) to his book, *The Tragic Finale*.
[3] *Existentialism and Religious Belief*, p. 225.
[4] French teacher, writer and philosopher. He was received into the Catholic Church
in 1929.

distinction between 'mysteries' and 'problems'. A *problem* is limited in its scope, it can be approached objectively from the outside, and it may be solved in a way that is susceptible of empirical verification. A *mystery*, on the other hand, cannot be grasped from the outside. Not only hope is a mystery, but so, for instance, are freedom, love, evil, and the basic mystery is that of being. Here we can only understand what is in question through becoming involved in it ourselves. This does not indeed rule out reflection, but it makes impossible any purely objective approach and any cut-and-dried solutions. The realm of 'mystery' in Marcel is something like the realm of the 'comprehensive' in Jaspers, a realm where subject and object are so involved in each other that they cannot be separated off. Just because we exist as human beings, we cannot evade these mysteries.

Somewhat parallel to the distinction between problems and mysteries is that between 'having' and 'being'. *Having* is an external egocentric relationship; it gives power over objects, whether these be material possessions or our own ideas. Yet the very things that we have or desire to have tend to tyrannize us. 'The more we allow ourselves to be the servants of having, the more we shall let ourselves fall a prey to the gnawing anxiety which having involves'; we concentrate our attention 'on the poor little counters spread out in front of us which we feverishly reckon up over and over again without respite, tormented by the fear of being foiled or ruined'.[1] We cannot indeed get away from having, but having must be transformed by *being*; and being brings us into a different kind of relationships, in which the sharp distinction of the self and its objects gives way to reciprocity, and existence transcends any narrow egocentricity.

We can already see the radical divergence of Marcel's thought from the egocentricity of Sartre. Marcel himself has summarized the train of his thought in the following sentence: 'Person—engagement—community —reality; there we have a sort of chain of notions which, to be exact, do not readily follow from each other by deduction (actually there is nothing more fallacious than a belief in the value of deduction) but of which the union can be grasped by an act of mind.'[2] This scheme of ideas may be filled out by noting that in Marcel's view what is typical of a person is that he is continually engaging himself—for instance, he says, 'I'll see you to-morrow at three o'clock.' But in doing this, he is already existing in a community. Like Buber, Marcel finds the *locus* of human existence not in the isolated 'I' but in the 'we'. The central virtue of the community is *fidelity*, and it is because of the high place which he gives to this idea that Marcel can be so much in sympathy with the philosophy of Josiah Royce, whose thought, it will be remembered, culminated in the idea of 'loyalty'.[3]

[1] *Homo Viator*, p. 61.　　[2] *Op. cit.*, p. 22.　　[3] See above, p. 37.

But fidelity itself has its ontological foundations, and points beyond the human community to the being of God. Thus when once the limits of a narrowly egocentric existence are transcended, we do not halt until we come to God. The metaphysic of hope is therefore like an escape from captivity, the response of man's finite being to the wider being of God.

If Marcel is reluctant to accept the existentialist label, it is still less applicable to another Catholic thinker, Louis Lavelle[1] (1883-1951). Yet his philosophical ideas are sufficiently close to those which we have been considering to justify his inclusion in this section. Lavelle's interpretation of human existence again presents us with a sharp contrast to the views of Sartre, for whereas the latter thinks that consciousness constitutes itself by an act of separation from being, Lavelle maintains that self-awareness is the discovery of participation in being.

Being is one and univocal. 'And if being is univocal, it is clear that one cannot discover the presence of the self without in that same act discovering the total presence of being.'[2] My being is inserted into total being, my thought into a universal thought, my will into an infinite will. Everything that is, is through its participation in a pure infinite act of being, which is God, and this is established not by rational metaphysical inference but from our experience of the participation of the self in being—'a metaphysical experience at once primitive and permanent'.[3] This experience is reciprocal in its nature. Being is present to the self, and it is through a subjective act of awareness that being can be known; but on the other hand, the self is present to being, which gives to the self its very existence. Thus it is the presence of the self to being that has ontological priority. 'The presence of being to the self has its foundation in the presence of the self to being.'[4]

Thus we live in the presence of being, a total being in which all finite existents participate. We pass from one instant to the next within the interior of a constant presence. But this total presence of being is obscured for us because of our tendency to concentrate attention on particular presences, whether of persons or things. Lavelle would agree with Heidegger at least in this, that forgetfulness of being disorients our relations with ourselves, with other people, and with our world. He thinks that the troubles of the self arise mainly from the fact that it hopes, by multiplying particular presences, to enlarge its nature and to give itself power and happiness. But when it follows such courses, the self is doomed to frustration, and what it seeks must flee from it indefinitely. Its way to renewal

---

[1] Professor at the Collège de France, 1941-51.
[2] *De l'Être*, p. 248. A section of this book is available in English translation by F. Crosson.
[3] *Ibid.*   [4] *Op. cit.*, p. 262.

and to right relationships lies in the realization that in every particular presence there is given the total presence of being.

107. EXISTENTIALISM AND THEOLOGY
R. Bultmann, F. Gogarten, F. Buri, P. Tillich

Rudolf Bultmann[1] (1884-   ) was associated with Barth and others in the revolt against the old liberal theology of Harnack and the 'Jesus of history' school.[2] Bultmann's work was mainly in the field of New Testament studies, where he took up and developed the form-critical method that had originated with Weiss,[3] and came to very sceptical conclusions about the New Testament documents as records of historical facts. 'The historical person of Jesus was very soon turned into a myth in primitive Christianity.'[4] It is this myth which now confronts us in the New Testament, and it is impossible to get behind it to the historical Jesus. The historical facts, whatever they may have been, have undergone an irreversible metamorphosis into the story of a divine pre-existent being who became incarnate and atoned by his blood for the sins of men, rose from the dead, ascended into heaven, and would, as was believed, shortly return on the clouds to judge the world and inaugurate the new age. The central story is embellished and illustrated by peripheral legends which tell of miracles and wonders, voices from heaven, victories over demons, and the like. These ideas belong to 'myth', the undifferentiated discourse of a prescientific age, when events both in the world of men and in the world of nature were assigned to the direct agency of occult force whether divine or demonic.

Such a mythical understanding has become impossible in our time, for we think of men as responsible for their actions, and of natural events as explicable in terms of factors immanent in nature itself. If Christianity is inseparably tied up with ancient mythology and cosmology, how can we still hold to it? Bultmann replies that the New Testament must be 'demythologized', that is to say, translated out of the mythical form of discourse. He believes that hidden in the myth is a *kerygma*, a divine word addressed to men. This word is obscured for us by the mythical framework in which it is set, but, by demythologizing, it can be disengaged from this framework so that it is set free to address the men of the post-mythical age.

But into what language can we translate the Christian myth? It is when we ask this question that we come to the relation between Bultmann

---

[1] Professor at Marburg, 1921-51.   [2] See above, pp. 84ff.   [3] See above, p. 145.
[4] *Primitive Christianity in its Contemporary Setting*, p. 200.

and the existentialist philosophers. The *kerygma*, he believes, sets before us a possibility of human existence for which we are summoned to decide. To demythologize the New Testament is to elucidate, in a form freed from myth, the understanding of our own existence which the *kerygma* sets before us. In order to do this, we need categories in which to express the structure of human existence. Bultmann believes that Heidegger's existential analytic provides us with the conceptual framework which we need for the task of demythologizing, and in his *Theology of the New Testament* he shows how St Paul's understanding of man can be given fresh relevance when it is related to the context of existentialist thinking. Pauline terms like 'sin', 'faith', 'flesh', 'spirit'—terms which have long since become obscure or trivialized—come to life when interpreted in the light of the Heideggerian *existentialia*, and we begin to see that the New Testament, in spite of its seeming remoteness from our ways of thinking, confronts us as much as the existentialist philosophers do with something that is thoroughly relevant and contemporary—the choice between authentic and inauthentic existence.

It is in the light of these existential concepts that the myths of the New Testament are to be understood. As an example, let us consider the eschatological myth, which the first Christians took over from Jewish apocalyptic. According to this myth, the cosmic drama was nearing its crisis. The present age would shortly be brought to an end through a supernatural intervention, there would be a final judgment, and men would be assigned to destinies either of bliss or torment. The first Christians' expectation of an imminent end turned out to be mistaken, and nowadays we do not expect this kind of thing at all. But the ideas of the myth can be interpreted in relation to the here and now of our own existence. Every individual—as Heidegger so strongly emphasizes—stands before the imminent end—his own death. In his everyday decisions, he works out his own judgment, as he lays hold on his authentic being or loses it. When transferred to actual individual existence, the ideas of the myth begin to make sense, and indeed recover something of their urgency, with its stress on our responsibility as we choose our unrepeatable possibilities in the face of the end. Bultmann points out that this kind of demythologizing begins in the New Testament itself. The Fourth Gospel, written after the hope of an early return of Jesus had begun to fade, brings eternal life and judgment into the here and now.

The centre of the Christian story lies in the death and resurrection of Christ. Here we have a historical core—the crucifixion of Jesus—but again it has been transferred into a mythological setting, and is exhibited as an atoning sacrifice. 'What a primitive mythology it is', says Bultmann, 'that a divine being should become incarnate, and atone for the sins of men through his own blood!'[1] The resurrection is likewise classed as myth, and its function is to bring out the significance of the cross. But here again Bultmann translates into the language of existence. The cross and resurrection are experienced as atonement and new life when we take them into our own existence, when we give up all worldly security for a new life that is lived out of the transcendent. St Paul already anticipates this demythologizing when he understands baptism as a dying and rising with Christ. This is the core of the Christian proclamation, and it may be described as a new self-understanding. It summons men to the decision of faith, whereby they die to the world in order to live by the unseen reality of God.

It might seem that Bultmann has entirely transformed the Christian message into the symbolic statement of a philosophy of existence, but he would reply that this is not the case. Christianity differs from any philosophy in that it proclaims a gracious revelatory act of God which makes authentic existence possible for sinful men. But this act is not just something past, something that happened once for all on a datable occasion. It is rather what Bultmann calls an 'eschatological event', that is to say, it is present in every proclaiming of the word, in the sacraments, in every decision of faith. 'In every moment slumbers the possibility of being the eschatological moment. You must awaken to it.'[2]

Very close to Bultmann in his general theological outlook is Friedrich Gogarten[3] (1887–1967). He too was a pioneer with Bultmann, Barth and Brunner in the revolt against the liberal theology that prevailed at the beginning of the century, but Gogarten derived his inspirations especially from Luther, whose insights he has tried to recapture. Luther, he believes, broke the hold of metaphysics upon theology, and directed the Church's thinking into what we would nowadays call 'existential' channels. But Luther's insights were lost in the period of Protestant orthodoxy which follows. These insights need reasserting in our time, and according to Gogarten they are often better understood by secular philosophers like Martin Heidegger than by theologians.

The classic Christian doctrines, such as the christological and trinitarian statements, were drawn up on the basis of metaphysics. But now there has taken place a shift from metaphysics to history. In the Middle Ages, history was understood as a process which takes place within a stationary metaphysical framework. But 'modern man is able to envisage history only from the point of view of his own responsibility for it'.[4] When it is

---

[1] *Kerygma and Myth*, p. 7.   [2] *History and Eschatology* [*The Presence of Eternity*], p. 155.
[3] He has taught at Jena and Göttingen.   [4] *Demythologizing and History*, p. 19.

understood that man creates history, then instead of interpreting history in the light of metaphysics, we see that metaphysical systems themselves are products of history.

Most Protestant theologians nowadays have in fact renounced metaphysics in favour of an historical approach to their subject. But within the historical approach to theology, two points of view are discernible, each guided by its own concept of history. The 'official' theology of the Church, as Gogarten calls it, thinks of objective historical happenings on which Christian faith can be based. But this approach mistakes the nature of history which is not an object that can be viewed from outside. Hence Gogarten himself favours an existential approach to history. From this point of view, history cannot be an object, for we ourselves are within history and participate in it. We can understand history only by overcoming the subject-object dichotomy, and by approaching it from within our own historical existence. As far as the sacred history is concerned, faith can never be established by demonstrating that certain objective happenings took place in the past. Faith arises on the basis of an existential interpretation of the sacred history, which lets us see it as the disclosure of our own historical existence, responsible under the word of God. And this, Gogarten thinks, is something that we learn not only from modern existentialists but also from a right understanding of Luther's central principle, *sola fide*.

The most radical application of existentialism to the problems of theology is found in the project for a 'theology of existence', put forward by Fritz Buri[1] (1907-   ). He wholeheartedly endorses Bultmann's proposals for existential interpretation and demythologizing of the New Testament, but thinks that Bultmann does not carry his proposals far enough. As Buri sees it, Bultmann is left with two difficulties on his hands. The first is a logical inconsistency, for having set out to translate the Christian message into a language which talks of possibilities of human existence, he comes to a halt with the *kerygma*, the proclamation of a saving act of God. Whatever this may be, it is not a possibility of human existence. In Buri's view, it is in fact the last remnant of myth. The second difficulty is a certain arrogance which attends Bultmann's sharp distinction between the Christian gospel and philosophical ideas of an authentic existence. Is it true that Christianity *alone* can bring men into the authenticity of their existence?

The way out of Bultmann's difficulties can lie, Buri thinks, only through a 'dekerygmatizing' of the Christian message. The idea that there is some special act of God in which he addresses his word to man must be given up.

[1] Professor at Basel.

Grace and revelation are not given in a special act, but are given with existence itself. Here Buri adheres closely to Jaspers, who stands in relation to his theology much as Heidegger stands in relation to Bultmann's. When the notion of a *kerygma* has been abandoned we are delivered not only from the logical inconsistency of Bultmann's view, but also from its arrogance; for there would now be no difference in principle between the Christian idea of authentic existence, and that of a philosopher like Jaspers, who also thinks of authentic existence as a gift from the transcendent, but without postulating any special act of God.

Does this mean the disappearance of Christian theology? In one sense it does, for theology gets merged into philosophy. 'Between our theology of existence and a philosophy which founds itself on the same concept of existence, there is in principle no difference.'[1] Yet in another sense Buri is willing to allow a distinctive task to theology. Whereas philosophy takes all human existence for its province, theology works within the tradition of the Christian religion, and in particular it elucidates the existential significance of that heritage of symbolic and mythological material which belongs to Christianity. Buri is willing to allow an almost unique depth of existential insight to the Christian myth, which has survived so many variations and is still experienced as 'revelation'. 'In the sea of mythological ideas and images, there are only a few really great redeemer-myths of the kind which we have in the story of the eschatological Christ.'[2] The task of theology is to bring out the wealth of existential meaning in the Christian myth, and in particular its intense awareness of existence as grace.

The theology of Paul Tillich[3] (1886–1965) also has an existential starting-point, but much more than the three theologians already considered in this section Tillich goes on from existential concepts to explore the ontological structures of theology. Tillich describes his theological method as one of 'correlation'. He takes the existential situation of man on the one hand and the message of the Christian revelation on the other, and 'tries to correlate the questions implied in the situation with the answers implied in the message'.[4] The answers are not derived from the questions, that is to say, Tillich would agree with Barth that there is no way from man to God and that God must from his side reveal himself. But the questions are not derived from the answers, that is to say, Tillich would disagree

---

[1] *Theologie der Existenz*, p. 28.

[2] *Op. cit.*, p. 85.

[3] After teaching at Marburg, Dresden and Frankfurt, he went to the United States and was professor at Union Theological Seminary, New York, 1933-55; Harvard from 1955.

[4] *Systematic Theology*, vol. I, p. 8.

with Barth's absolute denial of natural theology. Only if man is asking the question of God and therefore has some idea of God can the revelatory answer have any meaning for him. 'Natural theology was meaningful to the extent that it gave an analysis of the human situation and the question of God implied in it.'[1]

The question of God arises out of man's awareness of his own finitude. To be aware of finitude is already to have some idea of the infinite, the unconditioned, the absolute. Finite being, surrounded, as it were, by non-being, cannot escape the quest for the ultimate ground of being. This is man's ultimate concern. Of course, he has many concerns, and some of them may be erected into false ultimates; the nation, or even success may be the thing which concerns a man ultimately. But these ultimates are not genuinely ultimate, and to treat them as ultimate is a kind of idolatry. Tillich suggests that we can judge of any pretension to ultimacy by asking if that which claims to be ultimate can be an *object* to us. If it can, it is not the genuine ultimate. The genuine ultimate must be something in which we ourselves participate, something which transcends the subject-object relationship and rises infinitely above all existent objects. This ultimate, which we can alone call 'God', is being itself.

In equating God with being itself, the ground of being, or the power of being, Tillich makes it quite clear that God is not any particular being or entity, not even the highest being, if by this is meant one being among others.[2] Tillich's idea of God is therefore of the same order as Heidegger's idea of being, and Tillich would escape the charge which Heidegger directs against Christian theology in general—that of making God an entity.

Tillich's use of the idea of being has been repellent to many persons who otherwise find much to admire in his theology. We have already seen[3] how A. C. Garnett, for instance, while he thinks of Tillich as one of the more enlightened theologians of our time, considers his talk about being as sheer error, springing from an elementary failure to understand the logical function of the verb 'to be'. But surely this attack can be answered,

---

[1] *Op. cit.*, vol. II, p. 15.

[2] But Tillich's actual usage is not always clear. For instance, when it is said that God is 'being itself' and also the 'ground of being', the word 'being' must be employed in two different senses; for 'being itself', as an ultimate, can have no ground, and the 'ground of being' must be interpreted as the 'ground of entities, or particular beings', that is to say, the 'being itself' by participation in which any entity is. Still more obscure is the expression 'power of being'. Here there is a double ambiguity. The word 'being' has the ambiguity already noted, and in addition the genitive may be either subjective or objective, that is to say, it may mean either the 'power exerted by being' or the 'power to be'. Thus the expression could bear at least four different senses, though it is doubtful if they are all intelligible. Which sense is intended by Tillich the present writer will not venture to say.

[3] See above, p. 275.

in the same kind of way as Heidegger answered the similar attack upon him by Carnap. When Tillich and Heidegger talk about 'being' and 'nothing' or 'non-being', these terms are not to be understood in their abstract logical signification—if they were, we would indeed land up in nonsense. The terms are to be understood in relation to the significance which they bear in human existence; in the experiences of anxiety and finitude, which bring the shock of possible non-being; and in the wonder for being which this shock awakens, the wonder that there is something and not just nothing.

To say that God is being itself is the only univocal statement that can be made about God. 'After this has been said, nothing else can be said about God as God which is not symbolic.'[1] We are not to despise symbolic language, which has a power of its own. It can open up new levels of reality by pointing beyond itself to that in which the symbol participates. Since God is the ground and structure of being, and finite things participate in this being, they can serve as symbols for God. Yet even the most adequate symbols fall short of the reality which they symbolize, and must be both affirmed and denied at the same time, in the clear understanding of their symbolic character. Otherwise the symbols themselves can be made ultimate, and in that case they are idolized and given a demonic character. We can speak of God as personal, living, just, loving, but in each case the being of God transcends the symbol employed.

Symbols occur in the context of myths or stories of the gods. Myth is in fact the language of ultimate concern, and Tillich states that 'Christianity speaks the mythological language like any other religion.'[2] Just as symbols are to be understood in their symbolic character, so myths are to be deprived of their literal significance and understood as myths—they are to be 'broken', in Tillich's expression. In this sense he agrees on the need for demythologizing, but he claims that we cannot dispense with the mythical form or substitute some other kind of language for it. The important thing is that we should not take our symbols literally, so making ultimate something that is less than ultimate.

In revelation, being itself grasps us and manifests itself to us. Revelation does not work against reason, but rather raises reason to an ecstatic level on which the subject-object relationship is overcome. Tillich recognizes a wider revelation which, for the Christian, is preparatory to the final revelation in Jesus as the Christ. Jesus sacrifices himself, the particular manifestation, to become the Christ, interpreted by Tillich in typically ontological fashion as the 'new being'. The new being is the power from beyond man that heals his existential conflicts and overcomes

[1] *Op. cit.*, vol. I, p. 265.   [2] *Dynamics of Faith*, p. 54.

his sin, understood as his estrangement from himself, from others, and from his ground. Thus the new being manifested in Christ answers man's ultimate concern and his quest for the ground of being.

108. REMARKS ON EXISTENTIALIST PHILOSOPHIES AND THEOLOGIES

That existentialism offers remarkable scope for the interpretation of religion and theology has become apparent in our survey. 'Theology', says Paul Tillich, 'has received tremendous gifts from existentialism, gifts not dreamed of fifty years ago or even thirty years ago.'[1] The question however is whether these gifts should be received, or whether, to adapt Laocoon's advice to the Trojans, we should fear the existentialists even when they are bringing gifts. For existentialism is commonly charged with two grave faults: subjectivism and irrationalism.

The charge of subjectivism obviously has some weight. Existentialism begins from the situation of the existing individual, though we should remember that his existence is not that of an isolated subject but existence in the world. Nevertheless, we may think that sometimes the existentialist philosopher is so immersed in his personal existence that he has become quite egocentric. Some of Kierkegaard's writings can be properly understood only if we know about his love-affair, while among contemporary thinkers Sartre's philosophy is tied up closely with his own psychological make-up, as, for instance, in what he says about sticky substances. But the more objectionable kind of subjectivism disappears in thinkers like Marcel, Heidegger and Jaspers. They reach beyond an egocentric view of the structures of intersubjective experience. The subjective element that remains is ineluctable—it is the acknowledgement that all philosophizing is from the point of view of a finite human existence, and this cannot be exchanged for a divine eminence from which one might objectively survey all time and all existence.

The charge of irrationalism has in view the use which existentialist philosophers make of such affective states as anxiety, nausea, boredom and the like. Obviously we cannot be guided by our feelings, which are often quite inappropriate. But in the existentialists, these affective states are not mere emotions. They carry with them an awareness of situations in which we participate, and which cannot therefore be objectively perceived from outside. These affective states are, as it were, crises of heightened awareness, in which we *notice* something that ordinarily escapes us—

[1] *Theology of Culture*, p. 126.

our own finitude, the being of the world, or whatever it may be. Provided that we are willing to sift and clarify through analysis the insights afforded by such experiences, and to ask whether these insights are justifiable, there can be no objection to making use of them. A philosophy which ignored them in the name of rationalism would in fact be a singularly narrow and shallow interpretation of experience.

Existentialism perhaps lends itself to extravagances, but in the hands of its saner practitioners, these are avoided. Indeed, one might say that they save us from still wilder extravagances, and especially the extravagance of trying to construct a philosophy without first scrutinizing in all its accessible dimensions the *locus* in which all philosophizing takes place —our own human existence.

When we turn to the existentialist theologians, perhaps we are most impressed with demythologizing and the existential interpretation of the New Testament story, as advocated by Bultmann and Gogarten. This indeed makes sense of many things that had become unintelligible. But, as the direction in which Buri has moved shows us, existential interpretation by itself might lead to the transformation of the Christian religion into something hardly distinguishable from a humanistic ethic. It is here that Tillich's emphasis on ontological rather than existential interpretation is important. Tillich restores what Bultmann's stress on ethical and personal categories tends to lose—the suprapersonal and suprarational depth of God, as experienced in the whole mystical tradition of religion. Ontological interpretation here does not mean the construction of a new metaphysical system, but it does mean indicating the place of the idea of God on the ontological map—namely, as the correlate of man's existential awareness of finitude, as being itself beyond any possible entity. The idea of God, however, remains only an idea or a possibility until it is filled in by God's manifesting himself in a revelatory experience. Not being a metaphysic, existentialism neither proves nor disproves God, but it can exhibit the existential and ontological connections that bring us to the point where, in the light of all our experience, we decide either that being is gracious to us (the religious view), or that being is alien to us and we are cast entirely on the slender resources of humanity (atheism or humanism).

When we set out on this survey, it was said that it would be something like a tour through an exhibition of pictures. We have now come out of the last gallery, but before we part company, let us in a concluding chapter reflect a little further on what we have seen.

XXIII

CONCLUDING COMMENTS

109. SOME FINDINGS AND SUGGESTIONS

AT the end of our survey, the reader may well feel somewhat bewildered. We have met so many views of religion, some of them
sharply conflicting, others shading off into each other, and some of
them so diverse that they seem to be talking about quite different things
or at any rate very different aspects of the same thing. Out of this teeming
diversity, no common view emerges. At the beginning of the book[1] we
quoted the remark made by an English theologian at the beginning of the
century, in which he pointed to 'a multitude of incoherent and incompatible points of view, all of which may be called modern, but none of
which can claim to be typically representative of the age—currents and
cross-currents and rapids and backwaters of thought'. At the end, we can
parallel this with a quotation from a mid-century philosopher: 'To-day,
as always, a violent struggle is raging between antagonistic views of the
world, and it is possibly more violent in our own time than it was during
the past century. Rarely has it been of such intensity, with such a wealth
of opposing viewpoints or expressed in such elaborate and refined conceptual frameworks.'[2]

On the other hand, we can hardly fail to have been impressed by the
extraordinary ingenuity and power of thought shown by the philosophers,
theologians and others included in our survey. The conflict of views is not
a sheer chaos, for we have been able to trace lines of connection in it,
lines of action, reaction and interaction. Another interpreter of modern
thought—one of the most acute and learned, if we may say so—sees it as
'an uninterrupted dialogue among free men',[3] a dialogue which sometimes unites them and sometimes divides them. Genuine insights are
gained in the dialogue, and not by one party only. When we think of the
situation in this way, our initial bewilderment will not pass into an utter
scepticism.

[1] See above, p. 19.
[2] I. M. Bochenski, *Contemporary European Philosophy*, p. ix.
[3] Nicola Abbagnano, *Storia della Filosofia*, vol. II/2, p. 723.

Our survey, however, has undoubtedly pointed us in the direction of a degree of relativism. Absolute and final truth on the questions of religion is just unattainable. It is true, as we have seen, that some theologians talk of an absolute divine revelation to which they have access, but as they proceed immediately to quarrel violently among themselves over the interpretation of this revelation, and admit that in any case the revelation must be interpreted in fallible words, it is clear that we get no absolute truth from them. Equally we reject the absolute scepticism of the man who tells us that we can know nothing of these matters whatever, for by his own standards he already knows too much, and is no less dogmatic and arrogant than his theological counterpart. We must steer a course between these vain extremes, and we have seen good reason to hope that although absolute truth is denied us, we can have partial insights of varying degrees of adequacy, 'glimpses that would make us less forlorn'.

When we mentioned relativism, we had a further point in mind. It has become fairly clear in the course of our survey that the kind of philosophy or theology which prevails at any time is not independent of the contemporary social and historical conditions, that is to say, of the *mood* of the culture in which it arises. In our discussion of existentialism, it was said that a mood or affective state is not just an emotion but a state of awareness in which we *notice* things which otherwise escape notice. The difference between mid-century thinking about religion and the kind of thinking that went on in 1900 is partly due to a difference in mood, which makes the mid-century man *notice* problems that were *unnoticed* fifty years earlier, while the problems of that time have ceased to excite us now. What we are driving at is that just as we have no absolute answers, so we have no absolute questions, in which *everything would be noticed at once*. Only God could either ask or answer such questions. Our questions arise out of our situation, and both questions and answers are relative to that situation. This need not distress us for it could not be otherwise—it is part of what it means to be *finite*.

If, as we have seen, there are many possible ways of understanding religion, and if no one way is likely to be the final truth of the matter, then would not the most rational response be to suspend judgment about it altogether? This would be the most rational response if religion were merely a *theoretical* matter, like a scientific hypothesis. But we have had ample evidence that religion is more than that. It is also a practical matter, *an attitude of the whole personality*. To suspend judgment about religion, as William James pointed out, is to act as if religion were untrue. Just because here and now we have to act and live, we cannot sit around waiting for someone to present us with the final truth on the matter, if that were deemed to be possible. We cannot avoid coming to some kind of decision about religion, either dismissing it or identifying ourselves with it in one or other of its forms. In the light of the finite imperfect ideas that we have, or that are given to us, we must take either the risk of faith or the risk of unfaith. William James ended his essay, 'The Will to Believe', with a notable quotation from FitzJames Stephen: 'What do you think of yourself? What do you think of the world? These are riddles of the Sphinx, and in some way or other we must deal with them. If we decide to leave the riddles unanswered, that is a choice; if we waver in our answer, that too is a choice; but whatever choice, we make it at our peril. We stand on a mountain pass in the midst of whirling snow and blinding mist, through which we get glimpses now and then of paths which may be deceptive. If we stand still, we shall be frozen to death. If we take the wrong road, we shall be dashed to pieces. We do not certainly know that there is any right one.'[1] This is the situation in which finite man has got to make up his mind—an agonizing situation, if you like, but also a challenging and adventurous one. So Kierkegaard viewed Christianity—not as a cozy convention but as a decision to be taken and a leap to be made.

FitzJames Stephen talks also of a 'leap in the dark', but here we must demur. While we have denied that there can be absolute knowledge, some insights are available. A leap so important as this is not to be taken in the dark but in all the light we can get, whether from revelation or from rational reflection or from conscience or from any other area of experience. We cannot escape choosing some understanding of religion, even if it is to understand religion as an illusion, but the choice should be an intelligent one, made in the light of such criteria as are available. We must now say what some of the criteria seem to be.

1. Our understanding of religion should be a *reasonable* one. By this is not meant that some conclusive proof is to be given, for we have already rejected the possibility of absolute certitude. Nor do we mean that every mystery is to be laid open, for this too would be an absurd demand for the finite intellect to make. Nor do we mean that non-rational elements in our experience are to be ignored, for we have already specifically declared that they are not. In asking for a reasonable understanding of religion, we simply mean that it should involve no *sacrificium intellectus*, no flagrant contradictions, no violation of natural reason, no conflict with what we believe about the world on scientific or common-sense grounds.

2. Our understanding of religion must be *contemporary*. By this we do not mean that it must conform to the philosophical vogue of the moment. But we mean that there can be no escape from the twentieth century to the

[1] Quoted in W. James, *Selected Papers on Philosophy*, p. 124.

times of the New Testament or of the Middle Ages or of the Reformation. No doubt we can learn much from all of these times. But what is required is an understanding of religion relevant to our own time, that is to say, an understanding which comes to grips with the problems which—in the sense explained above—the current mood of our civilization causes us to *notice*.

3. An understanding of religion ought to be *comprehensive*, that is to say, it must be an understanding of religion as an attitude of the whole personality, not just an understanding of this or that aspect of religion. Religion can easily be salvaged if we treat it only as a practical, ethical affair, stripped of beliefs about God and the world. This is as much an exaggeration as the view that religion is simply belief, a world-view. Any adequate account must show religion in all its dimensions—cognitive and affective as well as moral and practical.

4. We may add that any understanding of religion must be *on the way*. This follows from the denial that we can possess absolute truth. One can be loyally and wholeheartedly committed to a religious attitude without believing that it embodies final and exclusive truth, and without abandoning the expectation of learning more. Indeed, we should expect of any understanding of religion that it leaves room for further development.

Do any of the current interpretations of religion which we have studied measure up to these criteria? Or, assuming that we accept the criteria, have we reluctantly to admit that no positive understanding of religion can survive in our time? This is a question which the reader must decide for himself. But if he has accompanied me thus far through the book, he has perhaps a right to ask me what I think about it. I shall not conceal from him that I think the criteria are best satisfied on the philosophical side in those philosophies of existence and being that have been developed by Martin Heidegger and other thinkers; and on the theological side in the related work of men like Bultmann and Tillich. Here I see the possibility of working out a philosophical basis for religion that makes sense, is contemporary, comprehensive, and capable of further development; and further, it is a philosophical basis which readily allies itself with the traditional Christian teachings that have inspired Western civilization from its beginnings, revivifying these teachings and making intelligible for our time their abiding truth. I think that religion and philosophy need each other. Without a philosophical basis, religion degenerates into superstition; while a bare religious philosophy, for the great majority at least, cannot be fruitful for life without the revelatory symbols and the communal worship of a concrete religion.

I may however be excused from pursuing the theme of the relation of

Christianity to the philosophy of existence here, for if the reader is interested, he may refer to the books in which I have developed and defended this point of view in detail.[1] But from all that has been said above, it is perhaps superfluous to add that although this is my conclusion, and although I hope that some readers will be persuaded to see in the thinkers I have mentioned the growing-point of contemporary religious thought, I do not expect everyone to think in this way nor do I think that there is nothing to be learned from other schools. In George Santayana's words: 'I do not ask anyone to think in my terms if he prefers others. Let him clean better, if he can, the windows of his soul, that the variety and beauty of the prospect may spread more brightly before him.'[2]

110. FUTURE OUTLOOK

Having been rash enough to write the history of the present in religious thought, and even to commit ourselves to some tentative conclusions, we do not propose to add to our sins by attempting to write the history of the future, as the title of this section may have suggested. Certainly we do not intend to speculate whether one school will oust another, or what will be the character of the new schools which already must be taking shape among younger thinkers—for we have included in our survey only men whose reputations are firmly established, and none born after 1910. Still less would we venture to predict what events may befall our Western civilization in the remaining decades of the century, or what changes of mood may bring to notice problems which at present lie dormant.

Our purpose here is simply to draw attention to a fact which must be encouraging to all who care for religion, to whatever school they may belong—the fact that in spite of all the shattering events of our century and in spite of the shallow secularism that has engulfed so many, religious thought continues to be vigorous, and gives every sign that it will not cease to be so. When we think of names like Maritain, Berdyaev, Barth, Marcel, Otto, Tillich, to mention only a few, we see that twentieth-century man has not fallen below the level of his predecessors in the earnestness and perspicuity with which he has addressed himself to the problems of religion. Some of us believe that this is because these problems belong to the very being of man himself, and that he cannot rest until he has come to terms with them. He can understand himself only if he looks

---

[1] *An Existentialist Theology* (SCM Press, London, and The Macmillan Company, New York, 1955); and *The Scope of Demythologizing* (SCM Press, London, and Harper & Brothers, New York, 1960).

[2] *Scepticism and Animal Faith*, p. vi.

beyond himself. 'The question of God and the question of myself', says Bultmann, 'are identical.'[1]

'How hard', said Plato, 'or rather impossible is the attainment of any certainty about questions such as these in the present life. And yet he would be a poor creature who did not test what is said about them to the uttermost, or who abandoned the task before he had examined them from every side and could do no more.'[2] The man of the twentieth century is not shrinking from the task. No more than the men of earlier times is he likely to come to the end of this voyage in quest of the truth of religion, or to stand on a firm shore, for then he would no longer be man in this world, man as we know him, man as you and I are, *homo viator*. But the important thing is that the voyage goes on and will go on.

[1] *Jesus Christ and Mythology*, p. 53.   [2] *Phaedo*, 85.

XXIV

POSTSCRIPT: 1960–1970

111. A WATERSHED?

I T has been said that history never begins a new chapter: only historians do. I hope that the truth of this dictum has been recognized in the main body of this book, which represented the story of contemporary religious thought as beginning in conflict and ending in conflict. Yet the historian's business is to distinguish among the tangle of events some recognizable periods and patterns. We have ourselves distinguished three phases of twentieth-century religious thought. But when we come to the most recent developments in the field, to the decade 1960–70, it seems that something new has come along. One can hardly speak of a fourth phase, for there is nothing definite enough to warrant that description—at least, not up till now. A characteristic of the decade under discussion has been precisely the rapid changes in religious thought. Positions have been scarcely set up when they are abandoned and there is a move to something new. Inevitably this has led to some superficiality, and I have been tempted to call the nineteen-sixties the 'decade of the dilettantes', so far as theology is concerned. On the other hand, the rapid changes of mood have been symptomatic of unrest and probing of a very radical kind. Some have even talked of a 'new reformation'. There has certainly been a break with the tendencies which prevailed quite recently. The previous phase has ended, though the new one has not yet clearly revealed its shape. 'Death of God', 'secular Christianity', 'black theology', 'Dionysian religion' are among the more startling phrases that have been heard against the relatively sober background of the new hermeneutic, transcendental Thomism and the theology of hope. These contrasting labels, descriptions and slogans, thus roughly juxtaposed, tell something of the chaos and bewilderment in contemporary religious thought, reflecting, perhaps, chaos and bewilderment in the wider human society itself. But they also testify that religion and reflection upon religion are far from dead. They prove the point made at the end of the preceding chapter that 'the voyage goes on'.

If we avoid tendentious language about a 'new reformation', we may speak of a watershed in the religious thought of the decade 1960–70. This watershed cannot be precisely assigned to a particular year or attributed to only one factor. In Protestant theology, we had come to the end of an age of giants. Barth, Brunner, Bultmann, Tillich, Gogarten, the Baillies, the Niebuhrs—these outstanding men who for a generation had dominated the theological scene had completed their work, and indeed most of them died during the ten years under review. To be sure, they left unfinished tasks and unexhausted resources, and their influence is by no means at an end. But these men of the theological renascence had enjoyed a long innings and some fresh thinking was needed. In Roman Catholic thought, the early years of the decade saw the Second Vatican Council, summoned by Pope John XXIII. This was another aspect of the watershed. The new stirrings in Roman Catholic thought, described in chapter XVIII above, were greatly stimulated. If Roman Catholic theology was once noted for its conservatism, it became in this decade the most exciting and important theology going on anywhere. The liberating influences of Vatican II inevitably produced much that was aberrant and ephemeral, but on the whole one might say that Catholic theology finally burst from those rigid categories in which it had been so long contained, almost like a butterfly out of its chrysalis, and, without ceasing to be loyal to the Catholic tradition, has sought to find expression in contemporary thought-forms. The defensive spirit in which the Roman Catholic Church had for long tried to hold the modern world at bay and had condemned so much of modern thought in a series of documents from *Syllabus Errorum* to *Humani Generis*, gave place to a new spirit of dialogue—dialogue with other Christians, with other religions and with non-believers. As John XXIII expressed it in his opening speech to the Council, the Church 'considers that she meets the needs of the present day by demonstrating the validity of her teaching rather than by condemnations'.[1] Cautious though this statement may seem, it opened the door to vast possibilities of change and renewal in Catholic thought.

To the specifically theological and churchly factors affecting religious thought in the decade, one must obviously add the many secular factors, though these are so numerous and complex that they can receive only a very inadequate mention. On the one hand, there were continued spectacular advances in science and technology. For example, to mention two of the most striking, man stood for the first time on the moon, and he unravelled the mysteries of his own genetic constitution. On the other hand, the ambiguities of technology were brought home in a new way with the

---

[1] *The Documents of Vatican II*, ed. Walter M. Abbott, S. J., p. 716.

serious threats to the environment through pollution of rivers, the oceans and the air, and the dangers of over-population. Conflict between the industrial nations and the so-called 'third world' became sharper as the latter demanded a larger share in the affluence which technology had made possible. At the same time, the youth of the affluent countries was beginning to rebel against the whole system of values on which secular technocracy has been founded. How these sometimes contradictory trends have had their influence on religious thought we shall try to understand. The contradictions have been reflected in theology which, it seems, has too often followed what looked like the popular trend of the moment.

The expression 'new theology' was used a good deal in the nineteen-sixties. Readers of this book will recall that there was a 'new theology' in England[1] in the first decade of the century, just about the time when the Roman Catholic Church was being rocked by the controversy over the Modernist Movement.[2] The new theologies of recent years are in some respects not dissimilar to those earlier movements. They resume the immanentist, humanistic trend of nineteenth-century theology, after its interruption by the Barthian period in Protestantism and the Thomist revival in Catholicism.

In the remainder of the chapter, we shall consider first the developments in continental Protestant theology (Section 112), then the somewhat stormy course of theology in the English-speaking world (Section 113), and then the Roman Catholic contribution (Section 114). The chapter ends with a brief evaluation (Section 115).

112. CONTINENTAL PROTESTANT THEOLOGY, 1960–70

It must be acknowledged that Germany and Switzerland seem to be still the seed-bed, as it were, of Protestant theology, and that the theology of the English-speaking countries is largely determined by what goes on in continental Europe. It is appropriate therefore to consider the continentals before turning to the British and Americans. Among the German-speaking theologians, we already find discussions of most of the themes that have bulked so largely in the theology of the nineteen-sixties—secularization, theism, the question of the continuing relevance of the Bible, history, the social responsibilities of Christianity, and the rest. For the sake of convenience, our treatment will be organized around two important movements, usually known by the somewhat loose descriptions, the 'new

[1] See above, p. 39.   [2] See above, p. 181ff.

hermeneutic'[1] and the 'theology of hope'.[2] The former of these was more prominent in the earlier years of the decade, the latter had come to occupy the centre of attention by the end. It would also be true to say that the former for the most part continued to deal with problems inherited from Bultmann, Bonhoeffer and others, while the latter represents something like a new departure.

It was Bultmann who revived the study of theological hermeneutics in this century, and his theory of demythologizing remains the most important contribution to the subject made in a long time. Demythologizing means a translation of mythical language into the language of existence and history, and it was Gogarten who claimed that metaphysical language too must be translated into the language of history. Like Bultmann, he saw this historicization as a consequence of the New Testament itself, but he went further in identifying the historicizing process with secularization and argued that, rightly understood, secularization is not anti-Christian but is precisely a taking over of responsibility for history in accordance with New Testament teaching. The historicizing or secularizing process is a liberation from law, a coming of age and the achievement of adult responsibility. This interpretation in turn links up with Bonhoeffer's last teachings on the autonomy of secular man, the end of religion and the need to communicate Christian faith in non-religious concepts.[3]

All of these influences have converged in the work of Gerhard Ebeling[4] (b. 1912) who may be regarded as the most influential representative of so-called 'post-Bultmannian' hermeneutics.

In the Lutheran tradition, Ebeling is (very much like Bultmann) greatly concerned with proclamation and preaching. The theological hermeneutic is directed towards proclamation. Thus it takes place in the spoken word, rather than in writing. Central to Ebeling's theology is his notion of 'word-event' (*Wortgeschehen*). This is a dynamic understanding of language as an event which takes place among persons. It is the capacity for language, Ebeling believes, that makes man distinctively human and that allows him to be open for God and for faith. The task of theology is so to listen and respond to the Word of God that the word-event is renewed in present existence. 'Proclamation that has taken place is to become proclamation that takes place.'[5] He can also express this by saying that the tradition is

---

[1] For introductions, see J. M. Robinson and J. B. Cobb, editors, *The New Hermeneutic*; Carl E. Braaten, *History and Hermeneutics*.

[2] For an introduction, see J. M. Robinson and J. B. Cobb, editors, *Theology as History*.

[3] On these three theologians, see above, pp. 331–2 and 362–5.

[4] The following works are available in English: *The Nature of Faith*; *Word and Faith*; *Theology and Proclamation*; *The Problem of Historicity*.

[5] *Word and Faith*, p. 329.

to be transformed from *traditum* (what has been handed down) to *tradendum* (what has to be handed down).[1]

But if there is to be a listening to the word, there must also be attention to the kind of world in which the contemporary word-event must take place. Ebeling recognizes that 'our situation today is determined by the fact that the fateful process of secularization .... has reached a certain completeness in every sphere of human life'.[2] Thus he accepts the challenge of Bonhoeffer to look for 'a non-religious interpretation of biblical concepts', understanding 'non-religious' as 'non-legalistic'. Christianity itself demands that there should be respect for responsibility and intellectual integrity.

An obvious weakness of Ebeling is his preoccupation with language. Important though language is, the word, spoken and heard, does not constitute the whole of human existence. More than this, he uses the expression 'word-event' to cover so many things that it becomes a very vague expression. Not only preaching, but the sacraments and even the Church become 'word-events'! Surely this is carrying the Protestant preoccupation with the word to fantastic extremes. Braaten has rightly remarked that the great events of the gospel narrative were not simply language events but rather events that were creative of language.[3] One sometimes gets the impression that even Jesus was a word-event—or, at least, that he became so in the proclamation of the Church. But, somewhat surprisingly, Ebeling comes out more strongly for the necessity of knowing something of the historical Jesus than does Bultmann.

Many other important continental theologians have been engaged in the hermeneutical discussion. Ernst Fuchs (b. 1903) has developed the notion of a 'language-occurrence' (*Sprachereignis*) which, like Ebeling's word-event, tends to become a catch-all. Heinrich Ott (b. 1929), successor to Karl Barth at Basel, has done important work in attempting to reconcile the hermeneutic approaches of Barth and Bultmann.[4] Bultmann's preoccupation with the question of human existence gave the formulation of the question a privileged position and paid too little attention to hearing the word of God. Only in his later writings did Barth begin to do justice to the human interest in interpretation. Ott claims to find in the work of the later Heidegger a model for reconciling the two approaches, especially Heidegger's claim that the most authentic kind of thinking is of a passive, meditative nature, listening to the voice of being.[5] On the other hand, Herbert Braun (b. 1903) has carried the interpretation of the New Testa-

---

[1] *Theology and Proclamation*, p. 27.
[2] *Word and Faith*, p. 128.
[3] *History and Hermeneutics*, p. 140.
[4] Cf. *Denken und Sein*.
[5] See above, p. 355.

ment in human existential terms to such a length that some have supposed that he has even demythologized God. At any rate, whatever was conveyed by the notion of God, Braun seeks to express in the non-religious concepts of 'I may' and 'I ought'.[1]

Whereas Bultmann himself was influenced by the earlier work of Heidegger, the exponents of the new hermeneutic have taken more interest in the later Heidegger and in the younger philosopher Hans-Georg Gadamer (b. 1900), author of the influential book *Wahrheit und Methode*. It would be true to say, however, that the general orientation of the new hermeneutic has been towards the philosophy of existence. By contrast, the theology of hope makes a break with the existentialist frame of reference, judging it to be too narrow at several points for the communication of the essential Christian teachings. It is argued with some justice that existentialism has been allowed to force theology into a stance that is too narrowly individualistic. Furthermore, the whole hermeneutic concern with the 'here and now' has (or so it is maintained) neutralized the future reference of Christianity, as essentially an eschatological and even apocalyptic faith. Among contemporary philosophers, the veteran quasi-Marxist Ernst Bloch (b. 1885) makes more appeal to the theologians of hope than does Heidegger. Bloch has written on the radical reformer, Thomas Munzer, and on the revolutionary apocalyptic elements in the Christian tradition. His long-winded *chef-d'oeuvre*, *Das Prinzip der Hoffnung*, develops the metaphysical significance of such categories as hope, the new, the utopian, as interpretative of the world-process. Not only Bloch, but the whole Hegelian and Marxist tradition has been influential for the theologians of hope. Hegel himself is frequently quoted with approval, and one has to ask whether he is acquiring a new importance for religious thought after a long time of eclipse. The Hegelian tradition offers, of course, a clear alternative to existentialism, especially in its doctrine of history.

One of the leaders of the school is Wolfhart Pannenberg (b. 1928). He declares the futuristic, eschatological character of Christian theology in these words: 'One must be clear about the fact that when one discusses the truth of the apocalyptic expectation of a future judgment and a resurrection of the dead, one is dealing directly with the basis of the Christian faith. Why the man Jesus can be the ultimate revelation of God, why in him and only in him God is supposed to have appeared, remains incomprehensible apart from the horizon of the apocalyptic expectation.'[2] Bultmann's attempts to demythologize this expectation are criticized on the grounds that

---

[1] 'The Problem of a New Testament Theology', *The Bultmann School of Biblical Interpretation: New Directions?*, ed. R. Funk, p. 169ff.

[2] *Jesus, God and Man*, pp. 82–3.

he separates history and significance and also deprives eschatology of its future character. What is required is an understanding of history in its wholeness. 'We must reinstate today the original unity of facts and their meaning.'[1] The Hegelian tendency of this sentence is clear. It is explicitly to Hegel that Pannenberg appeals for an understanding of 'person' that will clearly break out of individualism.[2]

Pannenberg assails Bultmann also over the latter's demythologizing of the idea of resurrection. Though he eschews any crude literalism, Pannenberg holds that both the resurrection of Jesus and the promised resurrection of the dead must have an independent reality beyond that which existential interpretation allows to them. He reopens the question of the historical evidence for the resurrection of Jesus and claims that it points to an event prior to the faith of the disciples and creative of that faith. He also holds that a phenomenological analysis of the being of man shows that the human essence requires for its fulfilment a community which does not yet exist and thus in his very constitution man is pointed beyond death. Whether or not one accepts Pannenberg's arguments, it must be conceded that once again the question of an adequate theology of resurrection is an open question.

Jürgen Moltmann (b. 1926) likewise calls for a more realistic or objective understanding of resurrection. He holds that 'Christianity stands or falls with the reality of the raising of Jesus from the dead by God'.[3] Likewise the resurrection of the dead in the future is a real event towards which history is moving—though Moltmann, like Pannenberg, is tantalizingly vague about the nature of resurrection, which is to be understood neither literally nor in the demythologized fashion of the existentialists.

Promise and fulfilment are the categories under which Moltmann interprets the Bible. God is the coming God, rather than a God abidingly present. Thus hope, as the distinctively eschatological Christian virtue, has the primacy. This hope, however, is not something otherworldly, though since it is a hope for the 'resurrection of the dead', for a new condition still hidden in the future, it is also more than a merely worldly hope. Actually, Moltmann's theology has powerful social implications. He has been accused, with some justice, of being so preoccupied with the future that he underrates the present. But to.this he would reply that only dissatisfaction with the present (even to the extent of finding it godless) will motivate men to seek a better future.

---

[1] 'The Revelation of God in Jesus' in *Theology as History*, ed. J. M. Robinson and J. B. Cobb, p. 127.

[2] *Jesus, God and Man*, p. 181f.

[3] *Theology of Hope*, p. 165.

The theology of hope has spread far beyond Germany. Not surprisingly, it has had a strong appeal in the struggling 'third world'—though perhaps it is surprising that this theology should have had its origin in the most prosperous country of western Europe. Among these third world theologians[1] the deficiencies of Moltmann are made good by bringing his thought into confrontation with that of another continental thinker, Albert Camus (1913–51)—though since he was born in Algeria, he might himself be claimed as a third world figure. To be sure, Camus was not a philosopher of hope. He believed that the human situation is essentially as absurd and hopeless as that of the mythical Sisyphus, and the starting-point of his philosophy is a pessimistic existentialism. But with Camus existentialism bursts out of its narrower forms. Hopelessness is not taken to mean resignation—and Moltmann is certainly unjust in his brief remarks on Camus.[2] On the contrary, Camus preaches 'metaphysical rebellion'. This is defined as 'the movement by which man protests against his condition and against the whole of creation'.[3] But in his political philosophy it becomes clear that for Camus rebellion must be of a profoundly humanistic and personalistic nature if it is to be acceptable. Metaphysical rebellion is essentially man's refusal to be treated as an object.[4] (Whether this implies a more affirmative metaphysic than Camus avows is matter for debate.)

This atheist philosopher's critique of every inhuman form of collectivism and depreciation of the present for the sake of a future offers needed correctives to the laudable attempts of the theology of hope to break out of individualistic Christianity and, as already mentioned, these correctives are being applied by some third world theologians.

Before we leave the continental scene, brief mention should be made of a few other religious thinkers, who stand outside of the groups already discussed. Paul Ricoeur (b. 1913), French Protestant philosopher, has applied the insights of phenomenology and existentialism to the interpretation of human nature, especially as this is revealed in mythology and symbolism. In particular, he has studied the phenomena of finitude and guilt, in such books as *Fallible Man* and *The Symbolism of Evil*. But in sharp contrast to Sartre (whom he charges with dualism) Ricoeur does not end in a pessimistic view of man. 'Sin does not define what it is to be a man; beyond his becoming a sinner, there is his being created . . . Sin may be "older" than sins, but innocence is still "older".'[5] Likewise he argues that among the 'ontological' affects, joy is more basic than anxiety.[6] These remarks, how-

---

[1] An example is the Brazilian, Rubem Alves, author of *A Theology of Human Hope*; and here too belongs the 'black theology' of the United States, such as James Cone's *Black Theology and Black Power*.

[2] *Theology of Hope*, pp. 23–4.   [3] *The Rebel*, p. 23.   [4] *Op. cit.*, p. 250.
[5] *The Symbolism of Evil*, p. 251.   [6] *Fallible Man*, p. 161.

ever, should not be allowed to give the impression that Ricoeur counters pessimism with optimism. His account of the human condition is much more dialectical and makes room for resignation. The German New Testament scholar Ernst Käsemann (b. 1906) began within the orbit of the Bultmann school. He broke with Bultmann on the question of the historical Jesus,[1] and has gone on to criticize the adequacy of existential concepts for the interpretation of New Testament Christianity. It is a kind of robust, undogmatic liberal Protestantism that finds expression in his popular book, *Jesus Means Freedom*. Finally we may take note of two men who have continued in the tradition of Karl Barth—Helmut Gollwitzer (b. 1908) and Eberhard Jüngel. Both of them have been concerned especially with the question of God. Gollwitzer debates with radical theologians and seeks at once to defend and to rescue from distortion the biblical understanding of God in such books as *Die Existenz Gottes im Bekenntnis des Glaubens*[2] and *Von der Stellvertretung Gottes*. Jüngel responds to the current demands for a dynamic rather than a static understanding of God in his book *Gottes Sein ist im Werden*. Basing himself on Barth, he holds that the inner life of God is essentially dynamic, as a self-relating within the Trinity, and to this we are afforded some analogy through God's action in the world.

113. Anglo-Saxon Theology, 1960–70

Throughout most of the decade, the question of God dominated religious and theological discussion in England and the United States. In 1960 there appeared a book by the American religious scholar, Gabriel Vahanian (b. 1927). It bore the title *The Death of God*. It was not itself a manifesto of atheism, but rather a cultural analysis. According to Vahanian, we have entered a post-Christian era. God is no longer a meaningful factor in human life. But with Kierkegaard Vahanian blames Christian religiosity for having brought about the death of God, for God, the wholly Other, has been reduced by Christianity to a mere idol and our culture has rid itself of this idol. Vahanian is not an atheist but he detests idolatry and sentimental religiosity. In a later book he dissociated himself from the Christian atheists and claimed that the cult of Jesus without God is simply another idolatry.[3]

Vahanian's book was the first of a line which opened up a vigorous debate on the continuing viability of theism—a debate which reached a much

---

[1] See his *Essays on New Testament Themes*, p. 15ff.

[2] Available in English, *The Existence of God as Confessed by Faith*.

[3] *No Other God*, p. 29.

wider circle than theological debates normally do. John A. T. Robinson (b. 1918) published *Honest to God* in 1963. The book took up the questions concerning God and God's action that had been raised by Tillich, Bultmann and Bonhoeffer, and Robinson called for a drastic revision of our understanding of God in the light of both the theology and the secular learning of our time. No doubt the fact that Robinson was a bishop of the Church of England had something to do with the sensation which his book caused. But the time was ripe for the kind of debate which he initiated. The radical questionings that had been agitating theologians for a long time needed to be brought to a focus. A later book by Robinson, *Exploration into God*, gave some constructive answers to the questions raised by *Honest to God*. These made it clear that the bishop was not (as some had alleged) an atheist. Indeed, he revealed an unsuspected strain of mysticism. But in place of traditional theism, in which God has usually been considered as a self-sufficient being transcendent of and independent of the world, Robinson favoured a form of 'panentheism'[1]—a view which considers God and the world as correlative. Of course, in opting for panentheism, Robinson was adopting a position not uncommon among philosophers and theologians of our time. Tillich and Hartshorne illustrate different forms of panentheism.

However, in the United States a more far-reaching revolt against traditional theism was in progress. A group of theologians there rejected all forms of theism, and set themselves the task (perhaps self-contradictory) of building a theology without God. These theologians never formed a coherent school. Each of them had his own reasons for rejecting belief in God, and each chose his own way of reconstructing theology without God. Following close upon *Honest to God* came *The Secular Meaning of the Gospel*, by Paul van Buren (b. 1924). Influenced by logical empiricism and especially by the demand for empirical verification, he came to the conclusion that language about God makes no sense. But although discourse about God is illegitimate, a form of Christian theology is still held to be possible. It would confine itself to history and ethics. It is based on the history of the truly free man, Jesus, who still imparts his freedom to others. Jesus takes the place of God. In some ways, van Buren is an echo of the Ritschlians, especially Herrmann.[2] In his most recent writing, he seems to have abandoned the position that one cannot intelligently discuss the question of God, but he regards this question as 'almost totally peripheral to the major concerns of our time'.[3]

[1] See above, p. 274.   [2] See above, p. 85.
[3] See his contribution to *Marxism and Radical Religion*, ed. John C. Raines and Thomas Dean, p. 144.

If God is treated somewhat academically by van Buren so that finally it does not matter very much whether he exists or not, this is not the case with the two men most prominently associated with the 'death of God' phase in American theology—William Hamilton (b. 1924) and Thomas J. J. Altizer (b. 1927). For them, the question of God is not a peripheral one but a very existential one. We must deny God in order to be liberated as human beings. Hamilton talks of an Orestean theology. In Altizer's quasi-Hegelian metaphysic, God completely incarnates himself in the world and by this act of dying liberates man from an alien transcendent power.[1]

Mention of this phase of American theology would be incomplete without a reference to the Jewish scholar, Richard Rubenstein (b. 1924). In contrast to the optimism of Hamilton and Altizer, Rubenstein inclines towards pessimism, for his loss of faith in the God of Israel has been due to the sufferings of the Jewish people in this twentieth century. Speaking of his relation to the Christian atheistic theologians, he writes: 'I suspect that we part company most radically over what I regard as the Christian radical theologian's inability to take seriously the tragic vision. The tragic vision permeates my writings. How could it have been otherwise after Auschwitz?'[2] Yet Rubenstein's atheism is not entirely bleak—indeed, one suspects it might be better called a kind of pantheism. He is sensitive to the rhythms of nature and of life, and believes in the need for their religious celebration.

In 1965 a new theological perspective was opened up through the publication of *The Secular City*, by another American theologian, Harvey Cox (b. 1929). Picking up his insights from Gogarten and Bonhoeffer, he argued that secularization, so far from being regarded as an enemy, should be counted as implied in the Bible itself. The doctrine of creation, he argued, by its repudiation of all forms of pantheism, makes the world profane and a fitting object for man's investigation and even exploitation. Man is to be co-creator with God. City life and technological advance were hailed as liberating factors which allow to man a new sophistication and responsibility. The business of Christianity is not to be a 'religion' (if by this is understood some cultivation of the inner life) but to participate fully in the life of the secular city.

This was another book whose time was come and which had, like Robinson's of two years earlier, an immensely wide circulation and influence. And although one might criticize its over-simplified derivation of secularization from the Bible and its uncritical admiration of technological

---

[1] Cf. T. J. J. Altizer and W. Hamilton, *Radical Theology and the Death of God*.
[2] *After Auschwitz*, Preface, p. xi.

advance, it was a needed corrective to the negative, fault-finding, almost 'sour grapes' attitude towards the modern world that had been characteristic of so many religious books and sermons. If technology has dehumanized life at some points, it has enriched it at others, and Cox pertinently demanded whether the critics of technology would in fact be willing to go back (if that were possible) to the pre-technological era whose virtues they were so fond of extolling.

On the British side of the Atlantic, the most able exponent of secular Christianity was Ronald Gregor Smith (1913–68).[1] Though he took an affirmative attitude towards secularization, he maintained a more balanced and critical attitude than did the American secularizers. He was sharply critical both of the optimism which characterized *The Secular City* of Cox and of the reductionism to be found in *The Secular Meaning of the Gospel* of van Buren. His own type of secular theology was nearer to the German sources in Gogarten, Bultmann and Bonhoeffer. For Smith, the secular is above all the historical; but to live fully in history is to relate to the past and to have a respect for tradition as well as to relate to the present and the future. God is not a metaphysical reality beyond history, but neither can he be reduced to a mythological expression for our co-humanity or anything of that sort. He is the 'more', the transcendent, that we encounter within history itself.

The more extreme forms of secular Christianity, so far as these praised technology and decried the transcendent, proved to be short-lived. The later nineteen-sixties were marked by a revulsion of youth against the values that had been gaining ascendancy in the West at least since the time of the Renaissance. To be sure, this revulsion took place only among a minority, and it was usually very confused. Nevertheless, some people were now answering Cox's question about who would be willing to go back to the pre-technological era by trying to do just that and by dropping out of affluent society. One of the prophets of the youth revolt was the veteran Hegelian–Marxist philosopher Herbert Marcuse (b. 1898). He questioned the common assumption that one can be selective about technology, accepting its benefits and rejecting its evils. He believed that whether its basis is capitalistic (as in the United States) or collectivist (as in the Soviet Union) the technocratic society has acquisitive motives which warp a genuinely free humanity. He calls for 'a new type of man, a different type of human being, with new needs, capable of finding a qualitatively different way of life, and of constructing a qualitatively different environment'.[2]

---

[1] His writings include *The New Man, Secular Christianity* and (posthumously) *The Doctrine of God*.

[2] *Marxism and Radical Religion*, p. 7.

Many of the youth have, of course, gone far beyond Marcuse. They turn their backs on material comforts and the traditional secular ideals. Some have sought an experience of the transcendent, either through drugs or through mystical religion. There has emerged something like a counter culture, in which the values of the secular West are turned upside down. The immediate demise of religion, expected by Bonhoeffer and the secular theologians, has not taken place. This whole counter culture has received a tremendous boost through the growing awareness of the ecological crisis brought about through the uncontrolled and unco-ordinated proliferation of technology.

Whether the new movement will have permanence or is only a temporary halting-place in the advance of secularism and technological society, it is impossible to say. But the new fashion of thought is already reflected in American theology. One might be cynical and say that this theology has no mind of its own and is simply dragged along at the heels of an uncertain culture. At any rate, now that secularism and technology are no longer regarded as unmixed blessings, theologians are less likely to come forward with the claim that these things have their origins in the Bible or extolling the virtues of 'religionless' Christianity. One of the most articulate spokesmen of the new trend is Sam Keen, the author of 'A Manifesto for a Dionysian Theology'.[1] In his belief, religion is celebration, dance, feeling, closely related to the rhythms of life. Such religion has to do with expanding the boundaries of personality and consciousness. A Dionysian theology stresses the immanence of God. All reality is sacramental, and God language helps to focus our awareness of the sacred dimensions of life. Harvey Cox too has been touched by the new religious spirit. In a *Playboy* article at the beginning of 1970, he wrote: 'I used to believe and even hope that mankind might some day outgrow its religious phase . . . but people have been predicting the end of religion and the death of God for centuries and I no longer seriously believe it will happen, nor do I hope it will.' He adds this observation: 'With a few exceptions, I am not very impressed with the level of imagination, compassion or human vitality of the people I know who claim they have left religion behind.' So the wheel has come full circle. One can only hope that the new stress on celebration and ecstasy will not be swallowed up in anti-intellectualism or lose the real insights of the earlier theology of the secular.

In these ferments, the influence of the Canadian student of contemporary society, Marshall McLuhan (b. 1911) has been considerable. In a series of books[2] he has argued that the age of immediate communication

---

[1] In *Transcendence*, ed. Herbert W. Richardson and Donald R. Cutler, p. 31ff.
[2] The best-known is *Understanding Media*, 1964.

and of electric immediacy calls for a new type of mentality. We have reached a stage where we need to think in terms of wholes rather than of fragmented problems. Thus the analytic tendencies of Western thought since the Renaissance need to be replaced by the drive towards synthesis. Correspondingly, there is a move away from the verbal to the visual, a move that has been greatly accelerated by the advent of television. Mc-Luhan's ideas have been seized upon by the advocates of 'Dionysian reli-, gion', while he himself in a more sober way has advocated a new look at the value of mythology and metaphysics.

This survey of the English-speaking lands has concentrated on the newer trends that have emerged in the decade under review, but it should not be forgotten that during the same years there was a great deal of solid work in theology and the philosophy of religion along lines that had been laid down earlier. In England, Ian T. Ramsey (b. 1915) emerged as the leading exponent in the application of analytic philosophy to the problems of theological and religious language. He has tried to show that even in an age dominated by empiricism it remains meaningful to talk of God, and he has shown how this talk, though 'logically odd', relates to some of the most important experiences of life. These experiences are described in terms of 'commitment' and 'discernment'. They are experiences in which we see things or people in a depth that carries us beyond the level of ordinary experience and in which we are also brought to commit ourselves to definite policies and attitudes. The mystery disclosed in such experiences— the mystery of God—we can represent to ourselves by 'models' or analogues, and Ramsey has explored the relation between those non-picturing models of religion and the similarly non-picturing models employed by modern physics. While Ramsey has worked in the empiricist tradition, which is native to the British Isles, Ian Henderson (1910–69) turned to the continent. He was the pioneer in the English-speaking countries of a Bultmannian type of existential theology. The Barthian tradition has been notably continued by Thomas F. Torrance (b. 1913), who has in particular stressed the objective and scientific character of theology.

The controversy in the United States over the 'death of God' stimulated efforts towards a better formulation of theism. The tradition of Whitehead and Hartshorne was notably continued and developed by Schubert Ogden (b. 1928), especially in his book *The Reality of God*. Closer to Tillich was the work of Langdon Gilkey (b. 1919). Applying the methods of phenomenological analysis to ordinary secular experience, he argued, especially in his book *Naming the Whirlwind*, that such analysis reveals depths of ultimacy and sacrality which demand expression in God language. Though different in method, a somewhat parallel approach is found in the work of the sociologist, Peter Berger (b. 1929). He has maintained, in a book called appropriately *A Rumour of Angels*, that sociological investigation uncovers but does not exhaust certain areas of the human experience which function as 'signals of transcendence'.

114. ROMAN CATHOLIC THOUGHT, 1960–70

Mention has been made above of the renascence of Roman Catholic thought which, already begun in the years before Vatican II, was greatly stimulated by that council. Some of the men whose views have already been discussed earlier in this book continued to exercise a notable influence in Catholic thinking, especially Karl Rahner and Jean Cardinal Daniélou.[1] But many new figures emerged and several men whose work had hitherto been left in obscurity now came to notice.

Among the latter, particular mention must be made of Joseph Maréchal (1878–1915), the pioneer of a new and vigorous form of Thomism, usually known as transcendental Thomism. This new version of the perennial philosophy is different from the neo-Thomism discussed in Chapter XVIII.[2] Some of the neo-Thomists mentioned there, such as Gilson, have been quite critical of the new developments. Generally speaking, it may be said that the new form of Thomism is much more dynamic than the earlier forms, though it claims equally to have its roots in St Thomas. As the adjective 'transcendental' suggests, Maréchal developed his ideas in dialogue with the transcendental philosophy of Kant. In doing this, he directed attention to the intellectual act. One could also express the change in terms of a movement from conceptualism to intellectualism, where intellectualism is understood in a dynamic sense to indicate the inherent drive of the intellect to keep moving out beyond any stage of understanding that has been reached. This has led to a measure of ambiguity in the expression 'transcendental Thomism'. This is a *transcendental* philosophy, in the sense that it investigates the conditions of understanding and knowing, as Kant's philosophy did; but it is also a philosophy of *transcendence*, in the sense that it recognizes that man has an open nature, so that he continually drives beyond himself. The 'whither' of this transcending drive is God.

Thus described, transcendental Thomism is seen to have a relation to existentialism, for which the ecstatic self-transcending character of man is fundamental. This kinship is indeed apparent in some Catholic writers,

---

[1] See above, pp. 293–4 and 297–8.   [2] See pp. 278–90.

such as the Dutch Dominican Edward Schillebeeckx (b. 1914) who writes of 'the ecstatic character of our self-transcendence'.[1] But whereas existentialism stresses the will and the affects, transcendental Thomism in the strict sense stands closer to the Thomist tradition in asserting the primacy of intellect and in locating transcendence especially in the intellectual drive. The intellectual and even scholastic nature of this school of philosophy is well seen in the writings of the Canadian, Bernard Lonergan (b. 1904). He defines transcendence as 'the elementary matter of raising further questions'.[2] He gives a detailed and impressive account of the complex intellectual drive by which man presses on towards perfect knowledge and therefore to the vision of God. Lonergan explicitly differentiates the drive of the *mind* towards vision in St Thomas with the restlessness of the *heart* in St Augustine,[3] but in such a way as to suggest that these are finally complementary.

The dynamic intellectualism of this new Thomism is important as a corrective to the dangers of subjectivism and sentimentalism to which some forms of existentialism can lead—and these are dangers which nowadays threaten some Catholic theologians as much as their Protestant colleagues.

Other representatives of the new thinking include Emerich Coreth (b. 1919), author of a book called simply *Metaphysics*, which has much in common with the thought of Lonergan though it shows also a strongly Heideggerian influence; and Johannes Metz (b. 1928), a disciple of Rahner, who has been especially concerned to break out of the individualistic categories of much traditional theology so that his teaching has some resemblances to Moltmann's theology of hope.

The Second Vatican Council gave a new impetus to ecumenical exchanges, though indeed these had been taking place for a long time.[4] Catholic theologians increasingly sought out dialogue not only with Protestant and Orthodox Christians but with representatives of the non-Christian religions and with Marxists and atheists. The result has inevitably been a reshaping and development within Catholic theology itself. A broader understanding of the Church under the image of the 'people of God' and new approaches to the theology of the scriptures, tradition and the sacraments, have been typical of these theologians. Here we can do no more than mention the names of the best-known: Yves Congar (b. 1904), Louis Bouyer (b. 1913), Hans Küng (b. 1928). To these may be added Henri de Lubac (b. 1896), who has devoted himself especially to the problem of atheism, and Heinz Robert Schlette (b. 1931), who

---

[1] *God and Man*, p. 166. [2] *Insight*, p. 635. [3] *Verbum*, p. 90.
[4] See George H. Tavard, *Two Centuries of Ecumenism*.

has explored new ways of relating Christianity and the non-Christian religions.[1]

Finally, one must mention the developments in moral theology. Here the outstanding figure has been Bernard Häring (b. 1912). His massive work *Das Gesetz Christi* (E.T., *The Law of Christ*) breaks out of formalism and legalism and stresses the interiority of law, charity and responsibility.

115. Some Comments on the Decade

In spite of the varieties in the theologies surveyed in this chapter, there do seem to be some common characteristics. Especially, there is a new concern with man, almost a new Christian humanism. In some respects, this may indicate a return to the trends of the nineteenth century, though one would hope that the intervening lessons would also have been learned. Nevertheless, there is overwhelming interest in man, his nature, his future and his destiny, and a disposition to turn away from problems which do not appear to be related to the problem of the human condition. Even so far as there is interest in the question of God, that interest has to do with God as active in the world and in human affairs. The favourite symbol of the new theology is depth rather than height. God, and with him the meaning of faith and religion, is to be sought in the depths—the depths that underlie our daily life, our relations with each other, the world in which we live. Theology is not a study that turns away from man and the world, but looks for the encounter of God mediated through these realities.

To be sure, this humanistic thrust has sometimes been carried to extreme lengths. The interest in man has occasionally become an exclusive interest, so that God has been eliminated and declared dead. Even in the more moderate forms of secular and humanistic theology (including some of the Catholic varieties) one has a feeling of being back in the time of nineteenth-century doctrines of progress, with the lessons of the twentieth century swept far too prematurely under the carpet. Especially among some of the Americans, there has been a tendency to think of the Kingdom of God as an idealization of the affluent society.

But when extreme aberrations occur, there seems to come into play a self-correcting mechanism. The new humanism, in turning from the distant God to the life of man, has uncovered in man the principle of

[1] Among the more important writings of the theologians mentioned in this paragraph are: Yves Congar, *Tradition and Traditions;* L. Bouyer, *L'Église de Dieu;* H. Küng, *Justification* and *The Church;* H. de Lubac, *The Drama of Atheist Humanism;* H. R. Schlette, *Towards a Theology of Religions.*

transcendence itself. In an impressive way, the different schools of thought today understand man as an unfinished being. He is continually going out beyond himself, and is therefore a being who carries within himself clues to the meaning of transcendence and mystery. The secret goad, of which St Augustine spoke, still drives the religious thinker towards a fuller vision of God.

INDEX

The numbers of the pages on which a writer's thought is expounded appear in italic.